Rewards Vulnerabilities Position Perspective Opportunities Probability Mistakes Situations Momentum

孫子兵法

Sun Tzu's
Art of War
Playbook

Book One
Volumes 1 to 4

Gary
Gagliardi

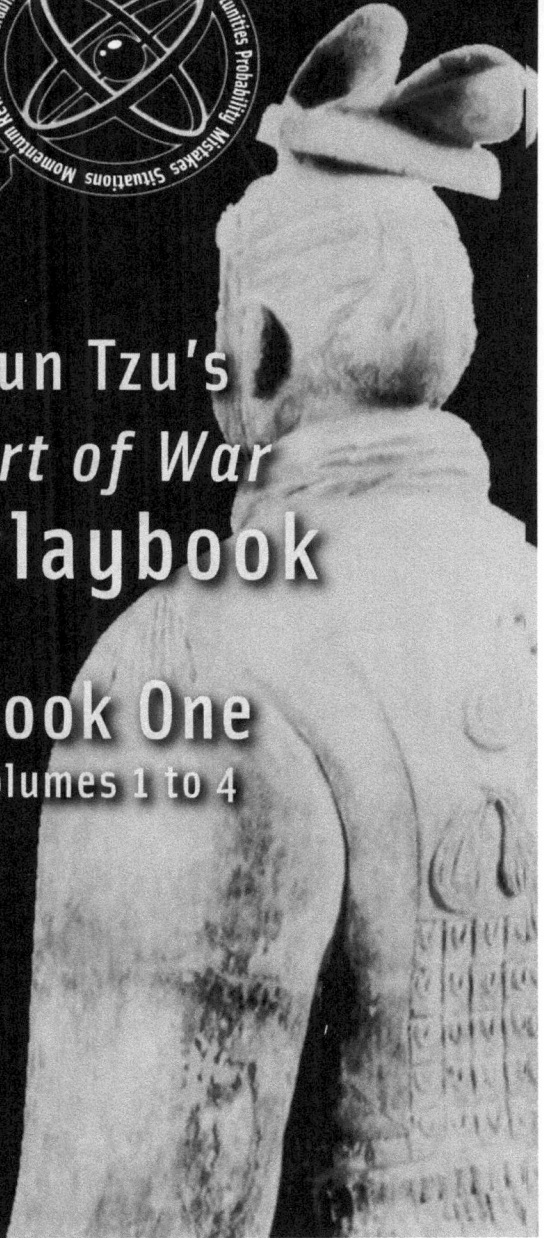

Sun Tzu's Art of War

Playbook

Book One
Volumes 1-4

by Gary Gagliardi
The Science of Strategy Institute
Clearbridge Publishing

Published by
Science of Strategy Institute, Clearbridge Publishing
    suntzus.com   scienceofstrategy.org

Sun Tzu's PlayBook - Book One Volumes 1-4
Library of Congress Control Number: 2014909969
First Print Edition
Also sold as Sun Tzu's Warrior Rule Book
Copyright 2010, 2011, 2012, 2013, 2014 Gary Gagliardi
ISBN 978-1-929194-85-8 (13-digit) 1-929194-85-4 (10-digit)

Registered with Department of Copyrights, Library of Congress.

Originally published as a series of articles on the Science of Strategy Website, scienceofstratregy.org. and
later as an ebook on various sites. Ebook ISBN 978-1-929194-63-6

PO Box 33772, Seattle, WA 98133
Phone: (206)542-8947 Fax: (206)546-9756
beckyw@clearbridge.com
garyg@scienceofstrategy.org

Manufactured in the United States of America.
Interior and cover graphic design by Dana and Jeff Wincapaw.
Original Chinese calligraphy by Tsai Yung, Green Dragon Arts, www.greendragonarts.com.

Publisher's Cataloging-in-Publication Data
Sun-tzu, 6th cent. B.C.
Strategy , positioning
    [Sun-tzu ping fa, English]
    Volume One: Art of War Playbook / Sun Tzu and Gary Gagliardi.
    p.197 cm. 23
    Includes introduction to basic competitive philosophy of Sun Tzu

Clearbridge Publishing's books may be purchased for business, for any promotional use,
or for special sales.

Contents

Playbook Overview

Note: This overview is provided for those who have not read the previous volume of Sun Tzu's Art of War Playbook. *It provides an brief overview of the work in general and the general concepts framing the first volume.*

Sun Tzu's **The Art of War** is less a "book" in the modern Western sense than it is an outline for a course of study. Like Euclid's Geometry, simply reading the work teaches us very little. Sun Tzu wrote in in a tradition that expected each line and stanza to be studied in the context of previous statements to build up the foundation for understanding later statements.

To make this work easier for today's readers to understand, we developed the **Strategy Playbook**, the Science of Strategy Institute (SOSI) guidebook to explaining Sun Tzu's strategy in the more familiar format of a series of explanations with examples. These lessons are framed in the context of modern competition rather than ancient military warfare.

This Playbook is the culmination of over a decade of work breaking down Sun Tzu's principles into a series of step-by-step practical articles by the Institute's multiple award-winning author and founder, Gary Gagliardi. The original **Art of War** was written for military generals who understood the philosophical concepts of ancient China, which in itself is a practical hurdle that most modern readers cannot clear. Our **Art of War Playbook** is written for today's reader. It puts Sun Tzu's ideas into everyday, practical language.

The Playbook defines a new science of strategic competition aimed at today's challenges. This science of competition is designed as the complementary opposite of the management science that is taught in most business schools. This science starts, as Sun Tzu did himself, by defining a better, more complete vocabulary for discussing competitive situations. It connects the timeless ideas of Sun Tzu to today's latest thinking in business, mathematics, and psychology.

The entire Playbook consists of two hundred and thirty articles describing over two-thousand interconnected key methods. These articles are organized into nine different areas of strategic skill from understanding positioning to defending vulnerabilities. All together this makes up over a thousand pages of material.

Playbook Access

The Playbook's most up-to-date version is available as separate articles on our website. Live links make it easy to access the connections between various articles and concepts. If you become a SOSI Member, you can access any Playbook article at any time and access their links.

However, at the request of our customers, we also offer these articles as a series of nine eBooks. Each of the nine sections of the entire Playbook makes up a separate eBook, Playbook Parts One Through Nine. These parts flow logically through the Progress Cycle of listen-aim-move-claim (see illustration). Because of the dynamic nature of the on-line version, these eBooks are not going to be as current as the on-line version. You can see a outline of current Playbook articles here and, generally, the eBook version will contain most of the same material in the same order.

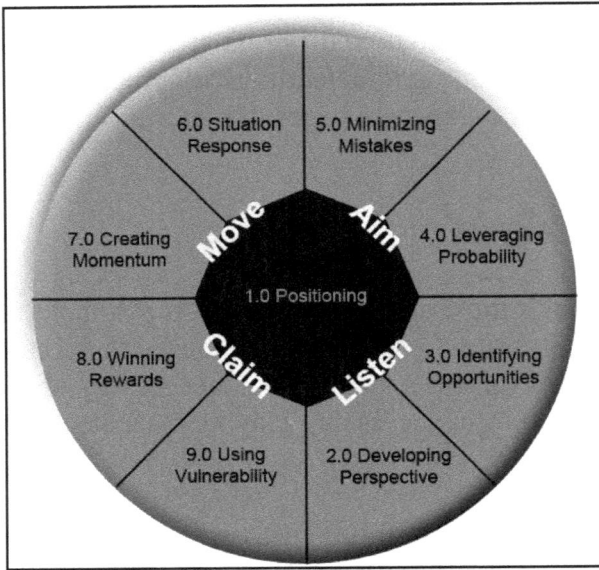

Nine categories of strategic skills define cycle that advances our positions:

1. Comparing Positions,

2. Developing Perspective,

3. Identifying Opportunities,

4. Leveraging Probability,

5. Minimizing Mistakes,

6. Responding To Situations,

7. Creating Momentum,

8. Winning Rewards, And

9. Defending Vulnerabilities.

These are the topic covered in the nine volumes of Sun Tzu's Playbook. Each book focuses on a single skill area.

Playbook Structure and Design

These articles are written in standard format including 1) the general principle, 2) the situation, 3) the opportunity, 4) the list of specific Art of War key methods breaking down the general principle into a series of actions, and 5) an illustration of the application of each of those key methods to a specific competitive situation. Key methods are written generically to apply to every competitive arena (business, personal life, career, sports, relationships, etc.) with each specific illustrations drawn from one of these areas.

A number identifies where each article appears in Playbook Structure. For example, the article <u>2.1.3 Strategic Deception</u> is the third article in the first section of the second book in the nine volumes of the Strategy Playbook. In our on-line version, these links are live, clicking on them brings you to the article itself. We provide them because the interconnection of concepts is important in learning Sun Tzu's system.

Playbook Training

Training in Sun Tzu's warrior skills does not entail memorizing all these principles. Instead, these concepts are used to develop exercises and tools that allow trainees to put this ideas in practice. While each rule is useful, the heart of Sun Tzu system is the methods that connect all the principles together. Training in these principles is designed to develop a gut instinct for how Sun Tzu's strategy is used in different situations to produce success. Principles are interlinked because they describe a comprehensive conceptual mental model. Warrior Class training puts trainees in a situation where they must constantly make decisions, rewarding them for making decisions consist with winning productively instead of destructively.

About Positions

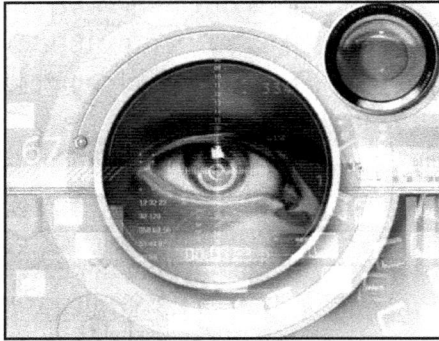

This first volume of Sun Tzu's Playbook focuses on teaching us the nature of strategic positions. "Position awareness" gives you a framework for understanding your strategic situation relative to the conditions around you. It enables you to see your position as part of a larger environment constructed of other positions and the raw elements that create positions. Master Sun Tzu's system of comparing positions, you can understand which aspect of your position are secure and which are the most dynamic and likely to change.

Traditional strategy defines a "position" as a comparison of situations. Game theory defines is as the current decision point that is arrive at as the sum or result of all previous decisions, both yours and those of others. Sun Tzu's methods of positioning awareness are different. They force you to see yourself in the eyes of others. Using these techniques, you broaden your perspective by gathering a range of viewpoints. In a limited sense, the scope of your position defines your area of control within your larger environment. In traditional strategy, five elements--mission, climate, ground, command, and methods--define the dimensions in which competitors can be compared.

Competition as Comparison

Sun Tzu saw that success is based on comparisons. This comparison must take place whenever a choice is made. For Sun Tzu, competition means a comparison of alternative choices or "positions". Battles are won by positioning before they are fought. These positions provide choices for everyone involved. Good positions discourage others from attacking you and invite them to support you. Sun Tzu's system teaches us how to systematically build up our positions to win success in the easiest way possible.

Competing positions are compared on the basis many elements, both objective and subjective. Sun Tzu's strategy is to identify these points of comparison and to understand how to leverage them. Learning Sun Tzu's strategy requires learning the details of how positions are compared and advanced. Sun Tzu taught that fighting to "sort things out" is a foolish way to find learn the strengths and weaknesses of a position. Conflict to tear down opposing positions is the most costly way to win competitive comparisons.

Today's More Competitive World

In the complex, chaotic world of today, we can easily get trapped into destructive rather than productive situations. Even our smallest decisions can have huge impact on our future. The problem is that we are trained for yesterday's world of workers, not today's world of warriors. We are trained in the linear thinking of planning in predictable, hierarchical world. This thinking applies less and less to today's networked, more competitive world.

Following a plan is the worker's skill of working in pre-defined functions in an internal, stable, controlled environment. The competitive strategy of Sun Tzu is the warrior's skill of making good decisions about conditions in complex, fast-changing, competitive environments. Sun Tzu's strategic system teaches us to adapt to the unexpected events that are becoming more and more common in our lives. We live in a world where fewer and fewer key events are planned. Navigating our new world of external challenges requires a different set of skills.

Most of us make our decisions without any understanding of competition. The result is that most of us lose as many battles as we win, never making consistent progress. Events buffet us, turning us in one direction and then the other. Too often, we end up repeating our past patterns of mistakes.

The Science of Strategy Institute teaches you the warrior's skills of adaptive response. There are many organizations that teach planning and organization. The Institute is one of the few places in the world you can get learn competitive thinking, and the only place in the world, with a comprehensive Playbook.

Seeing Situations Differently

Sun Tzu taught that a warrior's decision-making was a matter of reflex. As we develop our strategic decision-making skills, the critical conditions in situations simply "pop" out at us. This isn't magic. The latest research on how decisions are made tells us a lot about why Sun Tzu's principles work. It comes from using patterns to retrain our mind to see conditions differently. The study of successful response arose from military confrontations, where every battle clearly demonstrated how hard it is to predict events in the real world. Sun Tzu saw that winners were always those who knew how to respond appropriately to the dynamic nature of their situation.

Sun Tzu's principles provides a complete model for the key knowledge for understanding conditions in complex dynamic environments. This model "files" each piece of data into the appropriate place in the big picture. As the picture of your situation fills in, you can identify the opportunities hidden within your situation.

Making Decisions about Conditions

Instead of focusing on a series of planned steps, Sun Tzu's principles are about making decisions regarding conditions. It concerns itself with: 1) identifying the relative strengths and weaknesses of competitive positions, 2) advancing positions leveraging opportunities, and 3) the types of responses to specific challenges that work the most frequently. Using Sun Tzu's principles, we call these three areas position awareness , opportunity development , and situation response . Each area that we master broadens your capabilities.

- Position awareness trains us to recognize that competitive situations are defined by the relationship among alternative positions. Developing this perspective never ends. It deepens throughout our lives.
- Opportunity development explores the ground, testing our perceptions. Only testing the edges of perspective through action can we know what is true.
- S ituation response trains us to recognize the key characteristics of the immediate situation and to respond appropriately. Only by practice, can we learn to trust the viewpoint we have developed.

Success in competitive environments comes from making better decisions every day. Sharp strategic reflexes flow from a clear understanding of where and when you use which competitive tools methods.

The Key Viewpoints

As an individual, you have a unique and valuable viewpoint, but every viewpoint is inherently limited by its own position. The result is that people cannot get a useful perspective on their own situations and surrounding opportunities. The first formula of positioning awareness involve learning what information is relevant. The most advanced techniques teach how to gather that information and put it into a bigger picture.

Most people see their current situations as the sum of their past successes and failures. Too often people dwell on their mistakes while simultaneously sitting on their laurels. Sun Tzu's strategy forces you to see your position differently. How you arrived at your current position doesn't matter. Your position is what it is. It is shaped by history but history is not destiny.

In this framework, the only thing that matters is where you are going and how you are going to get there. As you begin to develop your strategic reflexes, you start to think more and more about how to secure your current position and advance it.

Seeing the Big Picture

Most people see all the details of their lives, but they cannot see what those detail mean in terms of the big picture. As you master position awareness, you don't see your life as a point but as a path. You see your position in terms of what is changing and what resources are available. You are more aware of your ability to make decisions and your skills in working with others.

Most importantly, this strategic system forces you to get in touch with your core set of goals and values.

Untrained people usually see their life in terms of absolutes: successes and failures, good luck and bad, weakness and strength. As you begin to master position awareness, you begin to see all comparisons of strength and weakness are temporary and relative. A position is not strong or weak in itself. Its strength or weakness depends on how it compares or "fits" with surrounding positions. Weakness and strength are not what a position is, but how you use it.

The Power of Perspective

Positional awareness gives you the specialized vocabulary you need to understanding how situations develop. Mastering this vocabulary, you begin to see the leverage points connecting past and future. You replace vague conceptions of "strength," "momentum," and "innovation" with much more pragmatic definitions that you can actually use on a day to day basis.

Mastering position awareness also changes your relationships with other people. It teaches you a different way of judging truth and character. This methods allow you to spot self-deception and dishonest in others. It also allows you to understand how you can best work with others to compensate for your different weaknesses.

Once you develop a good perspective of position, it naturally leads you to want to learn more about how you can improve you position through the various aspects of opportunity development covered in the subsequent parts of the Strategy Playbook.

Seeing the Invisible

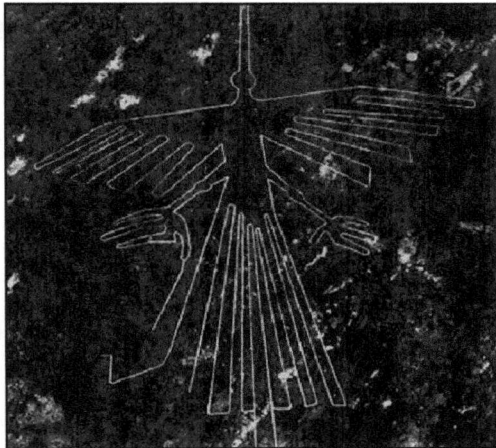

The "Nazca lines" are giant drawings etched across thirty miles of desert on Peru's southern coast. The patterns are only visible at a distance of hundreds of feet in the air. Below that, they look like strange paths or roads to nowhere. Just as we cannot see these lines without the proper perspective, people who master Sun Tzu's methods can <u>suddenly recognize situations</u> that were invisible to them before. Unless we have the right perspective, we cannot compare situations and positions successfully. The most recent scientific research explains why people cannot see these patterns for comparison without developing the network framework of adaptive thinking.[1]

Seeing Patterns

We can imagine patterns in chaotic situations, but seeing real pattern is the difference between success and failure. In our seminars, we demonstrate the power of seeing patterns in a number of exercises.

The <u>mental models</u> used by warrior give them "situation awareness." This situation awareness isn't just vague theory. Recent research shows that it can be measured in a variety of ways.[2] We now know that untrained people fall victim to a flow of confusing information because they don't know where its pieces fit. Those trained in Sun Tzu's mental models plug this stream of information quickly and easily into a bigger picture, transforming the skeleton's provided by Sun Tzu's system into a functioning awareness of your strategic position and its relation to other positions. Each piece of information has a place in that picture. As the information comes in, it fills in the picture, like pieces of a puzzle.

The ability to see the patterns in this bigger picture allows experts in strategy to see what is invisible to most people in a number of ways. They include:

- People trained in Art of War principles--<u>recognition-primed decision-making</u> --see patterns that others do not.
- Trained people can spot anomalies, things that should happen in the network of interactions but don't.
- Trained people are in touch with changes in the environment within appropriate time horizons.
- Trained people recognize complete patterns of interconnected elements under extreme time pressure.

Procedures Make Seeing Difficult

One of the most surprising discoveries from this research is that those who know procedures, that is, a linear view of events, alone have a ***more*** difficult time recognizing patterns than novices. An interesting study[3] examined the different recognition skills of three groups of people 1) experts, 2) novices, and 3) trainers who taught the standard procedures. The three groups were asked to pick out an expert from a group novices in a series of videos showing them performing a decision-making task, in this case, CPR. Experts were able to recognize the expert 90% of the time. Novices recognized the expert 50% of the time. The shocking fact was that trainers performed much worse that the novices, recognizing the expert only 30% of the time.

Why do those who know procedures fail to see what the experts usually see and even novices often see? Because, as research into <u>mental simulations</u> has shown, those with only a procedural model fit everything into that model and ignore elements that don't fit. In the above experiment, interviews with the trainers indicated that they assumed that the experts would always follow the procedural model. In real life, experts adapt to situations where unique conditions often trump procedure. Adapting to the situation rather than following set procedures is a central focus the form of strategy that the Institute teaches.

Missing Expected Elements

People trained to recognize the bigger picture beyond procedures also recognize when expected elements are missing from the
picture. These anomalies or, what the cognition experts[4] describe
as "negative cues" are invisible to novices *and* to those trained
only in procedure. Without sense of the bigger pattern, people are
focused too narrowly on the problem at hand. The "dog that didn't
bark" from the Sherlock Holmes story, "Silver Blaze," is the most
famous example of a negative cue. Only those working from a larger
nonprocedural framework can expect certain things to happen and
notice when they don't.

The ability to see what is missing also comes from the expectations generated by the mental model. Process-oriented models have
the expectation of one step following another, but situation-recognition models create their expectations from signals in the environment. Research[5] into the time horizons of decision-makers shows
that different time scales are at work. People at the highest level of
organizations must look a year or two down the road, using strategic models that work in that timeframe, doing strategic planning.
Decision-makers on the front-lines, however, have to react within
minutes or even seconds to changes in their situation, working from
their strategic reflexes. The biggest danger is that people get so
wrapped up in a process that they lose contact with their environment.

Decisions Under Pressure

Extreme time pressure is what distinguishes front-line decision-
making from strategic planners. One of the biggest discoveries in
cognitive research[6] is that trained people do much better in seeing
their situation instantly and making the correct decisions under time
pressure. Researchers found virtually no difference between the
decisions that experts made under time pressure when comparing
them to decisions made without time pressure. That research also

finds that those with less experience and training made dramatically worse decisions when they were put under time pressure.

The central argument for training our strategic reflexes is that our situation results, not from chance or luck, but from the instant decisions that that we all make every day. Our position is the sum of these decisions. If we cannot make the right decisions on the spot, when they are needed, our plans usually come to nothing. This is why we describe training people's strategic reflexes as helping them "do at first what most people only do at last."

The success people experience seeing what is invisible to others is dramatic. To learn more about how the strategic reflexes we teach differ from what can be planned, read about the contrast between planning and reflexes here . As our many members report, the success Sun Tzu's system makes possible is remarkable.

1 Chi, Glaser, & Farr, 1988, The Nature of Expertise, Erlbaum
2 Endsley & Garland, Analysis and Measurement of Situation Awareness
3 Klein & Klein, 1981, "Perceptual/Cognitive Analysis of proficient CPR Performance", Midwestern Psychological Association Meeting, Chicago.
4 Dr. David Noble, Evidence Based Research, Inc.In Gary Klein, Sources of Power, 1999
5 Jacobs & Jaques, 1991, "Executive Leadership".In Gal & Mangelsdofs (eds.), Handbook of Military Psychology, Wiley
6 Calder, Klein, Crandall,1988, "Time Pressure, Skill, and Move Quality in Chess". American Journal of Psychology, 101:481-493

Sun Tzu's Playbook

Volume 1: Positions

About Positions

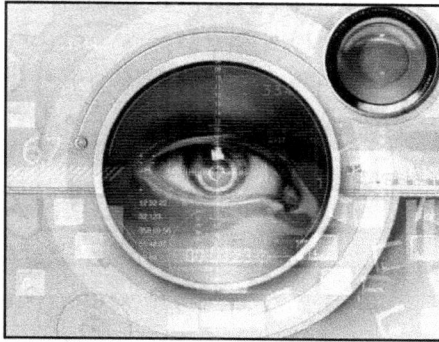

This first part of Sun Tzu's Playbook focuses on teaching us the nature of strategic positions. "Position awareness" gives you a framework for understanding your strategic situation relative to the conditions around you. It enables you to see your position as part of a larger environment constructed of other positions and the raw elements that create positions. When you master Sun Tzu's system of comparing positions, you can understand which aspects of your position are secure and which are the most dynamic and likely to change.

Traditional strategy defines a "position" as a comparison of situations. Game theory defines it as the current decision point (node) that is arrived at as the sum or result of all previous decisions, both yours and those of others. Sun Tzu's methods of positioning awareness are different. They force you to see yourself in the eyes of others. Using these techniques, you broaden your perspective by gathering a range of viewpoints. In a limited sense, the scope of your position defines your area of control within your larger environment. In traditional strategy, five elements--mission, climate, ground, command, and methods--define the dimensions in which competitors can be compared.

Competition as Comparison

Sun Tzu saw that success is based on comparisons. Comparisons must take place whenever a choice is made. For Sun Tzu, competition means a comparison of alternative choices or "positions". Battles are won by positioning before they are fought. These positions provide the choices for everyone involved. Good positions discourage others from attacking you and invite them to support you. Sun Tzu's system teaches us how to systematically build up our positions to win success in the easiest way possible.

Competing positions are compared on the basis many elements, both objective and subjective. Sun Tzu's strategy is to identify these points of comparison and to understand how to leverage them. Learning Sun Tzu's method requires learning the details of how positions are compared and advanced. Sun Tzu taught that fighting to "sort things out" is a foolish way to find learn the strengths and weaknesses of a position. Conflict to tear down opposing positions is the most costly way to win competitive comparisons.

Today's More Competitive World

In the complex, chaotic world of today, we can easily get trapped into destructive rather than productive situations. Even our smallest decisions can have a huge impact on our future. The problem is that we are trained for yesterday's world of workers who follow plans, not today's world of warriors who must make decisions on the front lines.

Following a plan is needed for working in pre-defined functions in an internal, stable, controlled environment. The competitive strategy of Sun Tzu is the warrior's skill of making good decisions about conditions in complex, fast-changing, competitive environments. Sun Tzu's warrior's principles teach us to adapt to the unexpected events that are becoming more and more common in our lives. We live in a world where fewer and fewer key events are planned. Navigating our new world of external challenges requires a different set of skills, those taught by Sun Tzu.

Most of us make our decisions without any understanding of competition. The result is that most of us lose as many battles as we win, never making consistent progress. Events batter us, turning us in one direction and then the other. Too often, we end up repeating our past patterns of mistakes.

The principles from *The Art of War* teaches you the warrior's skills of adaptive response. There are many books that teach planning and organization. Sun Tzu's work and more modern works based on its ideas teach you competitive thinking and how to advance your position in competitive environments.

Seeing Situations Differently

Sun Tzu taught that a warrior's decision-making was a matter of reflex. As we develop our strategic decision-making skills, the critical conditions in situations simply "pop" out at us. This isn't magic. The latest research on how decisions are made tells us a lot about why Sun Tzu's principles work. It comes from using patterns to retrain our mind to see conditions differently. The study of successful response arose from military confrontations, where every battle clearly demonstrated how hard it is to predict events in the real world. Sun Tzu saw that winners were always those who knew how to respond appropriately to the dynamic nature of their situation.

Sun Tzu's principles provide a complete model for the key knowledge for understanding conditions in complex dynamic environments. This model "files" each piece of data into the appropriate place in the big picture. As the picture of your situation fills in, you can identify the opportunities hidden within your situation.

Making Decisions about Conditions

Instead of focusing on a series of planned steps, Sun Tzu's principles are about making decisions regarding conditions. It concerns itself with: 1) identifying the relative strengths and weaknesses of competitive positions, 2) advancing positions leveraging opportunities, and 3) the types of responses to specific challenges that work the most frequently. Using Sun Tzu's principles, we call these three areas position awareness , opportunity development , and situation response. Each area that we master broadens your capabilities.

- Position awareness trains us to recognize that competitive situations are defined by the relationship among alternative positions. Developing this perspective never ends. It deepens throughout our lives.
- Opportunity development explores the ground, testing our perceptions. Only testing the edges of perspective through action can we know what is true.
- Situation response trains us to recognize the key characteristics of the immediate situation and to respond appropriately. Only by practice, can we learn to trust the viewpoint we have developed.

Success in competitive environments comes from making better decisions every day. Sharp strategic reflexes flow from a clear understanding of where and when you use which competitive tools methods.

The Key Viewpoints

As an individual, you have a unique and valuable viewpoint, but every viewpoint is inherently limited by its own position. The result is that people cannot get a useful perspective on their own situations and surrounding opportunities. Positioning awareness involves learning what information is relevant. The most advanced techniques teach how to gather that information and put it into a bigger picture.

Most people see their current situations as the sum of their past successes and failures. Too often people dwell on their mistakes while simultaneously sitting on their laurels. Sun Tzu's strategy forces you to see your position differently. How you arrived at your current position doesn't matter. Your position is what it is. It is shaped by history but history is not destiny.

In this framework, the only thing that matters is where you are going and how you are going to get there. As you begin to develop your strategic reflexes, you start to think more and more about how to secure your current position and advance it.

Seeing the Big Picture

Most people see all the details of their lives, but they cannot see what those details mean in terms of the big picture. As you master position awareness, you don't see your life as a point but as a path. You see your position in terms of what is changing and what resources are available. You are more aware of your ability to make decisions and your skills in working with others.

Most importantly, this strategic system forces you to get in touch with your core set of goals and values.

Untrained people usually see their life in terms of absolutes: successes and failures, good luck and bad, weakness and strength. As you begin to master position awareness, you begin to see all comparisons of strength and weakness are temporary and relative. A position is not strong or weak in itself. Its strength or weakness depends on how it compares or "fits" with surrounding positions. Weakness and strength are not what a position is, but how you use it.

The Power of Perspective

Positional awareness gives you the specialized vocabulary you need to understanding how situations develop. Mastering this vocabulary, you begin to see the leverage points connecting past and future. You replace vague conceptions of "strength," "momentum," and "innovation" with much more pragmatic definitions that you can actually use on a day to day basis.

Mastering position awareness also changes your relationships with other people. It teaches you a different way of judging truth and character. This methods allow you to spot self-deception and dishonesty in others. It also allows you to understand how you can best work with others to compensate for your different weaknesses.

Once you develop a good perspective of position, it naturally leads you to want to learn more about how you can improve you position through the various aspects of opportunity development covered in the subsequent parts of the Strategy Playbook.

Seeing the Invisible

The "Nazca lines" are giant drawings etched across thirty miles of desert on Peru's southern coast. The patterns are only visible at a distance of hundreds of feet in the air. Below that, they look like strange paths or roads to nowhere. Just as we cannot see these lines without the proper perspective, people who master Sun Tzu's principles can suddenly recognize situations that were invisible to them before. Unless we have the right perspective, we cannot compare situations and positions successfully. The most recent scientific research explains why people cannot see these patterns for comparison without developing the network framework of adaptive thinking.[1]

Seeing Patterns

We can imagine patterns in chaotic situations, but seeing real patterns is the difference between success and failure. In our seminars, we demonstrate the power of seeing patterns in a number of exercises.

The mental models used by warrior give them "situation awareness." This situation awareness isn't just vague theory. Recent research shows that it can be measured in a variety of ways.[2] We now know that untrained people fall victim to a flow of confusing information because they don't know where its pieces fit. Those trained in Sun Tzu's mental models plug this stream of information quickly and easily into a bigger picture, transforming the skeletons provided by Sun Tzu's system into a functioning awareness of your strategic position and its relation to other positions. Each piece of information has a place in that picture. As the information comes in, it fills in the picture, like pieces of a puzzle.

The ability to see the patterns in this bigger picture allows experts in strategy to see what is invisible to most people in a number of ways. They include:

- People trained in Art of War principles--recognition-primed decision-making --see patterns that others do not.
- Trained people can spot anomalies, things that should happen in the network of interactions but don't.
- Trained people are in touch with changes in the environment within appropriate time horizons.
- Trained people recognize complete patterns of interconnected elements under extreme time pressure.

Procedures Make Seeing Difficult

One of the most surprising discoveries from this research is that those who know procedures, that is, a linear view of events, alone have a *more* difficult time recognizing patterns than novices. An interesting study[3] examined the different recognition skills of three groups of people 1) experts, 2) novices, and 3) trainers who taught the standard procedures. The three groups were asked to pick out an expert from a group novices in a series of videos showing them performing a decision-making task, in this case, CPR. Experts were able to recognize the expert 90% of the time. Novices recognized the expert 50% of the time. The shocking fact was that trainers performed much worse that the novices, recognizing the expert only 30% of the time.

Why do those who know procedures fail to see what the experts usually see and even novices often see? Because, as research into mental simulations has shown, those with only a procedural model fit everything into that model and ignore elements that don't fit. In the above experiment, interviews with the trainers indicated that they assumed that the experts would always follow the procedural model. In real life, experts adapt to situations where unique conditions often trump procedure. Adapting to the situation rather than following set procedures is a central focus of the strategy that Sun Tzu teaches.

Missing Expected Elements

People trained to recognize the bigger picture beyond procedures also recognize when expected elements are missing from the picture. These anomalies or, what the cognition experts[4] describe as "negative cues" are invisible to novices *and* to those trained only in procedure. Without sense of the bigger pattern, people are focused too narrowly on the problem at hand. The "dog that didn't bark" from the Sherlock Holmes story, "Silver Blaze," is the most famous example of a negative cue. Only those working from a larger nonprocedural framework can expect certain things to happen and notice when they don't.

The ability to see what is missing also comes from the expectations generated by the mental model. Process-oriented models have the expectation of one step following another, but situation-recognition models create their expectations from signals in the environment. Research[5] into the time horizons of decision-makers shows that different time scales are at work. People at the highest level of organizations must look a year or two down the road, using strategic models that work in that timeframe, doing strategic planning. Decision-makers on the front-lines, however, have to react within minutes or even seconds to changes in their situation, working from their strategic reflexes. The biggest danger is that people get so wrapped up in a process that they lose contact with their environment.

Decisions Under Pressure

Extreme time pressure is what distinguishes front-line decision-making from strategic planners. One of the biggest discoveries in cognitive research[6] is that trained people do much better in seeing their situation instantly and making the correct decisions under time pressure. Researchers found virtually no difference between the decisions that experts made under time pressure when comparing them to decisions made without time pressure. That research also finds that those with less experience and training made dramatically worse decisions when they were put under time pressure.

The central argument for training our strategic reflexes is that our situation results, not from chance or luck, but from the instant decisions that that we all make every day. Our position is the sum of these decisions. If we cannot make the right decisions on the spot, when they are needed, our plans usually come to nothing. This is why we describe training people's strategic reflexes as helping them "do at first what most people only do at last."

The success people experience seeing what is invisible to others is dramatic. To learn more about how the strategic reflexes we teach differ from what can be planned. As those who are trained in Sun Tzu's science of strategy report, the success Sun Tzu's system makes possible is remarkable.

1 Chi, Glaser, & Farr, 1988, The Nature of Expertise, Erlbaum
2 Endsley & Garland, Analysis and Measurement of Situation Awareness
3 Klein & Klein, 1981, "Perceptual/Cognitive Analysis of proficient CPR Performance", Midwestern Psychological Association Meeting, Chicago.
4 Dr. David Noble, Evidence Based Research, Inc.In Gary Klein, Sources of Power, 1999
5 Jacobs & Jaques, 1991, "Executive Leadership".In Gal & Mangelsdofs (eds.), Handbook of Military Psychology, Wiley
6 Calder, Klein, Crandall,1988, "Time Pressure, Skill, and Move Quality in Chess". American Journal of Psychology, 101:481-493

1.0.0 Strategic Positioning

Sun Tzu's eight key methods defining competitive strategy in terms of developing relatively superior positions.

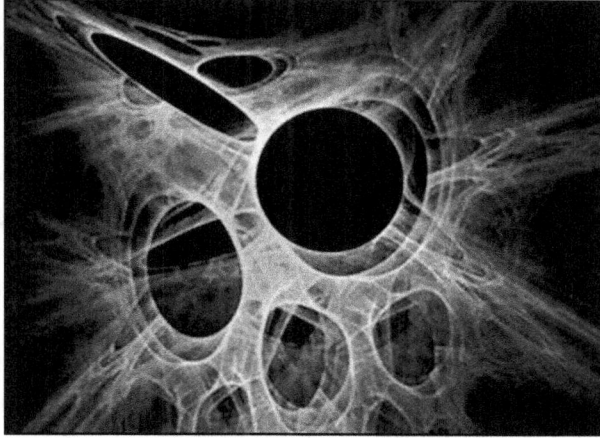

"Use your position as your war's centerpiece."
Sun Tzu's The Art of War 6:7:5

"When science finally locates the center of the universe, some people will be surprised to learn they're not it."
Bernard Bailey

General Principle: Strategy starts with understanding positioning.

Situation:

Sun Tzu's strategy explains the interactions of objects that we call positions. Like molecules or atomic particles, positions have various characteristics. We can analyze and compare positions and discuss how they "work" because we can discuss these general characteristics. While all positions may be a unique combination of characteristics, the characteristics themselves are not unique. Like all molecules consist of elemental atoms, all positions consist of elements that we can instantly recognize and evaluate. We can make decisions about the relative value and strength of various positions on the basis of these elements.

Opportunity:

Before Sun Tzu's *The Art of War,* success in competition was often explained solely by size. The rule was simple: the larger the force--whether an army or a single fighter, the more likely it was to win. The problem was that this rule did not explain what really happened in competitive situations where the smaller force often did win. It also didn't explain *how* some forces became larger than others. Sun Tzu saw that 1) size was not an advantage in many types of competitive situations, and 2) size itself could be explained by a more elemental concept, the idea of positioning. Positions with advantages create success easily. The size of an organization is a result of good positioning.

Sun Tzu's strategy defines the principles by which positions interact with other positions in the competitive environment. These principles are not deterministic, telling us what will always happen. Like the rules of subatomic physics, these rules are stochastic, that is, a matter of probabilities. These principles must also factor in our self-awareness and creativity. Unlike the interactions of subatomic particles which are naturally restricted to a finite set of reactions, we can consciously invent new reactions, reversing the expectations of others. This means probabilities are not fixed but constantly changing. However, all of these reactions are constrained by the basic nature of positions, which are defined by the following key methods.

Key Methods: The following eight key methods explain the basics of Sun Tzu's concept of strategic positions.

1. Competitive positions are paths. They are anchored in the past and have a direction toward a goal in the future (1.1 Position Paths).

2. *Competitive positions have both objective and subjective characteristics.* Competitive positions exist both in the external world and in the human mind. Both of these aspects of a position determine how competitive decisions are made (1.2 Subobjective Positions).

3. *Competitive positions can be compared on five key components.* Competitive positions are compared and interact with the competitive positions around them. These interactions take place in the competitive environment. Just as the environment of subatomic particles exists as other subatomic particles, the competitive environment is best viewed in terms of other strategic positions. The elements are mission, climate, ground, leader, and methods. Comparing these key areas are the basis of our competitive decision-making (1.3 Elemental Analysis).

4. *The external competitive environment drives change and provides rewards.* Without change, there would be no opportunities and without rewards, there would be no competition (1.4 The External Environment).

5. *The internal capabilities of a competitor are determined solely from making decisions and executing them.* We call these two internal components command and methods (1.5 Competing Agents).

6. *All positions are built around a set of motivations that determine both direction and strength.* This is the core of a strategic position (1.6 Mission Values).

7. *Positions are advanced through an adaptive loop of continually adjusting responses to events.* Events come from our external environment but our responses arise from our internal capabilities (1.8 Progress Cycle).

8. *The skills of external competitive success are the opposite of those of internal production.* The two skill sets are complementary opposites. However, both competitive and productive success depend upon each other (1.9 Competition and Production).

Illustration: These key methods of positioning govern every form of competition and every type of competitors. Each organization has a strategic position. The individuals that make up those organizations also each have their own strategic positions, both inside and outside of their organizations. We have positions in our personal relationships, in our career, in our social life, in our workplace, among our friends, and so on. Sports teams, military units, politicians, product brands, salespeople, negotiators, lawyers and every other profession in a competitive arena are actually working with competitive positions.

All of these positions are governed by the same eight key methods. As an application of these key methods, let's simply apply them to a career.

1. Competitive positions are paths. We can get jobs that our past jobs qualify us for and which take us toward our career goals. This is our career path.

2. Competitive positions have both objective and subjective characteristics. Our career path is determined both by our actual performance and how that performance is perceived by others. These two aspects of the job are related but they can be very different.

3. Competitive positions can be compared on five key components. Our career is judged by our career goals and values, job market changes, our current employer and industry, our decision-making skills, and our skill at performing our job.

4. The external competitive environment drives change and provides rewards. We can control neither industry trends nor how people are paid within our profession or industry.

5. The internal characteristics of a position determine its capabilities. We can develop our decision-making skills and our professional knowledge and abilities.

6. All positions are built around a set of motivations that determine both their direction and strength. We must balance our career choices depending on the relative importance of money, time with family, job risk, job stress, job satisfaction, and so on.

7. Positions are advanced through an adaptive loop of continually adjusting responses to events. Getting raises, promotions and a better position at another company are all based on the same adaptive process.

8. *The skills of external competitive success are the opposite of those used in internal productive success.* Competition focuses on adapting to people while production focuses performing tasks. Getting a promotion to a new position requires different skills than performing well in that position. Our ability to demonstrate our expanded abilities depends on getting promotions, but how well we perform determines our ability to get the next promotion.

1.1.0 Position Paths

Sun Tzu's six key methods defining the continuity of strategic positions over time.

"Use an indirect route as your highway.
Use the search for advantage to guide you."
Sun Tzu's The Art of War 7:1:9

"You cannot travel the path until you have become the path itself."
Gautama Siddharta

General Principle: Strategy requires predicting the direction of strategic positions.

Situation:

Positions rise and fall over time. The direction of strategic positions is affected both by conditions in the environment and the decisions that people in those positions make and act upon. Positions not only follow paths, rising and falling over time, but strategic positions are those paths. Their past and direction are critical parts of what they are and how they must be understood.

The problem is that positions change so slowly and gradually that we cannot see those changes easily. In our everyday lives, we often think of positions as static resting places. In everyday terms, we describe a person's "position" in a static way as part of a social hierarchy or as a clearly defined role in an organization or institution. This person is a department manager. That person is a priest or a lawyer. This is not the way we think about positions when we analyze strategic environments. We always attempt to look at positions not only in terms of where they are right now, but where they have come from and where they are going.

Opportunity:

The Chinese character that we translate as "mission" is *tao*. *Tao* literally means the "way" and the "path." Our method for using positions depends on understanding both their nature, their history, and their purpose. A strategic position is different from molecules or atomic particles because we are aware of our positions. Positions are created and directed by conscious beings not inanimate objects. We have come from somewhere in the past. Not only do we remember that past, but everyone in our environment remembers it as well. Our histories are part of our position, directing to some degree where we can go in the future. Strategic positions are always under someone's conscious control. This means that their direction is not random. It can be changed at any time by the choices and actions of those directing them. Positions have a direction because we care about our mission, that is, our goals and values. We make decisions to move toward our goals. We move into the future while making choices that shape the future.

Key Methods:

The following six key methods describe how we think about positions as paths.

1. ***Strategic positions are dynamic.*** The positions are temporary, a snapshot in time. What is harder to see is that positions are always changing, rising or falling, waxing or waning (<u>1.1.1 Position Dynamics</u>).

2. ***Strategic positions have persistence.*** People always defend their existing positions because we are all anchored to our past. Our histories are part of what we are and what we defend (<u>1.1.2 Defending Positions</u>).

3. ***Change is a key part of both the objective and subjective aspects of a position.*** In quantum mechanics and Sun Tzu's strategy, the concept of "at rest" doesn't even exist. All positions always have both speed and direction and our perception of that speed and direction shapes our decisions (<u>1.2 Subobjective Positions</u>).

4. ***Our decisions must be based on our view of the motion of position paths in our environment.*** All the strategic decisions that we make are executed in the future. We must make these decisions based upon where positions are in that future, not where they are now (<u>1.4 The External Environment</u>).

5. ***If we understand people's histories and motivations, we can approximate future position paths.*** This requires knowing our Art of War principles, what others have done in the past, and their specific goals (<u>1.5.2. Group Methods</u>).

6. ***As paths, future strategic positions are impossible to predict exactly.*** Unlike the paths of subatomic particles or baseballs, strategic paths are constantly changing because we are constantly learning. That learning affects the future vector of our positions. Skills are acquired and certain attitudes are formed. Mark Twain once described an education as the path from "cocky ignorance to miserable uncertainty." While learning our Art of War principles makes us keenly aware of what we cannot know, it also assures us that we will know more than those around us. Since these paths are under conscious control, their direction can be changed at any time (<u>1.5.1 Command Leadership</u>).

Illustration:

In sports, players must not think about where the ball is but where the ball will be. This is an extremely useful analogy for understanding the nature of strategic positions.

1. Strategic positions are dynamic. Both players and the ball move. The strategic situation is the changing configuration of the players' and the balls' positions.

2. Strategic positions have persistence. The goal posts do not move. Players have certain skills, reputations, and tendencies based upon their past experience.

3. Change is a key part of both the objective and subjective aspects of a position. A player acts based not only upon what the other players do but upon what he or she thinks they will do. Of course, players know that the other players have certain expectations about their behavior and they adapt their behavior based on that knowledge.

4. *Our decisions must be based on our view of the motion of position paths in our environment.* We do not play to where the ball and the other players are, we play according to where we think they will be.

5. If we understand people's histories and motivations, we can approximate future position paths. Even though we cannot know exactly what will happen when a player touches the ball, we can guess because we know the rules and goal of the game. The better we know the habits and skills of the player, the more accurate our prediction. The same is true of strategy.

6. As paths, future strategic positions are impossible to predict exactly. In sports, the path of a ball is relatively easy to calculate until a player touches it. After it is launched and before it is touched, the ball's path is controlled solely by the predictable laws of physics. Once a player touches it, however, all predictions are off. The balls future path cannot be predicted because its future path is controlled by the intentions and skill of the player.

1.1.1 Position Dynamics

Sun Tzu's seven key methods defining how all current positions are always getting better or worse.

"Positions turn around.
Nevertheless, you must never be defeated."
Sun Tzu's The Art of War 5:4:5

"Don't take life too seriously. It's only a temporary condition."
Bill Knapp

General Principle: All current strategic positions are temporary.

Situation: Since Sun Tzu teaches that all strategic positions are paths, we must see all current strategic positions as dynamic. While this sounds exciting, it really means that all positions are temporary. The temporary nature of strategic positions is a problem. It means that, given bad choices or just inactivity, our positions will naturally decline over time. It is easy to take our positions for granted.

As unpredicted events arise that seem to help or hurt our position, it is easy to make the mistake of thinking that our position depends on luck. The problem is that we think of these events as good or bad in themselves. We do not want to admit that our decisions put us in the path of these events. We do not want to admit that our response to every event is more important than the event itself.

Opportunity:

The temporary nature of positions also means that, given good decisions, positions can and do improve over time. Indeed, most of us generally improve our positions throughout our lives until age catches up with us. Most of us do this without knowing Sun Tzu's strategy. Our environment naturally provides both incentives and opportunities to improve positions. Even without a deep understanding of strategic positions, most of us improve our position if only because most of those we compete with also lack a deep understanding of strategic positions. It is our recognition of the opportunities in certain situations and our decisions to take advantage of them, not the situations themselves, that are the deciding factor in how our positions change. Our current position is always just the starting point. Our future paths are made possible by the conditions in our environment but it is determined by our skill at making decisions every day.

Key Methods:

To recognize and take advantage of situations, we must see them as a constellation of potential positions using the following seven key methods of Sun Tzu.

1. Shifting environmental conditions and our actions change our position. Our position changes automatically because conditions in the environment are always changing. As others around us act, their shifts of position affect our own because all positions are relative. As we prepare for events and respond to them, our own actions shift our positions and the relationships with others. Our environment and our reactions to it create constant elemental change (1.3 Elemental Analysis).

2. Our position changes even if we do nothing. We cannot stop the changes of nature and the actions of others. Sometimes these changes will improve our position, but more often, if we do nothing, our position changes for the worst. Strategy always involves making decisions about timing to adjust to this change. Change is built into our position because climate is always changing (1.4.1 Climate Shift).

3. *The most predictable of all changing conditions is aging*. We can predict with 100% certainty that all of us will one year older a year from now or dead, no exceptions. Aging can be many things. There is a difference between ten years of experience and one year of experience repeated ten times. Our use of aging determines the path of each individual's position. Our strategic position naturally improves after we are born because as we mature, we develop more abilities and more skills. After we physically mature, we enter into a long plateau where our aging has a much smaller affect on our position. However, toward the end of our lives, our abilities naturally begin to decline over time. Time limitations are built into everything (3.1.6 Time Limitations).

4. *Every position loses its capability over time by consuming its limited resources*. Everything ages. If not maintained and built up, every object that we build decays with time. This pattern of decay includes strategic positions, which are human constructs. The resources of every position are limited. If we use them without adding to them, the position loses its capabilities to support itself (3.1.1 Resource Limitations).

5. *Supporters change their decisions about our position over time*. Our existing positions are established based on the past choices by our supporters. When our supporters change their opinions about us, those changes undermine the positions that we have based on their support. Even without dramatic shifts in climate that necessitate re-evaluating their support, people eventually crave novelty. While people tend to continue doing what they have done in the past, they eventually make different choices (2.3.1 Action and Reaction).

6. *Unless we improve our positions over time, they will naturally tend to decay*. In Sun Tzu's vision, there is a natural balance in the universe that swings from fullness to emptiness. Aging, running out of resources and losing support are all symptomatic of this greater truth of balancing complementary opposites (3.5 Strength and Weakness).

7. ***Over time, the cumulative effects of our decisions have a greater impact on our positions.*** People are constantly acting to change their positions. The difference between levels of success has less to do with accidents of environmental conditions than the quality of the choices that people make on a day-to-day basis. Of course, the purpose of Sun Tzu's strategy is to explain how this is most easily accomplished in what we call the Progress Cycle (1.8 Progress Cycle).

Illustration:

Let us examine these principles by comparing them to a book by Malcolm Gladwell, called ***Outliers***, that makes the argument that success depends primarily on fortuitous environmental conditions beyond our control. His examples are the careers of people such as Bill Gates.

1. ***Shifting environmental conditions and our actions change our position.*** As Gladwell explains, Bill Gates was fortunate to find himself in a private high school with access to one of the first timeshare computers, enabling him to learn a technology unavailable to almost everyone else. This fallacious viewpoint focuses on the unusual, outlier successes like that of Gates. This hypothesis selectively filters out the typical success stories that are all around us. Drive down any business district in any town in America and the majority of the businesses that you see are not part of large corporations like Microsoft, but small businesses, started and built by individuals over the course of their lifetimes. These typical success stories built up their positions over time. These are the people that go on to become the "millionaire next door." For every Bill Gates, there are literally millions of these successes all over the world. Since all of these people are financially independent, the fact that they are not wealthy on the scale of a Bill Gates does not degrade their success.

2. ***Our position changes even if we do nothing.*** Forgetting all the decisions that led Gates from that school into the software busi-

ness, there were hundreds of other bright kids in that school with Bill Gates who had access to those same time-share computers. None of them went on to start leading software companies. Indeed, a few of those children, despite their advantages, almost certainly became alcoholics and drug addicts. Some of their positions ended up worse than those of their parents.

3. The most predictable of all changing conditions is aging. Like many "outlier" success stories, Bill Gates found his success early in life. This is not true for the average, everyday success story where most people's ability to earn increases throughout their lives as their capabilities increase. Even as their earning capability declines, most older people have accumulated many times the wealth of younger people simply because of aging.

4. Every position loses its capability over time by consuming its limited resources. The company that Bill Gates started, Microsoft, is completely different today than it was when Gates first made his fortunes. Had it kept selling its first product, the BASIC programming language for 8-bit microprocessors, it would have disappeared long ago. It was the subsequent positions of Windows, MS-Office, and other products that kept Bill Gates in his position as one of the most successful people in the world. Had his organization stayed in any of its early positions, it would have disappeared as certainly as Visicalc, DEC and Compaq, once the most dominating companies in their field.

5. Supporters change their decisions about our position over time. The untypical success of Bill Gates and typical success of the millions of millionaires-next-door have one thing in common: they are able to maintain their base of support over time. Millionaires cannot force customers and others to deal with them. Every day, those customers must be won anew.

6. Unless we improve our positions over time, they will naturally tend to decay. Many of the choices that people make can, of course, damage their position. Dropping out of school, using drugs and alcohol, not getting married, divorce, early pregnancy, a preference for self-indulgent activities, i.e. pleasing yourself, over productive activities, i.e. pleasing others etc. All of our choices have a predictable negative impact on our positions over time. While someone who makes bad choices can get lucky and win the lottery, these chance changes have surprisingly little effect on his/her position over time. Virtually all people who are in bad positions because of making bad choices quickly find themselves back in a bad position no matter how lucky they are.

Over time, the cumulative effects of our decisions have a greater impact on our positions. It was Bill's decisions that made the difference in the course of his life. Those decisions determined his position today as the world's richest man. Of course, one's actions are not guaranteed to advance a position.

1.1.2 Defending Positions

Sun Tzu's six key methods defining the basic ways that we defend our current positions until new positions are established.

"You are sometimes unable to win. You must then defend."

Sun Tzu's The Art of War 4:2:2-3

"If you are not prepared to use force to defend civilization, then be prepared to accept barbarism."

Thomas Sowell

General Principle: Current positions must be defended until new positions are established.

Situation: At its heart, Sun Tzu's strategy is based on simple economics. We get resources from our current position. We can use these resources to defend our position, advance, or extend it. These resources are limited. We must make choices about how we use them. The problem is that we can only advance our position when an opportunity presents itself. Until we discover that opportunity, we must maintain our existing position. We need our position because opportunities arise from our environment within the reach of our existing position. If we do not protect our existing position, opportunities cannot come knocking. Everything that has been part of our position in the past need not be defended forever, but we must always defend the parts of our position that touch on future opportunities.

Opportunity:

The more ground our positions control, the more resources we can access to advance our position. However, the more ground we control, the more resources we need to protect and maintain those resources. Defending positions competes for resources with advancing a position, but if we fail to defend our position, we lose resources and the connections needed to advance position. As the source of all our resources except for time, the ground that we control determines many of our basic capabilities (1.3.2 Element Scalability). The minimal ground that we can control is our own body. The minimal climate is our own attitudes and time. We extend our position by controlling more ground. We must defend our existing ground to hold onto our existing resources in order to have the resources to extend our position.

Key Methods:

Like so much in using Sun Tzu's principles, we are looking for the right balance. We need just enough defense, not too much or too little as expressed in these six key methods.

1. We know what we need to defend and what we do not need to defend. This means knowing what is worth defending. The basic standard is that we must defend the aspects of our ground that generate the most resources for the least effort and the most opportunities for the future (9.2 Points of Vulnerability).

2. We must avoid doing too little to defend our existing position. This usually means taking certain aspects of our position for granted. The most common mistake is taking our current position (and its resources) for granted. As we explained in the last post, positions naturally decay over time. If we are not maintaining that position, it can weaken to the point that its suddenly breaks. We can visualize an under-defended section of a position if we think of positions as a path. Imagine just a part of that path is weakening, growing thinner, and more fragile. If that part of the position is unimportant and unnecessary, outliving its value, this does not matter, but if that link ties together key parts of our current position, its loss can be devastating. In our practical wisdom, we recognize that a chain is only as strong as its weakest link (5.6.1 Defense Priority).

3. We must avoid defending every aspect of our position all the time. Being too defensive consumes valuable resources and creates strategic weakness. The other most common mistake is the opposite of the first: developing a defensive posture where we try to defend everything that has ever been part of our position all the time. The most extreme form of this defensive posture is a state of paranoia. This state of mind, while it is certainly defensive, can actually destroy the position that it seeks to defend. People that are too defensive find it impossible to let go of anything, especially the past. The position that they maintain (at least in their own minds) trails so far back into the past that it becomes a drag on moving forward. When we defend areas that do not require defending, we eat up the resources we need to advance our position (3.1.1 Resource Limitations).

4. We must see positions as stepping stones. In moving forward, we must sometimes leave things behind. However, we never give up all aspects of our current position. We never want to start developing a position over from scratch. Again, the key is balance. We must defend our existing position to get any opportunity to advance it. We must not defend it to such a degree that we destroy it or our opportunities to advance in the future (1.1.1 Position Dynamics).

5. We must move into new positions quickly but out of existing positions slowly. If a strategic position was a single point, this wouldn't be possible. A point cannot be in two places at once. However, since positions are a path, we always have a position to defend even when we are advancing to a new position (1.1 Position Paths).

6. We must avoid stretching ourselves too thin without abandoning the past. In these situations, we want to maintain and defend everything that is valuable in our existing position. Everything is a potential source of new opportunities (4.6.1 Spread-Out Conditions).

Illustration:

Let us illustrate these key methods with a variety of examples.

1. We know what we need to defend and what we do not need to defend. Our job, our current relationships, any assets that we control (money, house, car, etc). all represent parts of our position that we must defend. Certain aspects of our position consist of material property that we can use, but our resources also include all of the relationships that we have with other people. Everything everyone knows about us, that is, our reputation, is a part of our position. In strategic terms, fame is seen simply as an extension of position into more people's minds.

2. We must avoid doing too little to defend our existing position. For example, people's marriages get into trouble simply because they take them for granted and do not continue to work to defend them. They make the mistake of either taking their marriage for granted or thinking of a spouse as easily replaced. In fact, one of the most common keys to success is having a stable marriage. Divorce is a consistent predictors of failure because it indicates the inability to recognize what is valuable and defend it.

3. We must avoid defending every aspect of our position all the time. Think about Bogart's character of Commander Queeg in the movie, *The Caine Mutiny*. It was his concern about protecting his position that lead to its destruction. Maintaining positions requires maintaining relationships and nothing destroys relationships faster than exhibiting a lack of trust to those around us.

4. We must see positions as stepping stones. For example, to take a new job, we must usually leave our old one. When we mount steps, one foot must support our weight in the past while the other foot moves forward. Even when we take a new job, we bring as many skills, contacts, and resources with us from the old one as we can.

5. *We must move into new positions quickly but out of existing positions slowly*. For example, if we want to start our own home business, we can do so immediately but do it while maintaining our regular employment. We only quit our job when the home business has grown big enough to support us.

6. *We must avoid stretching ourselves too thin without abandoning the past*. For example in a business, we can add new customers and products without abandoning old ones.

1.2 Subobjective Positions

Sun Tzu's nine key methods describing the subjective and objective aspects of a position.

"When you are ready, you appear incapacitated.
When active, you pretend inactivity.
When you are close to the enemy, you appear distant.
When far away, you appear near. "

Sun Tzu's The Art of War 1:4:3-6

"More important than innate disposition, objective
experience, and environment is the subjective evaluation

*of these. Furthermore, this evaluation stands in a
certain, often strange, relation to reality."*

Alfred Adler

General Principle: Strategic landscapes and positions are neither objective or subjective but join aspects of both.

Situation:

Strategic positions on competitive landscapes exist in two planes at once. They exist both in the physical universe and in our minds. We say that they are "subobjective," simultaneously subjective and objective, consisting of both facts and opinions. This dual nature of positions and their competitive landscape is essential to understanding strategic positions. We can never know the complete objective truth about any situation. We can know facts, but the meaning of facts are filtered through our opinions of what those facts mean. We have our subjective perceptions, which capture a part of that truth filtered through our mental models.

Opportunity:

While there is only one objective reality, every one of us has a unique subjective perspective on that position. The gap between perception and reality can create opportunities (3.6 Leveraging Subjectivity). Very different perspectives on a situation give us different insights into the underlying, essentially unknowable, objective reality. Discovering the overlooked openings in that reality are the basis of all opportunity (3.1.4 Openings).

In an information economy, more and more people work with information and systems. and they are more disconnected from the underlying realities on which that information is based. This creates an opportunity for those who are closer to the underlying objective reality of a situation. The feedback loops connecting people to those underlying realities become longer, allowing greater deviations from reality over time (3.4.3 Reaction Lag). Larger organizations are especially vulnerable in this area (3.4 Dis-Economies of Scale). The larger they are, the greater the disconnect between objective and subjective aspects of their positions. This weakness is an opportunity for their competitors.

Key Methods:

Since we do not have complete information, we use the following nine key methods to improve our subjective judgments about positions.

1. We accept that we cannot know objective reality no matter how much information we have. There will always be a gap in our assessment of reality. The complexity of competitive situations is a potential trap for decision-making because we can always delay our decisions. There is always more information to be gathered (3.6 Leveraging Subjectivity).

2. We all have incentives to view and portray situations to our advantage. Sometimes this is intentional deception, but often it is self-deception as well. This fact tends to create more distance between objective reality and the subjective opinions that people hold about that reality (2.1.3 Strategic Deception).

3. The objective and subjective aspects of a position are "complementary opposites." This means that they are intimately joined and create one another in a loop. Each aspect of the dynamic shapes the other. Correctly understood, reality and opinion are not two separate things, but one thing with two components in dynamic balance (3.2.3 Complementary Opposites).

4. All subjective opinions are not equally close to their underlying reality. Some perspectives are very close to reality while other perspectives are total nonsense. (4.4 Strategic Distance).

5. Very different perspectives can be equally close to the underlying reality. Niels Bohr said that the opposite of a correct statement is a false statement, but the opposite of a profound truth may well be another profound truth. It is our breadth of perspective on a situation that allows us to see it with more clarity, especially in terms of understanding the forces shaping them (2.5 The Big Picture).

6. We must expect a larger gap between reality and perception when our information is older. It takes time to gather information. As we gather information, the situation is changing. The older our information, the more the situation has changed (1.1.1 Position Dynamics).

7. When stretched too far, events will snap subjective opinions back closer to reality. The further opinion stretches from reality, the greater the tension and instability of the situation. Opinion can snap back to reality almost instantly as events confront us with our foolishness (3.2.5 Dynamic Reversal).

8. Because of the subjective nature of our opinions, we test our perceptions against objective reality as soon as possible. We need to see the effects of our decisions on events. We want mistakes in our subjective judgments to be quickly corrected by events (1.8.3 Cycle Time).

9. Since reality is different than our opinions, we adapt our subjective views to better fit new information. This creates a constant loop between the objective and subjective nature of strategic positions. Our subjective view of positions changes the objective reality by guiding our actions. We run into problems when we cling to our subjective view when we get objective information that contradicts it. The objective reality of a position should change our subjective view when we observe an event inconsistent with our subjective view (1.8.2 The Adaptive Loop).

Illustration:

The gap between objective and subjective positions explains the financial/economic crisis of 2008-2009 that began with the worldwide distribution of bad real estate loans.

1. We accept that we cannot know objective reality no matter how much information we have. The objective reality of individual mortgage loans was relatively simple, but those loans were bundled to create complexity. On the objective level of reality, specific pieces of property were mortgaged to specific people who had a specific ability to repay these loans. The banks making those loans, who were closer to their true quality or lack thereof, were forced into these many questionable loans by the government edicts of the Community Redevelopment Act. However, they also knew that they could sell off those loans to government organizations such as Fanny Mae and Freddy Mac despite their underlying soundness. Though their immediate perception of the loans based on the property and people involved may have been that they were bad, that subjective judgment was mitigated by the implicit government guarantee.

2. We all have incentives to view and portray situations to our advantage. Those loans were sold, bundled, and "repackaged" by organizations such as Fanny, Freddy, and later on Bear Stearns to be sold as financial investments. In doing so, their subjective positions were enhanced, creating more distance between the subjective and objective reality. Organizations such as Standard and Poors and Moody were brought in to give their imprimatur of approval to these investments. This improves their value in subjective measure in people's opinions, making money in the process. Organizations such as AIG were brought in to insure these investments, improving their subjective worth, and making money in the process. These organizations gave plenty of money to the politicians who, specifically those like Chris Dodd and Barney Franks, who in turn, gave their blessing to the process and protected it from investigation.

3. The objective and subjective aspects of a position are "complementary opposites." These loan packages were both the investments that were sold by the investment banks and the individual investments by real people in individual pieces of property. Both aspects were different sides of the same things. Their difference was in the side we happened to be looking at. Investors were shown one side. Only those deep within these organizations knew about the real loans to real people and their performance.

4. *All subjective opinions are not equally close to their underlying reality.* One of the great delusions of the linear thinking of organizational age (discussed in several free articles starting here) is that objective reality can be completely reflected in our reporting

systems. As someone who built an accounting software company, I am keenly aware of what can and cannot be captured by general accounting procedures. While financial reporting and other forms of reporting such as the balanced score card seek to create the illusion that objective reality can be completely captured and analyzed, the series study of strategic science is based on the sure knowledge that no reporting system can ever capture all relevant information. We cannot treat information as anything but a limited subjective perspective on the situation.

5. Very different perspectives can be equally close to the underlying reality. There was a huge difference between the view of those investing in these loan bundles and the views of those selling them. This was reflected by Goldman Sachs shorting these investments at the same time that it was selling them to customers.

6. We must expect a larger gap between reality and perception when our information is older. It took almost ten years for the reality to catch up to the fiction. Bad loans were being made because the government required bad loans to be main. However, since those loans were being sold with an implicit government guarantee, it took a long time for rising rates of mortgage defaults to catch up to the subjective reality.

7. When stretched too far, events will snap subjective opinions back closer to reality. However, the loop will always complete itself. In the end, the objective reality of what those loans were truly worth caught up with the high flying subjective vision created by the institutional process. The crash was sudden, but the U.S. government came through, pouring hundreds of billions of taxpayer dollars into hiding the problem. The day of reckoning was pushed into the future again in the form of inflation potential and loan burdens.

8. Because of the subjective nature of our opinions, we test our perceptions against objective reality as soon as possible. Disconnect between the objective and subjective nature of investments can not grow unless the government enables these errors. One way that they do this is though guarantees insuring investments whose value is too complex to be understood.

9. *Since reality is different than our opinions, we adapt our subjective views to better fit new information*. This is the big problem with bureaucracies enabled by laws. Laws such as the Community Reinvestment Act lock in views of reality that cannot be adapted. So, people adapt to the law rather than the reality. This creates one crisis after another, but government is not deterred. It sees each crisis as proof of the need for more laws and less individual freedom that allows people to easily adapt.

1.2.1 Competitive Landscapes

Sun Tzu's seven key methods regarding the arenas in which rivals jockey for position.

"Some commanders are not skilled in making adjustments to find an advantage. They can know the shape of the terrain.
Still, they cannot exploit the opportunities of their ground."

Sun Tzu's The Art of War 8:1:16-18

"The real voyage of discovery consists not in seeking new landscapes but in having new eyes."

Marcel Proust

"It is only in appearance that time is a river. It is rather a vast landscape and it is the eye of the beholder that moves."

Thornton Wilder

General Principle: Competitive landscapes are alive, complex and continually changing requiring constant adjustments.

Situation:

When we think of "landscape," we think of the mountains and lakes that are fixed and stable. The problem is that competitive landscapes are made of living people who are constantly moving. These complex landscapes are continually forming and reforming. Sun Tzu taught that our positions are intimately connecting to these "dancing" landscapes of competition. In the modern world, we are raised at home and school where the relationships are well-defined, stable, and simple. We grow up poorly prepared for finding our way on the dancing landscapes of competition. The world in which we find success in is not only competitive and complex but growing more and more competitive and complex every day.

Opportunity:

The complex nature of the competitive landscape requires a different way of seeing positions (1.2.3 Position Complexity). Because our positions arise from our interaction with others, competitive landscapes are filled with novelty and opportunity. Because everyone who makes up the landscape is adapting to everyone else, these competitive landscapes are surprisingly robust. The adaptive agents in complex environments adjust to changes. When a competitor fails, another takes his or her place. The balance within the network assures that any holes are filled automatically by those looking for a new advantage.

Key Methods:

The following seven key methods define the unique nature of competitive landscapes.

1. A competitive landscape defines the space in which competitive positions exist. This space is defined by the relations of both competitors and various resources within a larger environment. The competitive landscape consists of both physical and intellectual components. It is both objective and subjective in its shape, existing both in the physical world and in our mental models of that world (1.2 Subobjective Positions).

2. The area of a landscape consists of the total number of potential combinations of its elements. These various combinations of elements are described as the niches in the environment. These elements exist in both competitors and their environments. The match between the competitor and the environment measures a competitor's "fitness." Competitive landscapes are also known as fitness landscapes. Each element has a range of possible characteristics within it. These characteristics interact in a huge number of combinatorial possibilities. Each of these combinations defines a different potential position in the competitive landscape. Sun Tzu's strategy analyzes these elements and their characteristics to compare various positions (1.3 Elemental Analysis).

3. Advantage in the competitive landscape is the superior fitness of a given position. A better position better serves our goals. The shapes of the landscape are infinite because every competitor has an infinite set of changing goals. It is also finite because the basic resources that are required for survival are limited. The basic goals of survival are shared by everyone in the environment. Others types of goals are shared by smaller numbers of competitors within the competitive environment. (1.6 Mission Values).

4. Competitive landscapes are inherently rugged, having many different local peaks within them. The various combination of characteristics within the environment create different forms of superiority. Those different forms of superiority combine with the different desires of various competitors to create diverse value points in terrain. Different combinations of characteristics offer different costs and benefits, creating many different types of local peak positions (1.6.2 Types of Motivations).

5. Competitors continually reshape competitive landscapes as they interact and adapt. This means that the competitive landscape is dynamic, constantly changing. Competitors are interdependent. As competitors move within them seeking advantages, the landscape itself is reformed, affecting the shape of the terrain for other competitors. This reformation changes the relative advantages in existing positions and opens up entirely new areas for exploration. This reshaping exists both in our subjective perceptions and in objective realities that create competitive landscapes. It arises from the new types of resources and new combinations of resources that are discovered and utilized by various competitors (1.1.1 Position Dynamics).

6. Good strategy improves our position within the local landscape moving us into more advanced positions. Our actions primarily affect our position in the landscape but they can also move us into landscapes that better suit our mission. Strategy explores the competitive landscape, trying to identify directions for improving our position (5.2 Opportunity Exploration).

7. External competitive landscapes are much more complex than internal controlled environments. Competitive environments are shaped by adaptive interactions of independent actors. Controlled environments are shaped for a given purpose, designed to limit interactions among actors. While no environment can be perfectly controlled for long spans of time, there is a huge difference in complexity between the two environments. This difference in degree creates a difference in kind. Beyond a certain level of complexity, environments go through a phase transition. The rules that work within relatively simple, controlled environments, i.e. the rules of production, no longer work. Instead, what works are the key methods of competition, the principles of adaptive strategy (1.9 Competition and Production).

Illustration:

Let us apply these principles to define a marketplace.

1. A competitive landscape defines the space in which competitive positions exist. Products, customers, and suppliers all hold positions within the marketplace. The positions of these elements consist of both objective facts and subjective opinions about each of these elements.

2. The area of a landscape consists of the total number of potential combinations of its elements. This includes characteristics of customers, suppliers, and products and emergent properties such as the climate of the marketplace.

3. Advantage in the competitive landscape is the superior fitness of a given position. In marketplaces, market share is one measure of fitness. Profitability is another.

4. Competitive landscapes are inherently rugged, having many different local peaks within them. Many different types of product characteristics meet many different facets of customer needs. Subjectively, the best product for a given customer may not be the most popular or profitable. Objectively, we can compare products meeting similar needs on the number of customers they satisfy.

5. Competitors continually reshape competitive landscapes as they interact and adapt. Marketplaces for specific product categories grow and shrink over time. Within a marketplace, different products rise and fall. The creation of markets and the rise and fall of products within them are based upon the decisions actors make in regard to the changing situation.

6. Good strategy improves our position within the local landscape moving us into more advanced positions. The goal of most products is to increase their popularity and profitability. There are dominant positions within weak markets and more profitable ones. Competitors try to improve their products position within a market, find broader markets, and move to more profitable markets over time.

7. External competitive landscapes are much more complex than internal controlled environments. The marketplace in which products are sold is much more complex than the factories in which products are made.

1.2.2 Exploiting Exploration

Sun Tzu's seven key methods on how competitive landscapes are searched and positions utilized.

"You must use the philosophy of an invader.
Invade deeply and then concentrate your forces."
Sun Tzu's The Art of War 11:3:1-2

"As mankind continues to explore and exploit the
realm of space there needs to be some accounting and
understanding of the medium. Space is a new realm to
the human experience. "

Bruce Bookout

General Principle: Progress requires both searching for new positions and harvesting existing ones.

Situation:

Each of us has a strategic position, but few of us understand clearly how positions are acquired and developed by crossing boundaries. Our educational system teaches us methods for using the resources within the boundaries of our control. These skills teach us very little about how to explore competitive landscapes outside of those borders. "Exploitation" is an interesting word, meaning both "to use" and "to misuse," "to develop" and "to corrupt". This confusion about exploitation comes from our confusion about boundaries.

Opportunity:

Sun Tzu simplified competitive strategy by developing the idea of positions and boundaries. Boundaries limit our position. Positions can only be advanced by crossing boundaries. When we exploit resources with our control, exploitation is productive. When we exploit resources outside of our control, it becomes destructive. As with all of Sun Tzu's concepts, exploring the competitive landscape for resources and exploiting the resources discovered are complementary opposites. We cannot have one without the other.

Sometimes we must make the most of our existing position through exploitation (8.3.4 Position Production). At other times, we must expand or advance our position through exploration (5.2 Opportunity Exploration). Human happiness depends both upon being productive and upon constantly improving our situation.

Key Methods:

We use the following key methods to balance exploring the competitive landscape with exploiting our position.

1. Exploitation satisfies our immediate needs while exploration satisfies future needs. Exploiting our current position seeks to get the most immediate benefits from our current situation. Exploration seeks to maximize the benefits available from our future situation. Exploration is a gift that our current selves give to our future selves by creating progress in our lives. Satisfaction cannot come only come from being happy with what we have. Research shows that the source of happiness is earned success. In Sun Tzu's terms, this means that constantly improving our situation is the source of happiness (1.8 Progress Cycle).

2. *Exploration of the competitive landscape requires adapting thinking and strategy.* Exploration is a systematic search of the competitive landscape for better positions. Sun Tzu's strategy exists because some methods have been proven to work better at doing this than others. Exploration includes both finding better positions and gaining control of them for exploitation. During exploration, we must make decisions about mysterious areas. We decide which areas are worth exploring further and which are worth exploiting (1.9.1 Production Comparisons).

3. *Exploitation of the competitive positions requires linear thinking and planning.* Exploitation utilizes the resources of a specific position on the competitive landscape to generate value. Exploitation includes both developing and executing methods for harvesting the value from a given position. During exploitation, we increase our control over our position, maximizing its production of value. We usually discuss exploitation in terms of "production" and "management" (1.9.2 Span of Control).

4. *We must strike a balance between exploration and exploitation.* If we are constantly exploring the landscape, we never get any value from it. If we never explore new territory, we can only maximize the value of our current position. This process reaches a point of diminishing returns. Without exploration, we cannot advance our position by expanding or moving into richer areas on the competitive landscape. The methods of competition and production sustain each other (1.9 Competition and Production).

5. *Positions are exploited and landscapes explored on both subjective and objective planes.* We explore the objective and subjective aspects of competitive landscapes looking for opportunities to improve our position. Opportunities to improve our position can exist in the physical nature of our environment, the opinions of other people, or in the gap between the objective reality and subjective opinion (1.2 Subobjective Positions).

6. *The relative advantages of positions for exploitation are constantly changing in the competitive landscape.* Dynamics are built into the competitive landscape. Change occurs both on the subjective and objective planes. The nature of superiority changes as our individual needs and goals shift over time. The relative advantages of specific positions also changes as people adapt, changing their position (1.2.1 Competitive Landscapes). ***The more dynamic the landscape, the more we are forced from exploitation to exploration.*** In other words, more static environments require more production while more dynamic environments require more strategy. The more dynamic our environment, the shorter the period of time a given position maintains its value. We are forced to move from old positions to new positions that are more valuable for exploitation. If there were not change in the landscape, there would be no new opportunities and everyone would be frozen in their existing positions (1.8.1 Creation and Destruction).

Illustration:

Let us make this very simple by considering a very small problem, finding the best place to eat.

*1. **Exploitation satisfies our immediate needs while exploration satisfies future needs.*** We can go to the best restaurant that we know or we can look for a better restaurant.

*2. **Exploration of the competitive landscape requires adapting thinking and strategy.*** Since there are a million restaurants, we need a method, that is, a strategy for finding the best ones. As we explore, we will discover new food preferences as well as new places so we will change our method as we learn more about our alternatives.

*3. **Exploitation of the competitive positions requires linear thinking and planning.*** If we are simply picking among the places we know, our job is much simpler: what are we in the mood for, what do we want to pay, what kind of time do we have.

*4. **We must strike a balance between exploration and exploitation***. If we are always trying new restaurants, our average eating experience is going to be, by definition, average. If we are always going to the best restaurants that we know, our eating experiences cannot get better without those restaurants improving over time, a relatively rare occurrence.

5. Positions are exploited and landscapes explored on both subjective and objective planes. The shape of the landscape depends both upon our personal tastes and the tastes of others in our local area. People must have the objective skills to open and manage the restaurants to which we go. Those restaurants must be run well enough to survive and be supported by customers for them to survive.

6. The relative advantages of positions for exploitation are constantly changing in the competitive landscape. Our tastes change both from day to day and year to year. Restaurants are constantly opening and closing.

7. The more dynamic the landscape, the more we are forced from exploitation to exploration.. In a very competitive market or in a volatile economy, our favorite restaurants are going to have a more difficult time surviving, so we are going to have to find new ones to replace them.

1.2.3 Position Complexity

Sun Tzu's seven key methods regarding how strategic positions arise from interactions in complex environments.

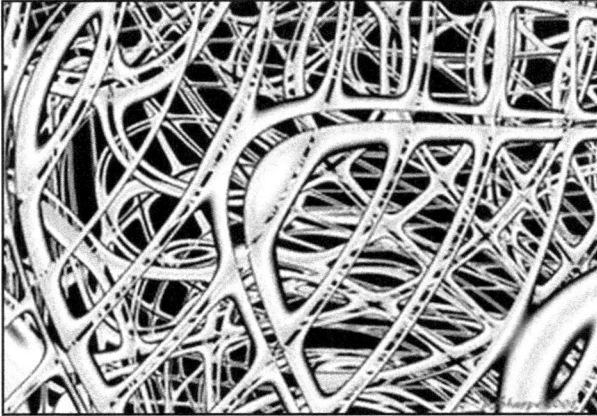

"War is very complicated and confusing. Battle is chaotic.
Nevertheless, you must not allow chaos."
Sun Tzu's The Art of War 5:4:1-3

"Out of intense complexities intense simplicities emerge."
Winston Churchill

General Principle: Positions emerge in unpredictable ways from their connections and interdependence on the positions of others.

Situation:

Positions exist as part of **complex, adaptive systems** that Sun Tzu called 'war' and we call 'competition.' His work explored the special nature of what we now call the "**science of complexity.**" Today this science explains different aspects of biology, economics, ecology, sociology, physics and many other fields. The nature of complex systems inherently limits both our knowledge and control over positions. Complex systems do not work mechanically in a linear, predictable way. Complex systems are unpredictable because every part of them is adapting to change. Though competitive events are based on probabilities, we can never know the exact probabilities involved because behaviors are constantly adapting. Chaotic systems are unpredictable in deterministic ways because they follow fixed rules, but complex systems are both unpredictable and non-deterministic.

Opportunity: The good news is that a little understanding of complex systems can give us a big advantage. Most people are playing with mindsets that assume fixed rules, Sun Tzu saw that we have a tremendous opportunity to exploit their narrow expectations. While we cannot predict complex systems, they work by their own rules. These principles create new opportunities in unpredictable ways. We can leverage these ideas to our advantage. Our success starts by accepting the limits created by complexity (2.1.1 Information Limits, 3.1.6 Time Limitations). We advance our position by working within the constraints of complexity rather than trying to impose our own rules (3.2.1 Environmental Dominance).

Key Methods:

The following key methods describe the complexity of competitive positions.

1. Competitive landscapes are determined by the interactions of agents, each with its own agenda. These agents are us, both as individual people and the organizations we form. As agents, we each have our own agenda, consisting of our unique goals. We are free agents to the degree we can seek our own ends. The ways in which we interact determines our position (1.2.1 Competitive Landscapes).

2. Our positions are inherently connected to the positions of others and to our physical environment. These connections consist of the exchange of resources and information. These connections create a many-to-many network, where actions are communicated from many positions to many others (1.5.2. Group Methods).

3. Our positions are interdependent on other positions and on our physical environments. Our positions depend on the conditions and events in our physical environment. Our positions also depend on the positions of others and what they do. Our presence also affects the environment and what others do. Our dependencies are both physical and psychological, consisting of both fact and opinion. (1.2 Subobjective Positions).

4. We all work to advance our positions based on our mental models. These mental models determine how we perceive our position and choose our actions. These mental models have memory. They contain a history of previous positions. We use these models over and over again, our mental models can change over time as we learn. The complexity of our positions arises from our interactions with others who may use the same or very different mental models (2.2.2 Mental Models).

5. Our actions generate reactions in the environment creating feedback loops. Positive feedback reinforces actions. Negative feedback discourages actions. Positive feedback encourages actions, magnifying their effect and the dynamism of the environment, perhaps creating emergent properties. Negative feedback discourages actions, decreases their effects, stabilizes the environment, and channels efforts into alternative directions. Economic theory assumes diminishing returns, but in complex systems, feedback loops create more rewards and different forms of progress (1.8.2 The Adaptive Loop).

6. As positions multiply, they become increasingly diverse, increasing the complexity of the landscape. The uniqueness of each position generates a unique perspective. That unique perspective creates different mental models. Different mental models create different responses. Positions differentiate themselves. We develop specialized skills and organizations, increasing the diversity of the environment. This increasing diversity reshapes the competitive landscape (7.3 Strategic Innovation).

7. New positions emerge from competitive landscapes in unpredictable ways. In complex systems, the whole is greater than sum of its parts. Features emerge from interacting agents to create entirely new features and forms of value. This is known as "emergence." More is not just more in complex systems. It is often different. Progress takes the form of a phase transition from one state to another. Potential is unknown. New breakthroughs encourages further developments. In complexity, this is known as "path dependence." We depend upon new paths to create new opportunities. When competitive landscapes create novel features, we describe it as opening up new opportunities (3.2 Opportunity Creation).

8. *The vast majority of changes in position will be small, but a few, rare big changes are possible.* Complex systems are non-linear. Small inputs can lead to major outcome swings. Results usually follow the power law distribution rather than a bell curve. The bigger the change, the more rare it will be. The more common the change, the smaller it will be (1.8.4 Probabilistic Process).

Illustration:

Let us illustrate these principles with a very simple illustration of a job position.

1. Competitive landscapes are determined by the interactions of agents, each with its own agenda. Our position at our workplace arises out of our interactions with other workers, customers, and everyone else we deal with in our job.

2. Our positions are connected to the positions of others and to our environment. We are connected to others by words and deeds. All jobs consist simply of exchanging information and materials with other people.

3. Our positions are interdependent on each other and on our environments. What we do affects what others do. What others do affects what we do. No man is an island if he has a job.

4. Our positions are advanced based on our mental models. We decide our actions directing our career based upon our mental models for managing our work life. These mental models affect how we see our native potential, our potential in the job market, and our potential at our current employer. We decide based upon those models whether to do what we are currently doing or seek a better position, either where we are or in another organization.

5. *All actions exist within feedback loops.* We hear about it when we make mistakes. We hear about it when we surprise people with a success. We hear about other opportunities in the job market.

6. *As positions multiply, they become increasingly diverse, increasing the complexity of the landscape.* Our work skills become more specialized as we deal with specific types of tasks. The more specialized our skill, the rarer it is and the more valuable it is.

7. *New positions emerge from competitive landscapes in unpredictable ways.* We cannot predict what opportunities will come our way.

8. *The vast majority of changes in position will be small, but a few, rare big changes are possible*. We will get many, many opportunities to improve our position in small ways. We will get very few opportunities to make a huge step up in responsibility.

1.3 Elemental Analysis

Sun Tzu's eight key methods defining the relevant components of all competitive positions.

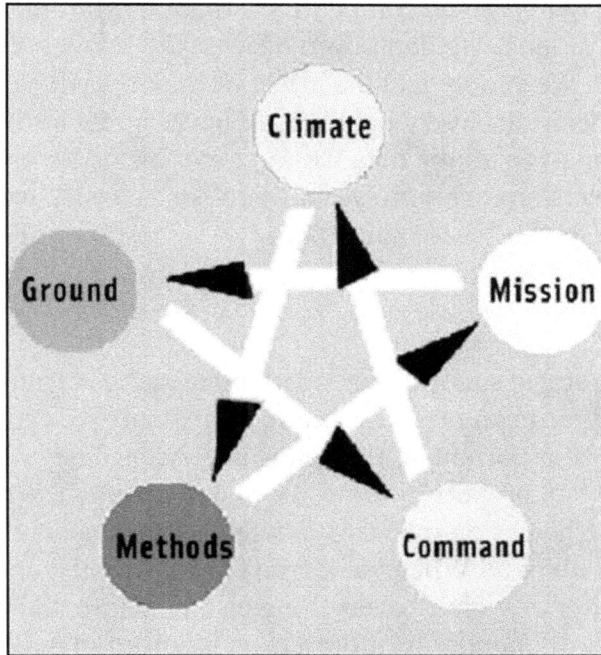

> *"Your skill comes from five factors. Study these factors when you plan war.*
> *You must insist on knowing your situation."*
> Sun Tzu's The Art of War 1:1:6-8

> *"Space and time are not conditions in which we live;*
> *they are simply modes in which we think."*
> Albert Einstein

General Principle: Positions are compared according to mission, climate, ground, command, and methods.

Situation:

The strategic challenge is to find methods to make faster decisions in highly complex environments. In these complex, fast-changing environments, the human mind cannot deal with the vast amounts of detailed information. Literally thousands of factors can come into play in a given competitive situation. Multiple agents affect our positions. We don't even necessarily know those actors or their actions. We simply feel the affect of their decisions. Still, we must make decisions every day. We are never going to have time to collect and analyze all the data we want to make those decisions. Many bad decisions are simply unavoidable. The only way to find out that they are bad is to make them.

Opportunity:

Seeing strategic situations as relative positions is valuable because positions can be compared in an instant. We can learn what information is important and which is irrelevant. The comparison of a few relevant properties of positions can tell us their relative advantages. Choices on the basis of a few key elements of positions can be made quickly. When we identify the properties that make a position "better or worse," everything else falls into place. While there are literally hundreds of principles involved in making the best decisions about conditions, a few properties that all positions share lie at their core. Those few key strategic factors enable us to understand the relative strengths and weaknesses of any competing set of strategic positions.

Key Methods:

In physics, Einstein's theory of relativity requires the concept of space-time, a union of the dimensions of three dimensions of space and time. In using Art of War principles, strategic relatively similarly requires the union of five different dimensions:

1. Mission is the dimension of the values determining strength and motivations. It is the organizing principle of a competitive force. Mission provides the core of a position's strength, connecting all the other elements. The values and goals of a mission determine its direction in the landscape. (1.6 Mission Values).

2. Climate is the dimension of change creating opportunities. It provides the temporary resources on which a position depends. It means all positions change over time. Without change, there can be no opportunities (1.4.1 Climate Shift).

3. Ground is the dimension of physical resources and persistent features. It is both where we compete and what we compete to control. The resources of ground provides rewards. Control of the ground gives a position stability ((1.4.2 Ground Features).

4. Command is the dimension of leadership and decision making. It is the realm of individual character. Decisions are not made by groups but by our individual choices. According to Sun Tzu, good warriors are distinguished by their ability to make productive decisions. The more productive our decisions, the more we extend our command (1.5.1 Command Leadership).

5. Methods are the dimension of group interactions for executing decisions. The most basic method is the division of labor. Methods define the realm of differentiated skills and our systems for putting them together to make the best use of resources. Methods are both competitive and productive (1.5.2. Group Methods).

6. All other principles for success relate directly to different aspects of these five key factors. Comparing strategic and competitive positions in the five dimensions of strategic space is the starting point for all meaningful strategic analysis. Most strategic analysis fails because it focuses on one or two of these areas, while ignoring the others (1.3.1 Competitive Comparison).

7. The five factors make it easier to envision a strategic situation in a tangible way. We can envision positions existing in a specific time and place. We can see them consisting of a group and a commander. We can understand the motivation that gives them purpose and direction. These elements allow us to understand the boundaries of positions, foresee their future directions, and predict the outcomes of meeting with surrounding positions (2.5 The Big Picture).

8. *These five characteristics can meaningfully map positions in any competitive arena.* Tools such as the Stratrix can help us map relative positions using these five dimensions. Just as Einstein's four dimensional space/time can be represented in a two-dimensional drawing to explain the operation of certain forces, the five dimensions of strategic space can be rendered in twodimensions, using the Institute's Stratrix tool (3.8 Strategic Matrix Analysis).

Illustration:

These five dimension affect every form of competition positioning: in business, relationships, sports, selling, military, and so on. Since every form of competition is a form of comparison, these factors always play into the conscious and subconscious ways positions are compared. As an illustration, let us contrast the areas of competition in business and personal relationships.

1. *Mission is the dimension of the values determining strength and motivation*s. Business mission is the goals and values the business shares with its customers, employees, and supporters. Relationship mission is what a given person is looking for in a relationship.

2. *Climate is the dimension of change creating opportunities*. Business climate is the forces of culture, technology, and economics driving business change in a market. Emotional climate is rise and fall of feelings over time that changes a relationship.

3. *Ground is the dimension of physical resources and persistent features*. Business ground is the marketplace of customers, suppliers, supporters, and competitors. The circle of intimacy is the personal connections that provide personal emotional resources.

4. *Command is the dimension of leadership and decision making*. Business command is the decision-making responsibilities of the organization. Character is attribute of personality that determine an individual's decision-making.

5. Methods are the dimension of group interactions for executing decisions. Business methods are the business processes, procedures, and other systems of producing value. Relationship interactions are the activities and habits of personal involvement on a daily basis.

6. All other principles for success relate directly to different aspects of these five key factors. The most successful businesses have relative strength in all five areas. The most successful relationships do as well.

7. The five factors make it easier to envision a strategic situation in a tangible way. Most businesses and most relationships focus on different aspects of their success formula, but usually miss the big picture of why it all works together around a core of mission.

8. These five characteristics can meaningfully map positions in any competitive arena. All such generic maps of businesses or relationships are over-simplifications, but they are useful. Their value is in simplifying complex positions.

1.3.1 Competitive Comparison

Sun Tzu's six key methods defining competition as the comparison of positions.

> *"Creating a winning war is like balancing a coin of gold against a coin of silver.*
> *Creating a losing war is like balancing a coin of silver against a coin of gold."*
>
> Sun Tzu's The Art of War 4:4:15-16

> *"There is no comparison between that which is lost by not succeeding and that lost by not trying."*
>
> Francis Bacon, Sr.

General Principle: Competition is based on the comparison of positions.

Situation:

People confuse competition with conflict because a lack of strategic skills leads inevitably to conflict. People think they hate competition because they prefer cooperation, but there can be no cooperation without competition. Most cooperation is inspired by our desire to be more successful in competition. We compete for the best partnerships, even the best spouses. In Sun Tzu's system, the opposite of cooperation is conflict not competition. Sun Tzu teaches "winning without conflict" as the most successful path in competition. Good strategy is impossible unless we understand what competition really is and why it is necessary.

Opportunity:

Science starts with clear definitions. In Sun Tzu's strategy, competition simply means making comparisons. Everyone makes comparisons all the time. Comparisons are necessary for decision making. Competition matters because our decisions matter. Since competition is comparison, information is critical to competition (2.1 Information Value). In the nineteenth century, the economist David Ricardo talked about competition as comparative advantage, which comes very close to Sun Tzu's ideas of relative positioning in competition. We all like being judges, but few us like being judged, but making comparisons and being compared are two sides of the same coin. The better we understand how competitive comparisons are made, the better we can understand where our opportunities lie (3.0 Identifying Opportunities).

Key Methods:

1. All competition is based on people making comparisons of characteristics. The elements of a position describe the most common points of comparison. Competition is the process by which people's positions are compared either in the judgments of others or by the physical outcome of events. Competing means seeking to advance our relative position in comparison to other positions. All strategic positions are judged by comparing them to other rival positions or alternative positions. This concept of comparison underlies *all* forms of competition. Unless a comparison is made, pitting one position against another, then no competition is possible (1.3 Elemental Analysis).

2. Comparisons are made among real alternatives. In competition, our position is measured either against the positions of others or our goals for our position. Positions are only measured relative to other positions, existing or desired. Though many forms of competition depend on the judgment of others, others do not. If we are alone on a desert island, we are competing against nature on the objective basis of an outcome, our survival (1.1 Position Paths).

3. Comparisons are based on past outcomes and judgments about future outcomes. The comparison among different positions is determined either by a physical outcome, by other people's judgment, or by a combination of the two. These comparisons are the basis of the objective and subjective natures of positions (1.2 Subobjective Positions).

4. Different areas of comparisons have different rules and standards for comparison. Every area of skill, every contest, and every other type of competition has rules by which its comparisons are made. When comparisons are made by outcomes, the rules govern what actions are allowed. When comparisons are made by opinions, the rules provide standards and guidelines for those judgments (1.2.1 Competitive Landscapes).

5. All rewards are attained from successful comparisons. For a comparison to be interesting, the comparison must be tied to a reward or payoff of some type. Competition is not just about winning any comparison, but winning those comparisons that pay according to our values (1.6 Mission Values).

6. *Both cooperation and conflict are based on comparison. Cooperating means working to a common goal.* We can join together with others to advance our position because by joining with others we can improve our relative position in many types of groups. Conflict means working for opposing goals. Direct competition means having incompatible goals, such as two competitors seeking the same, exclusive position. In evaluating relationships, we look for relationships that will support our goals and try to avoid conflicts that take us further from our goals (1.6.1 Shared Mission).

Illustration:

Let us look at how these key methods of comparison work for a wide variety of very different forms of competition.

1. All competition is based on people making comparisons of characteristics. A sporting event is a comparison of the capabilities of two opposing teams. A buying decision is a comparison of alternative uses of money. A job interview is a comparison of job candidates.

2. Comparisons are made among real alternatives. In sporting season, the position of one team is based on a comparison with the positions of the other teams in its group. In an evaluation of job performance, however, our position might be compared against our performance expectations, in the context of other employees' performances.

3. Comparisons are based on past outcomes and judgments about future outcomes. In sports, positions are based on outcomes of games. In a beauty contest, positions are determined by the opinions of judges. In a hiring decision, our position might be partly based on past outcomes and partly based on judgments of future potential.

4. Different areas of comparisons have different rules and standards for comparison. In sports, players must know the rules and what plays are allowed and which are penalized. In a dog show, judges must know the standards by which each breed is measured.

5. All rewards are attained from successful comparisons. In war, winning a costly battle can lead to losing the entire war. In a relationship, winning an argument can cost us a friendship.

6. Both cooperation and conflict are based on comparison. In sports, success is based upon the cooperation within the team. Military battles do not occur unless both armies think that they can win.

1.3.2 Element Scalability

Sun Tzu's seven key methods regarding how positions are analyzed by both component positions and elements.

"You control a large group the same as you control a few.
You just divide their ranks correctly."
Sun Tzu's The Art of War 5:1:1

"Two things are as big as the man who possesses them -
neither bigger nor smaller. One is a minute, the other a
dollar."
Channing Pollock

General Principle: Positions and their elements are scalable and self-referencing.

Situation:

We can get confused about strategic positions because they exist on a variety of different scales. Positions exist within larger positions. We can see positions close up or from a distance. A given nation's economy has a position within the world economy. An industry has a position within a nation's economy. A business has a position within an industry. An employee has a position within a business. The five elements defining the basic characteristics of a position also scale, reflecting each other at different levels. If we look at one of the key elements, for example, Mission, we can analyze it by breaking it down into the five elements.

Opportunity:

The mental models of Sun Tzu's strategy simplify complexity (2.2.2 Mental Models). We summarize volumes of confusing detail in a simpler picture. Looking more closely at a given element of a position helps us find the key element within the key element that we can best leverage as an opportunity (3.1.4 Openings). To do this analysis correctly, we must understand the principles about how positions and their elements scale. While there is always value in seeing the bigger picture, drilling down into the details can be useful only when we are trying to address very specific strategic issues (2.5 The Big Picture). Strategic positions contain a limitless amount of detail, but we only have time to access a very limited amount of it (2.1.1 Information Limits).

Key Methods:

The following seven key methods describe the different scales of positions.

1. Group positions can be broken down into the positions of its component groups and finally its individuals. We use these different scales in order to develop a more complete perspective.

2. Container positions provide the context for the relative comparisons of their component positions. Larger groups have positions that contain smaller positions of the smaller groups and individuals of which they are made. As individuals, we have smaller positions within the larger groups to which we belong (2.0 Developing Perspective).

3. An individual's position can be broken down into overlapping positions in different competitive arenas. As individuals, we have positions in a variety of family, career, business, and social circles. Looking at these overlapping positions gives us perspective on the balances that people strike in their lives (1.2.1 Competitive Landscapes).

4. Every element of a position can itself be broken down into the five key elements. Breaking down elements into more detailed sub-elements allows us to see more deeply into parts of positions and situations. Each element has unique characteristics that can be better understood in terms of the other four elements and self-reflexively, in terms of itself. We use the five key elements as different viewing angles to give us more perspective. Looking at elements within elements gives us depth of perspective (1.3 Elemental Analysis).

5. The elements from larger positions are greater than the sum of the elements of smaller positions. Elements within positions can add to the elements of larger positions, but new elemental characteristics can emerge from the group as a whole. Since some of the elements of component positions can cancel each other out, the resulting elements within a given group position can be very different than the elements of all the individual positions within it (1.2.3 Position Complexity).

6. The direction of a larger position is the sum of directions of its component positions. In other words, the element of mission must be shared to create direction in a larger position. The other four elements can reside in different parts of a position, but mission must tie the larger position together. The group falls apart or flies apart or stays where it is if mission is not shared (1.6.1 Shared Mission).

7. The direction of component positions is affected but not determined by the direction of larger positions. If a container position is improving or declining, all of its component positions will tend to improve or decline as well. This is very similar to the way the direction of the climate affects a position but doesn't determine it (1.4.1 Climate Shift).

Illustration:

These abstract key methods are easier to understand if we provide some examples.

1. Group positions can be broken down into the positions of its component groups and finally its individuals. An industry is made of component businesses. Those businesses are made of different product divisions. In the end, it all comes down to individual people.

2. *Container positions provide the context for the relative comparisons of their component positions.* The business position of an individual is best understood within their role in their business and their business's role in their industry,

3. An individual's position can be broken down into overlapping positions in different competitive arenas. A person can be very successful in their career and this fact can either help or hurt his or her family position. Since time resources are always limited, career competes with family, but since success in business produces other resources, such as money, it can help family position.

4. Every element of a position can itself be broken down into the five key elements. For example, we break the element of leadership into 1) caring about mission, 2) courage in facing climate changes, 3) intelligence to know the ground, 4) discipline in using methods, and 5) trustworthiness relating to leadership. Knowing that leader is weak in a given area, for example courage, we can better predict his or her behavior.

5. The elements from larger positions are greater than the sum of the elements of smaller positions. The mission of a company is not the sum of all of its employees' missions. It is the intersection of its employees' missions.

6. The direction of a larger position is the sum of directions of its component positions. If the majority of companies within a given industry are improving their position, the industry is improving its position as well.

7. The direction of component positions is affected but not determined by the direction of larger positions. A company's position can be declining along with its entire industry, but improving relative to its competition. Both of these factors are important in understanding the company's real position. If the position company is declining, the position of most but not all of its employees will be declining as well.

1.4.0 The External Environment

Sun Tzu's seven key methods defining the key external conditions shaping strategic positions.

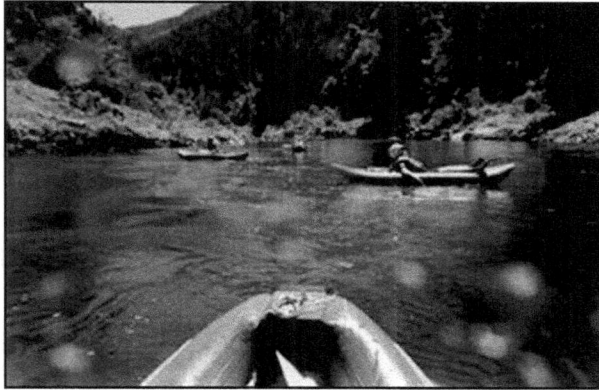

"You must know the battleground.
You must know the time of battle."
Sun Tzu's The Art of War 6:6:1-2

"Man must cease attributing his problems to his
environment, and learn again to exercise his will - his
personal responsibility in the realm of faith and morals."
Albert Schweitzer

General Principle: The key external conditions are the temporary and persistent features and resources.

Situation:

External conditions are all properties of our positions that we cannot directly control. We have three problems in dealing with these environmental conditions. First, there are a vast number of such conditions in a competitive environment. So many that all external conditions cannot be known. Our second problem is knowing which of these conditions are important to our position and which are not. Most of us fail to recognize the environmental forces that affect us. We are distracted by events that are recent and noisy while ignoring other conditions that are much more important. Finally, our last problem is knowing how to relate all these conditions to create a comprehensive picture of our situation.

Opportunity:

Given a clear mental model for understanding which conditions are strategically important and which are not, we can quickly filter out the most relevant information from the vast amount of data in the competitive environment (2.2.2 Mental Models). We can quickly see what key pieces we are missing. From a powerful model, we can develop a complete picture, not only of our competitive position in the context of the larger environment, but just as importantly the position of others and how their position relates and compares to our own. This mental model also gives us a framework for organizing a flood of information from our environment so that it facilitates making the right choices automatically. This organized picture allows us to see where our opportunities lie.

Key Methods:

The seven most general key methods for recognizing and categorizing these external conditions are:

1. We must first recognize the dynamic elements of the environment. Sun Tzu calls these temporary elements the conditions of climate. These are the formless resources, attitudes, and events that are constantly shifting and changing situations. The most important of such resources is our time. (1.4.1 Climate Shift).

2. We must then recognize the persistent elements of the environment. Sun Tzu calls these stable elements the conditions of the ground. These are the material resources, characteristics, and forms of our environment. These are the features that make a position valuable over time (1.4.2 Ground Features).

3. To better understand the changing climate, separate conscious choices from natural phenomena. Conscious choices arise from the strategic positions of others and can be analyzed by strategic methods. Natural phenomena are understood through other forms of science. Some climate events are a combination of both, the natural but unintended consequences of our choices. Natural phenomena are more predictable than human interaction. Such interactions create deep complexity of non-deterministic unpredictability (1.2.3 Position Complexity).

4. To categorize persistent fixtures of the environment, we separate actors from objects. Objects are more controllable than actors. Again, actors are amenable to strategic methods while objects are amenable to production methods. Groups of actors form a single actor when they work together. With the proper methods, we can shape objects in a highly predictable way, but in working with people, our results are always a matter of probabilities (1.8.4 Probabilistic Process).

5. We can rank all environmental conditions by their relative size. Conditions have size both in the physical sense and in the psychological sense. Psychological size depends on connections, the number of people affected by a condition and the degree to which they are affected. Events and temporary resources are measured in duration in time and the breadth of their impact. Stable features and resources can be counted and measured because they are tangible. These comparisons are the basis of all knowledge (2.6 Knowledge Leverage).

6. We can rank all environmental conditions by their proximity to our current position. Strategic proximity is measured in both physical distance and the amount of learning required. Proximity defines our immediate environment, that is, the conditions that have the largest and most immediate effect upon us. Events have proximity both in time and space while fixtures have proximity only in space. The concept of strategic distance is critical in understanding the impact of environmental conditions (4.4 Strategic Distance).

7. *Impact of external conditions is measured in their size times their proximity*. The amount of impact from events and actors is a combination of their proximity and size. Both their number of connections and the proximity of those connections are important in terms of impact (2.3.1 Action and Reaction).

Illustration:

The seven most general key methods for recognizing and categorizing these external conditions are:

1. ***We must first recognize the dynamic elements of the environment.*** Sunrise is a dynamic element. A purchase is an event. Our thoughts, actions, and emotions are all changing and shifting.

2. ***We must then recognize the persistent elements of the environment.*** The sun is a fixture of the environment. A buyer is a fixture of the economy. Our bodies, houses, and cars are persistent.

3. ***To better understand the changing climate, separate conscious choices from natural phenomena***. A purchase is a choice. Sunrise is a natural phenomena. A traffic jam is a combination of both, the result of many conscious choices interfering with each other creating an unintended event.

4. ***To categorize persistent fixtures of the environment, we separate actors from objects***. A buyer is an actor. The sun is an object. A company is an actor, but a city (separate from its government and buildings) is more like an object.

5. ***We can rank all environmental conditions by their relative size***. A big company of many people is a bigger actor than a small company of fewer people. In strategic terms, a hurricane that hits the coast is psychologically bigger than one that stays out at sea because it affects more people.

6. ***We can rank all environmental conditions by their proximity to our current position.*** A hurricane that hits a coast near us is more important than one that hits somewhere else. A company in our industry affects us more than those in unrelated industries.

7. *Impact of external conditions is measured in their size times their proximity.* A slowdown in an industry has a narrower impact than a general recession. A recession in America has more impact on Americans than one in Europe.

1.4.1 Climate Shift

Sun Tzu's nine key key methods regarding forces of environmental change shaping temporary conditions.

> *"You control your army by controlling its morale.*
> *As a general, you must be able to control emotions."*
>
> Sun Tzu's The Art of War 7:5:1-2

> *"Temperament lies behind mood; behind will, lies the*
> *fate of character. Then behind both, the influence of*
> *family the tyranny of culture; and finally the power of*
> *climate and environment; and we are free, only to the*
> *extent we rise above these."*
>
> John Burroughs

General Principle: Climate describes temporary external conditions, events, and the forces driving them.

Situation:

The passage of time plays a huge part in Sun Tzu's strategy. We experience the world as a series of events. Events affecting our strategic position come at us from many different directions. The problem is seeing these events in useful context rather than as a random series of happenings. Today's media makes this problem worse since it makes its living by bringing us more and more events. Our challenge is putting all those events into a coherent strategic picture. The world of events is the world of change. Most of us fear change because we fear the unknown. The more change we experience, the more chaotic conditions appear to be. The change seems without direction or meaning.

Opportunity:

Sun Tzu puts change into the context of the weather and climate. In the climate, changing events are both the cause and effect of all the energy in our environment. The energy of change creates opportunities. Without change, new opportunities to advance our position would not arise. All positions would be static. In societies that suppress change, people live and die in more or less the same state and, for most of them, that state is abject poverty.

The more dynamic external conditions, the more opportunities we have. The richest nations throughout history have been the fastest changing, that is, those at the center of events. The fact that most people fear change creates even more opportunities for those who are willing to embrace it.

Key Methods:

We use the concept of climate to help us discuss and evaluate the nature, direction, and the forces driving change.

1. Climate describes all external conditions that shift, evolve, and reverse themselves over time. In the simplest terms, *climate* describes what changes in our environment in contrast to the ground, which describes what is relatively stable. Of course, everything changes, especially our position, which changes even if we do nothing (1.1.1 Position Dynamics).

2. The primary resource of climate is time. We can only make decisions in the now, but those decisions factor in what has come before and what we expect in the future. Unlike all other resources, we each get the exact same amount of time every day. The only difference is what we do with it. Some of us kill time. Others of us are killed by time. The passage of time and its affect upon positions is all part of the cycle of the seasons in Sun Tzu's system (1.8.3 Cycle Time).

3. Physical changes in climate affect our capacities. The physical manifestation of time is movement. As time passes, movement changes the relationships of our physical proximity. This physical change affects our capability for various activities and our access to physical resources. Like the movement of pieces on a chessboard, the movement of people and objects over time affects what activities are possible. This is the objective side of climate (1.2 Subobjective Positions).

4. Intellectual changes in climate affect our attitudes which determines our activities. To categorize events, we separate conscious choices from natural phenomena. The choices in competition cannot be separated from emotion. Emotion is the trigger for action. The stronger the emotion, the more likely action is. The ability to get people to act is determined by the emotional climate. This is the subjective side of climate (8.5 Leveraging Emotions).

5. Except for the increase of methods knowledge, all trends reverse automatically when they reach an extreme. No trend keeps going up or down forever. Only learning and knowledge accumulate predictably over time. Many trends reverse themselves in predictable cycles that we can often recognize based on history. In straight-line trends, we do not usually recognize the potential for change, thinking that it will continue forever (3.2.5 Dynamic Reversal).

6. The most valuable trends for decision making are cyclic. They occur at regular intervals. These cyclic trends are driven by the balancing forces of complementary opposites. All such cycles eventually reverse themselves automatically because the underlying forces driving them balance each other. According to Sun Tzu's analysis, without these underlying balancing forces, all nature would dissolve into chaos. Only some cycles repeat themselves at regular intervals. Trends that depend on physical phenomena are more predictable than those that depend on choices. Physical trends are more predictable than emotional. (3.2.3 Complementary Opposites).

7. All positions age and are eventually destroyed as new positions are created. This is the cycle of birth and death. Everything that grows stronger eventually grows old and dies, including strategic positions (1.8.1 Creation and Destruction).

8. Every competitive arena is associated with its own climate. In the competitive environment, climate cannot be separated from ground anymore than time can be separated from space. However, we can talk about different characteristics and aspects of climate as distinct from ground, just as we can discuss aspects of the dimension of time as distinct from the dimensions of space (1.4 The External Environment).

9. Good timing depends upon understanding the trends of climate. Timing is knowing when to move and when to stay put. Many strategic moves are time sensitive. Situations are fluid. When a situation clearly demands a specific response, we must do so instantly, before the situation changes. It is also the knowledge of how to create and use strategic momentum. (7.4 Timing).

Illustration:

Each of these concepts is briefly illustrated below. We use the concept of climate to help us discuss and evaluate the nature, direction, and the forces driving change.

1. Climate describes all external conditions that shift, evolve, and reverse themselves over time. Business has a climate that is constantly changing. Relationships also have a climate. There is a job climate, industry climate, national climates and so on. All types of climate are both the result of change and the cause of it, affecting people's decisions.

2. The primary resource of climate is time. The business climate today is different from yesterday's and tomorrow's, but in each of these days, we all have only 24 hours to make our decisions.

3. *Physical changes in climate affect our capacities*. When it is rainy and muddy outside, we cannot travel as far, quickly, or easily. When it is light, we can see where we are going. When it is too cold or too hot, we tire more quickly.

4. *Intellectual changes in climate affect our attitudes which determines our activities*. If people are depressed, confused, or uncertain, it is difficult to get them to act, say in a depressed economy. If people are either very afraid or very confident, action is easy.

5. *Except for the increase of methods knowledge, all trends reverse automatically when they reach an extreme*. Day is followed by night, summer by winter. Happiness is balanced by sadness, courage by fear. A market that goes up will eventually come down, except to the extent it is driven by the growth of human knowledge.

6. *The most valuable trends for decision making are cyclic*. The timing of day and night are predictable but the rise and fall of markets is less so. However, the fact that markets rise and fall is critical in making good investment decisions.

7. *All positions age and are eventually destroyed as new positions are created*. People grow stronger and more capable as they mature from children to adults. As they get older, they begin to physically and psychologically decline. The same cycle applies to businesses, nations, and technologies.

8. *Every competitive arena is associated with its own climate*. The climate in California is different than the climate in Maine. The climate of the transportation industry is different from the climate in manufacturing. The climate of baseball is different from the climate of soccer.

9. *Good timing depends upon understanding the trends of climate*. The timing of day and night are predictable but the rise and fall of markets are not. The best time to start a business is during a recession. If we can survive financially during hard times, when the eventual reversal takes place, economic growth will grow the business. The worst time to start a business is during boom times when bad practices are forgiven by a favorable environment. Companies than can only survive during good times are weeded out during bad.

1.4.2 Ground Features

Sun Tzu's ten key methods defining the persistent resources that we can control.

"Some commanders are not skilled in making adjustments to find an advantage. They can know the shape of the terrain.
Still, they cannot exploit the opportunities of their ground."

Sun Tzu's The Art of War 7:1:16

"Innovation is the specific instrument of entrepreneurship. The act that endows resources with a new capacity to create wealth."

Peter F. Drucker

General Principle: Ground describes external conditions that persist over time and provide resources.

Situation:

Where we are now doesn't dictate where we can go in the long-term, but it does dictate where we can go next. We are confined by our position's location. We move according to the laws governing space. The challenge is understanding the laws that govern strategic space. Every location has its own shape and form. Every place is connected through space to nearby places. Place is inherently much more complicated than time. Understanding the complex nature of location and its many characteristics and capacities is at the heart of Sun Tzu's strategy. Without the resources that we get from our physical position, we could not continue to survive, much less compete. In a modern world, we make a mistake in taking these resources, such as food and water, for granted, not recognizing the work that has been required throughout history to attain them.

Opportunity:

The benefit of every location is the resources that it offers. Every physical location offers resources. The most basic resource that every position offers is its proximity to other positions. Proximity decreases our costs in moving to better position with more resources. We win that ability to use the resources of a given place through competition, but we translated that control into resources through production (1.9 Competition and Production). Strategic methods allow us to expand our control over our space. The more successfully we compete, the more area we control. We advance our position both by expanding our area of control and by moving to new, more bountiful areas.

Key Methods:

We use the concept of ground to help us discuss and evaluate the nature, shape, and properties of a given location when compared to other locations.

1. Ground is the term we use to discuss space, place, and location. Ground describes all external conditions that persist over time. In the complementary opposite *climate,* which describes what changes over time. The **ground** describes what persists despite the changes of time (1.4.1 Climate Shift).

2. Ground is the store of all persistent resources. The ground is a source of resources that persist over time. These resources are both physical and psychological. These resources are the rewards we get from controlling the ground (8.0 Winning Rewards).

3. We access the resources of ground through our control over it. To gain resources from the ground, we must first win control over it. This control allows us to use the ground productively. We win control of the ground through competition and get rewards from it through production (1.9 Competition and Production).

4. We earn control over ground through competition. The ground is both where we compete and what we compete for. For gladiators, the ground was the games in the coliseum because their performance in them was the source of all their rewards. In business, we define the ground in terms of marketplaces and their customers. In sports, the ground is the market for customers, the market for sports talent, and the actual playing field, depending upon your focus (1.3.1 Competitive Comparison).

5. The physical nature of ground determines the physical resources it provides. The physical characteristics of the ground affects how we can use it and what forms of resources it offers. Those characteristics start with physical space itself and its proximity to other locations. In terms of defending and advancing positions, the conditions of the ground is evaluated in terms of distances, obstacles, and dangers. We categorize different forms of the ground in terms uneven, fast-changing, and uncertain. Other conditions define the six extreme forms of ground. Still others discuss the terrain in terms of how it affects our relationships with others. This is the objective side of ground (1.2 Subobjective Positions).

6. The intellectual nature of ground provides psychological resources. In order to make decisions, people compare the characteristics of both objects and actors, positioning them in their minds. While emotional attitudes create climate, people's skills, knowledge, and opinions persist over time making them part of the ground, the mental terrain. This is the subjective side of ground (1.3.1 Competitive Comparison).

7. Most of the objective and subjective aspects of ground can be discussed in the same terms. The conditions of our mental terrain can be categorized using many of the same shape and form characteristics that we use to talk about physical space. We can only make good decisions about conditions when we have learned how to recognize them in physical terms (2.2.3 Standard Terminology).

8. The resources available in any one position are limited. A part is less than the whole. Some ground has fewer resources than all ground. Only a certain amount of resources can be produced over a given period of time from a given location. This limitation is partially driven by our limited knowledge. (3.1.1 Resource Limitations).

9. Our control over the ground is also limited. We never have complete control over the ground because our knowledge of nature is limited and because we compete with others (8.1.2 Control Limits).

10. We can only learn the value of controlling the ground after winning control. This problem creates one of the fundamental challenges of strategy because it means that we cannot predict the value of ground until we control it (2.3.2 Reaction Unpredictability).

Illustration:

Each of these concepts is briefly illustrated below.

We use the concept of ground to help us discuss and evaluate the nature, shape, and properties of a given location when compared to other locations.

1. Ground is the term we use to discuss space, place, and location. In terms of the physical space, locations in California are different than locations in Maine. In business space, the competitive arena in the transportation industry is different from the ground in manufacturing. As a playing field, the ground in baseball in different from the ground in soccer or American football.

2. Ground is the store of all persistent resources. The capabilities of our bodies are the minimum physical resources of the ground. Gold mines and oil wells produce other types of ground resources. Our reputations and knowledge are other forms of ground resources.

3. We access the resources of ground through our control over it. The only ground that we are born controlling is our own bodies. Our property, position at work, and position in the community are all forms of ground that we earn over time.

4. We earn control over ground through competition. If we were gladiators, the ground would be the coliseum because our performance there is the source of all potential awards. In business, we define the ground in terms of marketplaces and their customers. In sports, the ground is the market for customers, the market for sports talent, and the actual playing field, depending upon your focus.

5. The physical nature of ground determines the physical resources it provides. Food, water, metal, oil, and the invaluable resource of proximity come from the element ground.

6. The intellectual nature of ground provides psychological resources. People who have always bought a certain brand of car or voted for a particular party or to prefer doing a certain type of work all have a certain mental terrain.

7. Most of the objective and subjective aspects of ground can be discussed in the same terms. "High ground" is both a physical and a psychological strategic concept. Visibility, barriers, area, and almost every other aspect of the physical ground have their psychological parallels.

8. The resources available in any one position are limited. The abilities of a group of people are more than the abilities of any one person or subgroup of that group.

9. Our control over the ground is also limited. We control our bodies, but we cannot control our liver function. All jobs have limits on their authority. Even our control over our own property is controlled by a host of laws and conventions.

10. We can only learn the value of controlling the ground after winning control. We don't know how profitable a business is until we start it. We don't know the burdens of a management position until we win it.

1.5.0 Competing Agents

Sun Tzu's seven key methods regarding characteristics of competitors.

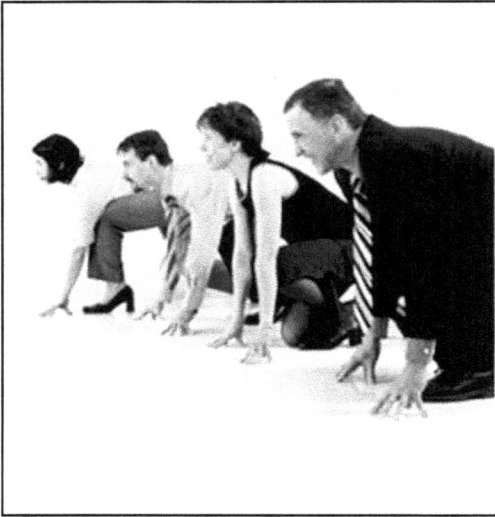

"Which method of command works? Which group of forces has the strength?"

Sun Tzu's The Art of War 1:2:7

"When once a decision is reached and execution is the order of the day, dismiss absolutely all responsibility and care about the outcome."

William James

General Principle: Competitors must make and execute decisions affecting their position.

Situation:

As competitors, that is, as agents or actors in a competitive landscape, we must make decisions and execute actions to improve our strategic position. Choices must be made, but those choices must be executed as well. Decisions and execution are two sides of the same coin. The problem is that most people do not have a clear mental model of what competitors are and how they interact. Competing agents consist of specific components. These characteristics play important roles in how a given competitor makes decisions and executes them. Without a model for understanding competitors, we skip from one competitive characteristic to the next, trying to figure out what role it plays. We miss certain important elements while fixating on a few. Only through luck and chance do we hit upon what is and is not important in a given situation with a given set of competing agents.

Opportunity: When we have a clear model of the key elements of a competitor, we can compare our abilities to the abilities of others. This comparison is the basis of competitive positions (1.3.1 Competitive Comparison). When we have a clear model about how competing agents interact, we can predict behavior much more easily. Sun Tzu provides a framework for understanding competing agents that we can refine over time. The skills that Sun Tzu teaches help competing agents make better decisions and better execute those decisions. Making decisions that we can execute and executing the decisions that we make are two sides of the same coin in Sun Tzu's system.

Key Methods:

The following seven key methods describe the key aspect of competing agents, ourselves, our rivals, and our supporters.

1. The competitive landscape is made up of competing agents who are compared. Competition is comparison. As agents, we act to improve our relative positions. As agents, we are compared by judgments. Those judgments are based both on opinions and outcomes. In many landscapes, we act as both agents and judges. In other landscapes, judgments are made apart from the agents themselves. Agents can be individuals or organizations made of individuals (1.2.1 Competitive Landscapes).

2. *Agents' decisions are motivated by their missions.* As agents, we all act with purpose. Our purpose is to satisfy our needs, values, and desires. All of us are motivated by our own personal mission. Individuals join into organizations to satisfy their mutual goals (1.6 Mission Values).

3. *Making competitive decisions requires the clear authority of command.* If the competing agent is one individual, that person is responsible for making his or her own decisions. If the agent is a group of people, the command role of making decisions can be divided into various areas of responsibility. Success of the organization demands clear lines of authority. People must know who has command in a given area. One individual must clearly have the final responsibility (1.5.1 Command Leadership).

4. *Methods for execution require methods combining personal skills and group systems*. Skills are the capability of an individual. Systems are the interaction of individuals within a group. Without skills and systems, decisions cannot be executed (1.5.2. Group Methods).

5. *Command and methods require each other.* Actions cannot be executed without a decision, but leaders cannot make decisions without taking into account how decisions are executed. Our ability to execute certain activities directs our decision making. Our decisions direct what actions we attempt to execute. These two components are complementary opposites, representing two different aspects of the same unified process (3.2.3 Complementary Opposites).

6. *Command and methods are always limited, specialized to fit in their position.* No person can do everything. No organization, no matter how large, can masters all skills and systems. A given set of decision-making and execution skills are developed to fit a given position (8.1.2 Control Limits).

7. *The model of command and methods is scalable.* It applies to an individual making and executing decisions about his or her position. It also applies the the largest organizations and how those organizations make decisions regarding their positions. At each level, the leader of a division picks the leaders under him or her.

Organization describes who has the authority for making specific types of decisions and who has the responsibility for executing those decisions (1.3.2 Element Scalability).

Illustration:

These ideas are fairly simple, but we offer some examples below.

1. The competitive landscape is made up of competing agents who are compared. In commercial society, we are both agents and judges. We compete either individually or as part of organizations for the dollars of customers. As customers, we judge other agents who compete for our dollars but we also compete for products in situations such as auctions. In sports, teams compete as agents, but the judgments are made by referees according to the rules of the game. In politics, politicians are agents who compete for the judgment of voters.

2. Agents' decisions are motivated by their missions. We work at our jobs to get an income. The more income we have the more desires we can satisfy. In romantic relationships, we compete for attention and commitment depending on the type of attention and commitment we desire. In sports, we compete to win games, but the individual athletes are also competing for recognition and attention.

3. Making competitive decisions requires the clear authority of command. Organizations flounder when they do not have a clear leader making clear decisions. I often see this problem when my family gets together. Since no one of us is in charge, we have a terrible time making decisions about what to do and who should do it. In the end, events only take shape once areas of responsibility are carved out.

4. Methods for execution require methods combining personal skills and group systems. In order to open a restaurant, we need to have access to a range of skills: cooking, menu-making, purchasing ingredients, selecting a location, negotiating a lease, and so on. While we can learn skills by doing, trial and error is an expensive form of education.

5. *Command and methods require each other.* It doesn't make any sense to decide to make cake if no one knows a recipe for making it. It doesn't make sense to bake a cake just because we know how if no one wants to eat cake.

6. *Command and methods are always limited, specialized to fit in their position.* Companies that have tried to master a wide variety of skills have consistently failed. The whole concept of "outsourcing" arises from the recognition of limits.

7. *The model of command and methods is scalable*. Large organizations run by distributing leadership and execution responsibilities to various groups. Within Wal-Mart, there are purchasing and selling divisions. In the selling divisions, there are geographic managers responsible for managing groups of stores. Each store has a manager. Each department within a store has a manager. At each time of day, someone is at least temporarily responsible for every area.

1.5.1 Command Leadership

Twelve key methods regarding individual decision-making (leaders).

"Next is the commander.
He must be smart, trustworthy, caring, brave, and
strict."

Sun Tzu's The Art of War 1:1:2829

"When once a decision is reached and execution is the
order of the day, dismiss absolutely all responsibility and
care about the outcome."

William James

General Principle: Leaders must make command decisions based on their training and character.

Situation:

In controlled environments, we are working with objects, and our success depends on knowing the right set of procedures to follow. Competitive environments are different. When we are on the front lines of competition, our success depends on the decisions that we make. Our decisions must take into account the changing conditions of our environment. Decisions must be made quickly, often with a minimum of information. Many of these decisions are automatic responses to conditions. The first problem that we must address is the one of taking personal responsibility. The second challenge is developing the personality characteristics that result in good decisions.

Opportunity:

Trained front-line leaders can recognize the key characteristics of a situation and respond instantly. They know which responses are the most likely to be successful. When we have a clear understanding of leadership, we can pick better leaders. When we understand the key characteristics of leaders, we can measure both ourselves and others against those standards. We can know who we can trust. We can predict who will make good decisions and what mistakes others are likely to make. When we understand how leadership really works, we can make the correct decisions more quickly without having to worry about making serious mistakes. The mistakes we do make are those from which we can learn.

Key Methods:

The following key methods apply to the element of leadership command:

1. Command is the responsibility of the individual. Leaders must make their decisions alone, and individuals must assume command within their own lives. There is no such thing as a group decision. Groups can only concur with a decision made by an individual. The individuals within a group each make their own decisions about whether to agree or battle with a suggested decision (1.5 Competing Agents).

2. We are in command when we are making decisions for our own goals. Even when we are following the command decisions of others, we usually find ourselves making decisions for ourselves through the course of the day. Even when following an organization's rules about how those decisions are to be made, we are using our own judgment in each moment (1.6 Mission Values).

3. *The more successful we are at making decisions, the more people turn to us as a leader.* The decisions of command with many followers may have a broader impact than the decisions of an individual, but every individual has to take command responsibility if only for the course of their own lives. The skills of decision-making are the same for a leader of millions and for each of us *leading* our own lives (1.9.2 Span of Control).

4. *As leaders, we must make decisions whether we want to or not.* When we are in command, we are making a decision even when we choose to avoid or delay a decision. The decision not to decide is also a decision. The decision to continue doing what we have been doing is a decision as well (1.8.1 Creation and Destruction).

5. *Command makes decisions to respond to events.* While we tend to think of "events" as the actions of others, more broadly "events" simply represent the discovery of new information about conditions in our environment. Our senses are constantly picking up information from the environment, but not all of it is new. It is the new information that triggers the leader's decision-making machinery. Some new information is generated by change. This is information from the climate. However, other information has been there all the time, but it is new to us because we discover it for the first time. This is information from the ground, specifically information from learning more about the ground (5.1.1 Event Pressure).

6. *Leaders must know which strategic areas require foresight and analysis.* The most basic command activities require working at building up a strategic picture of the situation. While many command decisions require snap, gut decisions, those decisions are based on a carefully cultivated strategic picture. Other decisions, such as the use of surprises, require preparation beforehand (3.0 Identifying Opportunities).

7. *Leaders must train their minds for snap decision-making.*
Our senses are exposed to a flood of information during the events of the day, and we are not necessarily consciously aware of it all. Our brains work on the pre-conscious level filtering that information to select the ideas that are important enough to penetrate our awareness. Our brains are continually making low-level decisions about what information is important enough to bring to the attention of the higher-level decision-making processes of our conscious minds (5.3 Reaction Time).

8. *Small command decisions have the biggest impact on our lives over time.* Success is less about individual decisions as it is about the general course of our decisions and the quality of the decision that we are making over time. No matter how well we analyze and train, we are going to make plenty of mistakes. The key is to learn from them. If we do, many individual decisions, even those that seem very insignificant at the time, can have a huge impact on the course of our lives over large spans of time. To stay in command, we must decide what is the best use of our time at every moment of every day (1.8.2 The Adaptive Loop).

9. *Leadership requires five qualities of character.* Since leaders are continuously making both subconscious and conscious decisions in an instant, command is a product of our character. The five qualities of leadership character are tied closely to the five key factors that define a strategic position (1.3 Elemental Analysis).

- *Caring* means devotion to the shared mission or goals.
- *Courage* means confronting the uncontrollable conditions of a changing climate.
- *Knowledge* means understanding the rules of winning resources from the conditions of the ground.
- *Trustworthiness* means honoring commitments to others in the realm of methods.
- *Discipline* means executing the decisions required of leadership.

10. *A lack of character qualities in a leader, show up in five different ways*. A leader who lacks these skills is unable to improve his or her position (3.5 Strength and Weakness):

- A lack of caring loses sight of the mission in dealing with events.
- A lack of courage cannot discover opportunities in adversity.
- A lack of knowledge fails to harvest the resources in the environment.
- A lack of trustworthiness cannot depend on others in executing decisions.
- A lack of discipline fails to persist in executing decisions.

11. A leader who has an excess of these characteristics also makes bad decisions. These excesses lead to a completely different set of weaknesses. (4.7.1 Command Weaknesses).

- An excess of caring is too rigid in ideology to join with others.
- An excess of courage results in foolhardy decision making.
- An excess of knowledge creates paralysis from analysis.
- An excess of trustworthiness makes us too particular about satisfying others.
- An excess of discipline loses flexibility in responding to events.

Illustration:

The following principles apply to the element of leadership command:

1. Command is the responsibility of the individual. Any organization, such as the UN, which has no clear leader cannot be effective.

2. We are in command when we are making decisions for ourselves. The less free people are to make their own decisions, the less productive their lives will be.

3. The more successful we are at making decisions, the more people turn to us as a leader. President Obama was elected because he was able to make better decisions than his opponents through the course of the campaign, winning more and more support as time went on.

4. As leaders, we must make decisions whether we want to or not. When a leader tries to delegate the hard decisions, as we are seeing with President Obama on healthcare, he is increasingly seen as ineffective and weak and loses support.

5. Command makes decisions to respond to events. When a leader flounders in the face of events, as John McCain did in the face of the financial crisis at the end of the campaign, they lose support.

6. Leaders must know which strategic areas require foresight and analysis. When a leader cannot produce a cohesive picture of a situation, as President Bush failed to do in Iraq, they lose support.

7. Leaders must train their subconscious minds for snap decision-making. On September, 11, 2001, when Rudy Guiliani was faced with dealing with the attack on the World Trade Center, he made a number of good decisions without good information, saving thousands of lives.

8. Small command decisions have the biggest impact on our lives over time. While it is the dramatic public events that get all the media, people such as Norman Borlaug, the promoter of high yield crops in the developing world saved more lives than any single man in history, winning the Nobel Peace Prize in 1970 for his contributions.

9. Leadership requires five qualities of character. All presidents has these characteristics in one degree or another or they would not have risen to the top political post in the nation.

10. A lack of character qualities in a leader, show up in five different ways. Neville Chamberlain's relative lack of courage compared with Hitler lead to WWII.

11. A leader who has an excess of these characteristics also makes bad decisions. Hitler's excess of courage led to the destruction of Germany.

1.5.2. Group Methods

Sun Tzu's ten key methods regarding systems for executing decisions (skills).

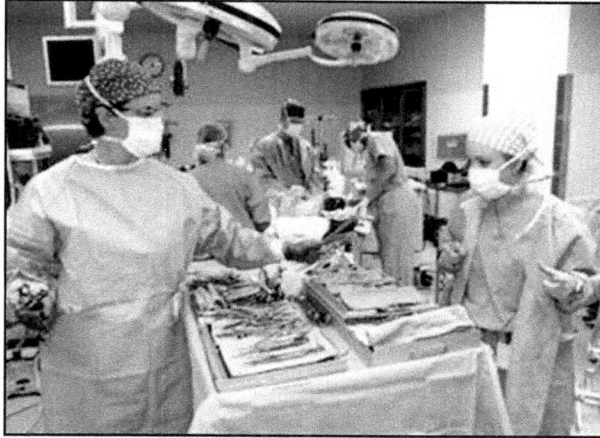

"Finally, you have your military methods. They shape your organization.
They come from your organization philosophy."
Sun Tzu's The Art of War 1:1:30-32

"An empowered organization is one in which individuals have the knowledge, skill, desire, and opportunity to personally succeed in a way that leads to collective organizational success."
Stephen Covey

General Principle: Methods of working with others are required to execute our decisions.

Situation:

Our decisions have no value until they are executed. If we decide to build a perpetual motion machine, the decision is meaningless. The task may seem desirable, but it is impossible. Decisions that cannot be executed by known methods are worse than worthless. Deciding to do something requires the knowledge that it can be done and an idea of how. As is so often the case with Sun Tzu, he sees this as a problem with understanding our boundaries and limitations. We can only accomplish what nature allows. The skills of any individual are limited. If we want to make valuable decisions, we must understand the chain of events that create value in our interactions with others. Knowing how to accomplish tasks starts with the challenge of finding the people who have the different types of knowledge we need. We can do little or nothing by ourselves.

Opportunity:

How well we execute our decisions depends on our methods. Methods describes both individuals skills and organizational systems. Sun Tzu's book is called "*The Art of War,*" but Sun Tzu didn't use the word "art." His title for his work was *Bing-Fa*. The term *fa* means methods, skills, and systems. His first emphasis is on mastering a known set of skills. Mastery requires practice. Mastering Sun Tzu's strategy means practicing methods and procedures that are known to work in competitive situations. We instantly make better decisions when we choose actions based on existing skills. Since we have limited skills ourselves, we are more capable when, instead of trying to do everything ourselves, we combine our skills with others.

Key Methods:

The following ten key methods define the nature of the methods that allow us to execute our decisions.

1. Our methods include all our capabilities to execute decisions. Methods include all the skills, systems, and procedures that we use to transform our decisions into action. These skills include what we can do ourselves and our ability to connect with others who have complementary skills. These skills come from our knowledge. Our skills represent what we know about the laws of nature and using the resources in our environment. This knowledge first exists in our heads but we put it in our procedures and machines. We can leverage our environment only in the ways that it allows (2.6 Knowledge Leverage).

2. All individuals gain skills as they grow. Individuals develop skills based upon their unique experiences and their unique position. No one except that individual really knows the extent and limits of his or her skills and experience (1.9.2 Span of Control).

3. Our methods connect our position to the positions of others. Skills and the positions based on them exists only within the larger competitive landscape. Our competitive and productive skills are not developed or used in a vacuum. They are based on the resources the we get from our landscape, that is, from those around us. In this world of interconnections, our skills are compared with the skills of others as a part of our position. To improve our position, our actions must, by definition, affect our relationship with others in either an objective or subjective way (1.2 Subobjective Positions).

4. *The most efficient methods divide tasks to develop individual expertise and group efficiencies.* Leadership is the realm of the individual decisions, but methods are the realm of the division of labor. Our decisions don't produce value unless we work with other people to execute them in the least costly way. This execution depends on our ability to work with others. We organize to develop interconnected systems and procedures to get tasks done. In other words, we create organizations. Some of these systems rely on hiring individuals with personal skills and know-how, but many of these systems are built on organizational knowledge that is passed from one worker to the another (7.2.1 Proven Methods).

5. All individuals and organizations are unique in terms of their particular knowledge and abilities. Every person and organization has different skills and abilities. While many skill sets overlap, every set of skills is specialized in some way to fit the unique position of the individual and organization (1.1 Position Paths).

6. Methods are embodied in our established procedures, tools, and machinery. Skills don't only exist in the human mind and body. They also exist in the machines and tools that we developed to accomplish a set of tasks. The knowledge about how to accomplish that task is given physical form in the machine or tool. Each component is designed to accomplish a part of the task (7.3.1 Expected Elements).

7. **The methods we use must be consistent with our goals.** We use our skills, systems, and machines to attain a specific set of goals so we cannot use methods that, while they accomplish a limited purpose, damage our ability to satisfy the larger mission (1.6.3 Shifting Priorities).

8. **Successful methods are copied by others**. We copy the best practices of others to improve our methods. Others copy our best practices to improve their methods (1.8.1 Creation and Destruction).

9. **Methods must be continuously improved by innovation**. Innovation is a major component of good strategy. We make decisions based upon new information and we improve our methods by implementing innovations. These innovations can come from internal sources or copied from external sources (7.1.3 Standards and Innovation).

10. **Both competitive methods and production methods are necessary for strategy.** Productive methods are the skills by which we produce the most value for others from the resources that we control. Competitive methods are the skills with which we position ourselves against competitors to win the control of more resources (1.9 Competition and Production).

Illustration:

Below we offer various examples to help illustrate these principles.

1. **Our methods include all our capabilities to execute decisions**. Our abilities start with knowing how to speak a language, use our hands and feet, and get desired reactions from others.

2. **All individuals gain skills as they grow.** We start as babies with limited control over our bodies. As we grow, we develop certain common skills, such as walking and talking, but our unique

position and experiences determines the specific skills we develop, such as what language we speak.

3. Our methods connect our position to the positions of others. We contact people at the grocery store because we need groceries. We connect to customers because we want to sell our products. While I can write a book alone, I need what others have already made (a computer, paper, pen, etc.). in order to do it. I also need their future efforts. Writing the book has no value unless it is manufactured, distributed, and sold.

4. **The most efficient methods divide tasks to develop individual expertise and group efficiencies.** Both McDonald's restaurants and the Mayo Clinic develop systems for the tasks they need to accomplish. Every type of organization has a different type of methods.

5. All individuals and organizations are unique in terms of their particular knowledge and abilities. A McDonald's restaurant doesn't have the same practices as a Burger King, but two McDonald's restaurants, no matter how similar, will operate differently because they employ different people with different skills who naturally balance their abilities. Each one of us is a unique constellation of skills gained from our unique path of experience.

6. Methods are embodied in our established procedures, tools, and machinery. A crowbar embodies a different form of knowledge than a computer but if the situation requires a crowbar, a computer won't do us much good.

7. The methods we use must be consistent with our goals. The simplest example is economic, we cannot waste money if we want to make money, but the most common example is moral: we cannot destroy people in order to save them. One of the most horrible examples are those who, in order to "save" people from the effects of DDT, condemned millions of poor, black children in Africa to death.

8. Successful methods are copied by others. Globalization is the current word we use for the spread of manufacturing methods throughout the world.

9. *Methods must be continuously improved by innovation*. The quality and variety of food at McDonald's is better today than it was fifty years ago and will be better ten years from now than it is today.

10. *Both competitive methods and production methods are necessary for strategy*. The competition of an election produces a winning politician or political party, but unless those winners are able to convert their election into better lives for their citizens, they will be replaced, one way or another.

1.6.0 Mission Values

Sun Tzu's eight key methods about the goals and values needed for motivation.

"It starts with your philosophy.
Command your people in a way that gives them a higher
shared purpose."

Sun Tzu's The Art of War 1:1:14-15

"The major reason for setting a goal is for what it makes
of you to accomplish it. What it makes of you will always
be the far greater value than what you get."

Jim Rohn

General Principle: Mission describes the motivations directing decisions and actions.

Situation:

We all have plenty of desires, but they change constantly and are often conflicting. Out of these conflicting desires comes our motivations, or what we call "mission" in Sun Tzu's strategy. An extremely common source of strategic mistakes is our failure to identify and clarify motivations. There are a whole list of problems associated with the lack of a clear mission. Without a clear mission, we drift with the situation at the mercy of our environment. We can react to events against our values and goals. Without understanding values and motivations, we will fail again and again in predicting people's behavior. Decisions and actions have no meaning outside of the context of goals and values that provide motivation.

If we don't understand motivations, we will get into trouble time and again without understanding why.

Opportunity:

The clearer our goals and priorities, the more likely we are to achieve them. If we don't know where we are going, any direction works as well. If we understand the motivations of others, we can work with them more effectively and predict their reactions (2.3.1 Action and Reaction). It is only our knowledge of goals and values that can change enemies into allies (1.5.1 Command Leadership). The better we understand values, our own and those of others, the easier it is for us to work together. Sun Tzu teaches that the best way to reach our own goals is to work with others in helping them reach theirs.

Key Methods:

These are the eight most important key methods that Sun Tzu offers regarding mission.

1. Mission is the central element of strategic position, connecting the other four key elements. The other four elements are the climate, ground, leader, and methods. In the original diagramming system of Chinese science and philosophy, the other four elements were the points in a compass and our goals were the center. Our mission defines the motivations that connect these elements and give them meaning. Our current position only has meaning in terms of our goals and values. The difference between our current position and desired position is defined by our mission. It is what gives our strategic position its direction (1.3 Elemental Analysis).

2. ***Our mission embodies our philosophy and our values in our goals***. Sun Tzu defined mission as our shared, higher values. Mission is based on a belief system, that is, on a philosophy. Our goals encapsulate what we think is important. In an absolute sense, our mission captures both our purpose in life and the way that we think the world works. When Sun Tzu wrote about mission, he used the Chinese character ***tao***, which is usually translated into English as "philosophy," but its literal meaning is "the path" (1.6.3 Shifting Priorities).

3. ***Everyone has a slightly different belief system based on their training and experience***. Belief systems are highly complex. We can agree on many beliefs and still disagree on many others. People's unique combination of beliefs are based on their unique life experiences. No two people can live the same exact life because every path is unique (1.1 Position Paths).

4. ***All our individual goals and values are inherently self-centered***. We can only see the world from our own, unique perspective. We only directly know our own thoughts and feelings. We value our beliefs because the are our own. Those who are willing to die for the one's they love are dying for their personal loves. Those who are willing to die for their beliefs are more dedicated to their personal vision than others. They believe that their physical life is less important than their ideal of self. Since everyone's beliefs are ultimately self-centered, disparaging anyone's goals as selfish is mere sophistry. The question is merely how many of our goals can we share with others (1.2 Subobjective Positions).

5. ***Our success depends on sharing our values with others.*** People can have goals and values that are completely selfish, but those goals and values are useless in terms of positioning. The important goals that create strength are those that can be shared. Organizations are impossible without a shared mission. The idea of a shared path captures many critical elements in creating a shared, higher mission. People can be on similar paths with different goals, just like people can share the same street going to different destinations. Everyone within an organization can have their own personal goals, but the organization's shared mission, values, and philosophy are the glue that holds those people together in a common business. Understanding the elements that can create a shared mission is critical to successful strategy (1.6.1 Shared Mission).

6. All shared missions are limited. Missions are always limited in scope of belief and often limited in time. We do not know or agree on the basis of a perfect Truth. We only agree on some limited aspects of our beliefs. If we think, "Everyone knows this is true," we are wrong. There is no such thing as a knowable and constant "common good." There are only temporary agreements about shared missions. At every point in human history, most things that everyone believed were eventually proven false. Much of what we believe today will be proven false eventually as well (2.1.1 Information Limits).

7. Both creating allies and positioning against our rivals requires empathy. Empathy is our capacity to see other people's mission from *their* perspective. We must get out of our own heads and into the mindframes of others. Without empathy, we cannot create winning positions. Empathy is the foundation of the warrior's creative mindset. If we cannot put ourselves into other people's shoes, we can never develop positions that win supporters. We cannot position against rivals unless we can predict their behavior by imagining what we would do in their positions. We must imagine both the range of possible values and changing priorities of both our potential supporters and opponents (1.6.3 Shifting Priorities).

8. Roles such as ally and enemy are defined solely by mission interactions. In its most abstract form, our *enemy* is any person whose mission conflicts with our own. An ally is someone with whom we share a mission. Positions that are complementary in one situation can compete in another situation (1.3.1 Competitive Comparison).

Illustration:

Let us illustrate these ideas discussing the general challenges of working in an organization with other coworkers.

1. Mission in the central element of strategic position, connecting the other four key elements. Everyone in the organization has a position. Each has their own ground (area), climate (attitudes), commands (decision-making), and methods (skills). All of these are united by each person's goals.

2. Our mission embodies our philosophy and our values in our goals. Everyone in an organization is working for their own individual goals.

3. Everyone has a slightly different belief system based on their training and experience. No matter how much we are like those with whom we work, it is our differences that create the strengths and weakness that make us better working together than apart.

4. All our individual goals and values are inherently self-centered. Each of us has an inflated sense of our own worth because only we know everything that we do. It is a trick of perspective. Closer things appear to be larger than things far away. We are all closer to ourselves.

5. Our success depends on sharing our values with others. We and our co-workers can share the "path" of making our company successful even though we may get different rewards from that success.

6. All shared missions are limited. Some will work for money, others for social approval, others to satisfy their own egos and so on. We can disagree about the right path to take both because our goals are different and because we see a different route as best. Agreement on goals does not mean agreement on means. What we all share at work is the belief that our organization is the best vehicle we have to satisfy our needs.

7. Both creating allies and positioning against our rivals requires empathy. We must understand what is important to those we work with. To motivate our co-workers more smoothly, we must put our needs in terms that address their missions.

8. *Roles such as ally and enemy are defined solely by mission interactions.* Our coworkers are our competition for internal promotions.

1.6.1 Shared Mission

Sun Tzu's ten key methods on finding goals that others can share.

"Trust only in yourself and the self-interest of others."
Sun Tzu's The Art of War 1:7:16

"If your imagination leads you to understand how quickly people grant your requests when those requests appeal to their self-interest, you can have practically anything you go after."
Napoleon Hill

General Principle: Higher values are the basis of shared missions that unite groups in powerful positions.

Situation:

When pushed, people push back. We cannot improve our position without the assistance of others, but everyone puts their own interests, goals, and opinions first. We cannot get people to commit to us unless we also make commitments to them. As Thomas Shelling said it in *The Strategy of Conflict*, "The power to constrain an adversary depends upon the power to bind oneself." People disagree about goals and values. Even when we agree on goals, we can disagree about methods and means. We can dissagree about where a given choice of path will lead. Even when we agree on means and ends, that agreement is often just temporary. Changes in climate shift a situation to create disagreement.

Opportunity:

Sun Tzu's strategy requires finding or constructing shared missions to bring people together as allies and supporters. Everyone's goals revolve around their own interests. Everyone is looking for friends, allies, and supporters.

People have an infinite number of desires. We can help them satisfy their own desires and in return they can help us toward our own goals, often unintentionally. Though people do often disagree about means and ends, there are a great many people in the world and their needs are constantly changing.

Opportunities exist in the short term, when we can temporarily agree on a means that suits our diverging goals. Opportunities exist in the long term. If we disagree on immediate actions, we still can always agree that the value of working together is greater and more certain than our differing opinions about actions.

Key Methods:

In constructing a shared mission, Sun Tzu provides the following key methods.

1. Shared missions are based on the current priorities that we have in common with others. When it comes to our personal mission, goals, and values, we all have a range of priorities. Shared missions are created by people who find common ground among those priorities. We can have areas of disagreement, but as long as our areas of agreement have a higher priority, we can create a shared mission. This higher priority is part of what Sun Tzu means by a "higher, shared purpose" (1.6.3 Shifting Priorities).

2. We must choose our methods based upon our shared mission. Tactics are the methods we choose to pursue our goal or mission. These methods can be based upon what is immediately convenient. They can bring people with different long-term missions together. Strategy requires a mission whose values are broad enough to share and enduring enough to persist (1.5.2. Group Methods).

3. A shared mission allows us to work with others to satisfy our mutual self-interest. In the original Chinese, the word Sun Tzu used to describe mission means literally "the way" or "the path." When we have serious disagreements over these means, we cannot find a shared mission even if we agree on all goals. The idea of means goes deeply into our philosophy of how the world works (1.6 Mission Values).

4. The depth of a mission determines how long alliances last. Without higher, longer-term goals, alliances will not hold. A group can never steer a consistent course and make any progress if they don't agree generally on direction. Without shared values, we cannot work with others, which makes success impossible (1.6 Mission Values).

5. We must avoid confusing a temporarily shared means for a shared longer-term mission. There is a difference between a tactical alliance of sharing the same means to different ends and a strategic one of sharing the same ends. Choosing the same path doesn't *always* mean a shared long-term goal. People can choose *some* of the same goals and *some* of the same parts of a path, working for mutual self-interest in some areas while competing in others. Our information about goals is never certain (2.1.1 Information Limits).

6. Trust arises when our actions demonstrate a priority on the shared values of the group. If everyone expects everyone else to stab them in the back at the earliest convenience, we cannot forge meaningful alliances. To create a high-trust group, we must visibly sacrifice our immediate self interest to those of the group. Such sacrifices occur naturally when our mutual self-interest depends upon each other. (2.3 Personal Interactions).

7. We can have the same general values but disagree on the best path to take. Shared values do not automatically create a shared mission. If people choose different paths, they cannot work together, helping each other along the way ((1.1 Position Paths).

8. Alliances based on shared values are not always possible. It is a mistake to think that we can always find common ground. There are goals that are absolutely diametrically opposed, where no shared means are possible simply because those goals lead in such different directions. Trusting in shared values without a demonstration of them gives people an invitation to deceive us (2.1.3 Misinformation and Disinformation

9. Empathy is the difference between selfishness and self-interest. The most obvious sign of the inability to find shared mission is a lack of empathy and understanding regarding differences in values and mission. Selfish values and goals leave no room for sympathy and empathy for those with different goals (1.6.2 Types of Motivations).

10. It takes creativity and perspective to construct shared goals to explore opportunities. Sun Tzu's system of innovation requires changing the order of things. We can do this by changing people's perception of the value of sharing a mission (7.3 Strategic Innovation).

Illustration:

Let us illustrate these principles with examples from a variety of areas.

1. Shared missions are based on the current priorities that we have in common with others. A good example is working with our coworkers in an organization. In an organization, our short-term opportunity comes from a shared mission with others who almost certainly have very different longterm goals. Some of us may be working simply for a weekly paycheck, while others are working to develop certain skills, while still others are working because they love the product the organization offers.

2. We must choose our methods based upon our shared mission. We use the methods of our organization, whether it is selling a product or converting people to a way of thinking, based upon the shared mission of the organization, not our individual goals.

3. A shared mission allows us to work with others to satisfy our mutual self-interest. Our differences in career direction over the long-term is less important than our agreement on the short term path. People within the same organization can have very different career paths over their lifetimes but work well together for the time they share the organization's goals.

4. The depth of a mission determines how long alliances last. The best example of our long-term opportunity is marriage. As two people in a marriage, we can agree the the value of our working together is greater and more certain than our differing opinions about the future.

5. We must avoid confusing a temporarily shared means for a shared longer-term mission. We can easily find a shared mission with those who have different goals. One person can join a company simply for the paycheck. Another can join for the professional experience. A third can join because of his or her personal relationship. However, all three of these people can work together because the mission of the company satisfies their different goals, at least for a period of time.

6. Trust arises when our actions demonstrate a priority on the shared values of the group. We all almost automatically sacrifice or our personal freedom to conform to certain social agreements. These agreements range from the use of money to the ban on public nudity. By our conformance, we earn the trust of others. Violating such agreements, in major ways, such as not paying our bills, destroys that trust. Even minor violations in our visible choices, such as a poor choice of clothing, undermines that trust.

7. We can have the same general values but disagree on the best path to take. For example, two opposing political parties can always agree on certain goals: reducing crime, poverty, improving health, and so on, but they cannot come to share a mission unless they can find some means to reach that goal that they can agree upon. Usually, one political party sees the other party's solutions as making the problem worse, not better. This is because of different views of how the world works.

8. *Alliances based on shared values are not always possible.* The classic historical mistake was Chamberlain's agreement with Hitler before WWII that was supposed to prevent war. It assumed that the two leaders agreed on the importance of avoiding the destruction of conflict.

9. *Empathy is the difference between selfishness and self-interest*. For example, religious extremists, including environmental extremists, are selfish because they cannot accept that others have the same right to opinions and choices that they do. Such extremists not only see their beliefs as the only acceptable beliefs, but they feel the need to force everyone to live by their rules. This requires not only putting their opinions above the opinions of others, but a belief that others must not be free to make their own decisions.

10. *It takes creativity and perspective to construct shared goals to explore opportunities*. A common method is to exaggerate the danger of a common enemy.

1.6.2 Types of Motivations

Sun Tzu's six key methods regarding hierarchies of motivation that define missions.

"You can exploit five different needs in a leader. If he is willing to die, you can kill him.
If he wants to survive, you can capture him.
He may have a quick temper.
You can then provoke him with insults.
If he has a delicate sense of honor, you can disgrace him.
If he loves his people, you can create problems for him."
Sun Tzu's The Art of War 8:5:1

"Motivation is the art of getting people to do what you want them to do because they want to do it."
Dwight David Eisenhower

General Principle: Five levels of mission form unique individual motivations.

Situation:

Sun Tzu teaches us to leverage people's motivations, but that can be a challenge. Everyone has a constellation of sometimes competing goals and values inside their head. One of the most challenging strategic problems is trying to understand what other people want. Sun Tzu's system is *allocentric*. This means that it focuses on the interests and concerns of others. We use their interests to further our own. The problem, of course, is that human beings in general have a complex array of motives, and each person is unique. Not only that, but their motivations can change from moment to moment as the situation changes. So the problem gets worse when we try to predict the interests of others in the future. Some motives are very changeable while others are more stable.

Opportunity:

Sun Tzu teaches us not to worry about understanding people perfectly. Our goal is only to understand the motives of others a little more clearly than most people do. Remember, in using Sun Tzu's principles, it is only our relative superiority of position that counts (1.3.1 Competitive Comparison). Sun Tzu model for motivation stresses 1) the external focus, 2) simplicity, and 3) interconnections to the other elements of his system. The external focus is important because most people are too preoccupied with their own wants and needs. The practice of strategy forces us to get out of ourselves and see the world from the perspective of others. Simplifying motivations is critical because human beings are unbelievably complex and we need a practical system. We handle this complexity by interconnecting motivations to every part of Sun Tzu's system. This perspective is so valuable that it is one of the nine major categories of strategic knowledge (2.0 Developing Perspective).

Key Methods: The six key methods that define different types of motivation are described below.

1. People's motives connect to every element of their strategic positions. All five elements act as our reference points for motivations. This system was designed to simplify the questions that we ask about people's motivations. It focuses on the motivations that we can use to make decisions in a well-defined way. Other systems, such as Maslow's hierarchy of needs, which Sun Tzu's system strongly resembles, have categories, such as "self actualization," that can neither be compared nor shared. This makes them difficult to use in strategic decisions (1.3 Elemental Analysis).

2. Our desire for meaning is based on our belief in ultimate goals and eternal values. This is the highest, deepest, and rarest form of motivation. We sometimes refer to them as "spiritual" missions. These are the missions for which people are willing to die, which is how Sun Tzu refers to them above. They are based on our very specific ideas of the meaning of life and how the world works. Because of the deep level of importance people attach to these motivations, shared spiritual missions can create organizations that last for millennia. We can kill the people, but not the mission. Spiritual or philosophical motives connect with the core of mission (1.6 Mission Values).

3. Our desire for survival arises from our physical and economic needs. This basic or "ground" level of motivation. It is the most common and predictable level of mission. We must meet our physical needs simply to survive. By "economic," we mean whatever we need to survive and thrive: food, shelter and our possessions. Money, of course, can get us any of these. This is the broadest level of mission. We all share the need to physically survive. Physical motives connect to Ground ((1.4.2 Ground Features).

4. The desire for predictability arises from our need for safety in dealing with change. We want to feel secure from unpredictable threats. The importance of predictability rises and falls with the changing cycles in the environments. As conditions worsen and become more unpredictable, safety becomes more important. Climate takes the subjective form of our basic emotions concerning the future. If we are worried and anxious about the future, we react with fear or anger. If we are secure and confident in the future, we are optimistic and relaxed. Safety motives connect to Climate (2.4.2 Climate Perspective).

5. *The desire for control arises from our need for respect and authority.* These are our motivations for individual recognition, attention, and social status. We can describe these motivations as either "social" or "personal" since they involve our desire for social

recognition of our individual qualities of character. This reputation is the basis for our credibility, especially our professional position. The more recognition and respect we receive, the more authority we are given by society. The result is more individual command over our lives. These desires are as common as our physical desires, but their importance depends on our individual character. Personal motives connect to the key element of command (1.5.1 Command Leadership).

6. *The desire for relationships arises from our need for belonging and friendship*. This motivation comes from our membership in a group, a team, or a marriage rather than our individual social reputation. Our membership in these relationships gives us personal meaning through our interconnections with others. These personal relationships are deeper than our social status. The relationships are more intimate and direct than our general social status. All motivations relate to emotion, but here we are really talking about the giving and receiving of love. These missions are the narrowest, exclusive to our circle of close relationships, i.e. friends and family, but they are very deep and important to us. Since these motives are defined by our interdependence on others, they connect to the key element of methods (1.5.2. Group Methods).

Illustration:

Different organizations exist to satisfy one of these levels of motivation. One of the most common mistakes we see in the organizations that we work with is that they lose track of their mission.

1. ***People's motives connect to every element of their strategic positions.*** A given person has motivations at all these levels, so they usually have positions in many different arenas in order to satisfy them.

2. ***Our desire for meaning is based on our belief in ultimate goals and eternal values.*** Churches, social movements, political parties, and all other religious organizations work at this level.

3. Our desire for survival arises from our physical and economic needs. Businesses that provide food, clothing, housing, and financial services all serve this level.

4. *The desire for predictability arises from our need for safety in dealing with change.* Political organizations exist to provide basic levels of security and safety.

5. *The desire for control arises from our need for respect and authority.* Every type of organization and professional association that recognizes authority and professionalism addresses this level of motivation.

6. *The desire for relationships arises from our need for belonging and friendship.* The family is the most basic organization here providing relationships, but the personal emotional connections can arise among people in any other type of group.

1.6.3 Shifting Priorities

Sun Tzu seven key methods about how missions change according to temporary conditions.

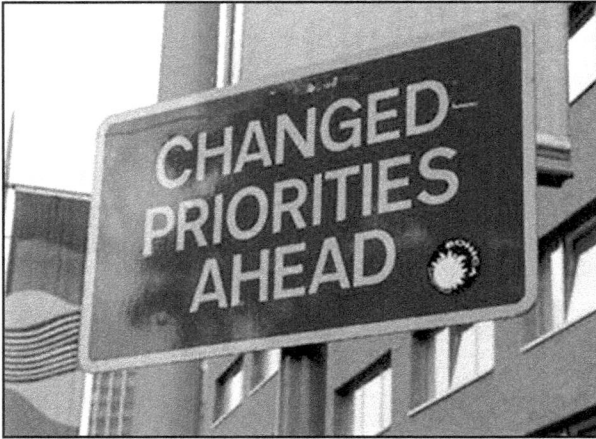

"You must predict the enemy to overpower him and win."
Sun Tzu's The Art of War 10:3:3

"Goals are simply tools to focus your energy in positive directions, these can be changed as your priorities change, new ones added, and others dropped."
O. Carl Simonton

General Principle: Changing conditions not fixed goal posts determine current mission priorities.

Situation:

People's motivation changes over time, both gradually and suddenly. Our goals and values change their relative importance depending upon our situation. For example, our long-term goals are suddenly very unimportant when we find ourselves in a life-or-death situation. Since strategy depends on predicting what others will do, this complex array of desires makes prediction difficult as it changes from moment to moment. We can never perfectly predict people's behavior because we can never understand exactly what is motivating them at the moment. This means that there are limits to how much we can depend on our alliance. Over time, allies can actually become enemies, depending on the situation. Most partnerships fall apart because our interests naturally diverge over time.

Opportunity:

Our mission *as a whole* is the most enduring part of our strategic positions (1.6 Mission Values). Sun Tzu's strategy gives us an easy-to-see system for understanding the hierarchy of motivations that relates to everything else we know about positions (1.6.2 Types of Motivations). While the specific order of priorities on this list can change from moment to moment, the list as a whole changes very slowly if at all. This hierarchy also tells us generally how the five different types of motivations tend to change over time, which are more temporary and which are longer lasting. This gives us a critical head start in terms of predicting the choices that people will make. We combine this understanding with another key aspect of our strategic model, knowing how changing conditions affect positions ((1.4.1 Climate Shift).

Key Methods:

There are many different levels to mission. Each person has their own private constellation of values and desires within a general framework. In everyday life, we can think of some of our goals as short-term and others as long-term, but we base much of our interaction with others upon knowing which of their motivations we can predict and which we cannot.

1. The priorities of our mission change as conditions change. This include both conditions in the external environment (1.4 The External Environment) and conditions within a person or organization (1.5 Internal Elements).

2. Both predictable and unpredictable changes in conditions affect motives. This means some changes in priorities will be predictable but others will not. (2.3.2 Reaction Unpredictability).

3. The most regular changes in priorities come from our cycle of internal needs and appetites. There is a natural cycle in our competing desires. The lowest levels of motivations are the most temporary because we know what our physical needs require and how we need to address them (1.8.3 Cycle Time).

4. Other predictable changes are linked to external cycles of climate. The external environment can also be predictable in its effect upon our priorities. We categorize these changes under climate, both the physical, social, and business climates (1.4.1 Climate Shift).

5. *These changes are predictable because they are linked to the external passage of time.* Whether we are looking at ourselves or others, we can understand that at certain times of day or year, we need to address different sets of needs (3.1.6 Time Limitations).

6. Unpredictable, non-cyclic internal and external events also affect priorities. These events can offer us either unexpected opportunities or unexpected problems. In either case, we must change our immediate priorities in order to address them (3.2 Opportunity Creation).

7. Knowing the events that affect others gives us insight into their current priorities. When we cannot predict changes in priorities, we must immediately adapt our viewpoint based on our knowledge of events. People cannot do everything at once and must change their priorities in order to address events (3.1.1 Resource Limitations).

Illustration:

Let us look at some simple examples of how priorities change in each of these categories.

1. The priorities of our mission change as conditions change. No matter how much more important our professional goals are over the long term, we must take time every day to eat and sleep to address our physical needs.

2. Both predictable and unpredictable changes in conditions affect motives. We can predict when we will get sleepy but not when we will get ill.

3. The most regular changes in priorities come from our cycle of internal needs and appetites. We will get hungry every day and sleepy every night.

4. Other predictable changes are linked to external cycles in the climate. For example, most of us work on economic and professional needs during the day because that is when we traditionally do business. Our emotional mission is more often addressed in the evening or on weekends. During summer, we take vacation. Certain business climate changes, such as Christmas shopping, are also predictable. At tax time, we will pay our taxes.

5. These changes are predictable because they are linked to the external passage of time. Day and night, winter and summer, taxes, and human aging are all predictable.

6. Unpredictable, non-cyclic internal and external events also affect priorities. We can get sick. An economic collapse in an industry can arise.

7. Knowing the events that affect others gives us insight into their current priorities. If we know someone has lost a lot of money, we can expect that they will focus more on activities relating to immediately raising money.

1.7.0 Competitive Power

Sun Tzu's ten key methods describing the sources of superiority in challenges.

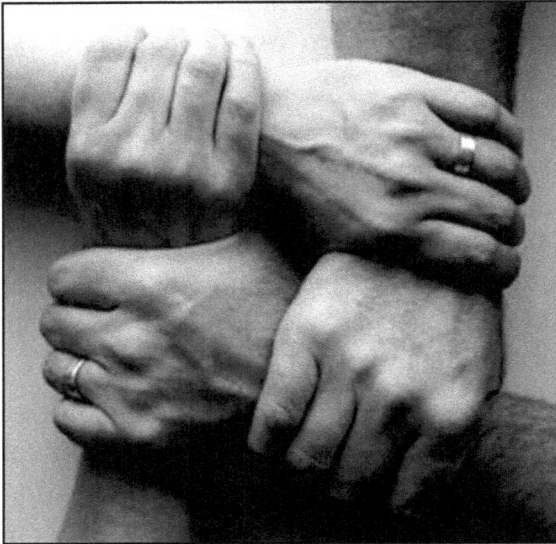

"Manage to avoid battle until your organization can count on certain victory. You must calculate many advantages."

Sun Tzu's The Art of War 1:5:1-2

"Build for your team a feeling of oneness, of dependence on one another and of strength to be derived by unity."

Vince Lombardi

General Principle: Strategic power comes from unity and focus, not size or the wealth of resources.

Situation:

How we determine if one strategic position is superior to another? How do we predict which strategic position will triumph in a comparison with competing positions? Our expectations are often very wrong. We expect larger organizations to be successful. We also expect organizations that have been successful in the past to continue to be successful in the future. We also expect the volume of resources used to have an impact. The problem is that these factors have very little effect on competitive outcomes. Size and wealth are the result of past success, but that success may have little relationship with the current mission. Sun Tzu teaches that size is not power and that past success is not momentum. In the real world, smaller forces often triumph over larger ones. Newer organizations often overcome established ones. Vast resources are often squandered in failed endeavors. This meant that something deeper was going on, something that isn't obvious to most of us without training.

Opportunity:

Sun Tzu developed his strategic system in part to explain our misconceptions about strength. Once we understand what a "strategic advantage" really means, we can predict which battles we will win and which we will lose. More importantly, we will stop wasting our efforts in areas that create as many disadvantages as advantages. This includes the size of an organization (3.4 Dis-Economies of Scale), past success (3.2.5 Dynamic Reversal), and expending resources (3.1.1 Resource Limitations).

Key Methods: The following ten key methods describe Sun Tzu's concept of competitive power.

Power means our capacity to move to a superior position despite meeting challenges and obstacles. Power is only required to overcome opposing conditions in our external environment.

1. When the opposing conditions come from the opposition of rivals, power is a relative comparison of the capacities of each party to move against another. Power is specifically the ability to advance a position toward a goal, as opposed to simply defending an existing position (1.1 Position Paths).

2. Power gives rise to relative strength of position in comparison to other positions. Strength comes from superior resources gained from controlling a given position, but it exists only as a comparison with other competing positions. There are many different types of strength, but all forms of strength are relative, arising from a comparison among potential alternatives and contesting positions. That comparison is based upon only a single criteria: the ability to a position to fulfill our mission of moving toward a goal. In making this comparison, some positions have advantages over others. An "advantage" can mean many different things in different situations, but all of them had to relate directly to supporting the mission. This realization lead Sun Tzu to develop a new idea about what the term "strength" really means in succeeding at a challenge (1.3.1 Competitive Comparison).

3. Strategic power arises from the unity and focus that comes from mission. Unity creates focus. Focus creates strength. Unity and focus together define all the advantages that can come from a strategic position in order to create strength (1.6 Mission Values).

4. Power is created when people focus their energy and other resources at a single place at a single time. This requires us to use the shape of the terrain since we all must be in contact with the focus point. We must have an opening in the shifts of climate to make it possible for everyone to act together at one time (1.4.1 Climate Shift).

5. The smaller the focus point in time and space, the greater the power. Intense efforts cannot last long so they must be kept short. Impact is dissipated over too much space (5.5 Focused Power).

6. Power is amplified when focused on relative weakness. We use the term "strength" to describe the advantage that results from targeting weaknesses. The weakness of the target emphasizes the relative power of the move (3.2.4 Emptiness and Fullness).

7. Power requires a leader clearly articulating the target, the direction, and the timing. Advantages come from a leader having the vision and communication skills necessary to rally supporters around the mission focusing on a single goal (1.5.1 Command Leadership).

8. Power requires methods that move people together at the same time. Good methods offer an advantage because they keep everyone together, focusing them on the goal. Disadvantageous methods create division, limiting focus to individual separate tasks rather than progress toward shared goals (1.5.2. Group Methods).

9. Every existing organization represents a formula of unity and focus. All success is built around using these aspects of power. An organization's formula addresses conditions in its environment creating the focus, the intensity, the clarity, and the unity success requires. Large, successful organizations grow and advance their position when their formula works better than other competing formulas for addressing the same values and goals (1.5 Competing Agents).

10. Size, success and wealth are a result of power not its source. Organizations, no matter how large and successful, fail when their formulas, which may have worked in the past, lose their potency. Those organizations may be strong in terms of resources, but they are not powerful unless they can move to positions that advance their position. Though strong, large organizations easily lose their focus and mission. Their mission becomes diluted, spread-out, muddy, and divided, at least when compared with other alternative organizations. Their success formulas get outmoded and outdated. Formulas grow outdated when they no longer generate the unity and focus that they have in the past. Without unity and focus on fulfilling a shared mission, the elements that make up a group's strategic position are weakly connected (3.4 Dis-Economies of Scale).

Illustration:

Let us illustrate these principles in the simplest form possible, discussing power in the terms of slicing bread and rowing a boat.

1. Power means our capacity to move to a superior position despite meeting challenges and obstacles. A tool works because it helps us make a move to a superior position. When our goal is cutting a slice of bread, we want the power to smoothly separate one piece of bread from the loaf.

2. *Power gives rise to relative strength of position in comparison to other positions*. Strength is having the bread in a more usable form to satisfy a weakness, in this case, our hunger. The power of a knife allows us get those resources.

3. *Strategic power arises from the unity and focus that comes from mission.* It is the unity, that is the solidity of the knife, and its focus, that is its sharpness that gives it its power. A knife made of butter will not work. A knife with a dull blade also will not work.

4. *Power is created when people focus their energy and other resources at a single place at a single time.* The edge of the knife focusing the power of our hand in a very narrow area.

5. *The smaller the focus point in time and space, the greater the power.* A knife requires less force than a club because it focuses force in the smallest possible space.

6. *Power is amplified when focused on relative weakness.* A knife cuts a loaf of bread but it will not cut a bar of steel.

7. *Power requires a leader clearly articulating the target, the direction, and the timing.* Since we are now talking about a group of people, let us change our illustration to a boat manned by a crew rowing through the water. In rowing, the coxswain steers the boat and provides the tempo.

8. *Power requires methods that move people together at the same time*. If some people are pushing or dragging their oars, the group's focus, unity, and strength are lost.

9. *Every existing organization represents a formula of unity and focus.* Different rowing crews can use very different formulas. Some can concentrate on agile members and speed of the stroke while others can depend on more muscular members who use more forceful strokes.

10. *Size, success and wealth are a result of power not its source.* Any sports team that wins consistently will become larger in terms of its supporters and get better candidates, in terms of its formula

for success for joining the team. However, this does not prevent better formulas using very different types of competitors from coming along and beating it. The larger and stronger a team gets, the more likely it is that a smaller, quicker team will eventually be able to beat it.

1.7.1 Team Unity

Sun Tzu's ten key methods for increasing our strength by the way we join with others.

Unity works because it enables you to win every battle you fight.

Sun Tzu's The Art of War 3:5:1

"Unity to be real must stand the severest strain without breaking."

Mahatma Gandhi

General Principle: The strength of a team's unity depends on leveraging individuality.

Situation:

What makes a team different than any random group of people? What should make it different is its unity, the internal bond that makes a group strong. Bringing a group together doesn't automatically create that bond. As easily as groups can come together, they also come apart. As humans, we have two opposing natures. Part of our nature is as social creatures. We are drawn into groups and look for group approval and support. However, we also have a strong drive toward individuality, and we are natural critics of the group. That side of our nature resists losing our identity to the group, forsaking the strength of the group for our own independence.

Opportunity:

The opportunity in unity for the individual comes from the strength of the group. Working with a group of people gives us access to broader skills and more resources than we have alone. The opportunity for the group is to bring people together in a way that their individuality strengthens rather than weakens the group. We can increase unity by celebrating individuality rather than suppressing it.

Key Methods:

Unity works when it brings a team together so that others want to join as well. A successful team makes the individual special, adding distinctiveness rather than subtracting it. While we can never win everyone over, if we win enough people, those that still oppose us will not attempt a direct meeting in competition. The strategy of unity encompasses a number of important concepts:

1. Unity increases if each person feels responsible for the group as a whole. When responsibility for the group as a whole is limited to management, the team will not be very unified. A team is unified when each individual feels responsible for the well-being of the group as a whole (1.7.2 Goal Focus).

2. Unity increases if individuals trust each other to handle their individual responsibilities. This means that each individual knows his or her area of responsibility, is capable of handling it, and is trusted by others in performing it (6.8.3 Individual Toughness).

3. Unity increases when individuals can work independently for the good of the team. External team processes are usually more disconnected than internal team processes. When the environment is controlled, unifying internal processes is easy. External activities are much more difficult to coordinate because the external environment is unpredictable and chaotic (1.9.2 Span of Control).

4. *Unity increases when member's contributions are regularly recognized.* The best programs recognize most people most of the time. This puts pressure on individual members who fail to contribute, making them more aware of their shortcomings even if the group itself doesn't make an issue of them (6.8.2 Group Strength).

5. *Unity increases from acting together under external pressure.* Shared danger, action, and success have a unifying power. Unity doesn't come from making speeches. Opposition creates unity because it can force a group to come together. Situations with less opportunity to act together and win battles together tend to pull organizations apart (9.3.1 Mutual Danger).

6. *Unity increases if individuals have complementary strengths and weaknesses.* Differences between individuals can increase unity more than similarity. Different personalities and skill sets depend on one another. Putting differences together in the right formula is the basis of strength in unity. A homogeneous group, where individuals have the same opinions and skills, will tend to agree on decisions, but it is limited in what it can do. A diverse group will tend to have broader perspective on a situation and more skills to apply to any given task, but it requires more trust in leadership to make decisions (3.5 Strength and Weakness).

7. *Unity increases when the mission minimizes differences in individual goals.* The construction of a common mission is often the most creative and important work in strategy. Individuals may belong to a group for very different reasons and have different goals, however, they must find a common goal in the mission of the group. The job of creating groups is largely the work of imagining shared missions (1.6.1 Shared Mission).

8. *Unity increases when new members become the responsibility of existing individual members.* Membership starts with direct personal relationships and responsibility. New members should feel responsible to their mentors and existing members should feel responsible to their wards (6.8 Competitive Psychology).

9. Unity increases with clear chains of command. Good leadership involves a number of issues. The three most important are 1) clear lines of authority, 2) decisions that can be executed given the situation, and 3) communication skills that unify people ((1.5.1 Command Leadership).

10. Unity increases when opponents are unable to exploit its natural divisions. Networked organizations with many connections between members are stronger than large organizations with clear divisions in the hierarchy that can be exploited (9.2.5 Vulnerability of Organization).

Illustration:

Some examples of how these principles are used or violated are below.

1. Unity increases if each person feels responsible for the group as a whole. A soldier's first priority is to the members of his or her unit.

2. Unity increases if individuals trust each other to handle their individual responsibilities. In NFL football, a defensive lineman can only defend his gap if he trusts his fellow linemen to defend their gaps.

3. Unity increases when individuals can work independently for the good of the team. Within most large sales organizations, there are constant conflicts between sales responsibilities among different territories and divisions but individuals are still able to work together.

4. Unity increases when member's contributions are regularly recognized. Most "employee of the month" programs are an example of too little, too seldom. Most people are always excluded so there is no pressure to perform.

5. Unity increases from acting together under external pressure. A dangerous common enemy has historically been the best glue holding together an alliance.

6. *Unity increases if individuals have complementary strengths and weaknesses.* Human beings have two separate physical forms: men and women. The oldest, more proven, and most successful team in human history, is a marriage based on uniting these differences.

7. *Unity increases when the mission minimizes differences in individual goals.* While golf is a great contest of individuals, team events, such as the President's cup, offer no individual awards. All proceeds going to charity.

8. *Unity increases when new members become the responsibility of existing individual members*. Groups that leave new members to find their own way lose most of their members.

9. *Unity increases with clear chains of command.* The reason that many ad hoc groups fail to accomplish their goals and fall apart is that responsibility is shared to the degree that it doesn't exist. Unity increases when opponents are unable to exploit its natural divisions. One of the reasons that American car companies ran into so many problems was that their divisions created internal politics and conflict.

10. *Unity increases when opponents are unable to exploit its natural divisions.* As organizations grow larger, internal separation in hierarchies create rival divisions who compete for resources within the organization.

1.7.2 Goal Focus

Five key methods regarding strength as arising from concentrating efforts.

"Where you focus, you unite your forces.
When the enemy divides, he creates many small groups."
Sun Tzu's The Art of War 3:5:1

"One reason so few of us achieve what we truly want is
that we never direct our focus; we never concentrate our
power. Most people dabble their way through life, never
deciding to master anything in particular."
Tony Robbins

General Principle: The strength of a team's focus depends on its concentration.

Situation:

Strategic strength depends on two characteristics: unity and focus. The problem is that from our ordinary, everyday perspective these qualities are opposite from one another. Most of us see unity as inclusive and focus as exclusive. To bring teams together, we must include other views, but to focus the team, we must exclude other views. The problem is that without both components, we cannot create strength. Unity without a sharp focus is weak. A sharp focus without unity behind it is also weak.

Opportunity:

Understanding competitive positions in terms of the five elements gives us a more specific and useful definition of unity and focus (1.3 Elemental Analysis). Our opportunity comes from clearly separating the external environment and the internal organization (1.4 The External Environment, 1.5 Internal Organization). Focus excludes most of the environment while including all of the organization. It works by concentrating group efforts in a very small external time and place.

Key Methods:

Focus enables easier decision-making because it eliminates what cannot be done given the limitations of space and time. If we know for certain what we should not do, it makes it easier to choose what we should do.

1. Creating focus requires recognizing limits. Our resources are inherently limited. Because our resources are limited, we cannot spread them too thinly. If we spread them too thinly, we create weakness relative to our competition. We cannot do everything and be everywhere at all times. Those that try to compete everywhere (ground) and do everything (methods) are weak everywhere in everything (3.1.1 Resource Limitations).

2. Creating focus requires concentration of resources. We limit the space and within that limited space we concentrate resources. If we concentrate many skills and resources in a limited space for a limited period of time, we create a competitive mismatch. In that place and time, you want to be in every way superior to your competition at the time of battle (3.1.4 Openings).

3. We use focus to create a mismatch at the focus point. *Battle* in Sun Tzu's strategy is defined as simply meeting a competitor or a challenge. It doesn't mean destructive *conflict*, which is a distinct concept and very different Chinese character. If we create a mismatch of resources at the time of the competitive meeting, we will have all the advantages in that time and space (3.2.4 Emptiness and Fullness).

4. Creating focus requires a limited mission. The more generic the mission is, the more useless it is in terms of focus. The more specific a mission is, the easier it is to see if an action falls within the scope of that mission. Strategy recognizes the problem of **mission creep. Mission creep** is the tendency of missions to broaden over time, losing their focus and, therefore, their strength and power. Interestingly, a limited mission also often works to creating unity, but while focus works by limiting ground, unity works by limiting time. People can have different destinations, but they can still share a path for a limited period of time (1.6.3 Shifting Priorities).

5. Creating focus over time is necessary to create persistence. Persistence is another form of concentration, but it isn't the same as continuing what isn't working for a little longer. To find success, even in a limited area, we have to persistently adjust our efforts to find the right method for success. The key question is always how long do we persist before we realize that we are doing something wrong and make adjustments (5.5 Focused Power).

Illustration:

The best analogy for focus is starting a fire using a magnifying glass. Starting a fire requires:

1. Creating focus requires recognizing limits. We must concentrate the heat of the sun, our limited resources, which is insufficient for starting a fire if spread out.

2. Creating focus requires concentration of resources. We must concentrate that heat in the smallest possible area of fuel.

3. We use focus to create a mismatch at the focus point. We don't focus on what is hard to ignite, a piece of wood, but what is easy, paper or soft tinder.

4. Creating focus requires a *limited mission.* We only focus until we get the fire smoldering, then we must immediately switch to broader activities such as blowing and adding fuel.

5. Creating focus over time is necessary to create persistence. It will take several tries to start the fire, adjusting our methods, to get the right angle and distance, and holding the focus motionless long enough to be effective.

1.8.0 Progress Cycle

Sun Tzu's ten key methods regarding the adaptive loop by which positions are advanced.

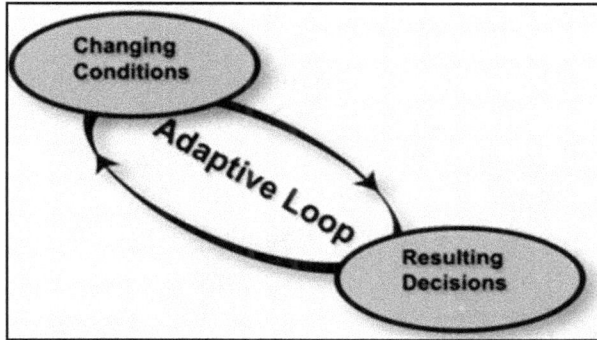

"End and yet return to start."
Sun Tzu's The Art of War 5:2:7 (literal translation of Chinese characters).

Failure is the opportunity to begin again, more intelligently."

Henry Ford

General Principle: Only a continuous loop of adapting to situations advances positions.

Situation:

Competitive processes are not linear. Production processes are linear. They convert raw materials step by step into a finished product. At the end of a production process, the product is finished. A linear process runs in one direction. The problem is that we are only trained in traditional schools for linear thinking, so we expect competitive processes to be linear, but they are not. They are cyclic. They continually loop back upon themselves, reincorporating feedback from the environment into our next choice of actions. Their processes are never finished. They have no true end point. Whether successful or not, each advance requires another advance. The process is always a loop. Every advance brings us back to the beginning where we start working on our next advance.

Opportunity:

Our opportunity is to embrace the loopy nature of strategy. This nature means that, though we never reach the end, we also can never truly fail. Each loop, whether it succeeds or fails, is a learning experience. Even if we fail to make the move we attempted, we still improve our position by learning more about our position and situation.

Key Methods:

1. The adaptive loop is the constant reaction to objective and subjective conditions in the environment. We take in information from the environment, make decisions, take actions, and establish positions. In the next cycle of the loop, we again adjust our information, decisions, actions and positions. In the first two stages, we work with subjective information, in the last two stages, with physical matters following the subjective and objective nature of positions (1.2 Subobjective Positions).

2. The adaptive loop is a two-part cycle of expansion and contraction. Like a beating heart or breathing, in half of the cycle we reach out to gather broadly from the environment then we narrow our focus by making decisions. We then open ourselves to events by taking action, then we narrow our focus again to establish a position. We can think of the expansion stage as the destruction of feeding off the environment and the contraction stage as the creation of something new in the environment (1.8.1 Creation and Destruction).

3. We call the adaptive loop the Progress Cycle because its only purpose is advancing a position. In its simplest form, we describe the adaptive loop as Listen > Aim > Move > Claim following the terms we developed in our most general work, *The Golden*

Key to Strategy. This short form is both easy to remember and easily applicable to a wide variety of areas. In The Playbook, we use a more sophisticated and detailed description of this cycle. This form was first developed in our work, *9 Formulas for Business Success.* In this form, understanding the nature of competitive positions sits at the center. The cycle itself is represented by the other formulas, breaking down Listen > Aim > Move > Claim into more detail: Listening to gather information to see positions more clearly (<u>2.0 Developing Perspective</u>).

4. The Progress Cycle starts with listening to put together a big picture to see openings. This is where we reach out into the environment. We open ourselves to the nature of the situation with the specific goal of seeing where we need to move (<u>3.0 Identifying Opportunities</u>).

5. The Progress Cycle requires aiming at only the opportunities that are the most likely to be successful. Unlike the productive moves of linear planning, we do not know exactly what will happen in any competitive move. Because our resources are limited, we must prioritize the opportunities that we explore, choosing those that are the most likely to be successful. (<u>4.0 Leveraging Probability</u>).

6. The Progress Cycle then aims at minimizing our mistakes. To explore new areas more successfully, we are going to make mistakes because success is only a probability. Many attempts will fail. We must learn how to handle those failures so they do not eliminate future success. (<u>5.0 Minimizing Mistakes</u>).

7. The Progress Cycle then acts, moving in standard ways to meet the challenges of the opportunity. This is the first component of the move part of the cycle. It is expansive, since our actions must move out of areas we control into new areas. In those areas, we must respond to situations in the ways that have proven to be the most effective in the past (<u>6.0 Situation Response</u>).

8. The Progress Cycle completes moves through creativity. While standard responses help us meet the challenges of the situation, we create the momentum we need to succeed only through creativity. This is the focusing stage of the moving cycle (7.0 Creating Momentum).

9. The Progress Cycle wins rewards by claiming them. Sun Tzu teaches that the rewards of a position must be claimed. This expansion stage again reaches out into the environment, in this case, for the benefits of the position to which we have moved (8.0 Winning Rewards).

10. The Progress Cycle claims rewards in order to defend our gains. This is the concentration stage, where we use the productivity of a position to secure it (9.0 Using Vulnerability).

Illustration:

1. The adaptive loop is the constant reaction to objective and subjective conditions in the environment. None of us are inventing this cycle. It exists in nature. Our job as scientists is simply to describe it so that people can recognize what is happening and use this knowledge for their own purposes. Once we understand the adaptive loop, we easily recognize its use in every form of competition.

2. The adaptive loop is a two-part cycle of expansion and contraction. The cycle is a feedback loop, continuously correcting our course as we navigate the environment. This cycle is scalable. For example, in sales, the large scale loop is often described as "qualification," "presentation," "overcoming objections," and "closing." Properly understood, this maps directly to Sun Tzu's description of "to learn," "to aim," "to march," and "to form."

3. **We call the adaptive loop the Progress Cycle because its only purpose is advancing a position.** Each "step" of the loop has within it smaller feedback loops. In military competition, recognizing the adaptive loop is a matter of life and death. 2,500 years ago, Sun Tzu in **The Art of War** described the cycle most generally as "to learn," "to see," "to march," and "to form." As a general, his focus was on the large scale movement of troops that took days or weeks. In other eras where different weapons and actions come into

play, strategists always see the complete cycle, but focused on different parts. In the 20th century, Col. John Boyd, saw the first part of the cycle as more important, He described the whole cycle as "to observe," "to orient," "to decide," and "to act," the OODA loop. As a fighter pilot, his interest was on loops that lasted a few seconds.

4. The Progress Cycle starts with listening to put together a big picture to see openings. For example, when we are in a period of gathering information, we are still acting, asking questions.

5. The Progress Cycle requires aiming at only the opportunities that are the most likely to be successful. There are hundreds of other competitive arenas where the adaptive loop is described in the specific language of the profession or the activity. Product design, political campaigns, military campaigns, sports events, and every other field in which people endeavor to improve their position have their own language for describing their version of the adaptive loop.

6. The Progress Cycle then aims at minimizing our mistakes. In military battles, we must preserve our army. In sports contests, we must keep the score close. In product design, we cannot create products that are too expensive to build.

7. The Progress Cycle then acts, moving in standard ways to meet the challenges of the opportunity. Every competitive arena has its own standard methods for dealing with different situations, but those methods are standards because they usually work.

8. The Progress Cycle completes moves through creativity. Those who succeed in every competitive arena are those that go beyond the standard to invent new responses. These responses are not merely superior execution of what is expected but a change from what is expected to what creates surprise.

9. The Progress Cycle wins rewards by claiming them. These feedback loops can take weeks or months or even years. For example, designing a new product and bringing it to market. But within these long loops are many little loops, some of which last only a few seconds. The cycle is only complete when the reward or benefit of the move is converted from potential to reality. Money is made. Opponents surrender the field.

10. The Progress Cycle claims rewards in order to defend our gains. When we win rewards, we set up a reason for others to want to take them from us. We now have a position to defend, so we must consider our vulnerabilities. Defending a position is easier than winning it, but it cannot be over looked. This defense, however, is also the basis for a new cycle of advancing our position.

1.8.1 Creation and Destruction

Sun Tzu's five key methods on the creation and destruction of competitive positions.

"It is the basis of life and death.
It is the philosophy of survival or destruction."
Sun Tzu's The Art of War 1:1:3-4

"Every piece of business strategy acquires its true
significance only against the background of that process
[of creative destruction] and within the situation created
by it. It must be seen in its role in the perennial gale of
creative destruction; it cannot be understood irrespective
of it or, in fact, on the hypothesis that there is a perennial
lull...."
Joseph Schumpeter'

General Principle: Competitive positions are continuously created and destroyed.

Situation: The problem is that it is difficult to see the continual process of creation and destruction that surrounds us. One of our training exercises is a demonstration of change blindness where we show the version of the same picture where a major feature has been eliminated in one of them. If we flash the picture with a second of white space in between, most people simply cannot see the difference. Similarly, we cannot see the changes taking place around us all the time. We expect conditions to be stable and predictable so we see them that way. Our perception of the world changes much slower than reality. Our mental models of the world are powerful tools when they are in sync with reality, but as they gradually fall out of step with the changes around us, they work less and less well. Positions are created and destroyed by the world's powerful process of change despite the limitations of our perceptions and the rigidity of our mental models.

Opportunity:

Just as there can be no opportunity without change, there can be no opportunity without destruction. Creation and destruction are complementary opposites: one requires the other (3.2.3 Complementary Opposites). For a new era to be born, an old era must die. Every act of creation is also an act of destruction. Creation and destruction are closely tied to the objective and subjective nature of positions (1.2 Subobjective Positions). The stubbornness of our opinions can maintain the reality of institutions long after the reality of their value has faded away (1.1.1 Position Dynamics).

One of the my favorite Sun Tzu strategists, Colonel John Boyd, wrote a paper on the role of creation and destruction in strategy. He saw the issue as primarily one of our subjective understanding of situations.

As we have said before, a position consists of two components: a physical reality and a subjective understanding of it. Boyd saw that, as we necessarily learned more, our existing understanding of a position was necessarily destroyed as we come to a higher level of awareness. As he wrote:

> *To comprehend and cope with our environment we develop mental patterns or concepts of meaning. The*

purpose of this paper is to sketch out how we destroy and create these patterns to permit us to both shape and be shaped by a changing environment. In this sense, the discussion also literally shows why we cannot avoid this kind of activity if we intend to survive on our own terms. The activity is dialectic in nature generating both disorder and order that emerges as a changing and expanding universe of mental concepts matched to a changing and expanding universe of observed reality.

So this creation and destruction of positions is, at its root, a necessary by-product of our learning. If we don't learn, our competitor's certainly will. We can either destroy our own positions by advancing them or we can wait for our competitors to destroy our position by catching up to us and surpassing us.

Key Methods:

The cycles by which positions are advanced not only creates new positions, but destroys old ones. Strategy exists to save us from the trap of thinking that the natural order of things is stable. Any stability in any competitive arena is just temporary, a temporary respite from the battle, nothing more. If the world was stable, we wouldn't need strategy.

1. Positions are continuously created and destroyed. We must move forward. We have no choice. We are all crossing the river, jumping from ice floe to ice floe, before they are swept away or melt from beneath us. As Sachel Paige said, "Don't look back. Something may be gaining on you." (1.1.1 Position Dynamics)

2. Creation and destruction begins and ends with our mental paradigms. Reality is continuously dynamic, but the human mind adjusts only in fits and starts. Our mental models, that paradigms explaining how the world works, are destroyed only after evidence mounts over time against them and new, better models are found. Those new, better paradigms are the basis for a new round of creations and destruction (2.2.2 Mental Models).

3. Periods of stability are temporary illusions. Because perception changes more slowly than reality, positions can seem set in stone. Every competitive arena--every country, industry, business, and person--may experience a period of quiet where the positions within it are stable. It is only a matter of time until this illusion of stability is destroyed (1.2 Subobjective Positions).

4. Positions that cannot adopt the new paradigm are destroyed. The computer revolution of the late twentieth century changed so many rules about how the world works, that it was only a matter of time until those changes caught up with us, wiping out a generation of organizations that were based on old rules that no long applied (2.1.3 Strategic Deception).

5. Positions grow under the emerging paradigm. As thinking shifts to the new paradigm, the value of these positions are better understood and more broadly appreciated (3.2 Opportunity Creation).

Illustration:

This is a particularly important lesson in today's climate of economic turmoil. We are witnessing the passing of an era where governments and large financial corporations thought that they were the master's of the universe because they were counting on the future being like the past, the trend line of, in this case, real estate prices continuing upward predictably forever. Unfortunately that never happens. Once everyone thinks prices are going up forever, that idea gets factored into the price, which means that the price is too high and the objective reality of what people can afford to pay will re-balance the scale.

1. Positions are continuously created and destroyed. The world's largest financial institutions and car manufacturers, the ones that are "too large to fail," are still in the process of being destroyed while smaller organizations who are more in touch with true risk and value are growing up to replace them.

2. Creation and destruction begins and ends with our mental paradigms. The endangered institutions were based on increasingly flawed economic models based upon the premise that the government could control certain factors, such as how affordable houses were or the standards for corporate accountability, that it could not be controlled.

3. *Periods of stability are temporary illusions.* Financial institutions and risky loans continued to grow for over a decade, but since the foundation of this growth was based upon broadly held misconceptions rather than financial reality, it was doomed. Organizations that aren't really advancing their positions, go the way of the Soviet Union, the buggy whip industry, Digital Equipment Corporation, and every worker who has lost his or her job by staying with a doomed industry.

4. *Positions that cannot adopt the new paradigm are destroyed.* The computer revolution of the late twentieth century changed so many rules about how the world works, that it was only a matter of time until those changes caught up with us, wiping out a generation of organizations that were based on old rules that no long applied.

5. *Positions grow under the emerging paradigm.* New financial organizations will base investments upon the real performance of the underlying assets, not upon the trust in organizations, including the government, who try to package and sell investments disconnected from financial reality.

1.8.2 The Adaptive Loop

Sun Tzu's nine key methods on the continual reiteration of position analysis.

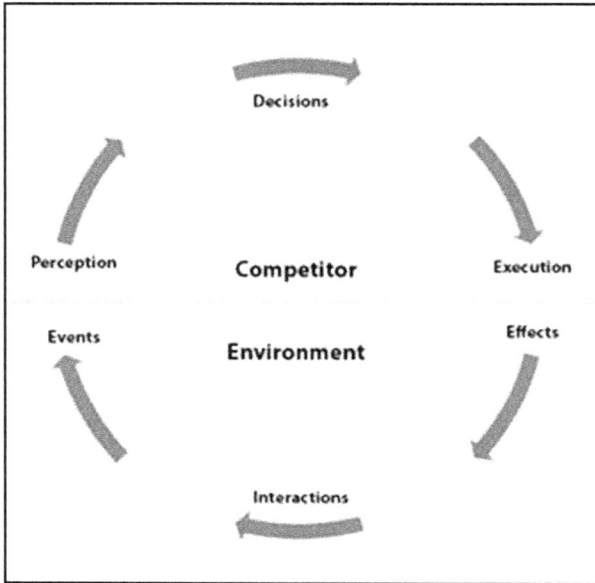

"Military leaders must be experts in knowing how to adapt to find an advantage. This will teach you the use of war."

Sun Tzu's The Art of War 8:1:14-15

"We can learn from experience if we are ready to adapt that experience to changed conditions."

J. C. Masterman

General Principle: Our picture of competitive situations is continually assembled over time.

Situation:

Our challenge is that we are never done adapting to changing conditions. We are flooded with information about change on a daily basis. On what information can we base our reactions? Without a system for filtering, organizing, and prioritizing that information, we end up with a confused, haphazard view of our strategic situation. We may see some aspects that are important but miss others that are much more important. This challenge is made more difficult by the continual distraction of events. To which events do we adapt? Events demand our attention because they are happening now. What is close to us seems bigger than what is far away so whatever is happening now seems more important than what happened yesterday or the day before. But, from this same logic, what seems so important now will seem less so tomorrow. The challenge is knowing which events are important and which are merely urgent.

Opportunity:

The system of elemental analysis gives us all the pieces we need to assemble a meaningful picture of our situation (1.3 Elemental Analysis). However, all strategic positions are paths, constantly moving (1.1 Strategic Paths, 1.1.1 Position Dynamics). Every time we formally analyze strategic positions, we are just getting a snapshot of the situation. That snapshot only shows where positions are now, not how they are changing. We can only see our situations and its opportunities when we assemble this series of snapshots. In doing so, we create a moving picture of the dynamics of the situations. We begin to see not only where positions are, but where they seem to be heading. This dynamic picture is the basis of our situation awareness.

Good situation awareness leads automatically to better decisions. While the other principles of Sun Tzu's strategy are important, even critical in certain situations, they are all based upon having a well-developed sense of situation awareness. We are continually making decisions based on our current level of knowledge, our current understanding of positions.

While we may need to do a formal analysis of strategic positions at certain times for specific reasons, real position awareness has to be a continual process, an integral part of gathering information, making decisions, taking actions, and harvesting the benefits of those actions.

Key Methods:

Living in an adaptive loop is a state of mind that sees the world according to the following key methods.

1. We are continually adapting our picture of our strategic situation and the positions within it. As new information comes in, we update our mental model of the situation, fleshing out our picture of the different missions, climates, grounds, leaders, and methods that affect us. As we move though the cycle of activities needed to advance our position, we continuously adjust our situation awareness. This is not analysis as a separate activity that starts and stops at a certain point in a linear process. It is literally our awareness, the framework within which we are constantly thinking (2.5 The Big Picture).

2. We recognize that the picture is hidden in its pieces. We should be driven by a constant itch that we are missing something important. Our information is always flawed. Our mental models never completely capture objective reality (1.2 Subobjective Positions).

3. We use the five elements as keys to unlock the key aspects of the situation. While we don't know what the strategic picture really looks like, we do know how the five elements fit together within it. By putting together these elements, we start completing blocks of the picture (1.3 Elemental Analysis).

4. We must increase our sense of size and proportion. As we collect more information from a wider variety of sources, we develop perspective, fitting the blocks of elements together, comparing positions. We see that picture from different perspectives. A well-rounded picture of the relationships among positions (2.0 Developing Perspective).

5. We must improve our ability to see where the pieces fit. As we build up our strategic picture, it gets easier and easier to add new pieces of information to it. As the picture takes form, we can see where new pieces of information fit more easily. We see where they reinforce the existing picture (2.6 Information Leverage).

6. We must develop our strategic awareness as an increasingly automatic, background sense. Through practice, we train our minds to sort incoming information. At first, we must do this consciously, working at it. Through practice, however, the process gradually becomes automatic, where we don't have to think about it because it is a habit (6.1.1 Instant Reflexes).

7. Though we can't always see it, we must sense that positions are always changing. Over time, adjusting the picture becomes habit. Things are changing whether we are looking at them or not. They are changing even when we are looking at them and can't see them changing (1.1.1 Position Dynamics).

8. We must sharpen our recognition of when pieces don't fit. As the picture takes shape, information that doesn't fit stands out. Misfit pieces can only be explained one of three ways: either our picture was wrong, the information is flawed, or the picture has changed (2.1.3 Strategic Deception).

9. We must heighten our awareness of the directions of change. As we assemble a series of snapshots of time, we get a moving picture of the dynamics of the situations: not only where positions are, but where they seem to be heading (1.1 Position Paths).

Illustration:

A good analogy for this process is putting together a jigsaw picture puzzle.

1. We are continually adapting our picture of our strategic situation and the positions within it. We cannot solve the puzzle all at once. We must settle on a method of building up our knowledge in small increments.

2. *We recognize that the picture is hidden in its pieces.* Picture puzzles make this easy by putting the picture on the cover. Competitive strategy requires assembling the pieces without a picture. The picture is both in the pieces and hidden by them.

3. *We use the five elements as keys to unlock the key aspects of the situation.* We use edges and colors as clues to assembling a picture puzzle. We start by putting pieces together in blocks of similar edges and colors.

4. *We must increase our sense of size and proportion*. As we get the edges of the picture puzzle completed, we can start seeing where the other blocks of pieces fit.

5. *We must improve our ability to see where the pieces fit.* As we build up our picture puzzle, it gets easier and easier to add new pieces because we see where the holes are. We start to recognize common shapes of pieces more readily and it takes less time to find the pieces we need.

6. ***We must develop our strategic awareness as an increasingly automatic, background sense.*** By practicing putting together puzzles, we sharpen all our recognition abilities. As the picture in the puzzle takes form, the pieces we need start to stand out from the pile. We find ourselves just picking up pieces and putting them right where they belong.

7. *Though we can't always see it, we must sense that positions are always changing.* This doesn't apply to today's jigsaw picture puzzles, but it suggests a whole new type of toy. Moving picture puzzles on the computer, where the picture is a repeating movie loop instead of a static picture.

8. *We must sharpen our recognition of when pieces don't fit*. We realize when we get off track by putting together two pieces that don't belong together. When the remaining pieces don't fit into the holes we have, we start looking for what we did wrong. If pieces from another puzzle are in the box, we wouldn't notice it at first, but as our picture takes form, those "wrong" pieces stand out more and more clearly.

9. *We must heighten our awareness of the directions of things*.
If we had, moving picture puzzles, we would only be able to see
how the movie "ended" after the picture gets put together.

1.8.3 Cycle Time

Sun Tzu's seven key methods regarding the importance of speed in feedback and reaction.

"Mastering speed is the essence of war."
Sun Tzu's The Art of War 11:2:16

"There are no speed limits on the road to excellence."
Anonymous

General Principle: Faster cycle times are the essential element of competition.

Situation:

In the unpredictable environment of competition, situations are unpredictable and turn around quickly. Actions often fail. Rewards are always uncertain. Though certain courses of action are more probable to succeed over time, any given instance can fail, sometimes spectacularly. The problem is that we simply do not have enough information or control in a competitive environment to direct events.

Opportunity:

When we think of all actions as a feedback loop rather than steps in a process, every action succeeds--at least in the sense of giving us more information. Even if the information is "that won't work," we learn from each experience. In using Sun Tzu's Playbook, every action is an experiment, an exploration. If we think of the goal in terms of gathering information, there *are* some things that will always work better, especially when comparing our situation to those of others.

Key Methods:

1. In every aspect of competitive strategy, nothing is more important than speed. This is especially important in the feedback loop. The faster we go through the loop of gathering information, making decisions, taking actions, and establishing positions, the more successful we will be. At each stage of this cycle, the use of speed makes success more likely and puts those who might oppose us at a disadvantage (5.3 Reaction Time).

2. The speed of the entire cycle is called cycle time. Cycle time measures how long it takes us to recognize and respond to the situations with which we are faced. In the adaptive world of strategy, faster cycle times *always* beat slower cycle times (1.8.2 The Adaptive Loop).

3. Speed in gathering information is critical. Since the environment is constantly changing, the older our information, the more out of date it must be. The faster that we acquire information, the more information we can get in the limited amount of time we have to make decisions. We must discover opportunities quickly because all opportunities only last for a limited period of time (3.1.6 Time Limitations).

4. Speed in making decisions is critical. Choosing the exact right form of action isn't nearly as important as deciding quickly so we can test our judgment against reality. Quick decisions require a good starting picture of the situation from which to judge changes. Leaders who cannot quickly recognize high-probability opportunities, react quickly, and choose actions that can be quickly executed are at a serious disadvantage (2.5 The Big Picture, 5.3 Reaction Time,).

5. *Speed in moving is critical*. The faster we move, the harder it is for opponents to respond and adjust to our movements. One of the most important aspects of strategy is situation response, where we recognize and respond the situations instantly (6.1.1 Instant Reflexes, 5.4 Minimizing Action).

6. *Speed in claiming positions is critical*. We cannot get rewarded until we clearly establish our position. The more time that elapses between our accomplishments and our claims of a reward, the less likely we are to get rewarded at all (8.1 Successful Positions).

7. *The faster our cycle time, the more quickly we can correct our course*. Since strategy is based on probabilities, we are going to make wrong decisions along with the correct ones. The faster our cycle time, the less time we waste in incorrect actions and the more quickly we are rewarded for correct actions (1.8.4 Probabilistic Process).

Illustration:

Let us look at how these ideas work when applied to investment.

1. ***In every aspect of competitive strategy, nothing is more important than speed.*** If we are going to be successful in investing, as opposed to lucky, we must respond to the up and down movement of the market. We must buy and sell before others do. If we are behind the market, we will lose money consistently, buying high and selling low.

2. ***The speed of the entire cycle is called cycle time.*** The cycle time of an investment is the time between buying and selling. A fast cycle time depends on the horizons we are working in. A day trader works on a faster cycle than weekly or monthly traders, but both must work ahead of their particular cycle.

3. ***Speed in gathering information is critical.*** It takes any news affecting an investment time to spread to everyone interested. Investors who get the news first, good or bad, always have an advantage.

4. ***Speed in making decisions is critical.*** To make good decisions about the news that we get about a particular investment, we have to start with some understanding of what it means to that investment. Without an existing picture of its situation, gathering the information to understand the impact of the news takes too much time.

5. ***Speed in moving is critical.*** It used to be that private traders were at a real disadvantage as far as executing trades. At one time, it took hours and even days to make an investment.

6. ***Speed in claiming positions is critical.*** The investment doesn't pay when the investment is made, it pays when the position is claimed or closed out. Taking a ten percent profit in a day is better than waiting a month for a twenty percent gain that may vanish.

7. ***The faster our cycle time, the more quickly we can correct our course.*** Not all of our trades are going to work. We must get out of our losing positions as quickly as we can. We must limit our losses if we are to profit from our gains.

1.8.4 Probabilistic Process

Sun Tzu's seven key methods regarding the role of chance in strategic processes and systems.

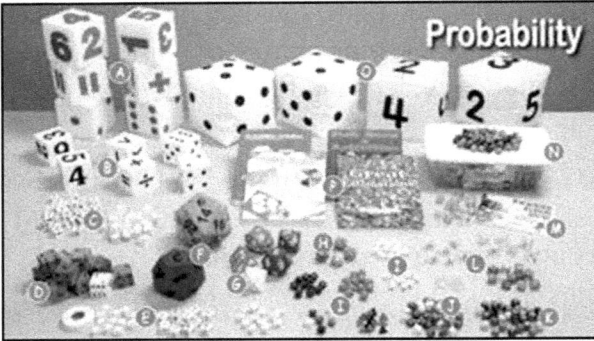

"Many advantages add up to victory.
Few advantages add up to defeat."
Sun Tzu's The Art of War 1:5:4-5

"It is a profitable Wisdom to know when we have
done enough: Much time and Pains are spared, in not
flattering our selves against Probabilities."
William Penn

General Principle: The adaptive loop leverages probabilities to make success more certain over time.

Situation:

If we expect the adaptive loop to advance our position in a predictable way, we will be disappointed. **Deterministic processes** solve problems working through a predictable linear process. Each step makes a change that gets us closer to our goals, like the steps in the manufacturing process. Every appropriate step has the predicted effect but *only* in a controlled environment. This linear thinking doesn't work in competitive environments where outcomes arise from the complex interactions of independent actors with different goals. Since every competitive situation is unique, their outcomes are also unique. Even if we could know all the conditions affecting a situation, outcomes would still be uncertain because the actors involved can create new responses that have never been tried before and whose affects are unknowable.

Opportunity:

Sun Tzu's process is a stochastic process based on probability not a deterministic process. Its probabilities are not fixed. In a competitive environment, we are always prepared for failure because of these uncertainties. We use methods that increase our chances of success over the alternatives but we avoid expensive failure. If we repeat high-probability actions recursively in the adaptive loop the probability of our success increases as long as we can continue to get new tries (1.8 The Adaptive Loop). Though we cannot know *exact* probabilities in the chaotic, competitive environment, we can know when one set of decisions have a higher probability of success than the alternative. The best strategic actions in a competitive environment have the desired effect more frequently than any alternative action.

Key Methods:

We identify higher-probabilities options over lower-probabilities options by using the following set of criteria. We increase our probability of success by choosing situations and options:

1. We increase our probability of success by knowing proven competitive methods. Sun Tzu's entire system defines a set of competitive moves that have been proven to work in different situations. It encompasses a large variety of situations, but it does not cover everything. The system simplifies competitive situations so that we can make quick, more correct decisions, taking into account all the major aspects of mission, climate, ground, command, and methods. Like all simplifications, this system can miss critical details, but knowing what works generally in a large variety of situations is the only way to increase our probability of success (<u>1.3 Elemental Analysis</u>).

*2. **We increase our chance of success over time by minimizing the impact of our failures**.* Since our information is always imperfect and our methods are generic, we will have failures. The key is to minimize the costs of those failures so that we get as many attempts as possible. We combine high probability methods with low-cost failures to increase the probability that we will find a way to succeed over time (<u>5.0 Minimizing Mistakes</u>).

*3. **We can know that high probability opportunities must minimize conflict because conflict is always costly**.* Logically, our success is more likely if no opponents are trying to stop us. Humans are endlessly creative. Creativity is the wild card in competitive probability. We want people to use their creativity in supporting us because we can never tell what our opponents will try (<u>3.1.3 Conflict Cost</u>)

*4. **We increase our chance of success by selecting relatively more solid information.*** Solid information means less complicated and more certain information. Information in competitive environments is always limited. Sun Tzu's entire system focuses our attention on just five key elements and other limited descriptions of situations. It is designed to solidify our information. We must avoid situations and choices with a larger number of unknowns or too much complexity (<u>2.1.1 Information Limits</u>).

*5. **We increase our ability to predict outcomes when we deal with relatively fewer people.*** The more people whose actions and reactions can affect the situation and its outcome, the less probability there will be that we get the results that we desire. In Sun Tzu's system, we focus more on those who judge our position than all our potential competitors because that group of potential supporters is usually much smaller (<u>4.5.1 Area</u>).

*6. **We increase our ability to predict outcomes when people have relatively few choices.*** The more number of choices the people involved have, the less probable every situation becomes. The minimum number of choices is always two: reaction or non-action. Much of Sun Tzu's system is designed to focus on a single, correct response to a single, dominant aspect of the situation (2.3.3 Range of Reactions).

7. *We increase our ability to predict outcomes when we know people's natural tendencies.* While every person is different, human psychology has certain tendencies. Our knowledge of tendencies comes primarily from the history of competitive experience and rules that have been developed from that experience (2.3.2 Reaction Unpredictability).

Illustration:

Let us look at these principles from the simple perspective of money management.

1. *We increase our probability of our success by knowing proven competitive methods.* Mathematically, probabilities mount over time like interest. Small differences at each iteration mount dramatically over time. For example, the difference between 8% and 11% annual interest on $1,000 over twenty years is the difference between $64,000 and a $1,000,000. Similarly, a method that has a 1.1% chance of success will be dramatically more successful than one with a .8% chance of success over twenty years.

2. *We increase our chance of success over time by minimizing the impact of our failures.* We build for diversified portfolios because we do not want to put all our eggs in one basket. We should avoid investing any sum that we cannot lose in speculative ventures whose value could go to zero.

3. *We can know that high probability opportunities must minimize conflict because conflict is always costly.* We avoid investing in firms that are in competitive battles where there will be clear winners and losers.

4. *We increase our chance of success by selecting relatively more solid information.* Personally, I stick to investing in ETFs rather than stocks in individuals firms because information is much better about what is happening within an industry as opposed to what is happening inside a business.

5. *We increase our ability to predict outcomes when we deal with relatively fewer people.* Again, by investing in ETFs, we reduce the impact of individuals on our investments. What happens to the price of Apple if Steve Jobs dies tomorrow? While the probabilities of Job's death are small over the short run, they are certain over the long run.

6. *We increase our ability to predict outcomes when people have relatively few choices.* Again, the dozens of different market sectors represented by ETFs represent a much smaller population than the tens of thousands of different stocks and bonds. In choosing all those stocks, people are choosing among relatively few market segments.

7. *We increase our ability to predict outcomes when we know people's natural tendencies.* There is a natural balance of forces in markets. When a certain investment goes up too quickly, people start developing a desire to sell and collect their profits. Even good investments will temporarily turn around when they are overbought. If we study the natural swings between various sectors, we see the cycle of these swings.

1.9.0 Competition and Production

Sun Tzu's seven key methods regarding the two opposing skill sets of competition and production.

"Supporting the military makes the nation powerful. Not supporting the military makes the nation weak."
Sun Tzu's The Art of War 3:4:**3-4**

"There will be hunters and hunted, winners and losers. What counts in global competition is the right strategy and success."

Heinrich von Pierer

General Principle: Competition is the complementary opposite of production.

Situation:

In the last several decades, the term "strategy" has been increasingly associated with planning and management control. The problem is that this confuses internal production with external competition. Production and competition are complementary opposite skill sets. Sun Tzu described the productive half of this dynamic as the "nation" and the competitive half as the "army." He warns that there is a tremendous danger in not clearly separating these two very different and yet complementary methodologies. In recent decades our focus of production has greatly overshadowed our understanding of competition. And, as the principles of complementary opposites requires, this imbalance creates a shift in the environment. Two centuries of advances in production have led to both the atrophy of competitive skills and the worldwide spread of production knowledge. At this point, we have diminishing returns from improving production, so the key advantages are shifting back to the competition side of the equation.

Opportunity:

Production and competition work together. Our opportunity is understanding when to use which set of skills. Our productive skills make the most of the resources that we control, but our competitive skills extend our span of control into new areas with additional resources. Production efficiencies can create a competitive advantage, but when production skills are equal, our advantage is in competitive positioning in the shared environment (1.2.1 Competitive Landscapes). Efficient production requires designing and planning systems. Effective competition requires making creative decisions about how to position ourselves in complex, fast-changing environments (7.3.3 Creative Innovation). Since competitive skills are relatively rare, studying Sun Tzu's methods has become increasingly valuable.

Key Methods:

We use the following seven key methods to use the differences between competition and production.

   1. Choosing the right methods requires knowing boundaries between competition and production. The methods of competition--adaptive thinking, expert decision-making, and big-picture problem solving--are very different from the methods of production—linear thinking, process planning, reductionist problems solving. Each set of methods only works well within the appropriate arena (1.5.2. Group Methods).

   2. *Competition adapts to external environments while production controls internal environments.* Competitive interactions are independent decisions while productive interactions are set procedures. This makes the external environment chaotic and unpredictable while the internal environment is organized and more predictable (1.4 The External Environment).

   3. Competition generally improves a human position while production shapes resources in a well-specified way. When we deal with those outside of our organization, we must think in terms of relative positioning. When we develop a position, we must think in terms of reshaping what we can control (1.1 Position Paths).

   4. Competitive methods explore and experiment while productive methods organize and systematize. Exploration is necessary because competitive resources are unproven. In contrast, productive resources are known and available. We need to explore a new area to discover its value. We need to experiment with a situation to its true nature (1.2.2 Exploiting Exploration).

   5. Competitive responses are event driven while productive steps are predetermined. In chaotic environments where actors are free to make their own decisions, we must adapt to events that arise unexpectedly at any time. In controlled environments, most events result from plans, which result from earlier agreements (5.1.1 Event Pressure).

6. Competition integrates details into a big picture while production reduces large process into detailed steps. The reductionist methods of production work so well because the environment is controlled and stable. This gives us the luxury of time for even more detailed analysis of how systems work. In competitive environments, we have neither the detailed information needed for reductionist methods nor the time to collect it. Situations simply change too quickly. Instead, we need to quickly develop a big, picture situation awareness that allows us to determine the dominant characteristic of a situation (2.5 The Big Picture).

7. Competition requires unique, custom solutions while production creates duplicate, standardized results. In competition, we must develop unique, custom solutions to a unique set of conditions. Since productive methods are based on duplication, they are easily copied, spreading through the environment. Since competitive methods are essentially creative, they create positions that cannot be exactly duplicated (7.3.3 Creative Innovation).

Illustration:

Let us illustrate these seven key methods with illustrations from a variety of competitive environments.

1. Choosing the right methods requires knowing boundaries between competition and production. A manager uses strategic skills finding and hiring the best people but he or she uses production skills in assigning them their duties and responsibilities.

2. Competition adapts to external environments while production controls internal environments. In our careers, we use strategic skills to search for a better job or get promoted, but we use production skills to get work from our in-box to our out-box.

3. Competition generally improves a human position while production shapes resources in a well-specified way. A salesperson uses strategic skills in working with customers but production skills covering his territory and reporting to his superiors.

4. Competitive methods explore and experiment while productive methods organize and systematize. In our personal life, we use strategic skills to find and develop our romantic relationships, but we use production skills to maintain a household.

5. Competitive responses are event driven while productive steps are predetermined. Usually only members of a highly bureaucrat organization can get pay raises and promotions in a predictable, pre-planned way. For those of us who want to move up within an organization more quickly than others, we must take advantage of openings that arise unexpectedly within the organization.

6. Competition integrates details into a big picture while production reduces large process into detailed steps. A salesperson can increase their control over a sales process by getting customer agreement to a specific set of detailed steps in the purchasing process. However, to make that process work, the salesperson must first choose the best possible prospect and overall sales strategy which requires a big picture perspective.

7. Competition requires unique, custom solutions while production creates duplicate, standardized results. Apple's competitive methods have created a unique position for them in the high-tech market, but their production methods create reliable, dependable products. A lot of people create unique, dependable products, but it is Apple's unique market position that makes their products more desirable.

1.9.1 Production Comparisons

Sun Tzu's six key methods describing how production naturally creates competition.

"Position yourself where you cannot lose. Never waste an opportunity to defeat your enemy."

Sun Tzu's The Art of War 4:3:22-23

"Our life is not really a mutual helpfulness; but rather, it's fair competition cloaked under due laws of war; it's a mutual hostility."

Thomas Carlyle

General Principle: Success in production is only determined through competitive comparison.

Situation:

Why is competition necessary for production? Can't we just be productive without being competitive? Such thinking represents a serious confusion about what competition and production are and how they depend upon each other. This problem starts with the failure to understand that competition is simply a matter of comparison. One of the most important aspects of life is that we compare our productive capacity. The comparison of production necessarily results in competition. The dynamics of comparing production evolves naturally into different levels of comparison. The problem is that most of us fail to understand the feedback loop of production and competition that defines our dynamic world of actions and reactions.

Opportunity:

Competitive arenas are necessarily defined as much by our productive skills as they are by our competitive skills. In the study of Sun Tzu, we focus on the skills of competition because they are much less familiar to us than the methods of production, but our opportunity for winning in competition arises from the unity of both (3.2.3 Complementary Opposites). In modern society, many of our competitive skills have atrophied because so much of competition is based on solely comparing our ability to produce. However, this comparison of productivity must naturally follow the underlying principles of competitive strategy. Our power arises from seeing how we leverage the balance between competition and production. To do this, we must understand all the different levels of competition inherent in the nature of production.

Key Methods:

There are six key methods that describe the competitive comparison of productive capability.

1. All competition is comparison, which includes the comparison of productive capacity. More production comes simply from improving systems, but rewards are won based upon the comparison of the relative value of that production. The five key elements of a strategic position naturally arise from this process of comparing productivity (1.3.1 Competitive Comparison).

2. Competition starts as a comparison of the natural resources of a position. This might be considered the natural state of a position. It compares our basic ability to choose the ground with the best natural resources for our natural capacities. In Sun Tzu's system, ground is the source of all raw materials. The relative quality of our position arises from the fit between our chosen ground and our natural capacities (1.4.2 Ground Features).

3. Competition extends to a comparison of what we produce from our natural resources. What we are able to produce from our resources depends upon our knowledge. We use that knowledge to transform the raw materials of our position into rarer and more valuable products. This is the beginning of that more advanced form of productivity that arises from what Sun Tzu calls "methods" (1.5.2. Group Methods).

4. Competition lengthens as the comparison of reputations for productivity. Our productivity creates not only products but, over time, our reputation. People judge our decision-making abilities based on what they see us produce. These judgments are generalized to include future expectations about the quality of our future decisions. What people are really comparing at this stage is our judgment itself. When positive, these comparisons lead to increased respect and authority in the community (1.5.1 Command Leadership).

5. Competition deepens as the comparison of our relative progress over time. Over time, we can become more productive through both learning and advancing our position. Changing conditions offer us the opportunity to learn and the opportunity to advance. If we see and take advantage of those opportunities, we win access to new resources. This will increase our productivity even more. Our increasing productivity is seen as progress (1.4.1 Climate Shift).

6. Competition evolves into cooperation from the comparison of direction. Once people can see our progress, they can judge our direction. Our direction reveals our goals and values in terms of productivity. If people share our goals and values, they will work with us. Working with others, we can divide our various tasks to further increase our productivity. Shared missions build organizations and relationships (1.6 Mission Values).

Illustration:

Let us look at some examples of competitive arenas based on these principles. Let us illustrate these different types of competition by looking at the increasingly complex aspects of human existence.

1. All competition is comparison, which includes the comparison of productive capacity. Every animate and inanimate object is a point of comparison.

2. Competition starts as a comparison of the natural resources of a position. Even animals are compared on the basis of "the ground" that they choose. Animals that choose better ground, eat better and have more offspring. Their choice of mates is also considered a form of ground, since that choice yields their natural capacities.

3. Competition extends to a comparison of what we produce from our natural resources. Unlike animals, humans consistently use methods to transform their resources into new, more useful products. Primitive humans created tools from the resources in their environment. Males and females in couples represented the first natural division of labor between two skilled specialists.

4. Competition lengthens as the comparison of reputations for productivity. The importance of reputations increased with the emergence of human societies. The larger the social group, the more important reputation became. Reciprocal altruism became intimately connected with reputation. Others shared with you because you shared with them.

5. *Competition deepens as the comparison of our relative progress over time*. This progress led to the competition among different civilizations. As some groups made faster progress than others, they naturally extended their territory into areas previously controlled by less productive groups. Farmers replaced hunters and gathers because their productivity increased faster.

6. *Competition evolves into cooperation from the comparison of direction.* As they found shared goals, groups of families became clans. Groups of clans became cities. Groups of cities became states. States were united based upon shared history, shared beliefs, and shared values.

1.9.2 Span of Control

Sun Tzu's eight key methods regarding the boundaries of competition leadership and production management.

"You must control your field position. It will always strengthen your army."

Sun Tzu's The Art of War 10:3:1-2

"Good fortune is what happens when opportunity meets with planning."

Thomas Alva Edison

General Principle: Planning works narrowly while strategy works broadly.

Situation:

Just as the skills of competition and production are intertwined by the nature of competitive comparisons, they are divided by our span of control. Only within our span of control do we have good information and control of our resources. Both physically and philosophically, the area that we control is relatively tiny when compared to areas we do not control. The most powerful person in the world can utilize only a tiny fraction of the world's resources. We live in a world with almost seven billion people and tens of millions of organizations. Each of these people and all their various organizations have their own spans of control. Each of these overlapping spans represents limits of information and capability.

Opportunity:

Production opportunities lie inside our area of control. Competitive opportunities lie outside our area of control. Our area of control is tiny compared to the vast expanse of areas where we have no control. This means that most opportunities lie outside of our span of control, where we cannot use the method of production to improve our position. A little circle of light represents where our skills at organization and production matter, and a vast ocean of darkness represents where our skills in positioning and competition matter. The good news is that this means that there are almost an infinite number of strategic opportunities. The challenge is discovering them, which is why so many of the principles of strategy involve collecting and filtering information.

Key Methods:

The eight key methods for resolving the challenges describe a repeating cycle of expansion and contraction.

1. We must listen to expand our strategic perspective. The appropriate strategy to deal with the vast amount of strategic area is a cyclic process of expansion and contraction. Starting with expansion, we use our current span of control as the starting point for gathering information to develop perspective on our position in the larger environment (2.0 Developing Perspective).

2. We then must focus our listening on identifying opportunities. We follow this broad perspective development by narrowing our focus. We must focus our listening to identify the opportunities in our external environment for advancing our position (3.0 Identifying Opportunities).

3. We aim to expand our position into the opening of the best opportunity. Improving our position within our tiny area of control requires more and more detailed knowledge about what we control. Because of the scope of the external environment, getting more and more *detailed* information about everything is impossible. We need to pick our best opportunity so we can focus on improving our knowledge of that area. This learning increases our chances of gaining control (4.0 Leveraging Probability).

4. We then focus our aim to minimizing our mistakes in exploring opportunities. This process is like breathing, expanding and contracting. We first broaden our knowledge in a specific direction, but then we must select only one action to focus our actions. We then narrow the scope of our activities to make the most of our resources (5.0 Minimizing Mistakes).

5. We move to expand our position by leveraging the conditions that we discover. As we cross the boundary into areas outside of our span of control, we discover new situations and sets of conditions. To move under these conditions, we must respond appropriately to these conditions (6.0 Situation Response).

6. We then focus our moves on innovation to create momentum. While appropriate methods are needed to start a move, innovation is needed to create the momentum necessary to complete it. This focus on innovation requires the courage of commitment to win the control of new position (7.0 Creating Momentum).

7. We claim to expand the rewards from a new position. Getting control of a position doesn't make it a valuable addition to our span of control. It must generate resources which we can control to produce value (8.0 Winning Rewards).

8. We then focus our claim to defend the value of our positions. This is the last step in the process, by which we consolidate our gains. At this point, we have expanded our span of control, but we must invest in activities that protect it (9.0 Using Vulnerability).

Illustration:

Let us illustrate these ideas by comparing the general business approach to expanding a business with the more specific sales problem of winning a single customer order.

1. We must listen to expand our strategic perspective. In business, we listen to discover how others see our market and how it is changing. In sales, we first listen to discover the broad needs of a customer.

2. We then must focus our listening on identifying opportunities. In business, we focus on identifying the best of new market opportunities. In sales, we focus to identify specific needs that our products can easily fulfill.

3. We aim to expand our position into the opening of the best opportunity. In business, we aim to expand picking the best market opportunity. In sales, we aim to expand our number of orders by meeting more of the customer's needs.

4. We then focus our aim to minimizing our mistakes in exploring opportunities. In business, we identify products and services that we can offer to test a small part of that opportunity. In sales, we aim to win the smallest possible commitment from the customer.

5. We move to expand our position by leveraging the conditions that we discover. In business, we expand by offering products and services to meet customers' unmet needs. In sales, we move by making a proposal to the customer that they can readily appreciate.

6. We then focus our moves on innovation to create momentum. In business, we offer something different to win customers away from alternatives. In sales, we use a novel approach to set up the close.

7. *We claim to expand the rewards from a new position.* In business, we use our new market position to create profitable sales. In sales, we ask for the order.

8. *We then focus our claim to defend the value of our positions*. In business, we focus on defending our new market positions and customers from arising vulnerabilities. In sales, we focus by making sure the order is handled well.

Sun Tzu's Playbook

Volume 2:
Perspective

About Perspective

Sun Tzu's science of strategy is, above all, an information science. Sun Tzu realized that the most important weapon in competition was the human mind. In Volume Two of the *Art of War Playbook*, we look at Sun Tzu's principles regarding the use of information. In his view, information shifts radically depending on the perspective from which one view it. These differences of perspective are one of the keys to creating powerful competitive strategies.

Today's new media brings us a flood of information, but the problem is that this information makes decision-making more difficult. Without the perspective that Sun Tzu provides, identifying what is important is like finding a needle in a haystack. The value of Sun Tzu's strategy is that its methods are designed to work where we know we can never have all the key information we need. Its methods are like a magnet pulling a few of the critical pieces of information from that haystack.

In a controlled environment, inside an organization, good information, especially about the plans of others, ensures good predictions about the future. However, in the larger, competitive environment, you cannot predict the future [1]*. Your position inside your company may seem secure, but in a marketplace customers are free to decide what they do. This means that while you may be able to predict that you can make a cake, you cannot predict that anyone in the marketplace will buy it.

In reality, we operate with incomplete information [2]* as a matter of course. Competitive environments are filled with misinformation. They are filled with outdated information. The limitations of information affect buyers as well as sellers. Our only guide to the future in competitive environments is the past. And while there is some continuity with the past, new alternatives are constantly being offered.

We can make decisions based only upon our subjective impressions [2]*. The less information we have, the more our subjective impressions differ from the physical reality. In chess, opposing players have access to all relevant information except each others' plans. In real-life competition, some people have information that others don't have. No matter how good our inside information, by definition we are outsiders to most of the world.

The strategic method [3] first gathers as much relevant information as quickly as possible. They then quickly filter that information so that actions can be taken safely, but each move is a probe designed to test our information and gain additional information that we could not have gotten without action. The final step is recognizing both our successes and failures.

Predicting the Future

In a controlled environment inside an organization, good information, especially about the plans of others, ensures good information about the future. The best way to predict the future is to create it. If you have a proven plan and access to the right ingredients, equipment, and skills, you can predict what your plan will create. For example, if you have a cake recipe, access to a kitchen, the necessary ingredients, and the time to make it, you can usually correctly predict that the future will have one more cake in it.

This is prediction is only possible because you control the process. You control the resources and the actions of those involved. This defines a controlled environment.

However, you cannot predict the actions of others and their use of their resources in the larger, competitive environment. In a marketplace, for example, customers are free to decide what they do. They control the key resource involved, their money. This means that while you may be able to predict that you can make a cake, you cannot predict that anyone in the marketplace will buy it.

In a competitive environment, you do not have access to the information that other people are using to make their future decisions. The environment is too large and complex. You often do not even know who the relevant actors in that environment are, much less the information that they have access to. When a business opens its doors in the morning, it doesn't know who, if anyone, will walk through them. Even if we could read each other's minds, there are simply too many people and possibilities to manage the vast amount of information involved.

We live in a flood of information. More information doesn't make the future more predictable. It makes the possibilities of the future even more confusing. In a controlled environment, the more information we have, the better our sense of control. However, in a dynamic, competitive environment, more information is just more noise.

The mental models taught by traditional strategy are designed to put a flood of information into a context where decisions can be made without a perfect knowledge of the future. Without these models, it is impossible to filter out what information is relevant in a given situation and what is just noise.

Incomplete Information

In competitive environments, we operate with incomplete information as a matter of course. No battle in history would ever have been fought if people had good information about their relative strengths. Both sides would know before the battle who would win. Battles are fought only because both sides think they can win.

Someone is wrong. At the most, only one side can be right. Both sides are often wrong when we consider the cost and value of most battles.

But no one knows who will win in competition. The information any group has is an insignificant portion of the total information in the environment. Getting all the information you need to bake a cake in a controlled environment is relatively easy. Getting all the information you need to sell cakes in the competitive market is much more difficult. There are always too many variables. There are always too many unknowns. Who can know how many people will decide they want to buy a cake today? Many who buy cakes in the afternoon didn't even have that information themselves in the morning.

Competitive environments are also filled with misinformation. Competitors try to mislead each other regarding not only their future plans but their current circumstances. Individuals distort the truth for a variety of reasons. As in a game of poker, any advantage you have is linked to what you know that the other players don't know.

The limitations of information affect a buyer as well as a seller. Internal resources are resources about which we have good information. We do not have good information about external resources, that is, the resources that others have. This makes finding the best product, the lowest-cost supplier, or a reliable service provider a challenge. The volume of unknown information in the external market is always much more than the known information available to any single decision-maker.

In controlled environments, everyone is relatively well informed about what is changing. In larger, more complex, competitive environments, it is infinitely more difficult to keep up with increasingly fast-changing information.

The past does not predict the future in competitive environments. Neither does planning. Conditions are fluid. New alternatives are constantly being offered. Everyone is continuously reacting to the changes around them, creating dynamic situations. Everyone predicts success, but actual results are unpredictable.

When people are successful, they think their planning worked. When they fail, they blame their plans. Most fail to see the effects of strategy because they don't understand the differences between strategy and planning.

Subobjective Information

Among the many powerful ideas that Sun Tzu teaches is that reality is always different than our subjective perceptions of it. We cannot know objective reality without filtering through our mental models. What is usually translated as "deception" in Sun Tzu's work is better described as the awareness that there is always a difference between perception and reality, but that we must deal with both at once, learning to make good decisions on "subobjective information."

Decisions Based on Perceptions

People make decisions based upon conditions, but everyone's idea of conditions is only based upon their subjective impressions. The less information we have, the more our subjective impressions differ from the physical reality. The fewer information sources we have and the more alike those information sources are, the narrower our perspective. The more information sources we have and the more variety in those sources, the broader our perspective.

"Insider" information is information about a situation that is held exclusively by one person or group of people. Insider information usually refers to information available only to those who are in a specific position. Outsiders are not privy to it. In chess, opposing players have access to all relevant information except each other's plans. This means that chess has very little insider information. This is very different from a contest such as poker, where each player has access to information about his or her own hand that no one else has. In real-life competition, insider information is critical to future events, but by definition most people do not have it.

Measures of Position

There are no absolute values in strategy. All judgments about positions are relative. These judgments are made by individuals from their own subjective perspective. There is no such thing as an objective condition that we call "strength." Strength and weakness are determined by comparing positions. From that comparison, we identify positions we suspect are stronger and weaker in one area or another. However, our judgments about conditions must be tested. Based upon that test, we can then say that various aspects of those positions are relatively stronger or weaker.

In these relative comparisons, insider information is always in play. We may have insider information about our own positions, but we do not have insider information about the positions that we are using for comparison. So no matter how good our inside information, we are always making decisions out of ignorance.

Sun Tzu's Strategic Method

How can we make good strategic decisions in an instant with limited information? Sun Tzu's Warrior's principles teach a number of sophisticated and yet practical models for decision making.

Knowing What is Relevant

Everything in Sun Tzu's strategy revolves around the idea of positioning. The only relevant question is: how do we advance our position? Our positions in all competitive arenas are determined by our decisions about conditions. Since information about conditions is critical to decisions, the first formulas of strategy are those designed to gather and organize as much relevant information as possible. By its nature, the environment frustrates information gathers. On one hand, it provides more information than we can handle. On the other, it seeks to hide the most critical information in a flood of data. Therefore, the tools of strategy limit our data collection to what is key and use methods that give us at least some insight into what we do not know. The concept of positioning is designed to limit the gathering of information to certain key areas where useful information can be found.

Focusing on Opportunities

The direction of positions is determined by motivation. What is an opportunity? It depends on our goal. Opportunities are determined by the opening that take us most easily toward our goals. The next formulas in Sun Tzu's strategy filter information to identify those openings so that decisions about actions can be made. This step requires its own specialized set of tools used for identifying opportunities and evaluating them. The process of advancing a position identifies the most likely areas where an advance can be made.

As Will Rogers once said, "It isn't what we don't know that gives us trouble. It's what we know that ain't so." Because each move is an experiment, Sun Tzu's first priority is experimenting safely. For example, the Minimizing Mistakes Formula teaches that initial moves should be small, limited, and local because they are the least risky.

Each move is a probe designed to test information in real time and determine its value. In making these moves, however, we must adapt to the situation as we find it. This systematic testing requires its own toolkit for adapting our experiments to the conditions we discover in the environment and that we can only discover by attempting something. Each strategic move seeks to make progress in a certain direction, but the immediate path to progress is discovered in the process of making the move.

Every Failure Is a Success

We win some and we learn some. If our goal is gaining a better understanding of our position, every exploration is successful. This requires recognizing both our successes and failures. As Thomas Edison recognized, most experiments fail. However, if conducted correctly, even failed experiments are helpful because they give you good information. Every move is successful in the sense of improving your quality of information about the competitive environment.

Though we must be prepared for failure, we live for success. We can often find success, however small, in every move. The final step is claiming our new position. Even when we have just gained knowledge, we have advanced our position in that aspect. These are the tools necessary to get every drop of value from a new position.

Developing Perspective

Given the proper methods, the chaotic nature of the environment becomes our ally. Sun Tzu's strategy doesn't change environmental conditions, but it changes our decisions in response to them. Small increases in the quality of our decisions can, over time, make huge differences in our position.

Our goal isn't understanding all the complexities affecting a situation. That power is beyond our capabilities. However, we can see the situation better than those around us. That is always our goal in developing our perspective. We use everyone's else's viewpoint to construct a more comprehensive big picture.

Many of the techniques first developed by Sun Tzu and developed over time allow us to use the shortage of information to our advantage. It is always easier and less expensive to control a situation by controlling the flow of information than by using physical force. For example, you create strategic momentum by introducing new information into the environment when you are prepared for it and your opponents are not.

2.0.0 Developing Perspective

Sun Tzu seven key methods for adding depth to competitive analysis.

"Discover an opportunity by listening.
Adjust to your situation.
Get assistance from the outside."
Sun Tzu's The Art of War 1:3:-1-3

"The manager has a short-range view; the leader has a long-range perspective."
Warren G. Bennis

General Principle: A strategic perspective requires systematically gathering outside opinions and facts.

Situation:

One person's perspective is narrow, seeing only one side of a situation. Our view of *our own* position is myopic. We are too close to our own lives to see them clearly. This makes comparing alternatives difficult. Adding to this problem, we naturally know, meet, and befriend people much like ourselves. Our "natural" networks are poorly suited from developing strategic perspective. Natural groups largely share the same perspective. Our friends and family see the world from more or less the same angle that we do. Our friends tend to be the same age and have the same background and interests. They usually share our opinions on a number of topics.

Opportunity:

Each person's opportunities are unique. Sun Tzu's principles teach us how to get the information we need to discover our opportunities. They are designed to filter information. Sun Tzu's methods of gathering information and creating contact networks seek to overcome their natural problems with having a narrow perspective. His key methods for information creates the well-rounded strategic perspective that helps us see the opportunities hidden in our situation. Sun Tzu's strategy tells us where to find those hidden opportunities.

Key Methods:

These are the seven key methods for developing perspective.

1. Our decisions are only as good as our information. The gathering of quality information is not tangential to making good decisions. It is a core skill. By definition, a good strategist is someone who is skilled at getting the right information at the right time. The goal of gathering information in Sun Tzu's strategy is the development of perspective. Perspective is the ability to see situations as completely and objectively as possible. A complete perspective is a perspective that sees a situation from as many different sides as possible (2.1 Information Value).

2. Developing a broad perspective requires systematic information gathering. We need specific forms of information. We all acquire information naturally in the process of living our lives. This natural information seldom meets our criteria for valuable information. Much of Sun Tzu's system is designed to address the challenges of getting the right information we need in chaotic competitive environments at the right time. To do so, we need a specific type of contact network and to use it to identify valuable information (2.2 Information Gathering).

3. Our information is only as good as our personal interactions. While information today is available from all types of sources, Sun Tzu focuses primarily on direct human contact. Only the human brain can compile information into a valuable form. All written and stored information was originally developed by people. Sun Tzu wants us to develop first-hand sources who can think specifically about our situation. In the world of direct relationships, we don't always get information directly. Our most valuable information comes from action, that is, seeing how people react to our actions (2.3 Personal Interactions).

4. We need five different types of contact to form a complete network. These contacts represent the five elements that define a competitive position. Our contact network is limited by our ability to organize and communicate competitive information. Bigger networks are not inherently better because of the costs of maintaining them. We are looking for more complete networks. One of the advantages of Sun Tzu's system is that it defines the key elements needed to understand our situations (2.4 Contact Networks).

5. To organize detailed information into a comprehensive picture we need distance. In developing our contacts, we want contacts who are close enough to a situation to get detailed information. We also need contacts who are distant enough from our situations to get perspective on them. Distance gives us a bigger picture, but the more distant we are from a situation, the more key details we miss. We need both detailed and generalized information on our competitive position. Our goal is to create a comprehensive picture of the situation (2.5 The Big Picture).

6. We gather information with the goal of creating leverage. Information is not valuable in and of itself. There is an infinite supply of information. Our information search must focus specifically on the types of information that give us leverage. This is information where subjective perspectives can be transformed into tangible positions (2.6 Knowledge Leverage).

7. Knowledge value and secrecy go hand in hand, both requiring the other. This means that they are complementary opposites in Sun Tzu's system. The more public information is, the less valuable it is. The more private information is, the more valuable it is (2.7 Information Secrecy).

Illustration:

Let us illustrate these ideas by looking at the situation of a typical small business owner.

1. Our decisions are only as good as our information. Small business owners find themselves in trouble when events catch them unaware. If an employee quits, a supplier runs out of products, or the city decides to tear up their street, they are in trouble if they don't hear about it until the day it happens.

2. Developing a broad perspective requires systematic information gathering. It doesn't matter if we run a restaurant, a grocery store, or a tattoo parlor, we are in the information business. *Our information is only as good as our personal interactions*. We can only hear about future plans of employees, suppliers, or the city if we are talking to the people who know those plans. The earlier we know, the more of an impact we can have. They may not tell us directly what we need to know, so we have to discern it from our interactions with them.

3. We need five different types of contact to form a complete network. It doesn't matter if we run a restaurant, a grocery store, or a tattoo parlor, we need information about the business climate, the customer marketplace, the lives of those we depend on, knowledge of methods in our industry, and knowledge of people's goals and values.

4. To organize detailed information into a comprehensive picture we need distance. We need information about the local business climate and the nation's business climate. We need knowledge about methods in our specific niche and knowledge of new technology that affects everyone. ***We gather information with the goal of creating leverage***. It doesn't matter if we run a restaurant, a grocery store, or a tattoo parlor, the new idea that takes our business to the next level will come from our information network.

5. Knowledge value and secrecy go hand in hand, both requiring the other. We must know which information that we need to communicate to attract customers and which information we must keep secret to maintain a competitive advantage.

2.1 Information Value

Sun Tzu's six key methods regarding knowledge and communication as the basis of strategy.

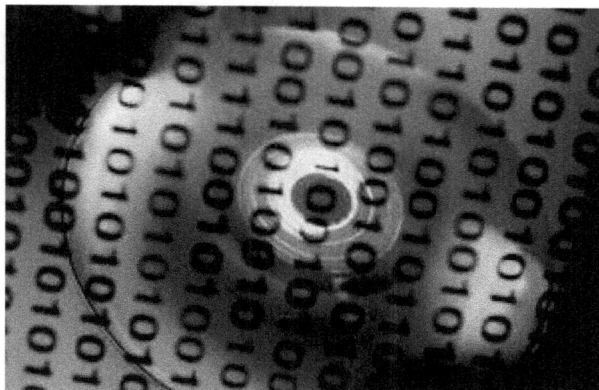

"The military commander's knowledge is the key. It determines if the civilian officials can govern. It determines if the nation's households are peaceful or a danger to the state."

Sun Tzu's The Art of War 2:5:-3-5

"Information is a source of learning. But unless it is organized, processed, and available to the right people in a format for decision making, it is a burden, not a benefit."

William Pollard

General Principle: Strategy depends on acquiring and using information to control situations.

Situation:

Our perception of reality is less than perfect. Our senses capture reality in an incomplete form. Our thoughts only partly comprehend what we sense. We must interpret what we see and hear. We organize that information based on very imperfect models of how the world really works. In a sense, we do not live in reality. We live in our limited perceptions and models of reality. Mistaking our perception for reality can be extremely dangerous. Since we all live within these limitations, information that goes outside of common perception and models is extremely valuable.

Opportunity:

Because we all live in our private worlds of perceptions, we all have the opportunity of finding unique advantages. We use information directly in two basic ways to create an advantage. First, we try to understand the true hidden nature of reality a little better than others with whom we are dealing. Second, we try to change people's perceptions so that they make decisions that give us an advantage for their own advantage. Our environment is rich in information, but our advantages do not come from more information but from better mental models for filtering and organizing that information. This is particularly easy in a world where people see only what is under control. We live on small islands of control in a vast sea of chaos. Control is the exception. Chaos is the larger reality.

Key Methods:

Sun Tzu's strategy was specifically defined to give us better mental models for accurately interpreting the strategic significance of the events that we witness. Many of these models were developed because people naturally confuse what they see happening in strategic encounters because much of what actually happens is non-intuitive. We must start with a basic understanding of what information is and why it is valuable.

1. We must identify valuable information out of too much information. Our information comes from our ability to discern differences between conditions. We experience events when we see, hear, smell, taste, and feel something change in our environment.

We cannot experience everything at once, even in our immediate proximity, so we are always filtering information. Because we cannot capture everything, we try to let what is valuable in while filtering out what is unimportant (Information Limits).

2. Valuable information is filtered and organized by imperfect mental models. Our minds convert immediate sensory experiences into generalized, symbolic forms. This generalized symbolic knowledge can be stored, shared with others, and duplicated. Direct sensory information cannot be stored, duplicated and shared in a similarly useful way. Language in the form of writing allows us to preserve and communicate information through time. Symbolic knowledge is organized to create our mental models. Our mental models are meta-information, information about information. They describes the principles that we use to understand how the environment operates (2.2.2 Mental Models).

3. Uncertainty is what makes information valuable. If we knew the future, we wouldn't need information. Our uncertainty drives us to want to learn more. What we see can be misleading, as anyone who has attended a magic show knows. Given that our mental models are imperfect, we are always imperfect witnesses. We are in a constant state of tension and attention because we want to know what the future will bring. New information can either confirm or violate our expectations of knowledge (2.1.2 Leveraging Uncertainty).

4. All preserved information about events grows less valuable over time. When we talk about the "information revolution," we are referring to the ability of modern technology to allow us to more easily capture information, duplicate it, and communicate it. All such preserved information is about the past. The information is used to create the mental models through which we predict the future. Our predictions about the future are based on outdated information from the past. These models work only because certain fundamental aspects of reality persist over time. Preserving and communicating information raises questions about when information is outdated. Many statements about conditions are time-sensitive. What was once true is not necessarily still true right now (1.8.3 Cycle Time).

5. *The value of information arises from the fact that all communication is guided by solely selfinterest.* Our ability to communicate with others depends upon the symbols that we share with them. We share information and keep information secret based upon what we see as our self interest. Information that is broadly known has a very different type of value than information that only a few people know. We are all constantly using information to our advantage. Even people who always tell the truth do so because they want the advantage of being known as truthful. Communicating information was once limited to the speed of human travel. Thanks to electronic media, duplication of information is virtually free and communication virtually instantaneous. (2.1.3 Strategic Deception).

6. *Surprise breaks through limitations, mental models, and uncertainty to create new value*. The ability to surprise and to be surprised is the wild card in the information deck. For the last two hundred years, people have begun to appreciate the value of radically new ideas. In productive environments, surprise is negative. In competitive environments, it represents an opening to new opportunities (2.1.4 Surprise).

Illustration:

Let us illustrate these ideas in a confusing, self-referencing form, dealing with you reading this site right now.

1. *We must identify valuable information out of too much information*. There are millions of pages that you could have accessed on the Internet, but if you are reading this now, you are doing so because you think it is more valuable than anything else you could find right now.

2. *Valuable information is filtered and organized by imperfect mental models.* You are seeing this word now through a mental model of language. If you cannot read English, you cannot understand this. These words are just symbols for shared ideas. When you start reading about a "fringlimest," you cannot understand what you are reading because it isn't part of your model. It is a nonsense word.

3. Uncertainty is what makes information valuable. Something is happening inside your computer right now, but you cannot see what it is. Real events are taking place in your room right now, but these words control you because you see them as important to your future. You are reading because you want to master the techniques for using the uncertainty of the world.

4. All preserved information about events grows less valuable over time. This sentence has been on the server for months. Is it still important? It is an event for you now, but it describes a timeless concept not a real world event. As you are reading this, the above sentence is old but is it outdated?

5. The value of information arises from the fact that all communication is guided by solely self interest. I am writing this sentence out of self-interest. I want to inspire you to learn more about Sun Tzu. However, just because this information is in my self interest doesn't mean that it isn't in your best interest as well.

6. Surprise breaks through limitations, mental models, and uncertainty to create new value. Surprise! I have nothing more to say.

2.1.1 Information Limits

Sun Tzu's eight key methods for making good decisions with limited information.

"Knowledge is victory. No knowledge, no victory."
Sun Tzu's The Art of War 1:1:36-37 (Ancient Chinese Revealed Version)

"Be willing to make decisions. That's the most important quality in a good leader."
General George S. Patton

General Principle: Strategic decisions are always made with limited information.

Situation:

We must be realistic about the quality of competitive information. There is an infinite amount of information that may be relevant to our competitive position. Much of this information is not only unknown but unknowable. The chain that brings us information consists of weak links. Unexpected events continually come from unforeseen directions. Information about these events is always limited. Our impressions about what is happening is filtered through our expectations, which are too often wrong. Sensory information is limited, not only by our senses, but by our focus and attention. Our mental models can filter out the wrong information. Our words never clearly express our ideas. Information is lost in communication: what is said is not necessarily what is heard. More information is lost in interpretation: what is meant is not necessarily what others think is meant.

Opportunity:

Despite the limitation of quality information, we must make decisions. The more quickly we make them, the better. We can gather only as much information as time allows. Many key decisions must be made in an instant. The time limits on making decisions is a key factor limiting our information about a situation (1.8.3 Cycle Time). While having better information than others is always beneficial, better information is seldom required to make better decisions than most people. All we need is better knowledge of what the key information is and a clearer focus on it than others (1.7.2 Goal Focus).

Key Methods:

Since complete and accurate information is never going to be available, we have to look at information differently in order to make our decisions. Good strategic decisions can be made with limited information, but only if we know the appropriate methods. To use those methods, we must:

*1. We make good decisions ith limited information by compar-
ing the relative value of making a decision against that of making
no decision*. If we have nothing much to gain or nothing much to
lose, we should avoid acting on information. Action is always costly.
Just having information doesn't demand that we act upon it. We
must ask ourselves, "Does a decision really need to be made now?"
(4.2 Choosing Non-Action)

*2. We make good decisions with limited information by esti-
mating the cost of making the wrong decision*. The potential value
of a decision is only half the equation. We make wrong decisions all
the time because we don't have perfect information about the future.
Wrong decisions are invaluable learning tools. We must ask ourselves, "Is any decision based on this information safe if the information is wrong?" (3.1 Strategic Economics)

*3. We make good decisions with limited information by ignor-
ing information that doesn't impact the decision*. In Sun Tzu's
system, we use the five elements to give us a solid guide. A vast
majority of information related to a decision or situation doesn't
affect our decision one way or another. If information doesn't
impact one of the five key elements, such information can be very
interesting, even distracting, arousing our curiosity, but that doesn't
make it relevant. When information does touch on one of the key
elements, the first question we should ask is: "If this information
were different, would it change my decision?" (1.3 Elemental Analysis)

*4. We make good decisions with limited information by weigh-
ing information based upon its relative importance to the decision*. In competition, everything is a comparison. All the remaining
information affects our decision, but not all of it is equal in its
impact. We must ask, "Which information is most influencing my
decision?" (1.3.1 Competitive Comparison)

*5. We make good decisions with limited information by testing
information consistency against our situation awareness*. People

often are influenced by the worst and most inconsistent information simply because it demands attention. However, that characteristic doesn't make it true. We must ask ourselves, given all we know about the situation and its history, is this information likely to be true?" (6.1 Situation Recognition)

6. We make good decisions with limited information by always suspecting that inconsistent information is wrong. Our information can be wrong because 1) it was garbled in communication, 2) events were misinterpreted, 3) people intentionally want to mislead us through secrecy or deception, or 4) the information has been outdated by more recent developments. We must ask ourselves, "How could this information be incorrect or how can it be quickly verified?" (2.1.3 Strategic Deception)

7. We make good decisions with limited information by balancing the cost of collecting more information against value of quick action. Action might be the quickest and least costly way to get better information. Often, it is the only way to get better information. If reliable, relevant information can be gathered more quickly and easily without action, we should gather it, but decisions can always be avoided by using the excuse that more information must be gathered. We must ask ourselves, "Is action the fastest and least expensive way to find out the truth?" (3.1.2 Strategic Profitability)

8. We make good decisions with limited information by having a prejudice toward acting to learn more. The best way to get better information is often through action not passing inquiry. Situations always change. It is a fantasy to think that we can always gather enough information to always make the right decision. If action is the best decision now, it is best to act now before the situation changes. We must ask ourselves, "Why wait?" The answer must never be, "For more information." (5.3.1 Speed and Quickness)

Illustration:

Let us use the example of gathering information about someone with who we are considering a serious relationship. The same principles work whether the relationship is personal or professional.

1. We make good decisions with limited information by comparing the relative value of making a decision against that of making no decision. If we do not see a great deal of potential value in the relationship, we should generally avoid it.

2. We make good decisions with limited information by estimating the cost of making the wrong decision. If rejecting the relationship is more costly than accepting it, we must consider that in our decision.

3. We make good decisions with limited information by ignoring information that doesn't impact the decision. Even if true, most past behavior in other relationships, good or bad, will have little impact on our future relationship.

4. We make good decisions with limited information by weighing information based upon its relative importance to the decision. We must know what is important in the relationship and which information that we have relates most directly to our values.

5. We make good decisions with limited information by testing information consistency against our situation awareness. Our picture of the person should come from all our information and, especially, from our direct, first-hand experiences. Most information should be consistent with a single picture. We must not fool ourselves, pretending that the general picture tells the story that we want to hear as opposed to the one we need to know.

6. We make good decisions with limited information by always suspecting that inconsistent information is wrong. Information about a person that seems out-of-character from our first-hand experiences should be immediately suspect rather than immediately believed.

7. We make good decisions with limited information by balancing the cost of collecting more information against value of quick action. In some situations, a closer relationship will generate more information than outside research. In others, outside research is a least costly path.

8. We make good decisions with limited information by having a prejudice toward acting to learn more. If is always better to say either "Yes" or "No" to the relationship than have it linger in limbo. Either path allows us to move forward, while making no decision leaves us stuck.

2.1.2 Leveraging Uncertainty

Sun Tzu's five key methods for leveraging the elemental nature of uncertainty.

Chaos gives birth to control."
Fear gives birth to courage."
Weakness gives birth to strength."

Sun Tzu's The Art of War 5:4:7-9

"Confusion is a word we have invented for an order which is not yet understood."

Henry Miller

General Principle: Strategic decisions are always made with limited information.

Situation:

All our early experiences in life are in controlled environments, where we are protected from competitive chaos. We are raised and educated in environments where the future is predictable and the information that we need most is readily available. In our first jobs outside the home, we only have to follow directions and do as we are told. These early experiences create false expectation of certainty. When we venture out from controlled environments into competitive environments, our mental model of a world in control is violated. We make the painful discovery that much of what happens is outside of anyone's control and unpredictable. Many of us can never accept this view of reality. We constantly yearn for the comfortable mindset of our childhood rather than get comfortable with uncertainty.

Opportunity:

Our opportunity comes from knowing that competitive situations always have hidden opportunities. No matter how certain, solid, or predictable the world seems, there are always new possibilities hidden in plain sight. Most people are untrained and unprepared for the fact. This gives us an advantage. We can train our mind to find new possibilities in what confuses others. We are all confused by the information that we get, but those who expect information to be reliable, complete, and what we expect miss what is possible. Instead of trying to "fix" the problem of making decisions with incomplete and inaccurate information by attempting to get perfect information, we can leverage the uncertainty of situations and of others. An expectation of uncertainty gives us a relative advantage in every situation (1.3.1 Competitive Comparison).

Key Methods:

We leverage uncertainty by understanding its inherent potential in every key element that defines a competitive position.

1. We leverage the fuzziness of values and goal to create shared missions. The opposing nature of goals that create rivals and enemies is uncertain and incomplete. We must avoid seeing situations in terms of black and white. Instead we look for areas of gray where we can find shared missions hidden in what appears to be conflicting situations (1.6.1 Shared Mission).

2. We leverage the uncertain direction of climate by seeing people's confusion as an opportunity. Most people fear change. They often fear it. Sun Tzu teaches us to embrace it because it is the source of all opportunities. Let others waste their resources trying to stop change. We adapt to change and surf on the waves of change. A constant opportunity in change is using it as a reason to change people's mind. New events require new decisions. By embracing change, we can leverage our superior knowledge against the confusions and uncertainty of others (1.4.1 Climate Shift).

3. We leverage the uncertainties of ground to utilize hidden resources. Our rivals expect us to use our obvious resources. Not all of our resources are obvious, even to us. We can easily overlook the potential of our resources. We must develop the mindset of automatically thinking about how we can utilize every resources that we control (1.4.2 Ground Features).

4. We leverage the uncertainties of character by expecting pressure to bring out the best and worst in people. Sun Tzu teaches that people's strengths of character are also the source of their weakness. When people are put under pressure, slight flaws can lead to them either cracking or breaking out (1.5.1 Command Leadership).

5. We leverage the uncertainties of methods by expecting the probable but being ready for the unlikely. We live in a world of probabilities, not certainties. While Sun Tzu teaches us to learn and use the most likely paths of competition, his teaching prepares us for what is highly unlikely. We avoid risking everything, even when the odds are in our favor because the unlikely will eventually happen. We are awake to uncommon opportunities because they will eventually happen as well (1.8.4 Probabilistic Process).

Illustration:

Let us illustrate these principles in a variety of competitive arenas.

1. We leverage the fuzziness of values and goal to create shared missions. Politicians constantly miss potential common ground because they see every situation in terms of partisan enmity.

2. We leverage the uncertain direction of climate by expecting the creation of new opportunities. In the world of technology, the confusion about new technology creates opportunities for high-tech companies. Some of the most successful firms in hi-tech didn't have the best technology, but they were able to leverage people's uncertainty, their hopes and fears regarding technology, better than others.

3. We leverage the uncertainties of ground to utilize hidden resources. During an agricultural age, land with oil was once considered a liability because it couldn't be farmed. Seeing the potential in oil required seeing the world from a different perspective.

4. We leverage the uncertainties of character by expecting pressure to bring out the best and worst in people. Capt. Chesley "Sully" Sullenberger always had the same character. He wasn't heralded as a *hero* until he successfully landed a crippled US Airways flight in the Hudson.

5. We leverage the uncertainties of methods by expecting the probable but being ready for the unlikely. Bill Gates ran a software company that sold programming languages when the opportunity arose to offer an operating system for the first IBM PC. This wasn't the opportunity he expected, but it was the one that he used. Even if we don't use this technique ourselves, we have to be constantly aware of when it is being used against us. It is more common than most people realize. We leverage uncertainty by understanding its inherent potential in every key element that defines a competitive position.

2.1.3 Strategic Deception

Sun Tzu nine key methods in misinformation and disinformation in competition.

Come a little closer

DECEPTION

"Hang on... I think it might be a trap..."

"Warfare is one thing.
It is a philosophy of deception."

Sun Tzu's The Art of War 1:4:1-2

"Now I believe I can hear the philosophers protesting
that it can only be misery to live in folly, illusion,
deception and ignorance, but it isn't --it's human."

Desiderius Erasmus

General Principle: Misinformation and disinformation are competitive tools.

Situation:

Knowledge is limited. Situations are uncertain. Nothing is more uncertain than what is hidden in the human heart. We are always seeking to shape the views of others to reach our personal objectives. From the time we are children, we recognize that we can control situations by controlling the information that others get about those situations. The point is that perception is not reality, but by controlling perception, people can control reality. Information does not necessarily reflect any objective reality at all but what others want us to think about reality.

Opportunity:

Information is valuable, and it is less costly to advance our position using information that it is using other resources. Physically changing a position is usually more costly than changing the subjective view of positions. By changing the viewpoints of others, we can physically advance our position more easily. Opinions change outcomes just as outcomes change opinions. Our ability to leverage information to advance a position inexpensively is the core of Sun Tzu's strategy. The point is that, since no one knows the ultimate truth, we have to think about the best way to represent situations in order to create a certain set of expectations. We are judged against the expectations that we create as much as we are by objective outcomes.

Key Methods:

Sun Tzu principles regarding the use of misinformation and disinformation are both a prescription and a warning. We must not only be willing to use these information tools as the situation demands, but we must also be constantly suspicious of the character of the information we are getting.

1. The possibility of deception must be considered in every competitive situation. Deception means nothing more than manipulating information to our advantage. When making decisions, we can never take information at face value. We must constantly ask ourselves how others might be using information to manipulate us or we might use a given situation to manipulate others (1.2 Subobjective Positions).

2. Deception can misrepresent conditions or motivations. Actions are always interpreted in light of the presumed purpose behind them. Misrepresentation of facts are easier to disprove than misrepresentations of motivations. Facts are external while motivation is internal. It is harder to prove a philosophy wrong than a simple fact (1.6.2 Types of Motivations).

3. Misinformation distorts the conditions of a situation. It does this by exaggerating or minimizing aspects of the situations. This can be intentional due to self-interest or accidental due to lack of knowledge. In Sun Tzu's system, we must misinformation to mean "missing information." Since all information is limited, all information is, to one degree or another, misinformation and must be evaluated in that light. Misinformation emphasizes some facts over others or leaves out critical details that impact a situation (2.1.1 Information Limits).

4. We must consider people's perspective and motivations when we interpret information from them. As we have said, misinformation can be created intentionally or unintentionally. People naturally create or pass on misinformation because it supports their position while leaving out or minimizing aspects that hurt their position. Thus, misinformation can represent their honest viewpoint, even when wrong. Information must always be judged by its source and especially their motivations. We automatically put information in the light that benefits us the most (1.6 Mission Values)

5. The biggest danger is not others deceiving us, but that we deceive ourselves. There is always a temptation to believe what we want to believe. We easily filter out information that runs contrary to our perspective and desires. The most destructive form of deception is always self-deception ([2.0 Developing Perspective](#)).

6. *Disinformation is information that represents a condition as the opposite of what it is.* The "[big lie](#) " is often more powerful and even believable than the slight lie. It is can be daring enough to cause us to drop our natural suspicions about misinformation. It can be grand enough to alter our perspective entirely. Disinformation works because of extreme situations naturally tend to reverse themselves. Sun Tzu recommends the constant use of disinformation in the first chapter of ***The Art of War.*** Many of the principles for using information to make strategic decisions are designed to avoid falling into the trap of disinformation ([3.2.5 Dynamic Reversal](#)).

7. *Deception is used to create expectations in others.* Those expectations affect both decisions and opinions. The same actions are evaluated very differently depending upon the expectations created. Depending on the mindset that we create, our actions can either disappoint or please people based on the level of their expectations ([2.1.4 Surprise](#)).

8. *The advantages of deception must be balanced against its impact on credibility.* Success requires the support of others. That support is impossible to get if we are not trusted. Deception can be used to create trust, such as when we under-promise and over deliver, as well as to destroy trust ([1.6.1 Shared Mission](#)).

9. *All opinions are eventually measured against objective outcomes.* This is why strategy teaches us to judge people by their actions and not by their words. Actions can still be designed to mislead us, but actions require more investment. As the old saying goes, "Talk is cheap." So information has both a short-term effect, creating expectations, ***and*** a long-term effect, when those expectations are evaluated in light of following events. We cannot consider the total effect of using information or misinformation without factoring in both the short-term and the long-term ([1.8.1 Creation and Destruction](#)).

Illustration:

Let us illustrate these principles in a variety of competitive arenas.

1. The possibility of deception must be considered in every competitive situation. The car salesperson may or may not know whether or not the car is a lemon, but his sales pitch is the same regardless of his knowledge.

2. Deception can misrepresent conditions or motivations. A car salesperson can be more concerned with his immediate commissions or with having repeat customers in the future. The first type of salesperson will misrepresent the facts intentionally, while the second type will do so only accidentally.

3. Misinformation distorts the conditions of a situation. Since a salesperson has chosen to work for a given car company, he or she begins with the belief in the superiority of that product, whether or not the belief is justified.

4. We must consider people's perspective and motivations when we interpret information from them. A car salesperson can provide lots of solid information, but his or her information about competing products is likely to have gaps that favor his or her own products.

5. The biggest danger is not others deceiving us, but that we deceive ourselves. It is not what the salesperson says, but what we want to believe. We may believe that a given model of car will make us more popular when, in fact, it has no such effect.

6. Disinformation represents a condition to be the opposite of what it is. Some cars were own by little, old ladies who drove them only once a week. Most are not.

7. Deception is used to create expectations in others. A good salesperson may describe a very quiet car as a little noisy so we are impressed on the test drive. A bad salesperson will over-promise, describing it as completely silent, which will set up a disappointment upon driving.

8. *The advantages of deception must be balanced against its impact on credibility.* A salesperson who says a very quiet car is a little noisy increases their credibility by demonstrating a higher standard for truth.

9. *All opinions are eventually measured against outcomes.* The most successful car salespeople in the world are those who care more about a long-term relationship than an immediate sale.

2.1.4 Surprise

Sun Tzu's five key methods on the creation of surprise depends on the nature of information.

"It is the same in all battles.
You use a direct approach to engage the enemy.
You use surprise to win."

Sun Tzu's The Art of War 5:2:1-3

"A true leader always keeps an element of surprise up
his sleeve, which others cannot grasp but which keeps his
public excited and breathless."

Charles de Gaulle

General Principle: Information can be used to create surprise.

Situation:

We are continuously bathed in a flood of new information, and yet little of this new information really surprises us. Our news comes from a worldwide network. Few of the events that affects our lives directly on a day-to-day basis are covered by the news. Like viewers of a television show, we think of ourselves as merely spectators, the audience, of the news. This is a dangerous and destructive attitude toward information. It distances us psychologically from the flow of information that Sun Tzu teaches is the key to our success. One problem is that too much of our information network lies outside of our competitive neighborhood where events do impact our lives. Another is that, despite the constant flow of events, we start to expect that our lives will continue much as before. This expectation sets us up for the surprise that completely undermines our position.

Opportunity:

Innovation is the attacker's advantage. Sun Tzu's strategy leverages innovation, identifying people's expectations and using those expectations as the basis for creating surprise. We must see ourselves as the actors not merely the audience. When we generate new possibilities, others must adjust to us and we have to worry less about adjusting to them. Our goal is simply to make consistently better decisions that those around us. Sun Tzu's strategy is about improving our chances over time. The more we use surprise and the less we are victims of it, the more successful we will be. Moves to a new position are best completed by using surprise (7.0 Creating Momentum). In both cases, we must know how the nature of information creates the expectations that makes surprise possible.

Key Methods:

These are Sun Tzu's five key methods describing the role information in creating surprise.

1. Surprise is only possible because events violate expectations. We are surprised because things don't happen as we expect. We use information to create expectations. Innovation is continuous, but people are largely blind to change. Surprise is sudden, discontinuous intrusion of an innovation in a situation. Innovation is unexpected because it is unpredictable. But, of course, it is not unpredictable if we are the ones doing the innovating. Surprise is how we use expectations (2.1.3 Strategic Deception).

2. The expectations needed to create surprise can be either unthinking or realistic. We can sometimes use unthinking expectations to catch people when they are unaware, but the consistent use of surprise requires intentionally creating realistic expectations (7.2.2 Preparing Expectations).

3. Unthinking expectations can be used to create surprise when people lose contact with their environment. We are doing something, but our attention is elsewhere. Since strategy is all about adapting to the environment, the failure to pay attention to what is going on around us is always a mistake (1.4 The External Environment).

4. Realistic expectations cannot be surprised when people respond in a commonplace way. Realistic expectations arise form knowing standard methods. In studying Sun Tzu, we learn competition's "standard methods," which are the range of typical actions that usually take place in a given situation. Standard methods are proven practices. People usually take certain actions in a given situation because those actions work. Often those actions work because the situation itself was designed for those actions to work (7.2 Standards First).

5. Realistic expectations can only be surprised by innovation. Innovation is a new idea, a new method, often unproven. It is the complementary opposite of standard methods. Like all complementary opposites, standard methods and innovation form a single system. In this system, these seemingly opposite and opposing forces generate each other in a continuous cycle. Innovation creates a new set of possibilities, which eventually become the new standard. That new standard becomes the basis for future innovation. Standard methods and innovation continually recreate each other in an endless stream(7.1.3 Standards and Innovation).

Illustration:

These ideas can be illustrated simply by thinking about driving a car.

1. Surprise is only possible because events violate expectations. As we drive down the road, the car ahead of us can go straight, turn right, or turn left. We don't know what it will do, but we are not surprised by any of these choices because we expect them.

2. The expectations needed to create surprise can be either unthinking or realistic. People can forget that they are driving and be surprised by a normal driving experience, but if we want to surprise drivers, it is best to create a situation that normally doesn't happen while they are driving.

3. Unthinking expectations can be used to create surprise when people lose contact with their environment. The car ahead of us suddenly brakes. We are surprised. It is not that we didn't know cars could brake. We are surprised because we had temporarily forgotten that we were driving.

4. Realistic expectations cannot be surprised when people respond in a commonplace way. It is realistic to expect the car in front of us to turn right, turn left, go straight, speed up, or slow down. If we are paying attention, when it does any of these things, we should not be surprised. These possibilities are standard methods, representing the range of what is normal and predictable.

5. Realistic expectations can only be surprised by innovation. If the car in front of us suddenly floats into the sky or sinks into the earth, we would be surprised. This is not what is realistically expected. These are not standard methods for a car. If we have set up a trick where a car that is driving is suddenly is lifted off the road by crane, people will be surprised.

2.2 Information Gathering

Sun Tzu five key methods on gathering competitive information.

"...bureaucrats worship the value of their salary money too dearly.
They remain ignorant of the enemy's condition.
The result is cruel."

Sun Tzu's The Art of War 13:1:12-14

"When action grows unprofitable, gather information; when information grows unprofitable, sleep."

Ursula K. LeGuin

General Principle: How we gather information determines how we see our positions.

Situation:

Sun Tzu puts the value of information higher than that of money. In most forms of competition, our definition of "winning" is far from obvious. It depends on what we consider valuable. Mistakes are even made confusing the most universal measures: money, time, and information. Our gathering of information starts with developing a broader perspective about what knowledge is the key to our success. The information that we gather shapes our very understanding of success. A limited perspective loses sight of both the broad possibilities and strict limitations of what is possible. When we do not see the possibilities, we miss finding a way to advance our position in unexpected ways. When we do not see the limitations, we make costly mistakes.

Opportunity:

Competition is based upon the idea of comparing positions (1.3.1 Competitive Comparison). The comparison is based only on the information that we gather. Before we can know how to compare positions, we must understand how our information affects our perception of positions. We gain our advantage by knowing what types of information are most important in comparing positions and identifying success. Success becomes easier when we understand all the dimensions in which it can be attained. The information that we gather defines and shapes our understanding of success.

Key Methods:

We must keep the following four key methods in mind when we gather strategic information.

1. Information gathering depends on our interactive relationships with other people. Competition is a human endeavor, dependent on subjective impressions as well as objective fact. Though there is an infinite amount of information available from impersonal sources such as the Internet, very little of that information is valuable for building our strategic perspective. In building a network, we have to think about two aspects of information: its quantity and its quality (2.2.1 Personal Relationships).

2. To know what information to gather, we need proven mental models. It is always easier and faster to use templates for gathering information. In a competitive situation, we do not have time to work through all the complexities of a situation. We cannot measure or analyze all potentially meaningful details in a give situation or position since many are unique. However, we can quickly work through mental models, comparing our current situation an existing model to identify key information. Sun Tzu's system is a generic model (2.2.2 Mental Models).

3. The five element model provides a universal template for gathering key information. The five elements provide a starting point for all information gathering. We must understand how the key aspects of mission, climate, ground, command, and methods generally determine position. Mastering this model assures that we don't miss key aspects that are important in all such comparisons (1.3 Elemental Analysis).

4. Every competitive field has its own "rules of the ground" for specialized information gathering. Sun Tzu's principles are generic, meta-rules, applying to every type of competitive comparison. Each competitive field also has its own, specialized measures for success. The rules of the ground can depend solely on people and their opinions. Other times, those rules are dictated by the physical constraints of the competitive environment. There are arbitrary rules and fixed rules. There are conditional principles and universal principles. (8.3 Securing Rewards).

5. We need a common vocabulary for information gathering. This allows us to communicate the key strategic issues more quickly. Much of this vocabulary may be unique to our competitive arena, but Sun Tzu's system provides a common vocabulary for discussing competitive issues more broadly (2.2.3 Standard Terminology).

Illustration:

Let us quickly apply these key methods to understand how information gathering works for a small business owner.

1. Information gathering depends on our interactive relationships with other people. The key competitive information that we need comes from talking to other business people, other people in our industry, our customers, our suppliers, and other such sources.

2. To know what information to gather, we need proven mental models. We will get a lot of information almost randomly as we talk to people. A customer will mention a product. Another business in our area will mention an accountant. Someone else will discuss a problem with employee taxes. We cannot keep track of these different pieces of information unless we have a mental model that organizes and prioritizes them. Those models also guide us to ask the right questions.

3. The five element model provides a universal template for gathering key information. Sun Tzu teaches us to identify the goals of those with whom we are working, recognize issues of business climate, learn aspects of the ground, parse people's character, and seek specific methods.

4. *Every competitive field has its own "rules of the ground" for specialized information gathering.* Consider what "winning" means for a business. The same business can be compared to its competition in many different dimensions. One business can be more successful than its competitors in market share. Another can be more successful in profitability. A third can be more successful in total growth. Another can be more successful in percentage of growth. Still another can be measure customer satisfaction in repeat business.

5. We need a common vocabulary for information gathering. Business accounting has its language. Various industries have their own more specific language. Sun Tzu's offers a standard for more generic communication.

2.2.1 Personal Relationships

Sun Tzu's five key methods on why information depends on personal relationships.

"You don't have local guides?
You won't get any of the benefits of the terrain."
Sun Tzu's The Art of War 11:7:5-6

"Personal relationships are the fertile soil from which
all advancement, all success, all achievement in real life
grows."

Ben Stein

General Principle: Only interactive personal relationships can discover quality information.

Situation:

Sun Tzu taught that success depends on the quality of our information and that our information depends solely on our personal relationships. In understanding our situation, we don't know what we need to know. Literally. From our limited perspective, we have blind spots when it comes to our situations. We cannot describe where those blind spots are and what we are missing because we don't know. The most basic challenge in developing a contact network goes back to the problem of information quantity versus quality. More contacts do not necessarily mean more complete information. In developing a contact network, we can only stay productively in touch with a limited number of people. Contact networks have limits. It takes time and effort to maintain the relationships upon which a contact network is built. If we grow our contact network beyond that limit, that network actually produces less useful information than a smaller network.

Opportunity:

For Sun Tzu, strategy is about making unique connections. In this regard, human relationships are uniquely powerful. The most powerful force in the world is people caring for other people. When others care about us, even a little, they turn the wonderful power of the human mind to our situation. When we care about others, we will move mountains for them. In looking for a needle in a haystack, more information doesn't help. It is just bringing in more hay. Our relationships harness the processing power of the human mind. Each of us has our own mental powers. Putting together a contact network is only partly about having people with right range of information. (2.4 Contact Networks). It depends heavily upon having the right human connections with the people involved.

Key Methods:

Personal relationship are the key to good information because of the following five key methods.

1. Our key information comes from our interactive personal relationships with other people. Though there is an infinite amount of information available from impersonal, non-interactive sources, sources like the Internet, very little of that information is valuable for building strategic perspective. In building a network, we have to think about two aspects of information: its quantity and its quality. Quality information comes from personal connections with other people (2.4 Contact Networks).

2. Our personal relationships harness the minds of others. Only a human mind can filter through the flood of information for what might be valuable to a specific other person. Our relationships with others focus their minds on our unique situation. That focus is only possible within a relationship. Given that focus, they can fill in our spotty and limited perspective and help us see where our opportunities might lie (2.0 Developing Perspective).

3. ***Personal relationships can identify important information that we didn't know was important.*** A machine can only search for the information the we know that we need. In competitive environments, we often simply don't know the key information that we need. We rely upon our personal relationships to fill in our blind spots. Unlike machines, people can find valuable information for us that ***we didn't know*** we were looking for but only if they care to do so (1.2.3 Position Complexity).

4. Personal relationships harness the power of caring about each others' goals. When we make a connection, the connection point is our shared philosophy. Our caring is where our common mission lies. That shared mission can start with something as simple as filling in each others' blind spots (1.6.1 Shared Mission).

5. There is an inverse relationship between the number of our personal relationships and their quality. Some people have a greater capacity for personal relationships than others, but there is always a limit. Relationships take time. Like all resources, our time is limited. We can know a lot of people well enough to know if we can trust them. Too many different views from to many different people who we don't know how to trust, doesn't help us. As with information, more is not necessarily better (3.1.1 Resource Limitations).

Illustration:

Let us look at all of these ideas from the perspective of people trying to their own small business and worried about government regulations.

1. Our key information comes from our interactive personal relationships with other people. Business people don't need to know everything as much as they need to know people who know what they need to know.

2. Our personal relationships harness the minds of others. There are hundreds of new laws under considerations with thousands of pages of text. Only someone who knows both the business person's industry and is experienced with the application of those laws is in a position to know about specific threats.

3. *Personal relationships can identify important information that we didn't know was important.* A business person who discovers new opportunities through its contacts focuses less on general news and more on the specifics of his or her situation. If that person has other contacts who have seen cycles of government activism come and go, he or she worries less about what cannot be controlled.

4. Personal relationships harness the power of caring about each others' goals. This is the basis of all "mastermind" type groups. The difference in Sun Tzu's strategy is that we try to take a more systematic approach to building a contact network. We use a more systematic approach because great contact networks do not just happen.

5. *There is an inverse relationship between the number of our personal relationships and their quality*. In the deluge of information today, if small business people know too many people, they are bound to get lots of contradictory advice, which creates more of a problem than it solves.

2.2.2 Mental Models

Sun Tzu's five key methods on how mental models simplify decision-making.

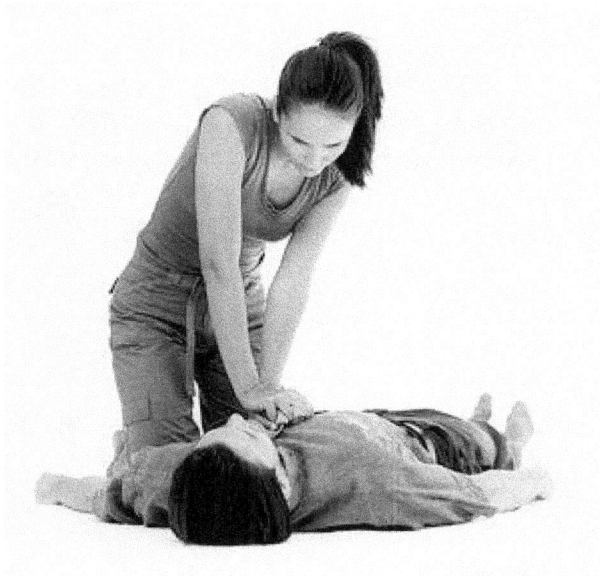

"Military leaders must be experts in knowing how to adapt to find an advantage."
Sun Tzu's The Art of War 8:1:14

"Even people who are not geniuses can outthink the rest of mankind if they develop certain thinking habits."
Charles Darwin

General Principle: Experts use mental models to quickly prioritize their responses to situations.

Situation:

Sun Tzu's system converts information into decisions. On the front-lines of decision-making, new situations are constantly arising. Amateurs try to reason their way through these situations. Sun Tzu taught that experts compare ther current situation with a large, set of common situations and recurring conditions to choose the best course of action. As modern research always shows , experts are able to make the right decisions almost instantly from mental models. Given the complex dynamics of competitive environments, simply picking through the information and putting together a plan is virtually impossible. When we work through the problem analytically, quickly knowing the appropriate response seems impossible. The challenge is understanding how experts work their magic.

Opportunity:

Sun Tzu's methods are best understood as a series of interconnected mental models.

Mental models describe common, generic situations and conditions that key us to make the right decision. To make good decisions, we compare our current situation with these mental models. It is always easier and faster to make comparisons than to figure things out. In a production environment, we have time to reason through situations. In a competitive environment, we do not have the luxury of time. Situations are too complex. We analyze all potentially meaningful details. We must quickly work through a list of mental models, comparing our current situation to these models, to quickly identify the appropriate response.

Key Methods:

This methods of comparing current conditions to generic mental models is used throughout strategy to make instant decisions. This method is founded on some key methods for making good decisions under pressure.

1. Sophisticated mental models describe a wide variety of common situations. People can either build their mental model over years of practice or though intense periods of training (7.2.1 Proven Methods).

2. Current situations are compared to mental models using a few key factors. As new situations arise, those using mental models aren't distracted by every aspect of the situation. They only have to compare the situations to their mental models to identify the key aspects (1.3 Elemental Analysis).

3. Mental models are first compared for situation identification. While many mental models may touch upon aspects of a situation, a given situation will match one mental model most closely. This allows us to quickly orient ourselves(6.1 Situation Recognition).

4. The situation is then compared to the mental model for any unexpected characteristics. Once we have a template, we can easily see what doesn't fit. Every situations is unique, but if there are too many points of mismatch, we must ask if we are using the right model (1.8.2 The Adaptive Loop).

5. The right model gives experts instant access to set of guidelines for making fast, good decisions. While decisions must still be adapted to unique aspects of the situation, the mental model offers a reusable template for success. This is much faster than other forms of decision-making and more often comes to the correct decision. (5.3 Reaction Time).

Illustration:

While this same process is used for making every decision in a front-line environment, perhaps the decisions of medical experts best illustrate how it works. In this illustration, we compare medical decision making with making any strategic decision.

1. Sophisticated mental models can describe a wide variety of common situations. Medical professionals are taught mental models as the key symptoms of a large number of specific medical conditions. Strategy professions are taught the key elements of a large number of specific strategic situations.

2. Current situations are compared to mental models using a few key factors. Medical professionals quickly check through the key areas of symptoms checking blood pressure, iris response, body temperature, etc. Strategy professions work through key aspects of position, mission, climate, ground, etc.

3. Mental models are first compared for situation identification. Medical professionals quickly connect a given symptom with the highest probability problem, for example, a high temperature with infection. Strategy professionals do the same, for example, connecting a lack of mission with a lack of unity and focus.

4. The situation is then compared to the mental model for any unexpected characteristics. Medical professionals then test to confirm the diagnosis, for example, confirming an infection by a blood test. Similarly, strategic professionals test for a lack of unity by probing alliances for potential defectors. If these tests prove negative, medical professional go back to looking for more key symptoms.

5. The right model gives experts instant access to set of guidelines for making fast, good decisions. If the diagnosis is confirmed, the standard treatments are used, i.e., antibiotics for infection or the use of division on disunity.

2.2.3 Standard Terminology

Sun Tzu five key methods regarding how mental models must be shared to enable communication.

"This is the art of war:
1. Discuss the distances.
2. Discuss your numbers.
3. Discuss your calculations.
4. Discuss your decisions.
5. Discuss victory."

Sun Tzu's The Art of War 4:4:4-10

"Philosophy is written in that great book which ever lies before our eyes.We cannot understand it if we do not first learn the language and grasp the symbols in which it is written."

Galileo Galilei

General Principle: Shared mental models improve communication by giving us a common language.

Situation:

Communication is based upon a shared understanding of how the world works. The problem is that most of us have no shared vocabulary for dealing with the concepts that Sun Tzu teaches. In some cases, the words fit the ideas poorly. For example, we see "competition" as "conflict" not "comparison." For other concepts, such as complementary opposites , we have no words. We have been all been trained to talked about problem solving in the terms of linear or industrial thinking. While we learned about Sun Tzu's strategy from our life experiences, people lack common terms even if they have learned similar lessons. Without a common conceptual framework and vocabulary, we have to work a lot harder in gathering information to develop our strategic perspective.

Opportunity:

Given a common conceptual framework and vocabulary, not only can we communicate the key strategic issues more quickly, but we can develop a powerful, shared perspective for identifying opportunities for each other. Our education may work against us, but our experience works for us. We all subconsciously recognize that step-by-step planning is only half the solution. The other half is our ability to instantly adapt to changes in environment. When we share this concept with our contact network, everyone in the network benefits and the quality of our strategic perspective improves dramatically.

Key Methods:

1. We must work with others to develop a common language for discussion competitive situations. The mental models used in Sun Tzu's strategy were designed to facilitate this process. The process of developing a common language regarding external strategy isn't difficult, but it demands a effort. Information gathering doesn't stop with the right range of personal relationships (2.2 Information Gathering).

2. Standard terminology can eliminate the confusion between *external challenges* **and** *internal control.* The value of information gathering is in its external focus. As special terminology can maintain that focus. While everyone has opinions about how others could better manage the controlled areas of their lives, our contact networks are more effective in helping us developed perspective on our environment (1.9 Competition and Production).

3. Standard terminology starts with the terms of elemental positioning. This means specifically covering all five aspects of a position-- mission, climate, ground, leaders, and methods. This assures us more complete information and a more complete perspective (1.3 Elemental Analysis).

4. The use of standard terminology gradually educate others in the models of Sun Tzu's strategy. Mental models are based in a certain description of reality. One of the Institute's missions here is to develop a standard vocabulary for discussing strategic situations based on the standards developed by Sun Tzu (2.2.2 Mental Models , 7.2 Strategic Standards).

5. Terminology models rely less on details such as specific measurements and more on relative comparisons. Our minds cannot keep track of too much detail. Relative comparisons are easier to visualize and remember, especially when limited to the five key elements (1.3.1 Competitive Comparison).

6. Terminology models restrict us to discussions of real alternatives. It is easy and seductive to compare elements of positions against imaginary ideals, but positioning takes place in the real world, among real alternatives. Nobody and nothing are perfect. The idea of perfection, especially thinking anything or anyone is perfect, is a form of self-deception. The more we restrict ourselves to real situations, the more useful a common vocabulary becomes (2.1.3 Strategic Deception).

Illustration:

Let us illustrate these principles in terms of our romantic relationships, especially in terms of identifying romantic opportunities within a community of people.

1. We must work with others to develop a common language for discussion competitive situations. No one really has a concrete language for discussing their position in relationships. Sun Tzu can help.

2. Standard terminology can eliminate the confusion between <u>external challenges</u> and <u>internal control</u>. While people love to gossip about the intimate details of other people's relationships, these are the areas where information is the very poorest. Information about the externals, i.e., who is going where with whom doing what is much more reliable and useful.

3. Standard terminology starts with the terms of elemental positioning. Relationships like all positions depend on a shared mission (philosophy and goals), the dynamics of climate (changes such as aging), ground (especially economics), leadership (matters of character or, so often, its lack or excesses), and methods (what people like to do in relationships).

4. The use of standard terminology gradually educate others in the models of Sun Tzu's strategy. We can be frustrated by a situation, but it helps a lot to know which of the nine common situations it represents. We can respond appropriately to a serious situation in a relationship differently than a difficult situation only if we understand the real distinctions between them. (Serious situations require more resources while difficult ones require persistence.)

5. Terminology models rely less on details such as specific measurements and more on relative comparisons. While physical dimensions (height, weight, etc.) are easily quantified, the most important characteristics defining people in relationships are not. Both types of characteristics make more sense in comparisons: Joe is taller than Jim. Jane is more outgoing that Jill.

6. ***Terminology models restrict us to discussions of real alter-natives.*** Perfect relationships are imaginary and imaginary relationships are for imaginary people. The tendency to compare people with idealized, imaginary versions in the media is very destructive to all relationships.

2.3 Personal Interactions

Sun Tzu's six key methods on making progress through personal interactions.

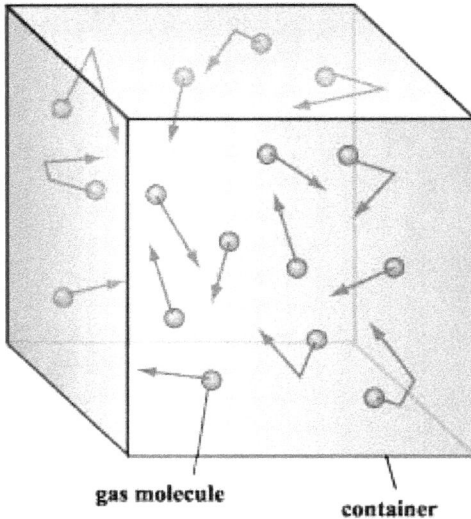

gas molecule   container

"Internal and external events force people to move."
Sun Tzu's The Art of War 13:1:6

"History is the record of an encounter between character and circumstances."
Donald Creighton

General Principle: We only advance our position through our interactions with other people.

Situation:

In a competitive environment, plans constantly collide resulting in situations that no one plans. The encounters are like molecules of gas bumping off of each other. As a gas is heated, its molecules become more energetic, bouncing off of each other more frequently. The same is true of positions in a competitive environment. As we put energy into our moves, our contacts with others becomes more and more frequent. In a more connected society (see Networked World), more and more types of interactions are possible over greater distance at less cost. People are frustrated because all these random events seem to continually knock them off course, but that is the nature of the environment.

Opportunity:

Sun Tzu's strategic methods use these random interactions with others to take us where we want to go. We cannot change the nature of our environment, so we must embrace it. Each interaction must become the source of our progress rather than an obstacle. The path in this environment cannot be planned. Each interaction will take us in a new direction, but if we know how to navigate this environment, the sum of all these changes takes us to our goals. Sun Tzu's strategy is not a game of solitaire. It is always played with, among, and off of other people. It is not about what we do alone. It is about how others react to what we do and how we react to their reactions.

Key Methods:

Perhaps half the concepts in Sun Tzu's work deal with the key methods regarding the predictable and unpredictable parts of human interactions, but the following six key methods are critical to having the right perspective.

1. Sun Tzu's methods utilize our interactions with others to advance our positions. In life, we can never move directly toward our goals. We only get to our goals by "bouncing" off of other people in our interactions with them. Sun Tzu's strategy isn't, as people often mistakenly think, simply a contest of "beating" opponents. It is about advancing positions which requires us to interact with others (1.1 Position Paths).

2. *We can only execute our decisions by interacting with others*. We do not compete on a deserted island. The methods of adaptive strategy is designed to work solely within the confines of human interaction. In terms of more economic, professional, personal, and social goals, advancing our position usually means winning the acceptance and support of others. We describe the process of positioning as building up our position so that others cannot attack it and ideally want to join. Our position is our rank, status, station, and standing formed from people's attitudes, views, opinions, and perceptions about us (1.5.2. Group Methods).

3. *These interactions create a game of discovery*. We discover our possibilities through our interactions with others. Others discover possibilities in their interactions with us. We do not approach interaction with the goal of controlling people. We approach interactions with a sense of unknown potential. We can only find our path to our goals through those interactions. Our path to our goals can dramatically change from these interactions (2.3.1 Action and Reaction).

4. *Each interaction we have is compared with all other interactions.* In every form of competition, our positions are always evaluated by comparison with other positions. Both we and the people with whom we interact are constantly doing these evaluations. This creates a highly interactive environment where each interaction creates expectations for future interactions (1.3.1 Competitive Comparison).

5. *We must consciously work <u>not </u>to get ahead of ourselves in our interactions*. This is one of the basic reasons why adaptive strategy isn't a form of planning. While we can look ahead, we must always decide and react to the here and now. Yes, we try to out-think other people, but that starts by thinking on our feet, during our interactions. When we get ahead of ourselves, we make assumptions about what other people will or will not do. Those assumptions are almost always wrong. People often know how they are going to react beforehand so we cannot as well. (2.3.2 Reaction Unpredictability).

6. ***Key information that we know we need comes only from our personal interactions.*** Sun Tzu's strategy teaches us the key elements of information. We need the help of others to get that information from vast quantities of information in the environment. Every contact is an opportunity for gathering that key information. The really valuable information is usually what is locked up inside of other people's heads (2.2.1 Personal Relationships).

Illustration:

The phone rings. An email arrives. It is a new contact. We don't know who this person is or whether or not the contact offers us an opportunity.

*1. **Sun Tzu's methods utilize our interactions with others to advance our positions**. Only through our contacts with others can we change their perception of our position. 99% of the emails we get may be meaningless in terms of our position, but that remaining 1% is critical to it.*

*2. **We can only execute our decisions by interacting with others**. In the end, our efforts must affect others or they affect no on. The most brilliant sales pitch, the most wonderful product, the most brilliant idea have no affect on the world until they touch the lives of others.*

*3. **These interactions create a game of discovery**. If we see the contact as an interruption, we will miss any opportunity that it might offer. Often, it will offer no opportunity, but we will never discover new opportunities if we assume every contact is a waste of our time.*

*4. **Each interaction we have is compared with all other interactions.** A person contacting us probably has very low expectations. That makes it easy for us to exceed those expectations by responding in a more positive way than they expect.*

5. We must consciously work _not_ to get ahead of ourselves. We must listen first and gauge where the person making contact is come from and respond in a way that itsn't so far outside their expectations that our response seemed inappropriate.

6. Key information that we know we need comes only from our personal interactions. Even if the contact offers no other opportunities long term, it is always an opportunity for gathering information about how others see our positions and why they are contacting us.

2.3.1 Action and Reaction

Sun Tzu's eight key methods on how we advance based on how others reaction to our actions.

*"You must force the enemy to move to your advantage.
Use your position.
The enemy must follow you."*

Sun Tzu's The Art of War 5:4:16-18

"To every action there is an equal and opposite reaction."

Sir Isaac Newton

General Principle: Our decisions about action must factor in the opposing reactions of others over multiple encounters.

Situation:

Good competitive decision-making seems convoluted to those who don't understand it. In a competitive environment , we cannot simply go in a straight line toward our goals. Instead, we reach our goals only through bouncing off of other people. When we want a specific reaction from someone, we often get the opposite. The more we push, the harder they push back. This is known in psychology as reactance. Each interaction changes our direction in some small way, putting both parties on a slightly different path. Each interaction take us both in a new direction. As others affect us, we also affect them. This is only a problem if we are trapped in the industrial mindset of linear thinking.

Opportunity:

When we developed the adaptive mind of a warrior, we can enjoy the uncertainties of interaction. It keeps life interesting. It makes it more of a challenge. Sun Tzu's strategy is sometimes a matter of anticipating the moves of others. Other times, it is realizing that there are opportunities in human interactions that we cannot anticipate. In our most important interactions, we don't bounce off of each other just once. We bounce off of each other again and again. Each iteration is an opportunity for learning on both sides. We learn about others and they learn about us. Knowledge gained from past interactions is factored into future ones.

Key Methods:

The following eight key methods describe how Sun Tzu sees the reactive nature of relationships.

1. Our actions must consider how people are free to react and what their freedom will mean to future interactions. While we sometimes describe strategy as out-thinking our opponents, it is more accurate to say that we want to include others and their freedom to act within our thinking. The competitive environment is defined by the interaction of people free to make their own decisions (1.4 The External Environment).

2. In a competitive environment, reactions to our actions are unpredictable. We can never count on others doing what we assume they will do. We cannot assume that they do what they say. We cannot even assume that they will do what is in their best interests, though that is a safer bet. Often, people don't know what they will do until the moment they act (2.3.2 Reaction Unpredictability).

3. It is always easier to predict negative reactions than positive ones to our actions. If we push people, we can be fairly certain that they will push back. From this fact we get the value of negative psychology. Sometimes it is easier to get people to do what we want if we pretend that we don't want it (6.8 Competitive Psychology).

4. *A single interaction makes it easier to set up future interactions.* While the chance that we encounter any given individual are small, the chances that we encounter someone again after encountering them once are much greater, especially if that is our goal (1.8.2 The Adaptive Loop).

5. Multiple interactions are much easier to guide than a single interaction. Over multiple reactions, we build up trust and certain expectations. While we can have some influence over a single reaction, the influence of both parties grows over the course of a relationship (1.8.4 A Probabilistic Process).

6. We seek multiple interactions that take us mutually in the direction of our different desires. Our bounces off of other people are guided. While we compete with one another in how we are compared, we can often work together to make faster progress toward our goals. This means that we can consider where each bounce takes us not only individually but as a group. The best relationships are those where the process of continually bouncing off of each other takes us where we both want to go. Organizations develop their external strength from the shared mission of their internal interactions. We bounce off each other within an organization so that as a group we make better progress in our shared external environment (1.6.1 Shared Mission).

*7. **One big positive interaction can make up from a lot of costly little interactions.*** This dynamic of mutual progress is not as simple as the concept of "win/win" suggests. The unspoken assumption in win/win is that each party gets something out of every single interaction. In real life, our interactions are seldom so simple. We are bouncing around, not going in a straight line. Even if the relationship is productive as a whole, many individual interactions are more costly than they are beneficial. However, one big positive bounce from a relationship can make up from a lot of little costly bounces (1.8.4 Probabilistic Process).

*8. **We can learn people's unique character from their reactions to our actions***. Every person is unique. This means that we need quality information about other people's character, habits, and attitudes. When we know that we are going to be running into a person (or the same people again and again), we have to take the responsibility for trying to figure out how they "bounce" in their interactions with others. This requires us to join our understanding of character (1.5.1 Command Leadership).

Illustration:

Let us illustrate these principles using one of our favorite topics, making sales.

*1. **Our actions must consider how people are free to react and what their freedom will mean to future interactions.*** In sales, we must accept that a sales encounter can go many different directions and that we cannot control that direction.

*2. **In a competitive environment, reactions to our actions are unpredictable.*** In sales, we should act as if we expect agreement, but we must be prepared for many other options as well.

*3. **It is always easier to predict negative reactions than positive ones to our actions.*** If we focus simply on getting the order, almost all of our interactions will be negative.

4. *A single interaction makes it easier to set up future interactions.* Asking questions in the sale qualification stage (the "Listen" phase of Sun Tzu's Progress Cycle) makes it easier to know what aspects of the product proposal to offer in the sales presentation stage (the "Aim" phase of Progress cylce).

5. *Multiple interactions are much easier to guide than a single interaction.* It is infinitely easier to get an agreement to future sales discussions than it is to get an agreement to an order after one discussion.

6. *We seek multiple interactions that take us mutually in the direction of our different desires.* Over many discussions, both the salesperson and the buyer have an opportunity to learn from interaction.

7. *One big positive interaction can make up from a lot of costly little interactions.* Over multiple interactions, salespeople have an opportunity to create the grounds for a mutually desirable agreement.

8. *We can learn people's unique character from their reactions to our actions.* Every person is unique. Continued sales relationships are built both upon both finding mutual goals and the pleasures of contact.

2.3.2 Reaction Unpredictability

Sun Tzu's seven key methods explaining why we can never exactly predict the reactions of others.

"Surprise and direct action give birth to each other."
They are like a circle without end."
Sun Tzu's The Art of War 3:2:24-25

"It's all about exploring the more unpredictable aspects in the character, not just fighting people."

Victoria Pratt

General Principle: People's reactions can never be predicted exactly because every situation is unique and people creative.

Situation:

The challenge in our interactions with others is predicting their likely reactions. This problem goes back to the difference between planning and strategy. In a internal, controlled environment, people are all working together and therefore try to keep each other informed about plans. In external, interactive environments, people are pursuing their own goals. People are free to do what they see as best. We cannot exactly predict their reactions because we cannot know their minds. That information is forever beyond our reach. People's reactions are not even completely rational. This is why Sun Tzu's strategy factors in a host of cognitive biases in people's reactions. Strategically, behaving predictably is dangerous. It can be just as dangerous to assume that we know what others will do.

Opportunity:

Our opportunity is to respect people's freedom to act. Once we accept the idea of freedom, we realize that we must adapt. We then realize that we need to think in terms of probability rather than certainties. When we choose our actions based upon probabilities, we remain free ourselves. We are free to adjust to other possible reactions. We must gauge our actions based upon all the potential reactions of others. People are not machines. The competitive universe is not deterministic. It is filled with people just like us, who do not behave in an easily predictable manner. Since our individual choices depend on array of circumstances and values that others cannot know, we are constantly making surprising and novel choices. The same is true of everyone else as well.

Key Methods:

The following seven key methods describe how Sun Tzu sees the unpredictable nature of reactions.

1. People's reactions are unpredictable because our knowledge is limited. While empathy is necessary for making good decisions, we must avoid risking too much on our assumptions. Our assumptions are based on how we would react to their situation. However we are not in their situation. Our perspective on their situation is different than their perspective. There are boundaries on what we can know (2.1.1 Information Limits).

2. Reactions are unpredictable because we cannot know people's current priorities. People's priorities change from moment to moment as different needs assert themselves over time. We cannot know for certain which needs will seem paramount to anyone at any given moment when a decision is made (1.6.3 Shifting Priorities).

3. Reactions are unpredictable because we cannot know how people will react to change. We cannot know what changes will capture people's attention nor how they will respond to those events. People often act out of habit but they only do so until they crave novelty. Every person feels the pressure of events in a different way (5.1.1 Event Pressure).

4. Reactions are unpredictable because we cannot know how well others understand a situation. Economics and game theory are based upon our acting rationally in our self-interest, but competitive environments are too complicated and chaotic for many people to discern where their interests lie. Since most people lack the mental models necessary put conditions into a larger context, their responses cannot be foreseen (2.2.2 Mental Models).

5. Reactions are unpredictable because we cannot know all aspects of character. This applies to both character flaws and strengths. It also applies to ourselves as well as others. Decisions arise at the intersection of knowledge and character. Knowing what to do isn't the same as having the courage or discipline to do it (1.5.1 Command Leadership).

6. Reactions are unpredictable because we cannot know what methods people use. We cannot even know exactly what skills people have or which skills they will apply to a given situation. People tend to use the methods to what they know best, even when those methods are poorly suited to the situation. Many keep their choice of methods a secret for very good strategic reasons. Others will simply try the first thing that pops into their head. Others will try to do things that they do not know how to do. Even when people use standard methods, they can change those methods to try and improve them (7.1.3 Standards and Innovation).

7. These uncertainties cannot be eliminated so they must be managed. We manage them in two ways. We learn the possible range of reactions (2.3.3 Range of Reactions) and we use a lot of questions (2.3.4 Using Questions).

Illustration:

These limitations can be illustrated in every competitive arena.

1. People's reactions are unpredictable because our knowledge is limited. People enjoy watching sporting events because we can never know what is happening next.

2. Reactions are unpredictable because we cannot know people's current priorities. At the moment we contact someone, they may be so hungry that nothing else we do or say will make an impression.

3. Reactions are unpredictable because we cannot know how people will react to change. A change that seems exciting and attractive to us can seem frightening to someone else.

4. Reactions are unpredictable because w e cannot know how well others understand a situation. Think of all the alcoholics who insist that they don't have a problem.

5. Reactions are unpredictable because we cannot know all aspects of character. How often are people surprised by someone they trusted stabbing them in the back?

6. Reactions are unpredictable because we cannot know what methods people use. To a man with a hammer, everything looks like a nail. A fighter will tend to start swinging whenever they are in trouble even when each swing creates an opening.

7. These uncertainties cannot be eliminated so they must be managed. Smart sales people asked both open-ended questions that can go any direction and closed-ended questions that limit possible responses.

2.3.3 Likely Reactions

Seven key methods regarding the range of potential reactions in gathering information.

"Another general fails to predict the enemy.
He pits his small forces against larger ones.
His weak forces attack stronger ones.
He fails to pick his fights correctly."
Sun Tzu's The Art of War 10:2:27-30

"The meeting of two personalities is like the contact of
two chemical substances; if there is any reaction, both
are transformed."
Carl Gustav Jung

General Principle: Choose actions based upon the most likely responses.

Situation:

Sun Tzu's methods depend on information, specifically our perspective on how people will react. While it is important to know that people's reactions are never certain, we must still predict others to succeed. Our challenge is identifying the situations in which reactions become relatively predictable. Competitive environments are defined by the fact that people are free to act and react how they desire. Our actions only produce their results through other people's reactions.

Opportunity:

Competitive strategy is based on probabilities (1.8.4 A Probabilistic Process). Probabilities are based on situations and conditions. Though we cannot exactly predict what people will do in every situation, some situations are more predictable than others. While we cannot know every potential reaction of any given encounter, we can recognize specific situations in which people's reactions become more predictable. We play those probabilities, working to make sure that the unpredictable outcome of a single encounter does not determine our fate. In using Sun Tzu's strategic principles, each move is a small experiment. We never gamble everything on a single outcome because experiments fail more often than they succeed. However, through the repeated attempts of the adaptive loop, where we learn from each failure and adjust our methods, success becomes more and more likely over time (1.8.2 The Adaptive Loop).

Key Methods:

We can know what people are most likely to do. We choose our actions based upon the range of most likely responses. In descending order of probability, people's general responses are :

1. If they have responded to a similar situation in the past, people are likely to do what they have done in the past. If people have chosen a given action before, they are likely to choose that action again. The more often they have chosen that action, the more likely they are to choose it again. However, at some point this behavior can switch to its opposite. However, usually something has to change in the environment for them to switch. People are creatures of habit. Developing new responses takes work. Unless we are given an incentive to change our responses, we will usually continue to do what we have been doing (1.1.1 Position Dynamics).

2. At predicable spans of time, people's reactions are more likely to address certain cyclic physical needs. These changes range from the daily cycles of hunger and the need for sleep to the annual cycles of the seasons to the long-term cycle of aging. People are the most predictable in terms of how and when they satisfy their physical needs (1.6.3 Shifting Priorities) and the demands of time ((1.4.1 Climate Shift).

3. When faced with a threat or direct challenge, people are likely to react with the flight or fight response. If people have very few strategic skills and little experience with a given situation, they are more likely to choose the flight and fight response. If we push people, they will either push back or flee. Which route they choose depends upon their character, but the greater the pressure on people who are untrained in situational probability, the more likely it is that they will choose one of these responses (Your Gut and Your Brain , 2.3.1 Action and Reaction).

4. If people have made verbal commitments, they are more likely to react according to their commitments. While people do lie in situations where it will give them an advantage, there are many more advantages in being seen as honest and trustworthy. When people commit to a course of action, they usually will follow that course of action, or at least try to do, what they said they will do. The value in getting verbal commitments is that is makes reactions more predictable (8.3.3 Rules of Engagement).

5. When they fail to honor commitments, their most likely reaction is the opposite of what was promised. When people break with commitments, they usually don't react a little differently than promised. They go the whole way. The commitments could have been an attempt to mislead, but they are also free to change their minds. However, they do not change their minds for slight adjustments. They do not change their minds unless the course they want to take is the reverse of what they promised (3.2.5 Dynamic Reversal).

6. *The more experience and trained people are in competition, their reactions are more likely to conform to Sun Tzu's principles*. Though most people are not trained in any systematic way in strategic decision-making, almost everyone discovers pieces of Sun Tzu's system through trial and error. As people learn a few of these principles and methods through experience, they will tend to apply them more broadly than they deserve, bringing us back to the first rule in this list. If we recognize patterns of response from someone, we can expect to see those same responses again, even when those responses are inappropriate to their situation. As Mark Twain said, "A cat that has sat on a hot stove won't sit on a hot stove again, or a cold one either." (6.0 Situation Response).

7. *People's reactions become more predictable if we can combine these elements*. People are more likely to do what they have said they will do if that is what they have done in the past. This is even more likely if their past actions fit into the flight and fight response. Which reaction they are likely to choose, depends on the specifics of their position: their motivation, the climate, the ground, their command, and their skills. Knowing people's motivations helps more than any other factor in understanding their potential choices. Knowing their skills and experience is the second most important factor (6.1.1 Conditioned Reflexes).

Illustration:

Let us apply these key methods to predicting the reactions of a prospect confronted by a salesperson.

We can know what people are most likely to do. We choose our actions based upon the range of most likely responses. In descending order of probability, people's general responses are :

1. If they have responded to a similar situation in the past, people are likely to do what they have done in the past. The prospect's most likely response to a sales proposal is to continue their past patterns of buying or not buying over time.

2. At predicable spans of time, people's reactions are more likely to address certain cyclic physical needs. A salesperson can use the opportunity of a lunch invitation to change a prospect's past behavior. A smart salesperson will identify physical changes in the environment that should make the prospect reconsider his or her past decisions. Those decisions can never be wrong so conditions must change to set up the potential for a different purchasing decision.

3. When faced with a threat or direct challenge, people are likely to react with the flight or fight response. A salesperson cannot get a prospect out to lunch if the salesperson has put pressure on the prospect. The prospect will either flee or flight the pressure, making lunch with the salesperson an unattractive proposition.

4. If people have made verbal commitments, they are more likely to react according to their commitments. A smart salesperson gets a small commitment first. Instead of asking for a lunch meeting at the spur of the moment, he casually asks for a commitment to it at some future date. After getting that commitment, most people will follow through with it, even if they don't want to at the time.

5. When they fail to honor commitments , their most likely reaction is the opposite of what was promised. When the salesperson calls to confirm the promised lunch appointment, the prospect can simply say that he never made the commitment and that the salesperson is confused. The salesperson should be prepared for this possibility, being prepared to admit confusion and simply asked again.

6. *The more experienced and trained people are in competition, their reactions are more likely to conform to Sun Tzu's principles*. It takes time to learn the patterns of response from a prospect so that we can use them to our advantage. The entire system of action and reaction is designed to build positions over time rather than win orders on the first encounter.

7. *People's reactions become more predictable if we can combine these elements*. A salesperson should seek to develop repeated patterns, such are regular lunch dates with clients, learning how a given prospect typically reacts in a given situation.

2.3.4 Using Questions

Sun Tzus five key methods for using questions in gathering information and predicting reactions.

"You must question the situation."
Sun Tzu's The Art of War 1:2:2

"To be able to ask a question clearly is two-thirds of the way to getting it answered."
Carl Gustav Jung

General Principle: Questions are a powerful tool in working with others.

Situation:

Sun Tzu's system of information gathering focuses on communication and leveraging people's reactions. We often keep our questions locked up in our head. We think of the questions that we have as internal. We fail to understand the value of getting those questions out of our head and communicating them with others. We avoid questions for a number of reasons. Often, we want to appear more knowledgeable than we really are. Even more often, we want avoid looking stupid. We are afraid of exposing our ignorance and therefore our vulnerabilities. When we ask a question, we are taking the risk of rejection. We sometimes prefer hearing ourselves talk rather than encouraging others to talk.

Opportunity:

Good decisions depend on our ability to ask questions. We choose our actions to get the responses that we want from them. We cannot expect people to tell us what we need to know without our first telling them what we need to know. The use of questions is a powerful tool for predicting people's reactions. Asking questions actually controls people's minds, directing their attention where we desire. They are perhaps the most powerful tool in our arsenal of working with others through action and reaction.

Key Methods:

The following key methods describe the use of questions in developing a strategy.

1. Good methods continually leverage the power of questions. Questions both gather information and control the direction on an encounter. We cannot make decisions until we have an idea about people's reactions to our actions. When we ask questions, people are forced to respond. Questions are a simple and powerful method to control other people's reactions to our actions (2.3.1 Action and Reaction).

2. We can ask open-ended questions to solicit unknown information and potential reactions that we cannot foresee. Our information is always incomplete. Our perspective is not that of others. The first and most valuable role of questions is harnessing other people's minds to help us fill in the blanks. As a result of our question and the thinking questions generates, many will offer alternatives that we could have never thought of on our own. Of course, we have to be open to hear these possibilities. These responses are extremely valuable, identifying new potential course of action working together (2.1.1 Information Limits).

3. We can ask people directly about specific information and potential reactions to the suggested course of action. We use these questions when we know what we want to know. A direct question gets people thinking. In many cases, people will not know what they will do. But by simply asking, we put them in a position where they have to think about their responses. Their initial reaction to the question is likely to be their initial reaction to the action. It is the least expensive test of an action (5.4.1 Value Tests).

4. We can ask questions to shape people's reactions. We cannot push people directly to do what we want. However, questions demand a response and to some degree, determine what actions people must consider. While there are principles about why peoples reactions **must** always have elements of unpredictability (2.3.2 Reaction Unpredictability) and other principles about the best ways to predict those reactions (2.3.3 Range of Reactions).

5. If we cannot ask questions of someone directly, we can ask others who are close to them. Information gathers in pools. While we want to get information, especially about people's plans, from the individuals involved, sometimes that isn't possible. In those cases, we need to go to those around them, those who have frequent contact with them. If we cannot contact those people, we can ask people who are in similar position. If we cannot do that, we can ask those who are more experienced in seeing similar people's reactions (8.4 Individual Contact).

Illustration:

The obvious illustration here is in sales where asking questions is the heart of good method, but let us use the illustration of government decision-making because it also illustrates the most common problems in this area.

1. Good methods continually leverage the power of questions. We can see this mistake of failing to ask questions about people's reactions to government policy. Legislators treat the situations as static environments instead of a dynamic ones. For example, one of the biggest forces shaping economic decisions is the tax policy itself. but politicians routinely forecast tax revenue based upon economic activity before increased taxation without asking questions about how changes in taxes will change reactions. Forecasts about government policy, especially its costs, are always wrong because as a result of policy changes, people's activities change. We should ask people about how they would change their behavior in reaction to a new law instead of asking about how they feel about the intentions of such laws.

2. We can ask open-ended questions to solicit unknown information and potential reactions that we cannot foresee. We can ask people about their likely reactions to a new government policy. For example, if we plan to move to a given government health care proposal, we can ask about all the potential problems that they might foresee either in implementation of the proposed program or in people gaming the new system for personal benefit.

3. We can ask people directly about specific information and potential reactions to the suggested course of action. For example, if the government requires a small penalty for not getting medical insurance while forcing companies to provide insurance despite health problems, we should ask if people would wait to get insurance until they have a health condition that requires treatment.

4. We can ask questions to shape people's reactions. In asking questions about recent government policies, the tea party and similar movements have been able to galvanize large, popular movements seeking to redirect government.

5. *If we cannot ask questions of someone directly, we can ask others who are close to them.* If we don't trust the answers that people give us about health insurance, we can ask economists. We can ask people generally to their and others'. Given that health insurance cannot be denied on the basis of pre-existing conditions, most economists would predict that if the penalty is less expensive than insurance, people would simply wait until they develop health problems. Such programs must coerce people to buy insurance so that they cannot game the system by waiting to get sick. So coercing insurance companies to insure those with pre-existing conditions leads to more coercion, forcing everyone to buy insurance.

2.3.5 Infinite Loops

Four principles predicting reactions on the basis of the "you-know-that-I-know-that-you-know" problem.

"They are like a circle without end.
You cannot exhaust all their possible combinations!"
                                    Sun Tzu's The Art of War 4:4:14

"Our minds are finite, and yet even in these
circumstances of finitude we are surrounded by
possibilities that are infinite, and the purpose of life is to
grasp as much as we can out of that infinitude."
                                    John Ruskin

General Principle: Thinking about the reactions of others cannot be an infinite loop.

Situation:

Before we act, we think about how others will react, but their reaction includes trying to foresee our reactions. There is a trap hidden in thinking about the cycles of action and reaction. It has no natural stopping point. As opponents plan, they naturally consider how we might do. So, in turn, before we act, we must consider not only how they will react but how they will think that we will react. They, in turn, know that we are thinking about what they are thinking about what we are thinking. In trying to find an advantage by thinking one step ahead of others, we find ourselves in an infinite loop of regression. Out-thinking others is not the same as out-positioning others.

Opportunity:

Sun Tzu's methods require anticipating the moves of others. They also depend upon acting, quickly and decisively. The prejudice is toward action, since only action puts us back in touch with reality. The mental loops of thinking about what others are thinking about what we are thinking about their thinking trap us in a world of infinite imagination. Quick responses often work simply because others get bogged down in the infinite loop of possibilities. Time is our most valuable resource. We cannot lose sight of the fact that our opportunity in dealing with others. Our advantage is often as simple as making good decisions more quickly than most do.

Key Methods:

The following five key methods describe how we handle the problem of over thinking a problem according to Sun Tzu's methods.

1. We must recognize the "ad infinitum" decision loop of possibilities before we slide into it. We cannot out-think our competition using a method of infinite regression and infinite possibilities while our lives, and especially the time we have for making a given decision, are extremely finite. Infinite loops consider more and more remote possibilities in each iteration. In a chess game, there are finite possibilities and only one goal. The number of potential actions and reactions in a game is large, larger than the number of atoms in the known universe, but they are still finite. In real life, there are infinite possibilities and infinite goals. The possibilities include moves that haven't even been invented yet but get invented because some enterprising individual sees new possibilities (1.8.3 Cycle Time).

2. To escape infinite decision loops , we limit the number of elements considered in action and reaction cycles. Every detail and direction can be entered into our calculations of what others will do if we let them. We do better if we limited our thinking to only the five key elements (1.3 Elemental Analysis). (2.3.1 Action and Reaction).

3. To escape infinite decision loops, we limit thinking about action and reaction cycles to three or four iterations. Experiments in human psychology and game theory show that almost everyone naturally looks ahead only two or three moves, so a single loop more is all we need to create a comparative advantage (1.3.1 Competitive Comparison).

4. To escape infinite decision loops , we add additional iterations based directly on experience level. Experienced people will tend to follow the principle above, which means we have to use four or five iterations. Of course, even more experienced people will use this rule as well. This give us the opportunity to see this entire lesson and infinite loop by referring to itself (2.3.5 Infinite Loops).

5. To escape infinite decision loops , we *rely on actions rather than mental gymnastics.* Imagination is a good and necessary part of competitive decision-making. However, it has a limit. At some point we must get real information and we can only get that from interaction not imagination. It is often better to ask others about potential cycles of actions and reactions rather than try to calculate these cycles alone. A crowd is better than the wisdom of any one person (2.3 Personal Interactions).

Illustration:

The obvious illustration here is in sales where asking questions is the heart of good method, but let us use the illustration of government decision-making because it also illustrates the most common problems in this area.

1. We must recognize the "ad infinitum" decision loop of possibilities before we slide into it. In our seminars, we have an exercise that demonstrates the ad infinitum problem in decision-making. We tell everyone that the maximum potential prize is $100, but the actual prize amount depends on how much you bid. The prize will go to the person who bids the amount closest to 70% of the *average* bid in the group. This sets up the infinite loop because the winning bid is 70% of the average bid, but the average bid is based on people calculating 70% of the average bid. If everyone bid $100, the winning bid would be $70, but everyone knows that $70 is the maximum winning bid, so they should perhaps guess 70% of $70, which is $49. Of course, if everyone does that calculation, the winning bid would be 70% of $49 or $34.

2. To escape infinite decision loops , we limit the number of elements considered in action and reaction cycles. This is limited by the game itself to a single element: what will the average person guess. People have their mission, to win. They have a climate, limited time to decide. They have the ground rules of the game.This is a question of character and methods: what does the average person do.

3. To escape infinite decision loops, we limit thinking about action and reaction cycles to three or four iterations. We use this number because the average person makes between two and three loops, say 2.5 iterations. In this case, this means they would bid between $34 and $49 dollars (see above).

4. *To escape infinite decision loops , we add additional iterations based directly on experience level*. After running this exercise once, we can ask the same question again, after they have seen the right answer from the first iteration. They will be less that $34 because they learned from the outcome of the previous round.

5. ***To escape infinite decision loops, we rely on actions rather than mental gymnastics.*** While the game always has a winner, played enough times, the "right" answer is not playing at all because the right answer regresses to zero.

2.3.6 Promises and Threats

Sun Tzu's six key methods on the use of promises and threats as strategic moves.

"You can make the enemy come to you.
Offer him an advantage.
You can give the enemy no advantage in coming to you.
Threaten him with danger."
Sun Tzu's The Art of War 6:1:5-8

"But as the arms-control scholar Thomas Schelling once
noted, two things are very expensive in international life:
promises when they succeed and threats when they fail."
Don Piatt

General Principle: We should only make threats to deter actions and promises to impel actions.

Situation:

Competition requires building up positions. This requires us to maximize our resources. In The Art of War, Sun Tzu constantly warns that we must judge people's intentions by their actions, especially when people communicate their commitment to future actions. We all communicate commitments in order to encourage people to act in a way that we desire today in order to get a reward or avoid a punishment tomorrow. The problem at the heart of any commitment is our believability. Making a threat or promise is easy, executing either commitment is costly. Making good on a threat requires punishing someone. Making good on a promise rewards someone. Both are costly to us.

Opportunity:

Leveraging information is the least costly way to build up a position. The main alternative, making physical moves, is much more costly. Our opportunity is to leverage the inexpensive threat or the promise in a way that eliminates the more costly forms of effort (3.6 Leveraging Subjectivity). If a threat is believed, we reduce our costs because we never have to act on it. If a promise is trusted, the cost of honoring is less than the value we gain both in the current situation and future interactions.

Key Methods:

The following six key methods describe the use of threats and promises from the perspective of Sun Tzu.

1. We threaten to increase the perception of the costs of doing what we don't want. Threats can help people avoid mutually destructive situations that would otherwise attract them. A threat would not be necessary if a move in a given situation did not potentially return benefits to one party at the expense of other (3.1.3 Conflict Cost).

2. We promise to increase the rewards of doing what we desire. Promises can help people achieve to mutually beneficial situations otherwise unavailable to them. A promise would not be necessary if a move was not more costly to one party that the other party. The reward balances the costs and rewards for both parties (3.1.2 Strategic Profitability).

3. *Both threats and promises depend totally on their communication and credibility*. Threats and promises must be heard and they must be believed. The most important aspect in being believed is our history. People judge our future behavior by our past behavior, or, as we say, our position is path with a history, not a disconnected point (1.1 Position Paths).

4. *In using threats and promises, others must believe that we are willing to sacrifice our future flexibility*. After the fact, executing a punishment or delivering a reward is going to be costly to us, so at that point in time, we would rather not do it. As Thomas Shelling wrote in ***The Strategy of Conflic*t** expresses, "The power to constrain an adversary depends upon the power to bind oneself." While these two ideas seem like opposites, they are actually two sides of the same coin (3.2.3 Complementary Opposites).

5. *Threats are better used for deterrence*. When successful, the undesirable action is deterred and the cost of extracting punishment is deferred. Threats designed to compel action encourage the minimum possible compliance and invite sabotage (2.3.1 Action and Reaction).

6. *Promises are better used to encourage an action*. When successful, the costs of the reward has already been "paid for" by the desired action. Promises designed to deter an action indefinitely require continuous payments for uncertain future rewards (2.3.2 Reaction Unpredictability).

Illustration:

Let us draw today's illustration from a little different competitive arena, parenting a teenager.

1. *We threaten to increase the perception of the costs of doing what we don't want.* We threaten to "ground" a teenager if they do not honor their curfew.

2. *We promise to increase the rewards of doing what we desire.* When we care more about getting A's than our teen does, we can promise are reward, such as extending driving privileges, for each "A's."

3. *Both threats and promises depend totally on their communication and credibility.* The teen needs to know the curfew and the punishment and trust that we will actually enforce it.

4. *In using threats and promises, others must believe that we are willing to sacrifice our future flexibility.* If the curfew is violated, we cannot suspend the grounding for "special events" or to relieve ourselves from constant nagging. If driving privileges are won by good grades, we must give up our own access to the vehicle during those times.

5. *Threats are better used for deterrence.* The threat works to deter staying out as long as the teen desires.

6. *Promises are better used to encourage an action.* The promise works to encourage more studying

2.4 Contact Networks

Five key methods regarding the range of contacts needed to create perspective.

"You need all five types of spies. No one must discover your methods.
You will then be able to put together a true picture.
This is the commander's most valuable resource."
Sun Tzu's The Art of War 13:2:7-11

"Networking is making links from people we know to people they know, in an organized way, for a specific purpose, while remaining committed to doing our part, expecting nothing in return."
Donna Fisher

General Principle: Contact networks gather information in the five key areas defining strategic situations.

Situation:

No matter how well connected with think we are, the networks of contacts that we naturally develop in our lives are inherently limited. Natural contact networks are myopic, consisting of people who largely shared the same points of view. This occurs because we tend to keep in contact with people who are like ourselves. Our contacts tend to be the same age, have the same interests and opinions, live in the same areas, and, more and more often, work in the same industry if not company as we do. We cannot develop a broader perspective from talking to people who share the greater part of our perspective.

Opportunity:

Sun Tzu based his design for information gathering around the five elements of a strategic position. We use the five elements our template for gathering information (1.3 Elemental Analysis). We need information about changing conditions (climate), our competitive arena (ground), those whose decisions affect our position (leader), the processes of the groups with whom we interact (methods), and the motivations guiding the people and groups who affect our position. Different types of people are better positioned to have these types information.

Key Methods:

Note: In Sun Tzu's *The Art of War,* his term for information sources is traditionally translated into English as "spies," but the Chinese character was originally closer in meaning to the concept "conduits,""channels," or "go-between." In my book, *Nine Formulas for Business Success* , we update Sun Tzu's five types of spies to a nonmilitary setting, but keeping their alignment with the five key elements of a position. We describe the five key methods for the type of information conduits that we need.

1. Old pros are people with experience in a specific competitive arena. They know the rules of the **ground** and the implications of those rules. There is no more important teacher than experience on the ground (2.4.1 Ground Perspective).

*2. Fresh eyes only belong to those who see the changes in **climate** from a fresh perspective*. As people get older, they develop a more fixed perspective and a point of view. We all need to connect our perspective to those who see things from the perspective of the next generation (2.4.2 Climate Perspective).

3. Insiders are those who know decision-makers whose decisions affect us. If we are a salesperson, these are people who know our customers and how they think. If we are an employee, these are those who know our boss. Only people who are close to those whose decisions affect us can give us insight into their character (2.4.3 Command Perspective).

4. Methods observers are people who can compare and contrast how we and our rivals operate. These contacts can tell us about the best practices used by our competitors. We must learn and understand competitive practices to understand our position(2.4.4 Methods Perspective).

5. Missionaries are those who carry our vision to others. This last group shares our sense of value with the world. They have a real interest in your shared mission (2.4.5 Mission Perspective).

Illustration:

These three types of people are needed in every contact network, whether we are talking about our business or our personal relationships. For our illustration, let us use the example of a person who is opening a small business. If we think that we want to open a new restaurant, what should our contact network look like?

1. Old pros are people with experience in a specific competitive arena. Before opening a new restaurant, we should definitely be talking to people with a lot of experience not only in running existing restaurants, but opening new ones. However, since this is the area of "ground," we should also be talking to people who know the specific location or area in which we are thinking of opening a restaurant.

2. Fresh eyes only belong to those who see the changes in <u>climate</u> from a fresh perspective. No matter what type of restaurant, we are opening, we want people to see it as new and exciting. This means we need to get in contact with young people, especially those who eat the kind of food we are thinking about offering to see what they find new and interesting in a restaurant.

3. Insiders are those who know decision-makers whose decisions affect us. In the restaurant, this category would include the food critics for the local paper, for popular blogs, and others who are in contact with your potential customers, perhaps even other businesses in the area you are working.

4. Methods observers are people who can compare and contrast how we and our rivals operate. These people are those who know restaurant operations, and it would include people who supply the restaurant business with equipment.

5. Missionaries are those who carry our vision to others. These people can be from any of the above categories, but who buy into the mission of our particular vision for a restaurant.

2.4.1 Ground Perspective

Sun Tzu's three key methods about getting information on a new competitive arena.

"You need local spies."

Sun Tzu's The Art of War 13:2:2

"Experience is the best teacher, but a fool will learn from no other." Benjamin Franklin

General Principle: Find old pros to learn the unique rules to the new competitive arena.

Situation:

Each competitive arena is unique. It has its own form and shape. We call the component of competition with form and shape "the ground." Most conditions affecting our strategic decisions are ground conditions. Unfortunately, our instincts and our egos combine to make seeking out local guides to the ground harder than it should be. We are naturally more comfortable with people who share our level of knowledge about the ground. If we are new to a competitive arena, we connect most easily with other new people. The problem is that those people cannot help us. Most people are deluded about the depth of their knowledge. We are shy about connecting with those a lot more successful.

Opportunity:

Sun Tzu's strategy teaches us how to organize ground characteristics into a meaningful picture (2.5 The Big Picture), but our contact network provides the pieces of information that we need to build that picture. Since our time is limited, we need to find the best and most comprehensive information as quickly as possible (3.1.6 Time Limitations). Our opportunity is making contact with the "old pros," who really know the territory. This is made easier because these old pros are too often overlooked today because youth is valued over experienced. When we seek out relationships with older people, we demonstrate that we value their experience. We make a positive impression when we do this because most older people would love the opportunity to pass on what they know.

Key Methods:

It is easy to find old pros who can act as mentors because they are easy to identify. They stand out in a crowd because they are older. However, to build the best contact network, we need to remember the following key methods.

1. The best source of perspective on the new competitive arena are those who have a track record of success in that arena. Actions speak louder than words. Most people learn the rules of the ground through painful trial and error, but a minority learn to avoid the errors more quickly than others. These people have demonstrated the ability to translate their knowledge into mental models (2.2.2 Mental Models).

2. The next best source of perspective on the new competitive arena are those who know a lot of other people in an area. Some people are natural connectors, who are great at naturally developing contact networks. These people are especially good sources of connection with others. Most of what happens in our competitive neighborhood never makes it into the official media, and, when they do, rumors pass information about the interesting developments long before it appears even on the web (2.4 Contact Networks).

3. The next best source of perspective on the new competitive arena are those who have a long tenure. Survival in an area demonstrates a level of competence and there is no more important teacher in life than experience. The longer people survive in a given competitive arena, the more they learn, even if they haven't been able to convert their knowledge into consistent success. Everything that is happening now in any competitive arena has happened before. It was in a little different form, but everything that is old is new again. These people have put in the time so that we don't have to (3.1.6 Time Limitations).

Illustration:

These three types of people are needed in every contact network, whether we are talking about our business or our personal relationships. For our illustration, let us use the example of a person who is opening a small business. If we think that we want to open a new restaurant, what should our contact network look like?

1. *The best source of perspective on the new competitive arena are those who have a track record of success in that arena.* When we are hired by a new employer, we need to make friends with

longtime employees. When our child goes to a new school, we need to make contact with other parents more experienced in working with the school. In a new relationship, we need to make contact with people who have known the person we are dating longer than we have.

2. The next best source of perspective on the new competitive arena are those who know a lot of other people in an area. In business, trade associations and trade shows are a great place to meet old pros and develop these relationships. People who are in the business of communicating, such as salespeople and PR people, are exceptionally good local guides. They also have an incentive to develop a relationship with us because communication is their business.

3. The next best source of perspective on the new competitive arena are those who have a long tenure. It can be easy to find old pros who can act as contacts because they are easy to identify. They stand out in a crowd because they are older.

2.4.2 Climate Perspective

Sun Tzu's four key methods on getting perspective on temporary external conditions.

"There are new conduits.
They see things differently."

> Sun Tzu's The Art of War 13:2:21-22
> [Chinese Revealed Version]

"It is the youth who sees a great opportunity hidden in just these simple services, who sees a very uncommon situation, a humble position, who gets on in the world."

> Orison Swett Marden

General Principle: Develop contacts who are in touch with what is changing.

Situation:

As we focus on our little corner of the world, we often don't see a change coming. If changes don't fit into our historic view of what is important, we can easily miss them. The longer we are in a competitive arena ourselves, the less sensitive we are to what is changing. In today's dynamic environment, our position can degrade quickly.

Our current strategic position is constantly degrading (1.1.1 Position Dynamics). These trends can help or hinder us. We don't know from which direction they will come. Change propagates itself like a wave. The changes of climate ripple back and forth, from one end of the world to the other, affecting one competitive arena after another. As this wave of change moves through different competitive arenas, it changes its form and shape but it keeps moving, affecting us all eventually.

Opportunity:

We want to see these changes coming from the greatest distance possible. Change is what creates our opportunities (3.2 Opportunity Creation). Our contact network gives us a broader perspective of time as well as place. Our opportunities lie not in the past or even the present but in the future (2.4.1 Ground Perspective). To get the right perspective on change, our opportunity is to see our competitive arena with fresh eyes. The faster we can learn about shifts in climate that affect us, the more of an advantage we have over others and the better positioned we are to deal with those changes.

Key Methods:

To keep in contact with what is changing in our local neighborhood, we need to develop special channels of information that focus on change. The people most interested in change are those with the least invested in the past.

1. Contacts who give us perspective on climate see changing trends earlier than others. The more advance notice we have of change, the more time we have to adapt to it. This is especially true of business people, who become more focused on control and planning instead of adapting to change. This is why so many young people see the business world as boring. Most businesspeople are focused myopically on the work at hand and the current process. They are more worried about the problems that happened yesterday than the opportunities that will open tomorrow (1.8.3 Cycle Time).

2. We need the fresh eyes of young people to provide a valuable perspective on climate change. Hot trends sweep through the culture. Young people are the best possible source for a fresh perspective on what is new and exciting. As we get older, we are not plugged into the hot trends. Young people devote a great deal of time to what is new because they have the time to invest. They also spend more time than most communicating with their peers. The emotions and energy of the young drives the biggest changes affecting opportunity (1.4.1 Climate Shift).

3. We must reverse our perspective to see the climate from the perspective of the young. Young people see the changes in climate to get a fresh perspective. We have to match this perspective to understand it. To be open to what is happening in the world, we have to have an open mind. As we get older, we develop our own perspective, responsibilities, and a point of view. After a wealth of experience, we tend to take change for granted, getting less excited about it. We filter information through a wealth of mental models. We have to work directly against this tendency (3.2.5 Dynamic Reversal).

4. We must have regular contact with young people to get a good perspective on climate. This contact adds an invaluable perspective to our contact networks. Throughout our lives we need to develop the habit of reaching out to the latest generation and developing relationships with them. This isn't necessarily easy because communication with young people isn't necessarily easy, but it is worth the effort. The process starts with communicating an idea that they haven't heard before, that we are interested in what they think (2.2.1 Personal Relationships).

Illustration:

The new world of computers and electronics provides some of the best illustration of these principles.

1. Contacts who give us perspective on climate see changing trends earlier than others. Catching a new communication trend is like catching a wave. If we don't start moving when the trend is first spotted, we can never get moving fast enough to get in sync with it and it just passes us by as the Internet passed by traditional newspapers.

2. ***We need the fresh eyes of young people to provide a valuable perspective on climate change.*** Many changes and trends are short-lived, but each new innovation in electronic communication, from Facebook to Twitter, that is changing the shape of our world caught on with young people first.

3. ***We must reverse our perspective to see the climate from the perspective of the young.*** IBM knew what other computer companies were doing, but Microsoft wasn't a computer company and it completely changed computers. The iPod did not start in the recording industry but it completely reshaped it. Starbucks did not arise from the coffee shop industry but it redefined what a cafe is.

4. ***We must have regular contact with young people to get a good perspective on climate.*** Some of us are fortunate to have young people in our family. Parents of young people, if they pay attention, tend to be better in touch with the latest trends. If there is a secret to including young people in our communication networks, it is not to tune them out. As our children grow up, we need new points of contact with the evolving culture. We need to reach out to young people who are relatives or belong to the same community groups that we do.

2.4.3 Command Perspective

Sun Tzu's six key methods for understanding developing sources for understanding decision-makers.

"You must first know the guarding general. You must know his left and right flanks.
You must know his hierarchy."
Sun Tzu's The Art of War 13:4:4-6

"The key is to get to know people and trust them to be who they are. Instead, we trust people to be who we want them to be- and when they're not, we cry."
David Duchovny

General Principle: Develop information channels about key decision-makers.

Situation:

Our success depends on the decisions of others. Their decisions depend on their unique motivations and character. Despite that, most of us invest too little on getting perspective on other people. We see their motivations and character myopically, from the point of view of our position and our friends positions. Some are so close to us that we lose our perspective. Others are so distant and anonymous that we think knowing them is impossible.

Opportunity:

We can get better information from key aspects of character and motivation by developing the right connections (2.2.1 Personal Relationships). As we get to know decision-makers or those close to them on a personal level, we get more insight into their needs, concerns, strengths, and shortcomings. The more we know, the better we can predict the future (2.3.2 Reaction Unpredictability). The more often our actions will get the response that we want (2.3.1 Action and Reaction). The better our information channels, the better our perspective and the better our decisions.

Key Methods:

We get to know decision makers from four different types of contacts.

1. Our primary source of command perspective is our direct personal relationships with decision-makers: When possible, we want to develop personal relationships with these decision makers who affect our position. This isn't always possible because some decision-makers, say our bosses, prefer to keep a distance, but often it is our shyness rather than the reticence of the decision makers that is the real problem (2.2.1 Personal Relationships).

2. Our secondary source of command perspective are "insiders" who see different aspects of decision-makers. People have many sides and show their different sides to different people. We see one side, others see another side. Having a range of contacts as friends helps us understand that all people are different, with different strengths, weaknesses, and challenges. If we want to get to know someone well, we are best served by developing relationships with others who know them (2.3 Personal Interactions).

3. We get a different aspect of command perspective from those who have regular subordinate contact with decisionmakers. One of the best techniques to get information on powerful decisionmakers is to find the "low people in high places" who come in regular contact with them. Sometimes we can get close to their secretaries and assistants, but even these direct channels can be guarded. However, there are usually a host of others, office workers and services providers (trainers, barbers, etc.) who can provide valuable insights about these people's concerns and character.

4. Historical perspective on the past actions of those in command has some limited value. Actions speak louder than words. Historical information is valuable because people will tend to do what they have done in the past. However, our true concern is the future. Character doesn't change often, but motivations do (2.3.3 Range of Reactions , 1.6.3 Shifting Priorities).

5. Public information is the least reliable source of perspective on those in command. While we cannot overlook it, we have to suspect what we learn from public sources. Most public information, including rumors, should be verified before we put too much faith in them (2.1.3 Strategic Deception).

6. Developing contacts that give us perspective on decisionsmakers are the most delicate of all networking. When getting to know someone, we collect evidence about their character, especially the five key aspects of character that relate to decision-making (1.5.1 Command Leadership). Of course, the most powerful weapon in gathering information is simply to ask questions (2.3.4 Using Questions). If these questions are based on a sincere interest in getting to know others, they will make us friends.

Illustration:

Let us look at two different business cases to illustrate the range of issues here: bosses and customers. We know our bosses but often have bad information on them. We too often judge them on their position rather than on their character and motivations.

1. Our primary source of command perspective is our direct personal relationships with decision-makers. People are often too shy to befriend their bosses or their boss's boss on a personal level. But people are people and we can find common ground with most people if we work at it to provide the basis of a relationship. Common interests, backgrounds, and histories from outside work are the best.

2. Our secondary source of command perspective are "insiders" who see different aspects of decision-makers. If we want to get to know our boss, for example, our fellow employees probably see pretty much the same side we do. However, another manager in a different department will know that individual in a very different way.

3. We get a different aspect of command perspective from those who have regular subordinate contact with decision-makers. Our bosses have secretaries, assistants, and other services providers with whom we can make a connection because we share a common contact: the boss him or herself.

4. Historical perspective on the past actions of those in command has some limited value. The more we can learn about our boss's own career, the more we can understand his or her character and motivation.

5. Public information is the least reliable source of perspective on those in command. Think of public information about the boss as a starting point for building the above types of relationships.

6. Developing contacts that give us perspective on decisions-makers are the most delicate of all networking. Getting information about a boss is extremely valuable, but we cannot let our boss know that we are making a project of researching him or her.

Everyone talks about knowing their customers. Unfortunately, most small businesses don't invest much in knowing their customers at all. Big businesses too delegate the task of "knowing the customer" to the "specialists" in marketing, who abstract customer motivations and care more about demographics than character.

1. Our primary source of command perspective is our direct personal relationships with decision-makers. Everyone who makes decisions in a business no matter what the size, should invest time in building personal relationships with some of their customers.

2. Our secondary source of command perspective are "insiders" who see different aspects of decision-makers. This means getting to know customers from the perspective of others who are close to them: friends and family. This is much more difficult.

3. We get a different aspect of command perspective from those who have regular subordinate contact with decision-makers. Where else do our customers do business? Who are their favorite service providers? We should talk to them.

4. Historical perspective on the past actions of those in command has some limited value. Sales histories are useful but only if we study them and their trends.

5. Public information is the least reliable source of perspective on those in command. Generic information about customers in the media is often too distant from our own competitive neighborhood to be valuable, but information affecting the local economy, such as plant closings, is always valuable for understanding changing motivations.

6. Developing contacts that give us perspective on decisions-makers are the most delicate of all networking. Customers don't like the idea that their suppliers are collecting data about their purchasing habits even when suppliers can service them better with that data.

2.4.4 Methods Perspective

Sun Tzu's five key methods for developing contacts who understand best practices.

"They remain ignorant of the enemy's condition. The result is cruel."

Sun Tzu's The Art of War 13:1:13-14

"Fools learn from experience. I prefer to learn from the experience of others."

Otto von Bismarck

General Principle: Learn best practices, especially from those who use systems, ideally those of our rivals.

Situation:

When learning the best practices in our competitive arena, trial and error is the slowest possible method of discovering what works. How-to books, like our own Playbook, can give step-by-step descriptions and examples, but they are limited. The best sources about best practices are those who have been successful in a given competitive arena. We may think of those people as our competitors, but that is the wrong mindset. Most people shy away from learning their competitors' methods out of a misplaced sense of competition.

Opportunity:

The world is filled with people who have practical experience in specific areas of skill. Many are willing to share their knowledge. The most important are those we might normally see as our competitors (1.3.1 Competitive Comparison). Strategy starts by mastering the best practices in any given competitive arena (7.2.1 Proven Methods). Those standards provide the basis for our strategic thinking. You wouldn't be reading this article unless you were interested in developing new skills in the system of strategy based upon the history of others success. The best way to learn new skills is to develop relationships with people who already have those or know the systems that we want to learn (1.5.2. Group Methods).

Key Methods:

The following five key methods describe how we get a better perspective on best practices.

1. *To get a perspective on best methods, we must to seek out and listen to people who have the skills and use the systems that are successful.* Our information comes through a contact network of a limited size. Part of the network must be reserved for those who understand the "best practices" in our competitive arena. Learning proven practices allows us to find opportunities to innovate. This is

a critical path to improving our position ([7.1.3 Standards and Innovation](#)).

2. *To get a perspective on best methods, we need personal relationships with our "competitors."* When we know our competitors as people on a personal level, we see them differently. We see that they aren't our enemies. We have more in common with our rivals than anyone else. They have more to teach us in terms of methods than anyone else. Competitors aren't known for being honest with one another, nor should they be, but everything we get to know about them helps us better understand our position ([1.3.1 Competitive Comparison](#)).

3. *To get a perspective on best methods, we need to have contacts with whom our competitors work.* These are people in touch with our competition and work with or even for them. These people can give us valuable insight in how our competition works. Of course that won't endear us to our competitors if we hire away their employees, but they are a terrific source of best practices and inside information about their character ([2.4.3 Command Perspective](#)).

4. *To get a perspective on best methods, we must learn complex systems from those using them daily.* If we need to understand a system, especially complex electronic, information or mechanical systems, it is best to learn from someone who has a skill and uses the system regularly on a nuts and bolts level. This category often includes people who sell systems of various types and are familiar with a wide variety of applications. People who understand the inner workings of systems can get a lot done with very little effort ([1.5.2. Group Methods](#)).

5. *To get a perspective on best methods, our relationships based on methods must be serious.* These relationships cannot be a simply a research project. When people actually become our friends, they care about our mission. They think about their systems from the perspective of our unique needs. Harnessing the intangible capital of the human mind requires a real connection ([2.2.1 Personal Relationships](#)).

Illustration:

We can illustrate with general observations about business that lead to very specific examples.

1. *To get a perspective on best methods, we must to seek out and listen to people who have the skills and use the systems that are successful.* We do not accidentally encounter the people we need to meet who know the methods that are behind success. We see successful organization, such as WalMart, but we must work to find out what systems, such as logistical systems, that are behind their success. We don't need to know the geniuses that created those systems, all we need to do is find people who know who those system work by using them When we do meet these people, we must be interested in them and listen to what they have to say.

2. *To get a perspective on best methods, we need personal relationships with our "competitors."* All business associations are groups of people who are potentially competitors. Associations are popular because no matter how competitive we are, we can learn from each other. Competition is not conflict. It is comparison.

3. *To get a perspective on best methods, we need to have contacts with whom our competitors work.* Many businesses naturally share common suppliers. Getting information about how our competitors work from these people often takes no more effort than simply asking.

4. *To get a perspective on best methods, we must learn complex systems from those using them daily.* Operators who do the actual work are often overlooked and undervalued within organizations. We can gain a lot simply by respecting the role they play.

5. *To get a perspective on best methods, our relationships based on methods must be serious.* As business people, we can get so focused on our own organizations that we don't have time to develop relationships outside of them. This is a mistake. Only those external relationships can give us perspective. At the Institute, we teach proven systems, but the principles of strategy are very general

at the Institute level. Many of our trainers take this knowledge down to the practical nuts and bolts level, applying it to specific problems in the real world. For example, Fred Leland draws upon a wealth of law enforcement and security experience working as a police officer in training other officers in strategic decision-making. The reason that we license our material to trainers like Fred is because their specific experience is as valuable as the general knowledge itself.

2.4.5 Mission Perspective

Sun Tzu's seven key methods on how we develop and use a perspective on motivation.

"Place people as a single unit where they can all see and hear. You must unite them as one."
Sun Tzu's The Art of War 7:4:7-8

"Sprinkled in every walk of life...are a handful of people with an extraordinary knack of making friends and acquaintances."
Malcolm Gladwell

General Principle: We focus on motivations to communicate a shared mission.

Situation:

We develop a contact network to collect the information that we need strategically, but the network does more than collect information. It also communicates it. We cannot get information without also communicating information. The value of information is 80 percent what comes in and 20 percent what goes out. In most areas, most of the value is in what we can learn. In one area, the area of goals and mission, the value is in what others learn about us. Many people try to keep their goals a secret, but the real power of goals comes from communicating them.

Opportunity:

People have to know our goals before they can help us (1.6 Mission Values). To help us, those in our contact network have to understand our goals and motivation. If we are asking questions, they want to know why. We have to communicate our mission in a way that gathers their support. Just as mission is the core of a strategic situation, it is the glue that holds together our contact network. Everyone within our contact network must find, in one way or another, a common cause with us (1.6.1 Shared Mission).

Key Methods:

The following seven key methods describe how we get a better perspective on people's motivation.

1. We cannot build a contact network without having a perspective on what motivates others to help us. The first type of information that we want to gather from every type of contact is information about motivation. However, to be successful, we not only have to gather information about the motivations of others, we must communicate information about our motivation as well (1.6.2 Types of Motivations).

2. Every type of contact can help us more if they understand our perspective on mission. Those who give us perspective on the ground can help us understand the rewards within a given competitive arena (2.4.1 Ground Perspective). Those who give us perspective on the climate can help us see our opportunities (2.4.2 Climate Perspective). Those who give us perspective on the decision makers can help us see what we have in common with others (2.4.3 Command Perspective). Those who give us perspective on the methods can help us understand the benefits of certain skills and systems (2.4.4 Methods Perspective).

3. Our perspective on motivation allows us to create shared missions. One form of opportunity is aligning people's motivations so they can work together. Incompatible motivations create conflicts, but different motivations can be aligned so everyone gets what they want (1.6.1 Shared Mission). This is the first step in identifying more specific forms of opportunities (3.0 Identifying Opportunities).

4. Our perspective on motivation allows us to make the shared mission exciting. People need stimulation and novelty. We tie together climate shifts, reward potential, character issue, and gimmicks to make the shared mission important and engaging. The higher our level of our mission and the more uniquely it is expressed, the better this works. The economics of making money is overdone and therefore boring."Professionalism"isn't much more interesting. Where we want to affect people is on the emotional and even spiritual levels of mission (2.1.4 Surprise).

5. Our perspective on motivation allows us to make the shared mission personal. We should connect our mission to our life stories and to the life stories of others. We must tell our life story in a way that helps people identify with us. Life experience creates stronger bonds than ideology. We want to give our mission an emotional connection. We connect our joy and pain to our relationships with others. We want to make it spiritual, in the sense of human spirit and destiny that we all share (2.2.1 Personal Relationships).

6. Our perspective on motivation allows us to transform personal contacts into missionaries. When our contacts support our mission, that is, share our mission, they will actively want to help us to fulfill that mission. People are interested in us because they see themselves in us and our mission. Missionaries are those who carry our message to others. Good missionaries are often able to articulate the value of supporting our mission better than we can ourselves (2.3 Personal Interactions).

7. Our perspective on motivation allows us to identify the natural "connectors" who make the best missionaries. Malcolm Gladwell, in his book *The Tipping Point*, explains that some people are extraordinarily well connected to a large number of others. Gladwell calls these people "connectors." We don't need to be connectors ourselves. We just need to connect with the connectors and win them over as our missionaries. Connectors are great missionaries. What makes us interesting to connectors? The same thing that makes us interesting to anyone else, our shared philosophy, our values, and goals (1.6.1 Shared Mission).

Illustration:

Let me make this illustration personal. Let us use this illustration to promote our Science of Strategy Institute's philosophy here.

1. We cannot build a contact network without having a perspective on what motivates others to help us. You can use our Science of Straetgy Institute contact page (http://scienceofstrategy.org/main/contact) ask about any aspect of our system and most of the time, I will answer you personally. From your questions, we understand your motivation.

2. Every type of contact can help us more if they understand our perspective on mission. When we were much smaller, we would send personal emails to those who download our free Ebook *Art of War* and ask them about their motivations. Unfortunately, we seldom have time any more to do that.

*3. Our perspective on motivation allows us to create shared mission*s. When we get the opportunities to visit our corporate customers to make live presentations, we always discuss how their organization's mission joins with ours in terms of helping people adapt to change.

4. Our perspective on motivation allows us to make the shared mission exciting. In recent years, we have increasingly focused on teaching Sun Tzu's concepts in our live presentation through activites and exercises rather than lecture. It is much more exciting for people to feel how these ideas work rather than simply hearing about them. We recognize the difference between doers and observers.

5. *Our perspective on motivation allows us to make the shared mission personal.* In my books, on the SOSI site, and occasionally in live presentations, I illustrate Sun Tzu's ideas using my battle with cancer. It was that battle that made me refocus my life on teaching strategy to regular people. Before, I just flew around the world working with large corporations. Of course, I still do, but that isn't why I write books or created the Institute.

6. *Our perspective on motivation allows us to transform personal contacts into missionaries*. We are support all those interesting in promoting Sun Tzu's ideas by offering them free memberships, materials, and other forms of support.

7. *Our perspective on motivation allows us to identify the natural "connectors"who make the best missionaries*. If you are one, contact me and let's talk about what we can do together.

2.5 The Big Picture

Sun Tzu's nine key methods on building big picture strategic awareness.

"If you can't see the small subtleties, you won't get the truth from spies. Pay attention to small, trifling details!"
Sun Tzu's The Art of War 13:3:7-8

"Each time we do a successful operation it allows us to slap new pieces of the puzzle in. We get a clearer picture. We're able to get more information."
Steve Russell

General Principle: Put together the strategic puzzle by building on the model framework.

Situation:

Developing strategic perspective is like putting together the pieces of a puzzle. We are exposed to a flood of information.Each piece of information seems disconnected. When we cannot fit information into a larger picture, it is quickly lost and forgotten. Everyone is trying to build up a picture of their strategic position. Most of these pictures lack a framework to give them structure. Information is loosely and randomly connected. The resulting picture is both sketchy and fragile.Without a framework, understanding is limited. Disconnected pieces of information are lost.

Opportunity:

Our minds recognize and remember patterns. We can see patterns even when we look at the random dots. Our ancestors looked at the stars in the sky and saw pictures. This is the way our minds work. The mental models of Sun Tzu leverage the way our minds work. His mental models were developed and preserved down the centuries because they work. Our opportunity is in making them work for us. They provide the framework around which we build our strategic perspective. With this foundation, we can manage more information. With this framework, we can quickly separate the relevant from the irrelevant. We can verify information because it is consistent with the framework (2.2.2 Mental Models).

Key Methods:

The following nine key methods describe how we put details into a larger, more comprehensive picture.

1. Sun Tzu's mental models are the framework, the scaffolding for creating a big picture perspective. To make them relevant to our specific situation, we have to flesh out that framework. We must fill these models with information from our unique situation, putting together the little pieces of information into a more comprehensive and powerful picture (2.2.2 Mental Models).

2. Big picture perspective requires a flow of information from a contact network. News is not information. We develop contact networks specifically to get the types of information most relevant to our situation (2.4 Contact Networks).

3. Big picture perspective sorts detailed information using the mental model of the five elements. This model gives us a structure for organizing what we learn. While we cannot remember a lot of separate details, we remember connected details. No detail is too small when it comes to putting together a puzzle. A piece of information that seems trivial by itself can be telling once we try to fit it into a larger picture. This picture allows us to understand our basic position, how it is changing, and how it is likely to change in the future. (1.3 Elemental Analysis).

4. Big picture perspective highlights the most relevant information as keys to advancing our position. This information is the most relevant because we can act on it. These models include identifying hidden opportunities, picking high-probabilities opportunities, responding to common situations, and so on (1.8 Progress Cycle).

5. As we flesh out our big picture perspective, it becomes easier to fit in new pieces and identify mission pieces. Going back to our puzzle analogy, each piece of information that we put in place makes it easier and faster to put new pieces into place. The blank areas in the puzzle also indicate where we must look for needed information. We learn the mental models of Sun Tzu's strategy to help us quickly sort the information that comes in so that it doesn't pile up but those models are more powerful as we flesh them out. The character of each piece can be identified quickly and put in a place where it provides us the most insight. (2.1 Information Value).

6. Information that doesn't fit into our big picture perspective draws our attention. As we put together our picture of the situation, the pieces have to fit. Pieces that don't fit tell us something important. Some pieces won't fit because they aren't right. If many pieces don't fit, they challenge our assumptions about how we are putting together the puzzle. A tiny piece of information can turn out to be the key in fitting everything together in a way that makes better sense. We know that much of our information is subjective and therefore prone to error.It is only by fitting the pieces of information together that we see how one piece of information confirms another (2.1.1 Information Limits).

7. Our decisions must be based on our big picture perspective, not separate events or elements. We can trust any specific data point at our own risk. We instead trust the picture. It is not the independent pieces that matter, but how they all fit together. None of the pieces of an airplane have the ability to fly, but when they are put together, that capability emerges. Knowing how to put the pieces together is the difference between a confusing series of events that pull us first in one direction and then another and having a map of the terrain (5.1.1 Event Pressure).

8. Our big picture perspective is more valuable when it joins our picture with those of others. When we work with other people using the same mental models, we amplify our abilities. We help them and they help us create our perspective of the strategic situation. Given common models and a common language, our pictures can quickly be connected with those of others to deepen and broaden our insight (2.2.3 Standard Terminology).

9. The process of building our big picture perspective never stops. We continue building and refining our picture of our situation throughout our lives. As some parts are outdated, new parts replace them but, correctly built, the picture grows more and more detailed and dependable over time (1.8.2 The Adaptive Loop).

Illustration:

Let us apply to these principles to the task of finding a better job.

1. Sun Tzu's mental models are the framework, the scaffolding for creating a big picture perspective. In searching for a job, most people are like pin balls, bouncing around randomly until they fall into a hole. Using the methods above in my personal career when I was in the job market, I managed to advance my position on the average of every eight months.

2. *Big picture perspective requires a flow of information from a contact network*. Starting with our current contacts, we should grow the network in the direction of where we want to go based on what we have done in the past.

3. *Big picture perspective sorts detailed information using the mental model of the five elements.* We begin to see our job area more completely, seeing where old opportunities are fading while others are opening up.

4. *Big picture perspective highlights the most relevant information as keys to advancing our position*. We start focusing on where opportunities are opening up, identifying where to look for the high-probability opportunities and how to best pursue them.

5. *As we flesh out our big picture perspective, it becomes easier to fit in new pieces and identify mission pieces*. As we look in more and more specific areas of opportunity, we develop an even more detailed picture. This picture helps us compare alternatives to see which hold the greatest opportunity for us personally.

6. *Information that doesn't fit into our big picture perspective draws our attention.* Rejection is information. Our ideas about what job we should be looking for changes as we realize that many of the opportunities we were pursuing have a very low-probability of success.

7. *Our decisions must be based on our big picture perspective not separate events or elements*. When we go to interviews, it is because we understand the job market and how we fit into it.

8. *Our big picture perspective is more valuable when it joins our picture with those of others*. We share our picture with our potential employers, demonstrating that we are not just looking for a job, but a career. If we demonstrate that we have a valuable perspective, we stand out dramatically from other applications.

9. *The process of building our big picture perspective never stops.* Not only does each interview improve our picture, but over our whole career, we use this process to continually advance our position.

2.6 Knowledge Leverage

Sun Tzu's five key methods for getting competitive value out of knowledge.

LEVERAGE

"Give me a place to stand, and I will move the Earth." - Archimedes

"Knowledge is victory.
No knowledge is no victory."

Sun Tzu's The Art of War 1:1:36-37
[Chinese Revealed version]

"As a small businessperson, you have no greater leverage than the truth."

Paul Keating

General Principle: Knowledge must get more value out of our resources.

Situation:

Despite the progress demonstrated by human history, there is a strong school of thought that claims that success is a zero-sum game. To advance our position, we must take from others. For those who see life as a zero-sum game, growth and progress can only end badly. It suggests that as the world grows and advances, we must all grow poorer because our limited resources are split among more and more people. Populations must therefore be controlled. People must be stopped from building and consuming because everything requires resources. From this perspective, the only moral strategy is to give up on personal progress and success.

Opportunity:

Sun Tzu's perspective on making choices maintains that real, lasting progress can be made, not only for the few but for all. He sees the only real resource as the human mind. The value of all other resources come from our knowledge of how to use those resources. The human mind can continually create more value out of once useless resources through learning. The only limited resources are our knowledge, our freedom to make decisions, and our capacity for understanding. More minds means more knowledge, freedom, and capacity, which means we get more value out of existing resources. This understanding turns our fears inside out. Population growth creates more minds that can create more value. Hong Kong and Singapore are rich despite their lack of resources. More progress creates less costly forms of value improving our environment. Our opportunity is to enrich the world by getting more value from undervalued resources, starting with our own time (7.6 Non-Zero Sum Games).

Key Methods:

The following five key methods describe Sun Tzu's perspective on the creation of value from knowledge.

1. ***Knowledge leverage means combining information with proven mental models to create value.*** Information alone is not knowledge. We must use this information to create knowledge and produce value. The old saying is that it takes money to make money.

The real truth is it takes knowledge to make money or, more precisely, to make progress. Money, like all resources, is wasted if it is not put into a model that works (2.5 The Big Picture).

2. *Our success depends directly on our ability to leverage knowledge.* Sun Tzu's system is built on getting rewards from making investments. Profit measures the value of our knowledge exactly. It is the difference between the value we purchase and the value that we generate. Profit depends on our knowledge. We must know what to buy, how and where to buy it, what to make, and how and where to sell it (3.1.2 Strategic Profitability).

3. *Information leverage requires an investment*. Though knowledge can replace every other cost, learning also has its costs. It must never be taken for granted. It requires time and effort to create and maintain the type of contact networks defined by Sun Tzu's strategy, but the costs of maintaining an information network goes beyond time and effort alone (2.2 Information Gathering).

4. *Leverage knowledge value by replacing other forms more costly resources*. The right knowledge saves time, materials, and effort. Good knowledge leverages available resources by allowing us to put those resources at the right place at the right time. The better our knowledge, the better our decisions about what to buy, where to buy it, what to produce, and how to produce it. This decision-making is the difference between success and failure (2.1 Information Value).

5. *When people who provide us with valuable information the we can leverage, we must share the rewards.* We must actively provide our contacts an incentive to think about us. When they hear information that might be valuable, we want them to think to pass it on. Knowledge is so valuable that no reward is too generous for those who can give us the right information at the right time. These rewards reinforce the relationship and communicate what we see as valuable. Rewards can be as simple as showing honest interest in the lives of our contacts. One of the best rewards is to pass on valuable information to them (2.3 Personal Interactions).

Illustration:

Let us look at the knowledge of competitive strategy, specifically at the knowledge that Sun Tzu teaches from this perspective.

1. Knowledge leverage means combining information with proven mental models to create value. We get a flow of competitive information from the environment, Sun Tzu's key methods give us proven mental models to convert that information into advances in our position.

2. Our success depends directly on our ability to leverage knowledge. Our success in competition depends on our knowledge of what competition really is and how it works. Being successful in external competition is simply a matter of knowing the principles of Sun Tzu better than those with whom we are competing.

3. Information leverage requires an investment. The most expensive way to learn competitive strategy is through trial and error. The materials and classes that the Institute offers are inexpensive in comparison, but they still require you to spend time in study and practice.

4. Leverage knowledge value by replacing other forms more costly resources. The real price that we pay for not learning competitive strategy is in the cost of lost opportunities. By not seeing our opportunities and not knowing how to take advantage of them, we pay a price in terms of our success in life.

5. When people who provide us with valuable information the we can leverage, we must share the rewards. If people didn't reward the Institute by purchasing our publications and training, we couldn't afford to provide this information. Because we can provide this value, more and more people are successful all over the world and we, in turn, are rewarded for the part we play in helping create that success.

2.7 Information Secrecy

Sun Tzu's nine key methods defining the role of secrecy in relationships.

"No work is as secret as that of spies."
Sun Tzu's The Art of War 13:3:5

"If knowledge is power, clandestine knowledge is power squared; it can be withheld, exchanged, and leveraged."
Letty Cottin

General Principle: We must know where secrecy is required to maintain our flow of valuable information.

Situation:

We can undermine our position by sharing the wrong information with the wrong people. People are not born with an inherent understanding of the principles of secrecy. These principles arise because knowledge is power. We must always consider how the power of our knowledge can be used against us. Knowledge about what we know or don't know is power over us. The challenge is that our ability to leverage knowledge depends on other people. We must give information in order to get information. People cannot support us unless they know us. We must therefore walk a tight rope, a dangerous balance of keeping information secret while sharing information.

Opportunity:

We all use secrecy to deny our rivals good information about our positions and direction. Skilled use of secrecy actually improves our ability to get information. It is critical in maintaining contact networks because our friends expect us to keep their confidential information secret. Our opportunity is in understanding when information is most valuable in public and when it is most valuable in secret. We do not have to publicize information in order to use it. We do not have to reveal what we know in making a move. This means understanding the different levels of relationships, the privacy expectations of each level, and the consequences of privacy being violated.

Key Methods:

There are nine key methods describing three different types of relationships and their requirements for secrecy.

1. We should keep all information secret unless we get leverage from publicizing it and then we must protect our sources.
Our default position should be secrecy. We give away information when we talk and when we act. We cannot leverage our knowledge

without communicating it. However, leveraging information is not as important as assuring that we continue to get new information. We must balance these two needs using the key methods below (2.6 Knowledge Leverage).

2. The principles of secrecy operate differently on personal relationships, authority relationships, and social relationships. One-to-one relationships are *personal connections,* where communication is the more free and the highest level of trust comes into play. One-to-many relationships are *authority connections,* where information flows are more filtered and controlled and the next highest level of privacy is expected. Many-to-many relationships are *social connections,* that provide us with the most general information and have the least expectation of privacy. These three areas can overlap. A social relationship can have a small element of personal connection. A authority relationship can have an element of social connection. These relationships are different because the motivations around which they are formed are different (1.6.2 Types of Motivations).

3. Secrecy is important because violating privacy expectations degrades higher levels of relationships. Each of us is constrained by the privacy expectations of others and they are constrained by us. A violation of those constraints always degrades the relationship, decreasing its importance. People leave personal and authority relationships based on these violations. When sensitive information from a one-to-one relationship is shared, what was once a personal relationship, entitled to private information, becomes an authority or social relationship. Serious violations destroy relationships and potentially creates enemies (7.2.2 Preparing Expectations).

4. Sensitive or secret information is a matter of personal opinion. All relationships include a variety of facts and opinions, but privacy expectations only extend to sensitive information. Unfortunately, what others consider sensitive is not always obvious. We must be very clear about what we consider sensitive information without expecting others to ask. On the other hand, we must ask to know what others consider sensitive without expecting them to be clear. Everyone has their own rules (2.3.4 Using Questions).

5. ***Key one-to-one relationships also have the highest expectations of secrecy and privacy***. These relationships are the most costly to maintain, but they are also the most critical to our success. We want to be able to share very private perspectives with others in our network and we hope that they will share their most private perspectives with us. The ability to keep confidences is a cornerstone of contact networks. Information from personal relationships, where the most confidential information is shared, cannot cross over into social or authority relationships where information is the less sensitive. If people within our contact network violate our confidences, we can no longer share confidential information with them (2.3 Personal Interactions).

6. ***Authority relationships have more complex expectations of secrecy and privacy***. Information from these relationships can be shared with our personal relationships but not in our social ones. Within the hierarchy, authority-based information can always be shared up (but information from personal relationships cannot). However, authority information can only be shared down with direction from above (1.5.1 Command Leadership).

7. ***When sharing information, the principles of secrecy depend on the other person's view of our relationship***. People do not judge us based upon our view of the relationship, but their own. We must be sensitive to their perceptions because relationships are subjective. We make mistakes when we act from our viewpoint rather than considering the subjective viewpoints of others (1.2 Subobjective Positions).

8. ***The principles of secrecy are most likely to be violated when relationships change.*** Relationships at every level not stable nor are they exclusive. People can move up and down among these three levels and within a given level. Even one-to-one relationships can rise and fall in importance. If a member of our contact network develops a closer relationship with one of our rivals, we must expect our confidences to be shared (1.1.1 Position Dynamics).

9. We must continually adapt our judgments about sharing information and secrecy. Both information and misinformation is shared within contact networks. Sharing information tends to strengthen relationships while misinformation tends to weaken them. In situations where relationships change and we are fortunate enough to learn about it, we have an opportunity to use the contact as a channel for misleading information or disinformation (2.1.3 Strategic Deception).

Illustration:

Let us illustrate how these principles work within romantic relationships because they offer the funniest examples.

1. We should keep all information secret unless we get leverage from publicizing it and then we must protect our sources. An engagement or marriage is a public announcement because it benefits both parties and society to publicize it. However, most of what happens between a couple is kept secret or should be.

2. The principles of secrecy operate differently on personal relationships, authority relationships, and social relationships. By romantic relationships we mean personal relationships.

3. Secrecy is important because violating privacy expectations degrades higher levels of relationships. If your romantic significant other tells you a secret, telling it to your best friend has painful consequences.

4. Sensitive or secret information is a matter of personal opinion. Sorry, you won't get out of it by telling someone you didn't know that the information was sensitive. If you didn't ask, you're an idiot for not knowing.

5. Key one-to-one relationships also have the highest expectations of secrecy and privacy. If your spouse tells you something sensitive, you do not share it with your boss.

6. *Authority relationships have more complex expectations of secrecy and privacy.* You must tell your spouse what your boss told you to keep a secret. There is authority and higher authority.

7. *When sharing information, the principles of secrecy depend on the other person's view of our relationship.* We may think the relationship is personal but the other person may think it is merely social and therefore free to tell whatever we confide in them to other friends.

8. *The principles of secrecy are most likely to be violated when relationships change.* When you break up a romantic relationship, expect those pictures to appear on the Internet.

9. *We must continually adapt our judgments about sharing information and secrecy.* If you think a relationship is in trouble, you might want to be a little bit careful about what you share.

Sun Tzu's Playbook

Volume 3:
Opportunities

About Opportunities

Competition is a comparison. People must compare alternatives before they can make choices. Potential supporters must compare before they can choose to work with you. You must compare before you can make choices about what opportunities to pursue.

Our last formula focussed on collecting better information for comparison. After collecting information, you use that information in this chapter's formula to identify opportunities.

This raises the serious question: what is an opportunity? The simplest definition is an opening in the environment into which you can expand and build up your position. You can only move into that space if it is open. This is why we use the term opening to describe strategic opportunities.

Success requires improving your position, moving from one opportunity to a better one. To move forward, you must find opportunities. These openings are stepping-stones to success. The Observe Opportunities Formula reveals the right times, proper conditions, and best places to find opportunities.

The Opportunity in Openings

To make progress, you need an opening. Openings are empty spaces in the environment. They are areas that are being overlooked by competitors. These spaces are not empty because of what you do or do not do. They are empty because of what everyone else is doing or not doing.

Sun Tzu states his view of the nature of opportunities simply:

> *You see the opportunity for victory; you don't control it.*
> The Art of War, 4:1:10

This short phrase raises three important points that you should understand about opportunities before proceeding.

The competitive environment creates and controls opportunities. Changes in the climate create opportunities. Openings are conditions in the environment. You do not control conditions in the environment. The environment is very large. The largest organization is microscopic by comparison. Thinking that you can create an opportunity in the environment is like a drop of water thinking that it can change the tides of the ocean.

Sun Tzu's principles teaches you to see opportunities, not to create them. Recognizing opportunities is difficult enough because an opportunity looks like nothing. Once you see opportunities, you can compare them. Creating opportunities is impossible. If you try to create opportunities, you are wasting your time and resources. You must use those resources to pursue opportunities that the forces in your environment create.

Finally, you cannot create opportunity. To become successful, you can create a campaign. You can create a position for an organization in the competitive environment. In Sun Tzu's Art of War Playbook, we have key methods for creating communication networks, momentum, sales, and lots of other valuable stuff for improving positions. When you think about what you can create, you must think about what takes advantage of existing opportunities. Before you can know what to create, you must recognize those opportunities.

Openings are like a black hole. There isn't anything to see. There are no competitors, no products, mo obvious resources, and no money being made in them. You cannot see nothing. Like a black hole, we must recognize an opening by what it happening around it.

The Choice Between Offense and Defense

Your first responsibility is to defend your existing position. Competition is a game you can only play while you have resources. When you run out, the game is over. Income from resources the lifeblood of an enterprise. You must preserve existing sources of income. You only look for new areas to conquer when your current base is secure.

Successful advances are like climbing a ladder. You gradually shift your weight from one rung to the next. The rule is that you move into new area quickly, but you abandon old bases slowly. In emergencies, you can be forced to move because your existing position has fallen apart, but normally you preserve your existing sources of revenue as you advance.

If your existing position is resource poor, you have to work more carefully. If moving into new positions hollows out your existing position, such a move can be fatal. In this situation, you focus less on external opportunities in the environment and more on internal opportunities in your systems. You need less strategy and more planning. Instead of looking for openings in the environment, you look for openings within your systems to control your expenses. As your systems improve, you eventually have more resources than you need to preserve your existing revenue stream. This is when you move into new opportunities in the environment.

Many organizations get this process backward. When their existing organizations are doing well, they devote their excess resources to internal systems, but they neglect pursuing new opportunities. They wait until their existing positions are in trouble before considering new opportunities. Putting more resources into profitable operations can be necessary to support growth, but frequently you are working at the wrong end of the law of diminishing returns. For every additional effort and dollar you put in, you are going to get less and less of a return.

People tend to let necessity dictate their attempts at advance. For example, people look for a new job at the worst possible time: when they are out of work. You are much more successful if you counter this tendency. It is a hundred times easier to find a new job when you are doing well in your existing job. It is also a hundred times easier to pursue new opportunities when your existing position is doing well.

New opportunities are more plentiful than most people think, but the best opportunities do not come on any schedule. Because of this, you must protect and build up your existing position and wait patiently until a new opportunity appears. When a new opportunity appears, you must let your existing position take care of itself while you concentrate on your advance.

Where to Look for Opportunity

You never fight competitors in the environment directly or try to control the environment. The environment is bigger than both you and your competitors. There are right ways and wrong ways to deal with the competition. The worst approach is to target a competitor's strong points.

The most common strategic mistake is to simply copy competitors who already dominate an environment. Imitation works in specific competitive situations that we cover later, but the success of your competitors in an environment never defines an opportunity.

What happens when you directly attack established competitors? You discover that you cannot make their position your own. You can try to duplicate their systems and contacts. You can try to offer a product that is superior in every way. You still won't win their supporters. This seems unfair, but it is the way it is. You can't let this frustrate and anger you. You can't change it by wasting money on marketing. All competitors must create their own unique positions. Trying to destroy the positions of others is a disaster.

People naturally follow the crowd. This is especially true in business, where every business tries to copy the latest popular product or idea. This never works because crowded areas create unprofitable positions. Following the crowd to find an opportunity is like trying to feed yourself on the scraps other leave.

If you want to be successful, go after empty spaces—openings—not areas that are already crowded. You must see openings in your environment and fill them before competitors recognize them. The power of this concept is that it moves you away from conflict with competitors. It moves you into areas where you can win their support without fighting them. It puts you in control because you are always picking your own supporters.

Your competitors can be well entrenched in their positions. You cannot beat them by going after their positions directly, succeeding in the same way that they do. Even though you share your competitive space or neighborhood with them, you must see the space differently than they do. You don't look at what competitors are doing. You look at what they are failing to do.

You don't want to fight your competitors for position. Battling over position is never profitable, even if you win. No matter how dominant your competitors are, some of their supporters are unhappy. This is certain because no one can do everything well. When you recognize this unhappiness and its cause, you are well on the path to finding your opportunity.

The bigger the organization, the more powerful the position, the more certain it is that that position has unhappy supporters. You must focus on the supporters that competitors have served the most poorly, the needs that they leave unsatisfied. Supporters choose you because you have first chosen them. When you choose to target a group of supporters, you choose to fill a particular type of need. The larger your competitors are, the more supporters they are trying to satisfy and the more specific needs they must neglect.

Competitors may be bigger, but if they are focused on satisfying the demands of their position how can their size hurt you? The larger their base of supporters, the more likely it is that some of those people are unhappy.

You beat competitors, no matter how large, by choosing where and when you compete. Positions that seem difficult are really easy when you understand the power of choice. Your choices control how much competition you have. You can divide the areas of competition to define where you compete best. You can fulfill the supporters' needs that competitors do not address.

Some competitors will always be much bigger than you are, but this means that they have many areas in which they can invest their resources. You want them to spread themselves too thin. You can then choose the opening that you want to address. You target supporters who are well suited to your mission and skills. You choose supporters whom your opponent has ignored because their needs are poorly suited to your competitor's mission and skill.

If competitors work globally, you focus locally. If they offer broad appeals, you can offer customized ones. If they deal in large volumes, you can offer more specialized releases. If they use standard terms, you can create special ones. The list goes on and on.

Your much larger, richer, more professional, more experienced competitors will continually overlook opportunities that are right under their noses. How can they hit a target that they cannot see?

You control where you compete. Your competition cannot control you unless you let them.

Sun Tzu's principles teach that strength can be a source of weakness. Only by studying the known strengths of competitors can you see where they are creating opportunities. All strengths create a complementary weakness. You must see how to put your strengths against your competitors' weaknesses.

Your competitors can have all types of different strengths. It doesn't matter what those strengths are. No one does everything well. People have to choose where to focus their resources. When they choose what strengths to develop, they are also choosing to develop weaknesses elsewhere.

Strength and weakness are another pair of those complementary opposites. Strength and weakness are two sides of the same condition. You discover opponents' weaknesses by studying their strengths.

This is simpler than it may sound at first.

For example, if a business focuses on having the lowest price, they must sacrifice some aspect of quality. If they focus on high quality, they are vulnerable on price. If they focus on doing specific things extremely well, they perform a broad range of services poorly. If they focus on a broad range of services, they lose the ability to perfect any one of those services. If they emphasize standards and speed, they must de-emphasize customization and personal service.

Whatever competitors do well, they are leaving an opening for you to do the opposite. Instead of envying their strengths, you can turn those strengths into weaknesses. Their packaging is more professional? Aim for a more natural look. Everyone knows who they are? Emphasize that only the select few know to work with you. If competitors attempt everything, they will do everything poorly and they will leave openings everywhere.

The truth is that human needs and tastes are infinite. All supporters have unmet needs. Solving one set of needs creates another. You pick your opportunities to address unmet needs. All competitors offer specific solutions. They cannot satisfy every customer.

The Role of Focus

If you look for opportunities arising from a competitors' strengths, you work their blind spots. If you target more obvious weaknesses, your competitors are already working to address these shortcomings. Your competitors must not recognize the opening that you see as an opportunity. You don't want to pin your hopes on weaknesses that they plan to address. You want to use opportunities that they cannot address without undermining their strengths.

You must keep your desire to leverage their strengths against them a secret. You don't want them to recognize their strengths as weaknesses. Don't give your competitors any ideas. They will be confident in their strengths if you don't draw their attention.

As you move toward these positions, do it quietly without competitors noticing. Do not let your competitors know what you are up to. Keep quiet about what you are doing. Make sales quietly. Avoid the media. Communicate to supporters directly so your competitors can't make adjustments to your moves.

You want to be assured that those to whom you are compared are too distracted to care about winning the supporters you target. You also don't want them trying to win those supporters back before you make them yours. This means that you have to know where competitors are planning to move in the future. You should know what new positions they are developing and in which positions they plan to expand.

The new plans divert competitors' limited attention from their existing supporters. Where competitors divide their attention, they create openings. If you know where they are expanding, you also know who they are forgetting. Focus your venture on gaps in their attention.

When you focus on a small area to develop your position among a limited group of supporters, you concentrate your resources. You must focus all your efforts into areas competitors serve poorly. You can then put a lot of resources into areas where others have put few. You can easily do a better job there than your much larger competitors.

In business, for example, your competitor's problem customers are not your problem customers. People tend to avoid problems, especially other people's problems, but your competitors' problems are not your problems. A few of your competitors' problems are your opportunities.

Problems are created by unsatisfied needs. Unsatisfied needs are openings. They are the true emptiness that creates opportunities. Every one of those needs points to an opening, an opportunity. To be skilled in finding opportunities, you must search out problems that others have left unresolved.

We all know that success come from satisfying people's needs, but we still don't recognize the opportunities hidden in every problem. Just like people thoughtlessly miss opportunities by following the crowd, most people miss opportunities by avoiding problems.

How can you tell if a competitor's problem is your opportunity? You have to consider how well those unmet needs match your mission, your resources, and your time constraints. Competitors leave gaps in the market because they cannot do everything well. However, you cannot do everything well either. You want to aggressively fill the gaps that competitors leave when those gaps fit your own resources.

You must be selective about what opportunities you pursue. You want to ask yourself three questions. Does satisfying these unmet needs meet your organization's mission? How well does the problem space match your resources? Will you solve the problem first?

You develop a mission to help you select the opportunities. If you are true to your mission, you will become better and better at solving a particular kind of problems.

Resource fit combines your enterprise's skills with your excess capacity. Your enterprise must have the right amount of excess resources to address the size of the market. The type of barriers blocking the opening must be well suited to your personal skills and your enterprise's systems. You must be able to easily contact the market and provide it a solution. If you cannot do both, the resource fit is not right.

Your affinity and proximity to the problem must give you a first-mover advantage. The best preparation for winning a market position is getting to the market first. In some market spaces, this is the single most important issue.

If you get to a market first, then you have time to build up your position and lay traps for your competitors. Since they are playing catch-up, it is easy to exhaust your new competitors. You can drain rich competitors. You can even push around bigger competitors. Didn't I say that strategy was fun?

Learn from the history of successful ventures. Success goes to those who make progress easy. Your ideal customer is one who is inexpensive to win. You don't have to become famous to win new positions. You also don't have to take chances in winning supporters.

You must engage only in successful campaigns. Find supporters that you can easily satisfy. Never pass by an opening that makes competitors look bad.

If an opportunity doesn't really play to my strengths, can I develop new skills to take advantage of it?

If you cannot see an opening that clearly fit your abilities, you must not move. You cannot always find a new opportunity. They may be there, but if you don't see them, be patient. You will eventually discover new opportunities. Then you can advance.

You must only go after positions that you are sure you can win. Avoid positions that are too large for you to dominate. Go after positions that are small enough for you to fill completely. You must have the resources to campaign for these positions. Go after a position when you have an easy solution to the problem that shapes it. Avoid crowded environments. Look for positions where you have a first mover advantage. Until then, you must conserve your resources so that you have plenty of ammunition when the right opportunity appears.

You may see new positions that you would like to win. However, you may not see an affordable solution for those situations. This means the opportunity isn't quite right. You may see how to win new positions by spending a lot of money. This also shows that the problem is not an opportunity.

You want to move into new positions effortlessly. You must avoid risking your current positions. Wait for the right time to move. Don't try to be too clever. Learning about potential opportunities is easy if you listen to your contact network. Don't imagine opportunities where you want them.

Success only requires enough faith to believe that people have an endless supply of problems. You will eventually observe opportunities that you can win without effort. Avoid highly competitive situations. Invest resources only if it is clear that a market can be profitable. You will succeed if you avoid making hasty decisions.

You build a great organization by first finding the right supporters. Only then do you worry about investing resources. Find the right supporters for your position and then invest only in what you absolutely need to win them.

3.0.0 Identifying Opportunities

Description: Sun Tzu's five key methods regarding the use of opportunities to advance a position.

"You can recognize the opportunity for victory; you don't create it."

Sun Tzu's The Art of War 4:1:1

"The reason so many people never get anywhere in life is because when opportunity knocks, they are out in the backyard looking for four-leaf clovers."

Walter Percy Chrysler

General Principle: A strategic perspective requires systematically gathering outside opinions and facts.

Situation:

This problem is identifying opportunities. One of the most common strategic mistakes is thinking that we have to duplicate the strengths of others in order to be competitive. The race goes to the swiftest. To win, we must be the fastest. However, strategic contests are more complicated than contests of skill. In competitive positioning, we seldom find opportunities duplicating the success of others. The opposite, finding success by focusing on the weaknesses of others, is the general rule.

Opportunity:

In normal usage, we use the word "opportunity" to describe any situation that offers an advantage or a combination of favorable circumstances. In Sun Tzu's strategy, we use the term "opportunity" to specifically to describe an opening in the direction of our goal. If we think in terms of advancing our position, openings allow us to move forward easily. Like all of strategy, an opening arises from a simple comparison (1.3.1 Competitive Comparison). An opening represents a vacant position that is relatively better than our current one. That position must be "open" because we don't want to get into contests to take positions away from those who already control them. These conflicts of strength against strength are just too expensive (3.1.3 Conflict Cost).

Key Methods:

To find opportunities, we must understand what they are and how they are created. The most basic key methods are:

1. Strategic economics dictates pursuing openings in our environment. No position is perfect. Relatively better positions offer a better balance of costs and rewards. Openings reflect unfulfilled needs in the environment. There are many specific types of costs and rewards, but, by pursuing openings, we avoid the most predictable cost, that of conflict and pursue the most predictable source of reward, the needs of others (3.1.0 Strategic Economics).

2. Opportunities are constantly created and destroyed by the natural shifts in needs. Once an opening is filled, a need satisfied, the opportunity is no longer there but moves somewhere else.

Phases such as a "window of opportunity" express our common sense appreciation for this.

3. Opportunities are generated by the natural dynamics of the competitive environment. No one creates their own opportunities. All we can do is position ourselves correctly to be in the right place at the right time when openings occur. Opportunity creation follows a pattern. We learn to recognize where opportunities are being created (3.2 Opportunity Creation).

4. An opportunity is only an opportunity if we have the resources to pursue it. Pursuing opportunities without understanding the constraints of our limited can be extremely dangerous. All openings are opportunities for someone, but we are interesting only in openings that represent *our* opportunities (3.3 Opportunity Resources).

5. Large competitors create lots of opportunities smaller organizations. One of the most common reasons that we fail to recognize opportunities is that we tend to think of size as an advantage. Large organizations reshape the environment in ways that create openings and opportunities for smaller competitors. In competitive arenas, size advantages turn into weaknesses that we can exploit (3.4 Dis-Economies of Scale).

6. A strength or fullness in one area points to the opportunity in a corresponding weakness or emptiness in another. Nature abhors a vacuum. We think of this emptiness as an unfulfilled need. Needs are vacuums that want to be filled. The ideal battleground is one that is empty but needs to be filled because of the nature of the opening. The most non-intuitive principles in strategy relate to how this emptiness creates wealth and power (3.5 Strength and Weakness).

7. Opportunities are hard to see because they sit in gaps in our perception. We cannot see openings because there is nothing to see. We see success, but success is what happens when someone fills an opening. We develop mental models that allow us to see the gap between objective reality and our subjective impressions of it to find opportunities (3.6 Leveraging Subjectivity).

8. *We can discover opportunities by redefining the nature of the ground*. Competition is based on making comparisons. The problem is that there are just some types of comparisons in which we are never going to look as good as we can. How comparisons are made is based upon a subjective decision. This choice either divides one set of contestants or one set of judges from another. This choice defines the advantageous "battle ground" (3.7 Defining the Ground).

9. *We can see opportunities by mapping the five key elements*. There are many types of openings, but we miss many of our potential opportunities because we cannot "see" the concepts involved. Given the right techniques, we can map the five dimensions used in Sun Tzu's strategic analysis into a two-dimensional picture (3.8 Strategic Matrix Analysis).

10. Illustration:

Let us use some business examples from the Internet to illustrate what opportunities are.

1. *Strategic economics dictates pursuing openings in our environment*. Yahoo, Google, PayPal, YouTube, Twitter, and all the other Internet companies found needs that no one else had satisfied on the newly created ground of the web.

2. *Opportunities are constantly created and destroyed by the natural shifts in needs*. The advantage that newspapers held since the invention of the printing press faded as electronic media rose. It simply uses less resources to deliver news and information via the Internet. Google saw that the business advantage of the Internet was in advertising. As buyer's eyes moved from papers to the Internet, sellers needed advertising to reach them. Old media dies. New media is born. ***An opportunity is only an opportunity if we have the resources to pursue it.*** The old media didn't have the intellectual resources to provide their customers with an entry into the new media. Time/Warner saw the opportunity. Time/Warner tried to get into the Internet by purchasing AOL, but they lack the intellectual resources do master the new area. Google had the intellectual resources of a new search algorithm and was the first to connect advertising with searching. _**Large competitors create lots of opportunities smaller organizations.**_ The culture of a large media organizations didn't allow it to adapt to the rapidly changing environment of the internet. Time/Warner/AOL at legitimized the new media and created opportunities for much smaller competitors. Those competitors rose up to eventually swamp the much larger company.

3. A strength or fullness in one area points to the opportunity in a corresponding weakness or emptiness in another. The vast number of places offering text information on the Internet created

4. an opening for the video information provided by YouTube. The detailed information on the internet created a need for brief information more suitable to phones offered by Twitter. *Opportunities are hard to see because they sit in gaps in our perception.* In a retail environment, we see shopping and buying as the same general process. The difference between the two processes becomes clearer on the Internet. We shop to learn what we want. We buy to get the best price and service.

5. We can discover opportunities by redefining the nature of the ground. The division between shopping and buying has created a host of new opportunities for both shopping services where we learn, such as C/Net for information on electronics, and buying services where we save such as Amazon.

6. We can see opportunities by mapping the five key elements. Using the matrix analysis, we can see both where the various competitors on the Internet sit and where potential openings are. *Knowledge value and secrecy go hand in hand, both requiring the other.* We must know which information that we need to communicate to attract customers and which information we must keep secret to maintain a competitive advantage.

3.1.0 Strategic Economics

Description: Sun Tzu's six key methods balancing the cost and benefits of positioning.

"Many advantages add up to victory. Few advantages add up to defeat."

Sun Tzu's The Art of War 1:5:5-6

"Wise men profit more from fools than fools from wise men; for the wise men shun the mistakes of fools, but fools do not imitate the successes of the wise."

Cato the Elder

General Principle: We must engage in only productive moves not destructive ones.

Situation:

Sun Tzu's competitive strategy is based on simple economics. One of the most destructive human tendencies is our ability to mentally separate the advantages of a position from its disadvantages, its benefits from its costs. The wost aspect of this tendency making decision on the basis of benefits without concerning ourselves with costs. Sun Tzu uses positioning to avoid wars of attrition because such wars are costly and "winning" does not assure a real pay-off. Decisions have consequences and all decisions have costs. Even deciding not to act has costs, the costs of missing opportunity. Experience has shown that the most costly decisions of all are those that focus on only benefits.

Opportunity:

Sun Tzu's competitive methods teach us to make profitable decisions. These decisions consistently yield more benefits than their costs. This can be more difficult than it seems. We start with the habit of seeing costs and benefit as two sides of the same coin. This thinking is ingrained into aspects of Sun Tzu's system because of its basis on Yin-Yang Philosophy. We call this concept complementary opposites. It teaches that the real world situations exist as a balance of opposing forces (3.2.3 Complementary Opposites). In economics, balancing costs and benefits is considered the basis of rational thinking. We study Sun Tzu to make this approach instinctive so all decisions are automatically based upon the balance without conscious consideration.

Key Methods:

The economics of Sun Tzu's competitive strategy are based on six general key methods.

1. Strategic economics always looks at our resources as strictly limited. Our decisions must take into account and make the most of these limited resources. Our most limited is our time, which means that even delaying a decision has a cost (3.1.1 Resource Limitations).

2. Profitable strategic economics requires separating what is knowable and what is not. Some things we can know for certain, such as the fact that our resources are limited. Other things, such as likely responses, we can know only as probabilities. Other things are simply unknowable before we make a decision. Making profitable decisions requires clearly separating these various realms of knowledge (3.1.2 Strategic Profitability).

3. Strategic economics always sees the biggest source of certain costs as conflict. Conflict means moving directly against opposition, especially fighting with them for positions. Conflict is always costly. While winning through conflict can put us on top temporarily, it always weakens us. If we improved our position by making ourselves weaker, we only invite more attacks. We face an unending supply of potential rivals. If we try to maintain our position through conflict, any seeming victory is strictly temporary. While we cannot know its costs exactly, we can always know that conflict is more costly than avoiding conflict. This may be the most non-intuitive of Sun Tzu's key methods. This is why so many decisions lead to disaster (3.1.3 Conflict Cost).

4. Strategic economics always uses openings to avoid costly conflict. An opening is not only absence of opposition but an empty position that nature rewards us to fill. Staying on top requires that the environment itself support us. An opening is inexpensive for us to fill because it generates more resources than it consumes (3.1.4 Opposition Openings).

5. Strategic economics teaches that neither the cost nor the value of pursuing a given opportunity can be predicted precisely. This means that we must make mistakes in calculating strategic profitability. This means that *all* of our decisions must minimize costs, avoiding fatal errors that consume our resources. We cannot predict costs so we must control them (3.1.5 Economic Unpredictability).

6. Strategic economics insists that the ultimate economic restriction is always time. Our current position is our source of our resources. We need excess resources, more than what we need to maintain our position, to pursue new opportunities. How quickly we can and must act and how long a campaign we can entertain depend on those economics. The longer we wait to move, the more our existing position can degrade over time, producing diminishing resources. The more opportunities we miss by waiting, the less opportunities we have left in the future (3.1.6 Time Limitations).

Illustration:

We often compare good strategy to a game like Go rather than a game like chess. Chess is designed as a war of attrition, where victory goes to the last person standing. Go is a game of building up positions, where victory goes to the person who is the most efficient in building up his or her position over time.

1. *Strategic economics always looks at our resources as strictly limited.* In chess, we have a limited number of pieces. In GO, a limited number of places on the board. As pieces or positions are "consumed" we get no more of them.

2. *Profitable strategic economics requires separating what is knowable and what is not.* We can know the key methods for placing pieces. We can know what our opponent has done in the past. We cannot know what either our opponents will do in the future or how we will respond.

3. *Strategic economics always sees the biggest source of certain costs as conflict.* While both of these games force conflict because of their limitations, we constantly avoid conflict because we cannot exactly predict its results. In chess, a forced exchange of pieces changes the situation so much that it can have implications that are impossible for us to foresee. In GO, we waste positions by continually challenging an opponent's moves instead of building our own positions.

4. *Strategic economics always uses openings to avoid costly conflict.* In both chess and GO, the openings are moves that we can make without forcing conflict. In both games, good moves open up our position to more open moves while pinning down our opponents to fewer open moves.

5. *Strategic economics teaches that neither the cost nor the value of pursuing a given opportunity can be predicted precisely.* All the possible paths in the future are more than we can foresee. The number of possible moves in a single game of chess exceeds the number of particles in the universe.

6. *Strategic economics insists that the ultimate economic restriction is always time*. In any strategic games like Go or chess, the winner is always concerned about wasting moves. A wasted move is a move that can be easily reversed by an opponent. In the end, the winner is the player who makes the most moves advancing his or her position that cannot be reversed.

3.1.1 Resource Limitations

Description: Sun Tzu's six key methods regarding the inherent limitation of strategic resources.

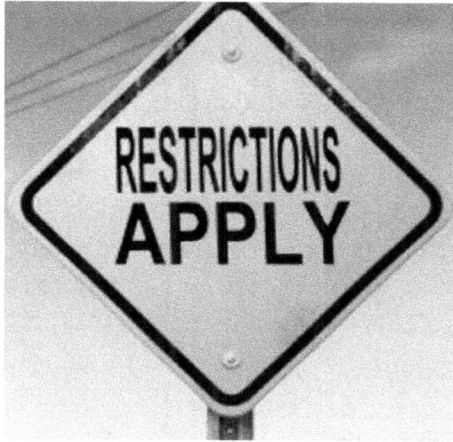

"If you exhaust your wealth, you then quickly hollow out your military."

Sun Tzu's The Art of War 2:3:5

"Genius has limitations; stupidity is boundless."

Anonymous

General Principle: Each of the five elements of a postition provides different resources and different limitations.

Situation:

Competitive decisions are choices about how to use limited resources. Our decisions often squander our limited resources. Most of us don't understand 1) what strategic resources are, 2) how they are limited, and 3) how they are consumed. Economic resources, such as money or property, make up only one of the five categories of strategic resources. Each category of resources is inherently limited, but they are limited in different ways. Some are consumed by using them. Others are multiplied by using them. Some are consumed by doing something. Others are consumed by doing nothing.

Opportunity:

When we understand the true nature of a strategic position, we get a much clearer understanding of what strategic resources are. Each of the five elements that makeup a position contributes a type of critical resource (1.3 Elemental Analysis). To understand our opportunities, we must see these resources more clearly, what these resources are and how they can be unintentionally wasted. Once we recognize their value, we are much more likely to protect our resources (1.1.2 Defending Positions). The mental models of strategy are devised to enable us to recognize not only the five major categories of resources but all their many different characteristics.

Key Methods:

We get our resources from our current position. Each of the five elements that define a position (mission, climate, ground, leader, and methods) define a different major category of resources. These resources are what we use to advance our position.

1. Values are the limited resources that we get from our mission. We need values to find supporters. Promoting goals and values that others cannot share destroys this resource. Our values allow us to join with others for our mutual benefit. We must choose one set of values. To do that, we must reject other sets of values. The refusal to choose values is the rejection of all values (1.6 Mission Values).

2. Limited temporary resources come from the climate aspect of our climate position. The key temporary resources are time and trends. All temporary resources expire over time. We are limited to only 24 hours in a day, but we use them up each day no matter what we do. Temporary resources are easier to waste because they expire simply by not using them. The problem with killing time is that it will kill us right back (1.4.1 Climate Shift).

3. Limited physical resources are what we get from our ground position. These include both our economic and social resources. Our material resources are limited. We can only have so much money, space, and connections with others. The ground offers a tremendous variety of resources, but they are all limited because we control limited ground ((1.4.2 Ground Features).

4. Limited character resources come from our decision-making capabilities. Strategy defines five types of character resources--courage, discipline, trustworthiness, caring, and intelligence. While all these reservoirs of character are limited, we need these limitations of character. The danger in terms of decision making in an excess of resources in these five areas. Too much courage leads to foolhardiness. Too much discipline to rigidity. (1.5.1 Command Leadership).

5. Limited skills and reputation are the resources we get from methods. Skill and reputation are just the objective and subjective sides of the same coin. No one can know how to do everything. However, unlike other resources, the more we use our skills and reputations, the more of them we develop. Their limitations come from outside. Our values, time, ground, character limit the type and number of skills we can master. Working outside of those limitations is costly and dangerous (1.5.2. Group Methods).

6. *No matter how many resources we have, the environment always has incalculably more.* People together are always much more powerful than individuals. All the resources of the most powerful person in the world are minuscule when compared with the power of the world as a whole. If we do not leverage our resources with opportunities created by the environment, those resources are wasted. One of the reasons that we seek to advance our position is to increase our resources, but no matter how far we advance, our resources are still limited and still insignificant in terms of controlling the environment as a whole, but more resources allow us to extend our control further and further (3.2.1 Environmental Dominance).

Illustration:

Let us look at the problem with limitations of resources from the aspect of someone pursuing a career in sports.

1. Values are the limited resources that we get from our mission. If a player thinks more of his or her own success and stats than the success of the team, their support within the team will decline.

2. Limited temporary resources come from the climate aspect of our climate position. As a player gets older, their abilities can grow or decline depending how they use their time, but no matter what they do, their careers are limited in terms of their ability to play the game.

3. Limited physical resources are what we get from our ground position. A player's natural physical abilities come from the nature of their body but those skills no matter how great are limited in many ways. Also, no matter how much money a player makes, he or she can still get into financial trouble.

4. Limited character resources come from our decision-making capabilities. A player with all the physical abilities in the world can get into trouble because of character flaws. Those flaws affect his or her decisions on and off the field.

5. Limited skills and reputation are the resources we get from methods. A player can master new skills as time goes on. A player with the right character and use of their time, can move from playing to coaching.

6. *No matter how many resources we have, the environment always has incalculably more.* The greatest player in history is eventually overshadowed by a newer player. Time provides a steady stream of new players and eventually one of them will surpass any past player in any given category (unless the games changes beyond comparison).

3.1.2 Strategic Profitability

Description: Sun Tzu's nine key methods for understanding gains and losses.

"Make no assumptions about all the dangers in using military force. Then you won't make assumptions about the benefits of using arms either."
Sun Tzu's The Art of War 2:2:1

"The best plan is to profit by the folly of others."
Pliny The Elder

General Principle: All key principles focus on making our average decisions profitable.

Situation:

Competition is uncertain and difficult. In competition, our resources are always limited. Running out of resources is fatal. We can know neither the costs nor benefits of a given move before we make it. Because of the uncertainties involved, we do know that every move will have costs and not all our moves will generate benefits. Many moves will consume more resources than they generate. We are taught in school that events can be foreseen and actions planned, but the predictability of plans are very different in a controlled environment than in a competitive environment. This mindset that assumes that the profitability of our actions can be predicted exactly is not only wrong but it can be fatal.

Opportunity:

Sun Tzu's The Art of War was the first work to recognize that success is always based on relatively simple economics. In modern science, the concept of strategic profitability is known as Minimax Theory , which is used in decision theory , game theory , statistics , philosophy. The idea is minimizing the possible loss while maximizing the potential gain. From the perspective of the competitive strategist and, fortunately for us all, the Sun Tzu's minimax model is much simpler than the one used in traditional game theory. It requires no math. It requires mastering only a few key principles. We don't worry about calculating only about minimizing and maximizing. We compare probabilities. We worry about time.

Key Methods:

To make profitable decisions, each of the nine formulas of Sun Tzu's system are all based about a profit strategy:

1. Understand the difference between competition, battle, fighting, and conflict. These four terms are used interchangeably in casual conversation, but we require more precise definitions so we can understand what is necessary and what is not.

- *Competition* is a comparison of alternatives positions of opponents.
- *Battle* is a meeting of potential opponents where positions are compared.
- *F ighting* is expending resources to overcome a challenge.

- *Conflict* is the attempt to damage our opposition so we can take their position. Conflict is a meeting, i.e, battle, that requires resources, i.e, a fight, but it has the specific goal of hurting opponents enough so that they will surrender a position to us.

2. All competition requires battles. Since all all competition is a comparison, such meetings are eventually necessary. By this definition, every buying decisions and sporting event is a battle, a situation where alternatives are compared. (1.3.1 Competitive Comparison)

3. B*oth advancing and defending our position requires various types of fights.* In other words, we must always use resources to overcome challenges. Battles are just one type of fight. There are many types of fights such as overcoming barriers in moving to a new position. Facing challenges and the use of resources are equally unavoidable (3.1.1 Resource Limitations).

4. All conflict is the result of a miscalculation. Conflict doesn't occur unless both parties think they can triumph. Opponent will always surrender or evade a battle rather than enter into costly conflict that they know that they will certainly lose. The problem is that, because of our limited information, we naturally over estimate our own advantages and underestimate those of our opponents. Conflict (2.1.1 Information Limits).

5. Conflict is always unnecessary. There are an infinite number of opportunities that exist as unfilled positions that others desire to be filled. Conflict results from the mistake of zero-sum thinking, that we can only advance our position by taking someone else's position away. The environment is continually creating new opportunities as new needs (3.2 Opportunity Creation).

6. Conflict always creates costs. The specific problem with our trying to damage opponents is that opponents must defend themselves. When two opponents fight each other, both are diminished by the effort, losing resources that could be better utilized by finding other ways to advance their position. Since both positions are damaged, creating opportunities for others outside of the battle. Since defending a position is always less expensive than attacking it, this is most costly way of trying to advance a position (1.1.2 Defending Positions).

Illustration:

Let us look at these key methods in terms of business conflict. In business, battling over customers is never profitable, even if we win them. Whenever two businesses get into, for example, a price war, we can predict that the most likely outcome is that both will end up losing profits. For decades a whole series of companies battled IBM for dominance in the mainframe computer industry. None of them were successful and their investors lost a staggering amount of money. Then a series of companies challenged Microsoft only to fail. Now the same thinking causes people to want to challenge Google directly in the search engine business.

Let us look at the specific battles of Microsoft and Apple over computers and MP3 players.

1. Understand the difference between competition, battle, fighting, and conflict. All businesses compete because their products are compared with other alternative uses of money. Apple and Microsoft will always compete.

2. All competition requires battles. A business battle occurs at every point of sale, when the customer makes a decisions to buy one product instead of another. The computer store is a battlefield.

3. B*oth advancing and defending our position requires various types of fights.* Businesses such as Microsoft and Apple fight by spending money on advertising, merchandising, product development, etc. These fights don't become conflict until one competitor starts attacking the other.

4. All conflict is the result of a miscalculation. Conflict only occurs when one company tries to take away another's customers by positioning their products as a direct replacement for the products of others. Recording artists compete with each other without conflict in selling their music, but Microsoft and Apple engage in conflict in their sales of computers and MP3 players.

5. Conflict is always unnecessary. Most customers of Microsoft and Apple but their different products for very different reasons, but rather than go after different customers, Microsoft and Apple choose to go after conflicting markets.

6. Conflict always creates costs. These battles have cost both companies but both are profitable that they think that they can afford the luxury.

3.1.3 Conflict Cost

Description: Sun Tzu's six key methods on the costly nature of resolving competitive comparisons by conflict.

"You must avoid disasters from armed conflict."
Sun Tzu's The Art of War 7:1:5

"We must work to resolve conflicts in a spirit of reconciliation and always keep in mind the interests of others. We cannot destroy our neighbors! We cannot ignore their interests! Doing so would ultimately cause us to suffer."
Dalai Lama

General Principle: The biggest and most certain source of costs in advancing a position is conflict.

Situation:

Conflict defines wars of attrition. In such wars, the party that sustains the least damage is the technical winner. The problem is that, according to the economics of strategy, both parties in a conflict are much more likely to be losers in the long-term. These Pyrrhic victories occur when winning the battle costs us our success over the longer term. These "victories" cost much more than any benefit that we can ever hope to win from them.

Opportunity:

We avoid conflict not out of altruism but for the pragmatic reason that that success is much more likely without it. Strategy is the economics of advancing our position and in that economics, conflict is simply too costly (3.1 Strategic Economics). When competition is properly understood, we can advance our position while avoiding all the costs of competition. Competition is always a comparison (1.3.1 Competitive Comparison). We do not have to damage our opponents in order to come out on top in that comparison. The ideal position is one that others do not want to attack and ideally want to join. Correctly understood competition embraces cooperation because allies support our position. Conflict, not competition, is the opposite of cooperation.

Key Methods:

Our strategy is to meet a potential opponents under the right conditions so that we can win battles and even fights without conflict. This means that we can win the competition, i.e. comparison, without having to damage our opponents to demonstrate our superiority.

1. Understand the difference between competition, battle, fighting, and conflict. These four terms are used interchangeably in casual conversation, but we require more precise definitions so we can understand what is necessary and what is not.

- ***Competition*** is a comparison of alternatives positions of opponents.
- ***Battle*** is a meeting of potential opponents where positions are compared.
- ***F ighting*** is expending resources to overcome a challenge.

- *Conflict* is the attempt to damage our opposition so we can take their position. Conflict is a meeting, i.e, battle, that requires resources, i.e, a fight, but it has the specific goal of hurting opponents enough so that they will surrender a position to us.

2. All competition requires battles. Since all all competition is a comparison, such meetings are eventually necessary. By this definition, every buying decisions and sporting event is a battle, a situation where alternatives are compared. (1.3.1 Competitive Comparison)

3. B*oth advancing and defending our position requires various types of fights.* In other words, we must always use resources to overcome challenges. Battles are just one type of fight. There are many types of fights such as overcoming barriers in moving to a new position. Facing challenges and the use of resources are equally unavoidable (3.1.1 Resource Limitations).

4. All conflict is the result of a miscalculation. Conflict doesn't occur unless both parties think they can triumph. Opponent will always surrender or evade a battle rather than enter into costly conflict that they know that they will certainly lose. The problem is that, because of our limited information, we naturally over estimate our own advantages and underestimate those of our opponents. Conflict (2.1.1 Information Limits).

5. Conflict is always unnecessary. There are an infinite number of opportunities that exist as unfilled positions that others desire to be filled. Conflict results from the mistake of zero-sum thinking, that we can only advance our position by taking someone else's position away. The environment is continually creating new opportunities as new needs (3.2 Opportunity Creation).

6. Conflict always creates costs. The specific problem with our trying to damage opponents is that opponents must defend themselves. When two opponents fight each other, both are diminished by the effort, losing resources that could be better utilized by finding other ways to advance their position. Since both positions are damaged, creating opportunities for others outside of the battle. Since defending a position is always less expensive than attacking it, this is most costly way of trying to advance a position (1.1.2 Defending Positions).

Illustration:

Let us apply these nine key methods to the simple and common goal of making more money in a career to see how they change the nature of the challenge.

1. ***Our profit strategy starts by advancing our goals by finding more profitable positions.*** Instead of working harder or even smarter to get more money, look for ways to advance your position.

2. ***Our profit strategy relies on leveraging knowledge being less costly than using physical resources***. Learning more about the job market and employers is less costly than going to more interviews.

3. ***Our profit strategy utilizes "openings" to reduce the costs of advancing a position***. Find positions that are looking for applicants instead of positions that have more than they need.

4. ***Our profit strategy finds the openings most likely to produce profits based on our current position***. Look for positions that are connected to your current situation through people, skills, or intellectual topography.

5. ***Our profit strategy uses many small moves rather than a few large ones to reduce cost and risk.*** Do not look to find a perfect position but a position that allows you to gradually improve your position little-by-little.

6. ***Our profit strategy uses proven responses to increase the percentage of successful moves***. Know the common challenges you will face in getting promotions and be prepared with the right responses.

7. ***Our profit strategy creates momentum to reduce the costly friction in establishing a position***. Build up tension and use surprises to release it to break down the usual resistance to promotions.

8. *Our profit strategy maximizes benefits by knowing the steps needed get the most rewards out of a move.* Continually package and repackage the benefits that you offer others in expanding your ground.

9. *Our profit strategy defends rewarding positions because defense is less expensive than offense.* Always defend your current job situation before attempting to find a better one.

3.1.4 Openings

Description: Sun Tzu's seven key methods on seeking openings avoids costly conflict.

Advance where he can't defend.
Charge through his openings.

Sun Tzu's The Art of War 6:3:6-7

"A good deal happens in a man's life that he isn't responsible for. Fortunate openings occur; but it is safe to remember that such "breaks" are occurring all the time, and other things being equal, the advantage goes to the man who is ready."

Lawrence Downs

General Principle: Advance positions by using openings to avoid costly conflict.

Situation:

Competition seeks rewards. Rewards come from positions that control ground. Conflict is a mistake based on two misconceptions. The first is that there is only a finite amount of ground. The second is that existing ground can yield only a limited amount of rewards. If the ground and its resources are limited, conflict is unavoidable.

As the number of people increase, they can only win rewards by taking from others. This would mean that the costs of conflict are also unavoidable and that all of humanity is locked into a war of attrition in which we all must grow poorer protecting what we have. Sun Tzu taught that this viewpoint was simply wrong.

Opportunity:

Sun Tzu taught that the ground as the stable source of rewards is infinite. He also taught that the climate as the changing source of opportunities is also infinite. Sun Tzu predicted that we would never run short of new, valuable ground. If he could see this truth from an agrarian culture 2,500 years ago, why do we still have problems seeing it today when the hottest real estate is the brand new terrain of the Internet? Sun Tzu recognized that the value of the ground came only from our knowledge about how to use it. As our knowledge grows, new resources become available from new types of ground. The only key resource is the human mind and its ability to learn.

Key Methods:

Conflict avoidance leads directly to the deeper lessons of strategy, especially a deeper understanding of the nature of positions and opportunities. Understood correctly, we can advance our positions in any direction. Once we stop focusing on what others have, there are undiscovered opportunities all around us. The wisest way to direct our energies is to look for rewards in areas where we have no opposition.

1. Opportunities exist as empty positions?openings?not positions that are already taken. We move into openings. We must especially avoid areas that are crowded with potential competitors. The conflict model of strategy focuses us on our perceived opponents instead of the larger environment where our opportunities lie. While we must be aware of our opponent's position in the environment, we use that awareness to help us identify where our opportunities might lie (1.3.1 Competitive Comparison).

2. Openings exists both in physical space and the psychological landscape in people minds. Positions always have both a physical and psychological dimension. When new physical ground is opened by discoveries, new psychological ground is always opened as well. Strategy works on both levels but it often focuses on the less visible psychological dimensions because its importance is easily missed (1.2 Subobjective Positions).

3. The easiest way to find psychological openings is to look for unsatisfied needs. Success means making victory pay and nothing pays better than satisfying people's needs. As we cannot say too often, a successful position is one that others cannot attack and ideally want to join. The power of looking for openings as needs is that it moves us away from conflict with others and into areas where we can win people's support (2.3 Personal Interactions).

4. There are an infinite number of potential open positions in the environment. The ground is unlimited because the knowledge that opens new ground is unlimited. Psychological ground is infinite because human needs are infinite. As soon as one need is filled, another one opens up. No matter how dominant our opponents are, they always leave plenty of openings for us to exploit. The future is not predictable because no one can know all the forms opportunity can take in the future (2.1.2 Leveraging Uncertainty

5. Openings leverage the forces of the environment to work for us rather than against us. Nature abhors a vacuum. By seeing opportunities as openings in the larger environment, we leverage the natural forces in the environment that are seeking to fill that opening. This is particularly easy when we are working on the psychological level of people's unfulfilled needs. People reward us to fill their needs (3.2.1 Environmental Dominance).

6. Our discovery of new ground is limited only by our imagination. Our creative ability is the source of discovery. Innovation creates new methods. New methods opens new ground. This is what Sun Tzu refers to as "surprise" in the quote. Creativity is not a rare skill, but a task that we can learn to do in a systematic way (<u>7.3 Strategic Innovation</u>).

7. Creatively using openings takes control from our opponents. When we fight over existing ground, we put our opponents in control of our situation. When we explore new ground, we take the initiative away from our opponents. The creative approach to opportunities puts us in control of our own position and situation. The more inventive we are in creating our own position, the less competition that we have. As we advance our position by exploring new ground, we gain greater and greater control over time. The idea that creativity creates momentum is one of the major principles of strategy (<u>7.0 Creating Momentum</u>).

Illustration:

This idea of openings exists in every competitive arena, but it is especially easy to see it in high-technological businesses since their very existence is based on it.

1. Opportunities exist as empty positions, i.e. openings, not positions that are already taken. It wasn't the companies that challenged IBM in the mainframe industry who became the new leaders in hi-tech. They all lost money. From Microsoft to Google, the winners are those who found open positions and developed them.

2. Openings exists both in physical space and the psychological landscape in people minds. When a new technological world like the Internet is opened up, our minds start immediately to populate it with the names of the companies and products. The map of the terrain isn't only the technological products themselves but how we place them in relationship to each other.

3. The easiest way to find psychological openings is to look for unsatisfied needs. As the Internet grew, searching it became the dominant need for users but advertising became the dominating need for providers. While others addressed each of these needs separately, Google brought them together.

4. There are an infinite number of potential open positions in the environment. Technology will open new areas like the Internet and new companies will arise to fill the needs in those areas.

5. Openings leverage the forces of the environment to work for us rather than against us. Companies such as Amazon and Ebay grow without even having to advertise because their users promote their products.

6. Our discovery of new ground is limited only by our imagination. We cannot even imagine the products of the future because the pioneers are so far ahead of us.

7. Creatively using openings takes control from our opponents. Apple's computers are doing better than ever but their success is driven by the iPod, a product that took Apple entirely away from the competitive fray.

3.1.5 Unpredictable Value

Description: Sun Tzu's seven key methods regarding the limitations of predicting the value of positions.

"Keep your army moving and plan for surprises."
Sun Tzu's The Art of War 11:3:8

"Greatness is a road leading towards the unknown."
Charles de Gaulle

General Principle: The cost and value of positions is unpredictable before exploration.

Situation:

Since strategy is the economics of advancing a position, moving into unoccupied and unexplored territory carries its own risk. When it comes to dealing with the unknown, there are two bad assumptions that we can make. Both lead to dangerous mistakes. First, we can think that because no one is currently occupying a position, there is no value to that position. This leads to conflict. The opposite mistake is to think that every open territory is valuable, some kind of gold mine. This leads to another costly mistake: our waste of limited resources.

Opportunity:

We avoid these mistakes by avoiding assumptions. We accept our ignorance about new territory (2.1.1 Information Limits). We avoid conflict and waste by refusing to make assumptions about the costs or potential value of a given opening. Imagination is a wonderful thing but it is a double-edged sword. While it requires imagination to see our opportunities, we have to be careful not to imagine what we cannot know: the potential profitability of a new position. We cannot advance our position without faith and optimism, but, since we are exploring new territory, we must balance our faith and optimism with methods that avoid disaster (5.0 Minimizing Mistakes).

Key Methods:

Opportunities represent the *potential* for rewards, but what do we know for certain about openings? We must understand the natural limits of the potential profitability of a move before we make it.

1. We know that openings offer no apparent direct opposition. This means that they are potentially less costly to explore than moving against occupied positions. This could be a relative advantage, but, while *seeming* empty, these positions may not actually *be* empty. As we move into them, others can be drawn to them as well. This fact forms the basis of a very common strategic situation (6.4.3 Contentious Situations).

2. Knowing that an opening exists doesn't tell us anything of its value. Open ground is not necessarily valuable ground. When we move to unoccupied positions, we must admit that we know nothing about either the cost of exploring those positions or their potential value. We know that exploring openings is less expensive than conflict, but lower costs do not mean making profit. To make a profit, the position must produce value. We cannot know that. This uncertainty is the main reason that people make the mistake of pursuing occupied positions. We know what those positions are worth. Their value has already been proven (3.1.2 Strategic Profitability).

*3. **We cannot extrapolate from the known into the unknown.** Unexplored positions will be similar to nearby positions in some ways and different in other ways. The problem is that we cannot know in which ways they will be similar and in which ways they will be different. Our fears project the worst into the unknown while our hopes project the best but neither brings us nearer the truth (2.1.1 Information Limits).*

*4. **Knowing probabilities is not the same as knowing actualities**. We can know what areas are **likely** to have relatively lower costs and high rewards but this doesn't tell us the real value of any opportunity. We must make decisions about where to explore based on these probabilities but even the highest probability gamble is still a gamble. Those who treat a gamble as if it was a sure thing are soon out of the game (4.0 Leveraging Probability).*

*5. **We have to go to a place to know a place.** Absence is the ultimate barrier to knowledge. We only get solid information about the cost and value of positions by exploring them. Since by definition no one is occupying an empty position, we cannot get information about it from anyone else. Until we make the trip, we are savages looking up at the moon and guessing what it might be like. This is why it is always necessary to make a move (5.6.2 Acting Now).*

*6. **The only value we are assured is that of more information**. The goal is experimentation and exploration. The competitive world is a maze and many of its branches are dead-ends. When we explore a dead end, we get a little better picture of our situation. We want to make as few wrong turns as possible but when we make a wrong turn, we must learn from it. Each piece of the puzzle helps us put together the big picture (2.5 The Big Picture).*

*7. **We cannot deem exploration a mistake on the basis of knowledge gained from it**. Even though many of our explorations will prove to be fruitless, we can only get that information from making the journey.*

Illustration:

We are going to illustrate these principles with a discussion about the value of the Iraq war in terms of costs and benefits. Though this illustration may prove to be controversial, it is an extremely good example of economic unpredictability.

1. We know that openings offer no apparent direct opposition. It was assumed that after the mission was accomplished in deposing Saddam, that Iraq would be an open for the creation of a Arab democracy, but that opening attracted opposition that raised the costs dramatically.

2. Knowing that an opening exists doesn't tell us anything of its real value. Even though the costs of the opposition are largely behind us, we still do not know if the democracy in Iraq is yielding any benefits. There appears to be a movement toward democracy in the region, but even the future of Iraq in that regard is uncertain.

3. We cannot extrapolate from the known into the unknown. Iraq is different than building democracies in post-war Europe or Japan, but we cannot yet know how it is different.

4. Knowing probabilities is not the same as knowing actualities. We knew that Saddam probably had weapons of mass destruction because he had had them in the past, but we did not know anything about the real nature of his capabilities at the time of the invasion. We especially did not know about the nuclear proliferation program out of Pakistan that was active not only in Iraq, but Syria, Libya, and Iran.

5. We have to go to a place to know a place. We turned over a rock and instead of finding the expected scorpion of chemical and biological weapons we found a much more deadly snake nest of Pakistani nuclear proliferation.

6. The only value we are assured is that of more information. Knowledge helps, but it is what we do with it that matters. Knowing about the nuclear proliferation helped put an end to it in Libya and Syria, but Iran still hasn't been dealt with.

*7. **We cannot deem exploration a mistake on the basis of knowledge gained from it**. To attack the war in Iraq because we didn't find the **expected** weapons of mass destruction makes no sense because we couldn't have know what weapons were there without the war itself. We cannot criticize our ignorance by saying that that ignorance didn't justify the actions that were the only possible way of ending that same ignorance.

3.1.6 Time Limitations

Description: Sun Tzu nine key methods for understanding the time limits on opportunities.

"Each day passes quickly.
A month can decide your failure or success."
Sun Tzu's The Art of War 6:8:15

""Four things come not back: the spoken word, the sped arrow, the past life and the neglected opportunity."
Arabian Proverb

General Principle: The time limitations of opportunities depend on economics.

Situation:

People inherently realize that all opportunities are temporary. We talk about "windows of opportunity" opening up and then closing. Because only our environment creates opportunities and is always changing, the temporary nature of opportunities is unavoidable. However, these basic ideas tell us very little about how to recognize whether an opportunity is waxing or waning.

Opportunity:

The temporary nature of opportunities evolves from economics (3.1 Strategic Economics). There is an economic life cycle in which opportunities emerge, mature, and eventually disappear. We define nine stages in this life-cycle that follow the nine stages of a campaign (6.4 Nine Situations). Once we master these stages, we can pretty quickly get a fix on where a given opportunity is in its evolution and what the best strategy is for exploring it (6.3 Campaign Patterns).

Key Methods:

The cycle of an opportunity starts in ignorance. In the beginning, people can know neither the location of an opportunity nor if it is valuable nor the method for exploiting it nor the size of the opportunity. As the opportunity is explored, all four of these areas--location, value, methods, and size--are resolved through the economic life cycle. In the beginning of this cycle, the opening is the greatest but the rewards are the least certain since so much is unknown. However, those who get into this cycle at the earlier stages always have a first mover advantage over those who come later. The ability to survive one stage and make it to the next depends upon understanding what each situation requires.

1. The climate changes, creating new open ground, but no one sees it. This is the first stage during which location of the opportunity is unknown. People fight over what they can see instead of going into the new area that is as yet invisible (3.2.2 Opportunity Invisibility).

2. A few innovators see the opportunity and start exploring it. At this stage, these early explorers don't know whether or not the ground is valuable. Early exploration simply looks for value. This is the easiest stage because few competitors are involved and the opportunity is still wide open (6.4.2 Easy Situations).

3. *The ground proves valuable and more are drawn to it.* If an opening does not prove valuable, it is no longer an opportunity. If early explorations do discover value, others will find out about it and be drawn to the opportunity. The increase of people exploring the ground increases the potential for conflict even though the method and size of the ground are not yet know (6.4.3 Contentious Situations).

4. *Different people explore different methods to make the new ground rewarding.* This is the stage in which people begin to explore different methods for getting rewards out of an opportunity. At this stage, no one knows the best method or even if there is any one best method. They look for different paths for controlling the ground but keep an eye on what others are doing in the area, trying to keep pace with them (6.4.4 Open Situations).

5. *A single best method emerges and people compete for control.* At this stage, location, value, and methods of the ground have been proven. The remaining issue is the size of the opportunity and how many people will share in controlling it. Competitors now look to put together dominating positions in competition with each other. This is the end of the opportunity for those who are not already in contention (6.4.5 Intersecting Situations).

6. *Economics begins to squeeze out competitors*. At this stage, those exploring an opportunity must become self-funded from within the opportunity itself. Outside funding for exploration dries up as the leaders emerge in the previous stage. Those who remain are those who are supporting themselves from their positions within the new area of opportunity (6.4.6 Serious Situations).

7. *The size limits of the opportunity are reached.* Some ground never reaches this stage because new areas off of it keep opening up, but most areas have limits. This stage marks another point at which the opportunity is fading. At this stage, a few dominate players have positions controlling all the valuable ground. The situation shifts from a true opportunity to a local zero-sum game. This is the end of the growth phase and the beginning of a contraction phase. Competitive skills begin to become less important than production skills (6.4.7 Difficult Situations).

8. *The climate begins to shift, and profitability diminishes*. At this stage, the opportunity reaches a point of diminishing returns. In the previous phase, conflict became more likely, but now it becomes a matter for survival. As the size of the competitive area itself begins to shrink in an absolute sense with the changes in climate, competitors are forced into conflict, destroying the profitability of the ground (6.4.8 Limited Situations).

9. *The ground is no longer profitable*. This is the final stage. It is reached when the cost of maintaining a position on the ground outweighs its value. If this point is reached, the ground must be abandoned. Those occupying it are forced to find new positions elsewhere. The ground is returned to its original empty state (6.4.9 Desperate Situations).

Illustration:

Let us follow this life cycle through a technology that has come and gone, that of traditional "mainframe" computers for data-processing.

1. *The climate changes, creating new open ground, but no one sees it*. This is the era of mechanical machines that are limited to doing mechanical mathematical calculations but not data processing. IBM was a maker of such mechanical adding machines.

2. *A few innovators see the opportunity and start exploring it*. The work in WWII on early computers makes it appear that something is practical but IBM says the market is limited to perhaps six such machines in the world.

3. *The ground proves valuable and more are drawn to it*. More than six machines are sold and more and more companies are drawn to the market as more and more people see its potential. ***Different people explore different methods to make the new ground rewarding.*** Many different types of architectures and designs are tried as issues regarding memory, storage, and programming are addressed.

4. A single ***best method emerges and people compete for control.*** Standard architectures and languages emerge. Companies begin to vie for dominance with IBM coming out on top. ***Economics begins to squeeze out competitors***. Companies that invested large amounts in trying to establish a mainframe business such as Sperry Rand with Univac cannot make it pay and begin to drop out in the 50s.

5. ***The size limits of the opportunity are reached.*** While the limits of computing were not reached, the limits of mainframe architecture were. Because of their cost, only certain organizations were able to support them. IBM and two or three other companies control the market.

6. ***The climate begins to shift, and profitability diminishes***. Mainframes started to be replaced first by minicomputers and then networks of servers. The cost of building and supporting the traditional architecture, operating systems, and languages begins to outweigh their value.

7. ***The ground is no longer profitable***. The traditional mainframe fades away and IBM becomes primarily a service company.

3.2 Opportunity Creation

Description: Five key methods regarding how change creates opportunities.

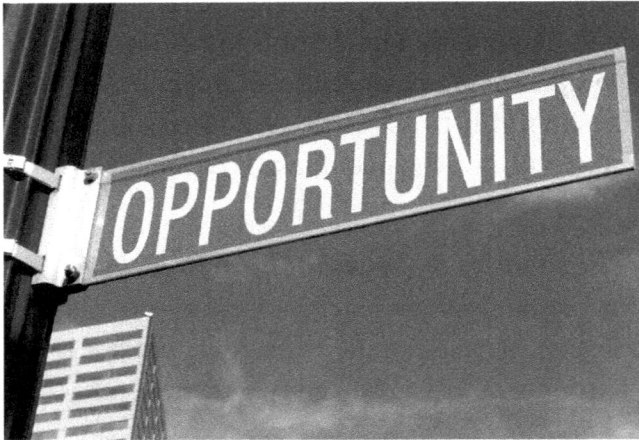

"Know when the terrain is open."
Sun Tzu's The Art of War 11:1:5

"There exist limitless opportunities in every industry. Where there is an open mind, there will always be a frontier."
Charles Kettering

General Principle: Opportunities are created by the natural forces of desire.

Situation:

Our world consists of 6 billion people constantly shifting through a rapidly changing kaleidoscope of actions, encounters, plans, and desires. Each competitive arena plays a part in this turbulent dance and cannot be separated from it. Larger and tiny opportunities are constantly arising and disappearing in this rich bubbling stew, but predicting where these opportunities will arise and where they will go seems impossible. This turbulence of change is both frightening and enticing. It threatens our current position at the same time it offers the possibility of improving it. We want to ride these changes, but they are always different, their paths seem random, and our encounters with them largely a matter of chance.

Opportunity:

Opportunity is created by two opposing natural processes. On one side, nature abhors a vacuum. On the other, dynamic environments continually create openings (3.1.4 Openings). We leverage nature's "desire" to fill openings by advancing our position into these openings. These forces continually degrade existing positions while continually creating new opportunities. Joseph Schumpeter called this process "creative destruction" (1.8.1 Creation and Destruction). The more dynamic the environment, the more opportunities it creates, but the shorter the life-span of any existing position.

Key Methods:

Nature's desire to fill a vacuum is echoed in our human desires. While we can occasionally leverage physical open spaces, we usually use the openings of need and desire. We all have unfulfilled desires. As one desire is met, another desire takes its place. While we can complain about this "greed," it is an unchanging force of nature. Even those who are quick to criticize the selfish desires of others do so because they desire to control others based on a "common good" that only reflects their selfish desires.

We need a powerful set of mental models to help us understand this complex interplay of often conflicting desires. It is the general key methods of change driven by complementary opposites and the specific principles of opportunity.

1. Only *the environment creates the openings of opportunity.* Nature gives us certain resources but creates the need in us for other resources. Trying to create our own opportunities is a waste of our effort because they come from within other people. We do not create the needs of others any more than we create our own needs. We cannot advance our position unless others support us. People do not support us unless they desire to do so. We are only rewarded for satisfying the needs of others (3.2.1 Environmental Dominance).

2. *Opportunities are difficult to see because they are empty.* We can see exchanges, when people are rewarded for satisfying needs, but new opportunities that no one is satisfying is nearly impossible to see. Emptiness is invisible. There are small openings all around us, but we usually cannot see them because we are too occupied with our own larger desires to notice the minor desires of others around us (3.2.2 Opportunity Invisibility).

3. *Opportunity exists in the potential of balancing of opposites.* This balance is easier to see as an exchange of resources. We trade what we have in abundance for what we lack. This is how value is created: a surplus in one place is exchanged for a different surplus somewhere else in the environment. This exchange is motivated solely by need but is possible because people have different needs and different resources that complement each other. Value is created by putting these complementary resources where they are the *most* needed. Our positions enable these exchanges of complementary opposites (3.2.2 Complementary Opposites).

4. *All opportunities can be described in terms of emptiness and fullness.* There are a million different forms of need. Each need requires different resources, but the general principle is that desire and resources are always balancing. Emptiness describes any state of need or lack of resources. Fullness is its opposite, a state of satiety and a surplus of resources. Both states are temporary, where one must give way to the other over time, creating one another in a constant cycle. The advantage in seeing the world as a cycle of emptiness and fullness is that it simplifies that kaleidoscope of different needs into just two possible states (3.2.3 Emptiness and Fullness).

5. *Abundance suddenly reverses into new forms of need*. New needs emerge not from an accumulation of older needs but from the satisfaction of need. Abundance arises because we improve the exchanges that move resources to where they are needed. This abundance provides the resources for addressing existing needs, but in doing so, always creates new types of needs, often spilling over into entirely unforeseen areas of desire. Another way of saying this is that desire is an emergent property of abundance (3.2.5 Dynamic Reversal).

Illustration:

Let us consider how the opportunity for manufacturing, selling, and using MP3 players was created.

1. *Only the environment creates opportunity because need arises from nature*. If the enjoyment of music was not born within us, the MP3 player would not exist. If we didn't desire more music in more places at more times, we wouldn't want MP3 players.

2. *Opportunities are difficult to see because they are empty*. The advantages of music in a digital form instead of a physical form was difficult for people to understand until they were exposed to it over time and is still very difficult for the music industry.

3. *Opportunity exists in the potential of balancing of opposites*. Thousand of resources must be exchanged to provide the resources necessary to create an MP3 player. All of those resources have value because people value music and are willing to exchange the value that they create for the MP3 player to have it.

4. *All opportunities can be described in terms of emptiness and fullness*. Music is a form of fullness satisfying the emptiness that is the desire for music.

5. *Abundance suddenly reverses into new forms of need*. The abundance of smart MP3 players has created the need for more portable application beyond just music.

3.2.1 Environmental Dominance

Description: Sun Tzu's five key methods on why openings must be created by others.

"Your war can take any shape.
It must avoid the strong and strike the weak.
Water follows the shape of the land that directs its flow.
Your forces follow the enemy who determines how you
win."

Sun Tzu's The Art of War 6:8:4-8

"Ability is of little account without opportunity."
Napoleon Bonaparte

General Principle: The competitive environment creates all our opportunities for us.

Situation:

If we think we can create our own opportunities, we are wrong. Within our span of control , we can always improve ourselves and our operations in terms of efficiency and effectiveness. The problem is that these improvements may or may not have any affect upon our external position, which is realm of opportunity. Only external conditions make our internal improvements valuable to others. The problem is that we do not create or control these conditions in our competitive environment. We especially cannot control the "openings" in the environment that represent opportunities. Whether we think about these openings as open spaces or as unfulfilled psychological needs, efforts to create opportunities always waste resources. They are driven by the illusion of control.

Opportunity:

Sun Tzu's strategy leverages the forces within the environment. For better or worse, we are moved forward by events and conditions like a sailing ship is moved by the wind. We cannot control these condition, but we can know how to use them. We control our progress and direction in the same way a sailing ship does, by knowing how to use these forces. We take the actions that work these forces in our advantage. In Sun Tzu's system, "an advantage" means a position that is favored by the forces in the environment over alternative positions. An opportunity is an opening that allows us to move into a position that has more advantages that our current position.

Key Methods:

1. We cannot create opportunities from our own skills and efforts alone. A need for our skills must exist in the environment and we must know where and how to find and use that opening. An opportunity is an opening, an empty space. We do not create that space. The decisions of others that leave that space open. In psychological space, we do not create the needs that others feel. We also do not create the situation by which that need is left unsatisfied. We take advantage of openings, but we do not create them (3.1.4 Openings).

2. *The environment makes the rules that define opportunity.* We can't fool Mother Nature. Every battleground has its own rules and those rule arise from the nature of the environment. We don't make these rules. Even in a sports contest the most important rules, the laws of physics, are not made or enforced by officials. Some are straight forward and obvious, such as the law of gravity. Others arise as emergent properties of complex systems, unforeseen and unpredictable. We not only don't make these rules, we can never completely understand them. Despite all our progress, we describe most of the universe as "dark matter" and "dark energy" to express our vast ignorance (1.4 The External Environment).

3. *The forces creating opportunities are larger than they seem.* Opportunity creation involves interactions between all parts of our environment. Our local situation is not separated from this larger whole but intimately connected to it though our knowledge of those connections is extremely limited (2.1.1 Information Limits). The amount of force required to open up opportunities in this vast network to depends on the size and duration of the opening, but the force required to make any change is larger than it appears. A trick of perspective can make us seem more relatively powerful than we are. What is closer to us appears larger than what is distant, confusing us about our relative influence to form our external environment on our own (1.2 Subobjective Positions).

4. *Nature makes us overconfident about our ability to control.* We need confidence to see and act on opportunities around us, but Sun Tzu teaches confidence is as dangerous in excess as it is in absence. In psychology and economics, this problem is known as overconfidence bias. All the research demonstrates the we systematically are overconfident about the likely success of our plans, discounting the effect of factors outside of our control (4.7.1 Command Weaknesses).

5. Opportunity cannot exist without external rewards. Competitive goals always include reward from the outside. Advancing positions also means gaining control of more resources and these resources must exist in the environment. We don't put them there ourselves. We cannot advance our position unless others support us. People do not support us unless we help them meet their needs. We are only rewarded for satisfying the needs of others. The size and complexity of the competitive environment makes its potential in terms of hidden resources impossible to know (3.1.1 Resource Limitations).

Illustration:

Let us simply look at the opportunity to start your own business.

1. We cannot create opportunities from our own skills and efforts alone. If we are good at doing our job, we are tempted to think we can start our own business to do it. Let us look specifically at the problem of a good cooks, that thinks that he or she can open new restaurant on the basis of their skill alone. We pick this example because many people, including many professional chefs, think that because they know their skill, they can create an opportunity for themselves.

2. The environment makes the rules that define opportunity. Even if we know the rules for making good food, we still have all the other rules for opening and running a successful restaurant. This includes everything from good restaurant design to the laws of economics. Many of these rules are non-intuitive, including the rules that openings for restaurants exist near other different types of restaurants.

3. The forces creating opportunities are larger than they seem. With modern travel, today's diners have more dining options and broader experience than ever before. The most difficult challenge in running a restaurant is drawing diners to it to try it for the first time but diners have too many choices, they cannot try them all. Advertising is an extremely expensive way to do this, so restaurants open near other restaurants to take advantage of existing flows of diners.

They can be seen by those who dine out by choosing the right location.

4. *Nature makes us overconfident about our ability to control.* Chefs, like all people in the "arts" almost always over estimate the quality of their product from the perspective of others. They expect the tastiness of their cooking to create "word of mouth" in influencing others to try it. This effect is almost always smaller than anticipated. There is a lot of good food. People eat out a lot. Even good food doesn't make as much of an impression on diners as a chef will assume.

5. *Opportunity cannot exist without external rewards.* Chefs, like many who consider themselves artists, work to satisfy themselves rather than their customers. The result is that 80% of new restaurants go out business within the first few years as their savings slowly run out.

3.2.2 Opportunity Invisibility

Description: Sun Tzu five key methods on why opportunities are always hidden.

"You can never see all the shades of victory."
Sun Tzu's The Art of War 5:2:16

"To see what is in front of one's nose needs a constant struggle."

George Orwell

"Opportunity is often difficult to recognize; we usually expect it to beckon us with beepers and billboards."
William Arthur Ward

General Principle: Opportunities are hidden, and, once discovered, are no longer opportunities.

Situation:

Opportunities are like phantoms that we can only glimpse out of the corners of our eyes. When we look for them directly, they disappear. We want to see patterns that make the future predictable, but the future is not predictable. We only know one thing about the future for certain. It will be different from the past. Making this problem worse, we often see patterns that do not exist. In psychology, seeing patterns that do not exist is known as the clustering illusion. Our desire to see opportunities can lead to conflict. Another problem is the bandwagon effect , our tendency to follow the crowd. This leads us to see opportunities where others have already had success. The problem is that an opportunity that someone else has already used is no longer an opportunity at all.

Opportunity:

Seeing opportunities is a special skill that we must be trained to master. We cannot see them by looking at them directly. Like black holes, we can only infer their existence from the effects they create around them. Seeing opportunities is an act of imagination, and, done correctly, prevents us from charging after expired opportunities that others have already used up. The mental models taught by Sun Tzu require knowing our limits so we can work within them (2.2.2 Mental Models).

Key Methods:

The key methods relating to the invisibility of opportunities sets the boundary conditions for seeing opportunities.

1. The nature of opportunities as openings makes them difficult to see. Opportunities are openings. They are empty spaces and unmet needs. How do we see emptiness? What is it that we are looking for when we try to see an opportunity? There is literally nothing there. We cannot see the opportunity directly because it is literally nothing (3.1.4 Openings).

2. *Seeing an opportunity is an act of imagination.* What we see is an empty place in the puzzle. We then have to imagine the shape and color of the piece that fills that emptiness. Sometimes we are right. Often we are wrong. We don't know if anything really fills that hole until something clicks when we try to fill it (7.3.3 Creative Innovation).

3. *People only see expired opportunities, other people's opportunities.* They are not thinking about imagination. Instead, they are thinking about imitation. They see a situation that was once an opportunity and think that they can take advantage of it by duplicating the success of others. These people can see opportunities only once they have been filled with something. In other words, they only see situations when they are no longer opportunities but other people's successes (3.1.6 Time Limitations).

4. *Once identified, it is impossible to know the extent of an opportunity.* Some opportunity doesn't mean enough opportunity to reward us for our efforts. We can know only one thing about the potential size of an opportunity at the beginning. We will only know its extent when when it begins to run out. It grows and grows until it reaches it limits. When it reaches those limits, that growth stops, sometimes quite suddenly. We can only guess at size until the excavation is done 3.1.1 Resource Limitations).

5. *Opportunities exist only in the future and the future is invisible.* We cannot know the future. Future potential of shifting climate is just one part of this problem. Thinking that we can know the future is what is known as hindsight bias. The past looks as though it was predictable when it wasn't. Some of the cycles of climate are predictable, but innovation is also part of the future and it changes patterns of potential. We never know when the next creative bolt of insight is going to strike, suddenly opening up new competitive landscapes and changing our situation forever (7.3 Strategic Innovation).

Illustration:

Since we recently saw the collapse of the housing bubble that so many saw as an opportunity, let us use that as an example of the dangers here. Was buying a house at that point in time an opportunity?

1. The nature of opportunities as openings makes them difficult to see. House prices go up 300% in a short period of time. A lot of people have made money flipping houses. Mortgage requirements and interest rates are at record lows. In the last, more dangerous years of the bubble, everyone saw the opportunity. That alone should have been the clue that the opportunity was gone.

2. Seeing an opportunity is an act of imagination. It took no imagination to see the value of housing and how it had increased. The real opportunity in housing existed before houses went up 300%, but who could see the opportunity then? Prices were stable. Interest rates were high. Financing hurdles were significant. Nobody was making money.

3. People only see expired opportunities, other people's opportunities. There was an opportunity, but it was gone. What was left was not an opportunity. As too many people have discovered, it was more of a trap than an opportunity as they bought houses that were soon worth less than their mortgages.

4. Once identified, it is impossible to know the extent of an opportunity. When did the opportunity end? The answer was different in different places, but the only important answer is that the extent of the opportunity was impossible to know before the bubble burst.

5. Opportunities exist only in the future and the future is invisible. Now everyone says that it was obvious that the housing market was oversold, but it wasn't.

3.2.3 Complementary Opposites

Description: Sun Tzu five key methods regarding the dynamics of balance from opposing forces.

"Know the enemy and know yourself. Your victory will be painless.
Know the climate and the ground.
Your victory will be complete."

Sun Tzu's The Art of War 10:5:15-18

"The opposite of a correct statement is a false statement. But the opposite of a profound truth may well be another profound truth."

Niels Bohr

General Principle: Look for new opportunities in a balancing of opposites.

Situation:

We are trained in linear thinking , which leads to "straight line" predictions. When a trend continues in one direction for a period of time, we naturally begin to think that it will always continue in that direction. The problem is that in the real world, we more commonly see a regression toward the mean , a return to balance. In the West, we have a deterministic and reductionist view of systems, but Plato was the first to recognize that these linear methods have natural limits. Sun Tzu based his system for discovering opportunities on the Chinese philosophy of yin-yang.

Opportunity:

While we cannot predict the future exactly, looking for the balancing forces dramatically improves our ability to find opportunities (1.4.1 Climate Shift). The future does not flow in a straight line, but in an undulating cycle arising from the contest between opposing forces. Many forms of opportunities can be found in positioning ourselves to take advantage of the reversing of these cycles. As our herd instinct takes most people in one direction, openings arise in the opposite direction. These cycles swing between opposite extremes that are the heart of Sun Tzu's system. When conditions swing too far in one direction, it is highly probably that they will start back in the opposite direction.

Key Methods:

There are a great many balancing forces that affect competitive advantage. In Sun Tzu's strategy, we call these balancing forces complementary opposites. Using Sun Tzu's methods we find opportunities in predictable cycles. These cycles repeat themselves in similar ways. This is because they are driven by complementary opposites, where the extremes are known and the balancing forces are understood at least to some degree.

1. All natural systems consist of a balance of opposing forces called complementary opposites. If nature didn't consist of a balance of forces, the universe wouldn't exist. All strategic conditions reflect the waxing and waning of these opposing forces. These underlying forces cannot always be known, but they are always there. Sun Tzu's strategy identifies dozens of complementary opposites that come into play in specific situations. Even the most basic elements of a strategic--ground and climate, command and methods--are defined as complementary opposites (1.3 Elemental Analysis).

2. No trend continues forever because its extension naturally exhausts the force of the dominant opposite. A trend in one direction is driven by the currently dominant half of a complementary pair. Over time, it requires more and more resources to drive the trend forward. All resources are limited, even those of natural forces. Eventually resources of the dominant half are stretched too thinly and the trend begins to reverse as the other half grows relatively stronger. We don't know what those limits are before we reach them, but their limitations are certain (3.1.1 Resource Limitations).

3. The stronger the trend, the shorter the life span of the opposing force. Gradual trends last longer than dramatic trends simply because resources of the dominant half are expended more quickly. Accelerating trends do not necessarily decelerate before they reverse themselves. Resources can suddenly reach their limit. This often leads to sudden crashes of the most dramatic trends (1.1.1 Position Dynamics).

4. Opportunities are created at the extremes of shifts between complementary opposites. Because most people make straight line predictions, the greatest number of people expect the dominant trend to continue at those extremes. This creates an opening. Few are prepared for that trend to reverse itself. Our opportunity is positioning ourselves so that the rising force of the other half of the balance carries us with it, harnessing the force of nature to advance our position (4.0 Leveraging Probability).

5. The growth of human knowledge is outside the natural balance of forces. Human progress is possible because knowledge stands apart from the balancing forces of nature. It is our understanding about those natural forces and how to leverage them. Each new type of knowledge or technology has its limits, but the extension of our knowledge itself can go on indefinitely. The end of one cycle in learning, opens up the potential of a new cycle of learning in a new direction. This makes the direction of these cycles of innovation beyond the time-line of S-curve itself impossible to predict (7.5.2 The Spread of Innovation).

6. Complex systems isolate us from the underlying balance of forces on which they are based. This is the one sense in which our knowledge creates its balancing force of ignorance. We embody our growing knowledge in systems. As our systems grow in complexity, we lose track of the natural forces on which they are based. We live in the artificial world that we have created. In this artificial world, we develop new mental models based on artifice instead of reality. Utopian systems of perfect control and predictability only seem possible because we are cut off from the underlying balance of forces on which our world is based (2.1.1 Information Limits).

Illustration:

There are all types of complementary opposites, but we can't cover them all. Since we are interested specifically in making progress, let us look specifically at technological growth.

1. **All natural systems consist of a balance of opposing forces called complementary opposites.** The positive and negative electrical charges, the opposite sexes, the economic cycles of greed and fear, our left and right hands are all different natural demonstrations of this rule.

2. **No trend continues forever because its extension naturally exhausts the force of the dominant opposite.** In the strategy of stock picking, this principle is called contrarian investing. In statistical analysis, it is reflected in the idea called "regression to the mean." When automobile and airplane technology is advancing as dramatically as they did in the 30s, we predicted rocket cars. We didn't get rocket cars because the physics of flight and economics of the assembly line have natural limits. When housing prices go up for a few decades, we start thinking that they will always go up.

When the climate gets cooler or warming for a few decades, we think that trend means the doom of civilization (see this post for a good chart showing a IPCCs straight line projection against real historical trends of heating and cooling). As computer technology improves dramatically, we start predicting " technological singularity " of limitless artificial intelligence.

3. The stronger the trend, the shorter the life span of the opposing force. The housing boom and the.com trends were dramatic, but each lasted less than a decade. The gradual improvements in breeding agricultural crops, in contrast, have continued for hundreds of years. The gradual increase in the value of gold has continued since currency was disconnected from the gold standard and will continue as long as governments can create money at will.

4. Opportunities are created at the extremes of shifts between complementary opposites. As the boom accelerates, sell the house as the boom trend accelerates. Buy houses as foreclosures increase. Though not technically a.com, I sold my software company in late 1997, before the software down slide that started in 1999.

5. The growth of human knowledge is outside the natural balance of forces. Never bet against human progress over the long-term. People will continue to learn and find methods that work better than older methods.

6. Complex systems isolate us from the underlying balance of forces on which they are based. In the middle of a boom, no one sees its underlying natural constraints. As money is printed, its value seems to hold for awhile but like a rubber band that is stretched and stretched, something eventually snaps. Money's artificial nature must pay homage eventually to underlying stores of natural value. Thus the rise of gold prices.

3.2.4 Emptiness and Fullness

Description: Sun Tzu's nine key methods on the transformations between emptiness and fullness.

"Avoid full and yet strike empty."
Sun Tzu's The Art of War 6:8:5 (Chinese Revealed).

"Strength is just an accident arising from the weakness of others."

Joseph Conrad

General Principle: Success in comparison arises naturally from focusing the fullness of strength on the emptiness of weakness.

Situation:

The saying is that opportunity never knocks twice, but opportunity is always knocking. The problem is that opportunity never repeats itself in the same way. All opportunities are unique in time and place. Another's opportunity is never exactly the same as our own. This makes identifying opportunities a challenge. Reality is too complicated for us to identify and analyze every possible condition that might represent an opportunity. Sun Tzu's strategy identifies many common opportunities indicators but he understood that such a list could never be complete. Opportunities are often based on the most unique aspects of the situation.

Opportunity:

Sun Tzu provides a simple mental model for searching for opportunities in a wide variety of unique situations. Our opportunities always arise in the transition back and forth between emptiness and fullness. We simplify our search for opportunities by changing our minds to think of everything in terms of emptiness and fullness. Emptiness is any lack, or vacuum, most commonly a human need or desire. Sadness, insignificance, hunger, slowness, and ignorance are types of emptiness. Fullness is whatever fills that lack, that vacuum, satisfying a particular need or desire. Happiness, significance, satiation, speed, and knowledge are forms of fullness. Happiness fills sadness. Satiation fulfills hunger. Knowledge fills up ignorance, and so on.

Key Methods:

Sun Tzu's concepts of emptiness and fullness are built on more basic key methods but extend beyond them.

1. We must avoid the full and seek the empty. All opportunities must be openings, positions that others have not occupied. By moving into openings, we avoid costly conflict (3.1.4 Openings).

2. Emptiness and fullness can take may different forms. Emptiness is any state of need or desire. Fullness is its opposite, a state of satiety and surplus. The advantage in seeing the world as cycles of emptiness and fullness is that it simplifies that kaleidoscope of different needs into just two possible states (3.2.3 Complementary Opposites).

3. Opportunity arises from the eternal shift among different forms of emptiness and fullness. Both states are temporary, where one must give way to the other over time, creating one another in a constant cycle. This cycle is endless. As one human need or desire is filled, another automatically arises. Needs that were once filled become empty again over time. We can use these constant shifts to our advantage (3.2 Opportunity Creation).

4. *The shift among emptiness and fullness cannot be exactly predicted.* When one need is filled, we do not know what new desire will take its place. We often cannot predict this for ourselves, much less others. The interplay among human priorities is inherently complex beyond human comprehension. Our opportunities exist at the juncture of what we have failed to foresee and others have also overlooked. People only need what they are not getting. We must see the opportunity, we cannot predict it (5.2 Opportunity Exploration).

5. *Emptiness becomes our opportunity when we can fill it for others.* The only forms of emptiness that create opportunities for us personally are those that we are in a position to fill for others. Emptiness is only an opportunity if it exists outside of ourselves, in others. Others will feel that emptiness in a way that we do not. This is why listening is the first step in the adaptive loop of listen>aim>move>claim. The openings that interest us as those that we can reach from our own position and fill using our internal resources of character and skill (1.5 Internal Elements).

6. *Emptiness is a temporary state so opportunity requires speed*. Emptiness is naturally balanced by nature. Depending on the type of need involved, the emptiness is either replaced by a greater need or grows until it must be addressed. Emptiness opens up and closes constantly. However, different types of emptiness reoccur in a pattern: the need to breath, the need to drink, the need to eat, and so on. We cannot aim at a specific opening for a specific person at a specific type because this cycle is based on probabilities not certainties, but the goal of strategy is to position ourselves for a certain type of emptiness. We want to be in the right time at the right place when that opening appears (1.6.3 Shifting Priorities).

7. *Small empty spaces are much more common than large*. Opportunity consist mostly of small, immediate forms of emptiness in the general direction that we want to move. These small openings are all around us, but we usually cannot see them because they are small and we are too occupied with our own larger desires to notice the minor needs of others around us. Often we can see them more easily if we focus on our own small needs because we often share them with others (3.2.2 Opportunity Invisibility).

8. Small openings lead to larger ones. Large openings that fit our skills are much less common than a smaller one, but are rare. In taking advantage of small openings. We undertake campaigns in order to gradually shift to better and better positions over time, making new, currently distant, resources attainable (1.8 Progress Cycle).

9. One form of emptiness can require other different forms of fullness. The concepts of emptiness and fullness are more universal than their specific forms. The opposite is also true. One type of fullness can create many forms of emptiness (3.2.5 Dynamics of Reversal).

Illustration:

Let us apply these ideas to building a small business.

1. We must avoid the full and seek the empty. If we run a small business, our opportunity to improve our business in a strategic sense (as opposed to operationally) exists in finding the empty places in our customers that we can fill.

2. Emptiness and fullness can take may different forms. Customers may want more service or less interruption. They may want lower prices or more value. They may want more selection or an easier decision.

3. Opportunity arises from the eternal shift among different forms of emptiness and fullness. People want what they don't have and cannot currently get. Those who have lower prices may want more value or they may want more selection. Those who have more value may want lower prices or an easier decision. They may want one or more of these forms of emptiness, depending on what they can already get.

4. The shift among emptiness and fullness cannot be exactly predicted. If a customer need is predicted, it would have likely been filled. As a business, our opportunities exist in customer needs that both we and our competitors have overlooked.

5. Emptiness becomes our opportunity when we can fill it for others. If we cannot offer more service, or sell for less or offer more selection, those forms of emptiness do not offer an opportunity for us. We must concentrate on making their decisions easier, offering more value, and offering less interruption,

6. Emptiness is a temporary state so opportunity requires speed. Rather than planning complex changes that require time to develop, we must offer quick, little changes in policy to see what strikes the right chord with customers.

7. Small empty spaces are much more common than large. Rather than trying to solve big but rare problems, we must offer little changes that address smaller but more common problems.

8. Small openings lead to larger ones. If customers see continual improvement in our operations, they will return more frequently to see what else has changed.

9. One form of emptiness can require other different forms of fullness. As we get more attention from customers, we will be able to address more and more of their needs over time.

3.2.5 Dynamic Reversal

Description: Sun Tzu's six key methods regarding how situations reverse themselves naturally.

"War is very sloppy and messy.
Positions turn around."
Sun Tzu's The Art of War 6:8:5 (Chinese Revealed).

"The reverse side also has a reverse side."
Japanese Proverb

General Principle: We see opportunities by thinking back-wards and upside-down.

Situation:

We are taught linear thinking but Sun Tzu's strategy is its oppo-site: seeing everything as a loop. We are taught that more is better, but in competition less is more. When we look at opportunities as openings, we are not looking for something but for nothing. Because of this, identifying competitive opportunities is counter intuitive. From this perspective, an opportunity never looks like an opportunity. It looks like a problem.

Opportunity:

Once we understand the nature of opportunities, we can use a simple mental trick to find them more easily. Opportunities are openings, empty spaces of unfilled potential. Since they are a form of negative space, the identification of opportunities often requires us to reverse the normal, obvious, and "common sense" everyday way that we normally see situations. This "backwards thinking" usually seems foolish until an opportunity is proven. However, once an opportunity is proven, everyone sees it as obvious.

Key Methods:

These following six key methods help us harness the dynamics of reversal.

1. We find opportunities by imagining the world reversing itself. Seeing opportunity is an act of imagination. Complementary opposites re-balance situations. Opportunities shift among different forms of emptiness and fullness. What is full today will be empty tomorrow. What is empty today will be full tomorrow (3.2.4 Emptiness and Fullness).

2. We must see every problem as an opportunity and seeming opportunities as a potential problem. If something is a problem for us, it is also probably a problem for others. All problems represent needs that must be addressed and we can get rewarded for addressing (3.2 Opportunity Creation).

3. We must envision what is old as new and what is new as if it was old. Opportunity is created by change, but change is a cycle, recycling what has come before. When people see things as new, they are missing the connection to the past. When they see it as old, they miss the connection to the future. Our opportunity is seeing what most people miss (3.2.2 Opportunity Invisibility).

4. We must see every strength as a weakness and every weakness as a strength. Every coin has two sides, a positive and a negative. Since one side usually commands the attention of most people, it gets plenty of attention and cannot be an opportunity. To find the opening we need, we have to look at the other side that every one is overlooking (3.2.3 Complementary Opposites).

5. We must imagine doing the exactly opposite of what others do and acting where others avoid acting. This lesson is a little tricky because we don't want to go the wrong way on one-way streets or drive through stop lights when everyone else stops. The controlling rule here is that we must avoid costly conflict. Doing the opposite or acting when others don't is an opportunity when it eliminates conflict. It is not an opportunity when it creates conflict (3.1.3 Conflict Cost).

6. We must think about offering less instead of more and working slower rather than faster. This is the ultimate in reverse thinking because it contradicts two key principles of opportunity and strategy themselves. Opportunity is filling openings. How can offering less fill a hole better than more? Speed is the essence of competition. How can going slower ever offer an advantage? However, everyone sees the value of more and more speed, even when they don't understand opportunity or strategy. This rule plays to a higher standard, that of strategic profitability. Less and slower consumes less resources creating a new potential for profitability that others often miss (3.1.2 Strategic Profitability).

Illustration:

Let us illustrate these idea in terms of investing.

1. We find opportunities by imagining the world reversing itself. While stocks may or may not be a good or bad buy right now, these principles provide a more strategic way of thinking about stock investing.

2. We must see every problem as an opportunity and seeming opportunities as a potential problem. One of the most common mistakes in investing is selling the winners and holding the losers. This is logical in the sense that selling winners makes a profit while we can wait for losers to turn around. However, it is poor investment strategy. Much better to sell losers asap and hold winners (setting stop points in case they turn around and become losers).

3. We must envision what is old as new and what is new as if it was old. When an adviser tout the latest hot stock, avoid buying it. Look for old, tire stocks (of good, solid companies, of course) that no one cares about any more. This is the logic behind the Dogs of the Dow philosophy, which have historically outperformed the Dow.

4. We must see every strength as a weakness and every weakness as a strength. A strong stock has a high price. A weak stock has a low price. If the goal is to buy low and sell high to create a profit, what do you prefer?

5. We must imagine doing the exactly opposite of what others do and acting where others avoid acting. Sell what most people are buying. Buy what most people are selling. Trade more when others are trading less. Trade less when they are trading more.

6. We must think about offering less instead of more and working slower rather than faster. Buy fewer stocks (or ETFs) and hold them longer. Make fewer trades after more deliberation. It is like playing poker, if you bet on every hand, you are going to lose.

3.2.6 Opening Matrix Tool

Description: Six key methods using for building a matrix to help us identify unseen openings using Sun Tzu's elements of a position.

	Climate	Mission	Ground	Leadership	Methods
Opening Type		Unmet	Unclaimed	Missing	Needed
CHANGES	Change Reversal	Needs/ Values	Resources/ Rewards	Leader/ Decision	Methods Shift
Change 1					
Change 2					
Change 3					
Change 4					
Change 5					

"Many advantages add up to victory.
Few advantages add up to defeat."
Sun Tzu's The Art of War 1:5:5-6.

"Opportunities? They are all around us: there is power lying latent everywhere waiting for the observant eye to discover it."
Orison Swett Marden

General Principle: Analyzing the effects of various changes on the five elements of positioning reveals hidden openings.

Situation:

People have a difficult time seeing opportunities because they are looking in the wrong place. They see what is already there rather than what is missing. Nature abhors a vacuum but vacuums are invisible. They see what is being used rather than what is being overlooked for use. They are frightened by change, turning away from their uncertain future rather than turning toward it and peering into its darkness. When they do look in that darkness, they imagine monsters and phantoms rather than its potential for magic.

Opportunity:

People must adapt to change. By organizing our thoughts on change, we can see the potential for new positions that it is creating. Without change, people will continue to do what they have in the past. Change motivates them to support new positions, positions we can create from the openings created by the change. Sun Tzu's five element model offers us a new way of seeing change and its potential for the future. We can use this model as a tool for seeing what is normally hidden. Like a telescope that allows us to see what is very large but too far away to be seen with our naked eyes, this model brings reveals new universes of possibility. Like the microscope, which shows what is very close but too small to be seen, this tool allows us to see the easy path forward that is normally hidden from us.

Key Methods:

The following key methods construct a matrix that we can use to see the resources and opportunities made possible by change. The idea is to identify all possible openings in a given situation.

1. List the most important changes affect your situation in the first column of the matrix. Change is the source of all opportunities. Look for changes that have a broad impact but which are easy to overlook. These changes are the source of all future opportunities (3.2 Opportunity Creation).

2. In the column next to each change, post the ways in which its trend might reverse itself or what people expect from the change might produce the opposite effect. This column represents the effect of the Climate column. While change itself is driven by climate, a future change in the current change is also caused by the continual shifts in climate. It most people are adjusting to the current change, we can get ahead of them by preparing for that changes reversal. Sun Tzu teaches that most trends tend to reverse themselves because of balances in nature driving change (3.2.5 Dynamic Reversal).

3. In the next column, list the new or unmet needs or values created by the change or its reversal. This is the Mission column. Meeting these needs or addressing those values is an opportunity. Others are likely to see these new needs or values are a problem rather than an opportunity. These needs and values follow an hierarchy of mission values (1.6.2 Types of Motivations).

4. In the next column, list the unclaimed resources or rewards made possible by the change or its reversal. This is the Ground column since Ground is the source of all resources and rewards. Sometimes, we can easily fill this column with ideas for getting rewarded for addressing the needs in the previous column. However, sometimes all we can see from change is the damage it does. However, "damage" to some area also often means that resources are being made available that were, in the past, being used elsewhere. These resources are available for our use if we can imagine how to use them (7.6.1 Resource Discovery).

5. In the next column, list the missing leadership or decisions for which the change or its reversal creates a need. This is the Leader or Commander element in Sun Tzu's model. When a number of different groups are effected by a change, all with different needs, they often are simply looking for a leader who can get them all pointed in the same direction, working together using that change. By providing that leadership, providing a vision or a project with a shared goal we can mobilize a force for positive change, we can leverage people's hunger for leadership (1.5.1 Command Leadership).

6. In the final column, list the outdated methods or the new methods that are necessitated by the change or its reversal creates

a need. This is the Methods part of Sun Tzu's model. Ideas for projects or campaign utilizing change are often more easily imagined by looking at how change outdates old methods or requires new ones (1.5.2. Group Methods).

Illustration:

This tool emulates a mental process that I personally use all the time. Recently, I have been working on community development using these ideas.

1. List the most important changes affect your situation in the first column of the matrix. Our local community 0of Shoreline (north of Seattle), has been affected by the following changes:

- Disappearance of Community Media
- Improvements in Shoreline's Main Artery
- Continued Economic Slump
- New Local Government Roles for Business Development and Events
- Local Community College in Trouble
- Donations to Non-Profits Down
- Decline in Local Service Organizations (Rotary, Kiwanis)
- Less Easy to Travel to Seattle For Events

2. In the column next to each change, post the ways in which its trend might reverse itself or what people expect from the change might produce the opposite effect. The following are potential reversals of these changes:

- New community media centered around internet
- None
- Local economy turns around
- Local Government cuts back on Business Development and Event Promotion
- College is closed down
- Donations begin to climb again
- People will begin joining local service organizations

- Government will fix travel problems to downtown Seattle

3. *In the next column, list the new or unmet needs or values created by the change or its reversal.*

- Local people need to know about community events/ Local business need advertising outlets The new look makes it possible to create a new image of city
- Local businesses need help to reach customers in and outside of city
- Local government needs ideas for "place-making" to distinguish community
- Local college needs to make money selling their unused facilities
- Worthy causes in the community are increasing need
- Local service organizations need more visibility and membership
- People in area need entertainment and events that don't require travel to Seattle downtown

4. *In the next column, list the unclaimed resources or rewards made possible by the change or its reversal.*

- Business will pay for advertising on some sort of local media
- The new highway is an advertising venue for local businesses and events
- Local business are willing to donate to causes to get visibility
- Local government has resources to help put local businesses and promote local events Local college is willing to offer their facilities to local business and service organization to generate revenue
- Local needs can be used to mobilize local interest through venues like schools
- Local service organizations are willing to offer manpower and work together on projects
- There is a market for local events and entertainment

5. *In the next column, list the missing leadership or decisions for which the change or its reversal creates a need.*

- Business need someone to give them ideas for promoting their businesses
- Those controlling signing on highway need to be convinced of community need to change policies
- Local business need to be asked to contribute
- Local government needs to be given some ideas in terms of how to promote the city
- The college president and administration needs to be given some ideas about how to utilize their facilities
- The local charities need to be contacted and contribute assets such as mailing lists.
- Local service organizations need to be contacted and lead to join together.
- The local market needs to offered a series of entertaining events put on by non-profits and local businesses to support local charities and bring business into the area.

6. In the final column, list the outdated methods or the new methods that are necessitated by the change or its reversal creates a need.

- All groups (local businesses, service organizations, local government, charity organizations, local college) need to develop methods for putting on a series of local events that they can grow year after years, following the example of other communities that have built successful events attracting dollars and attention from the surrounding area.

3.3.0 Opportunity Resources

Description: Sun Tzu's eight key methods regarding the nature of the excess resources needed to fill openings.

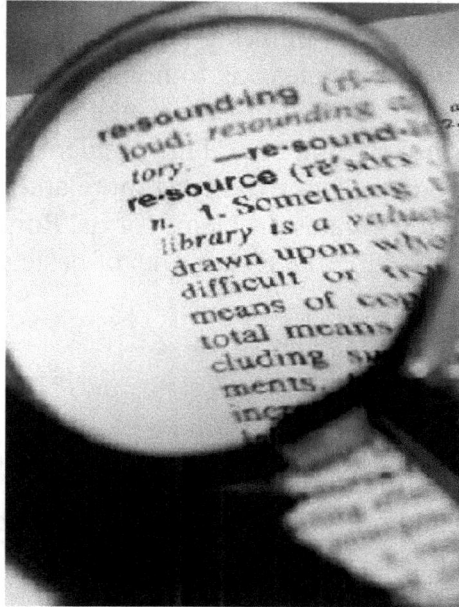

"If you are too weak to fight, you must find more men. In this situation, you must not act aggressively."
Sun Tzu's The Art of War 9:6:1-2

"The courage to imagine the otherwise is our greatest resource, adding color and suspense to all our life."
Daniel J. Boorstin

General Principle: We must pursue opportunities only when excess resources are available.

Situation:

There is a downside in learning to see openings. We can get sucked into situations that we should avoid. An opening has power. As Aristotle first observed , a vacuum pulls us in. How susceptible we are to this problem depends upon our character, but we all have a number of natural tendencies that create the problem. The first is known simply as wishful thinking , our tendency to make decisions based upon what it is pleasing to imagine. We also tend to over estimate our own ability to restrain ourselves. In research, this problem is known as restraint bias. This problem is amplified irrational escalation , our tendency to invest more and more in a past decision, even when it creates problems for us. Pursuing opportunities without understanding the constraints of basic positioning can be extremely dangerous.

Opportunity:

All openings are opportunities for someone, but we are interesting only in openings that represent our opportunities. Seeing openings in emptiness and need is a powerful and valuable skill (3.2.4 Emptiness and Fullness). We work at it because openings are so difficult to see (3.2.2 Opportunity Invisibility). Our success, however, depends upon keeping our priorities straight and seeing the big picture of our situation (2.5 The Big Picture). Knowing a few simple principles in looking for opportunities helps us protect our limited resources and helps us recognize which of these opportunities are right for us (2.1.1 Information Limits).

Key Methods:

An opening is a necessary condition for us to pursue an opportunity, but it is not a sufficient one. In addition to an opening, we obviously need the complementary resources necessary to fill that opening. The following mental model must guide us in knowing when to act and when not to.

1. We need enough resources to pursue an opportunity. Everything requires resources. It requires resources for us to maintain our existing position. It also takes resources to explore any opportunity. It may not take a lot of resources, but some resources are always required. The problems is that our resources are always limited (3.1.1 Resource Limitations).

2. We must _not_ act if we do not have "excess" resources. Defense of our existing position always has the first claim on our available resources. Excess resources are those that we don't need to sustain the key aspect of our current position. When we don't have the excess resources, we must concentrate simply on defending our current position. (1.1.2 Defending Positions).

3. We must often readjust our priorities to create excess resources. Our resources are devoted to all sorts of things, all of which we can describe as "maintaining our position." When an opportunity comes along--and often before--we often must sacrifice one desire in order to get the resources to pursue a more important desire. This is always a matter of priorities, but we will never pursue any opportunity if we don't have a high priority on improving our position rather than simply maintaining it (1.6.3 Shifting Priorities).

4. We can improve our internal production to create excess resources. We perform our existing responsibilities more efficiently to generate the excess resources we need. This falls within our span of control. The more productive we are, the more resources we free up for using in competition, which is outside of our control (1.9 Competition and Production).

5. Our excess resources must fit _all_ the requirements of the opportunity. Openings are the hole. Our resources are the peg. The peg must fit the hole. Opportunities often require several different types of resources, both temporary resources and physical resources. If our excess resources only match some of what is required, we must avoid the opportunity because it will inevitably take vital resources needed to maintain our current position (3.2.3 Complementary Opposites).

6. We must have excess resources at the right time. Opportunities are limited. We cannot control when openings appear or how long they last. Having or making the resources required depends largely on the timing involved. Unlike temporary resources, we can save up physical resources so they are available when opportunities appear (3.1.6 Time Limitations).

7. We must resist event pressure in evaluating our resources. Events, especially events that create opportunities, pressure us to act, even when it isn't in our best interest. We cannot act simply because of event pressure. We must act because our situation requires action (5.1.1 Event Pressure

8. When we have excess resources, we _must_ act on a high probability opportunity. We cannot act without an opportunity. We cannot act without excess resources. We must act when we have both the opportunity and the resources when there is a high-probability of our action being successful (4.0 Leveraging Probability).

Illustration:

Let us illustrate these principles in thinking about how we can expand our current responsibilities to get a promotion or work toward getting a promotion.

1. We need enough resources to pursue an opportunity. Expanding our current responsibilities requires time and effort. It is emotionally demanding. We must have the time and energy to do more without decreasing our overall performance.

2. We must _not_ act if we do not have "excess" resources. In our career, our first priority is performing our current responsibilities well. We cannot get promoted if we hurt our current performance in pursuing a promotion. If we decrease our existing job performance, we create an opening for others to attack us. If we cannot do our existing job well, we will not be given more responsibilities.

3. We must often readjust our priorities to create excess resources. We can easily be spending time on tasks that are really a part of our responsibility and aren't helping us get promoted because the need for them is not recognized by others.

4. We can improve our internal production to create excess resources. We need to find faster, easier ways of performing our current responsibilities. Aside from freeing up our resources, finding faster ways to work qualifies us for promotion.

5. Our excess resources must fit <u>all</u> the requirements of the opportunity. We shouldn't pursue opportunities at work for which we really aren't qualified either objectively or subjectively. In my career, I was promoted an average of every eight months and when I reach a level where I had to "pay my dues" by just doing time in my current position before being qualified for promotion, I would move to another company.

6. We must have excess resources at the right time. We cannot control when jobs open up. We have to be ready and positioned to take over those responsibilities when they do.

7. We must resist event pressure in evaluating our resources. We shouldn't just go after another position because it opens up. It must fit our skills and goals.

8. When we have excess resources, we <u>must</u> act on a high probability opportunity. If we can satisfy our existing job responsibilities with plenty of time and energy left over, we ***<u>must</u>*** use our excess time to pursue additional responsibilities of some kind. There are always valuable things that need doing. We must identify those that are most likely to advance us and go after them. If we don't pursue additional responsibilities, others will eventually notice that we are underemployed. This again, hurts our existing position.

3.4.0 Dis-Economies of Scale

Description: Sun Tzu's six key methods on opportunities created by the size of others.

"Small forces are not powerful.
However, large forces cannot catch them."
Sun Tzu's The Art of War 3:3:19-20

"Strength does not come from physical capacity. It comes from an indomitable will."
Mahatma Gandhi

General Principle: The size of large organizations must create opportunities for smaller organizations.

Situation:

One of the most common reasons that we fail to recognize opportunities is that we tend to think of size as an advantage. When we see a large organization, we think that it naturally dominates its competitive area. We talk about the power of economies of scale. Our expectations regarding the value of size are constantly frustrated as one large company after another fails, while new smaller companies rise up to take their place. What is happening? Our problem is that we fail to understand most of the advantages of size are advantages in production, not competition. While size is a great advantage in any controlled areas of production, as an areas of contention becomes more and more competitive, size turns into a disadvantage.

Opportunity:

Competitive opportunities are openings. The actions of large competitors tend to create new openings, but most of these openings are too small for the large competitor themselves. As we master Sun Tzu's principles, we see that every characteristic, especially size, has both advantages and disadvantages (3.2.4 Emptiness and Fullness). In competitive arenas, size advantages turn into weaknesses that we can exploit. Dominant large organizations change the environment but, in doing so, they become easy targets for smaller, more adaptable competitors. One of the secrets in identifying opportunities is studying the nature of the large organizations. The advance of their position drives out smaller direct competitors in markets they move into, but that advance also creates a whole new set of openings in their wake.

Key Methods:

The following key methods describe how the large size of a competitor creates opportunities for smaller competitors.

1. The same size that is an advantage in production is a disadvantage in competitive maneuvering. The skills of production and competitive adaptability are complementary opposites. Size creates advantages in production. For this reason, small organizations cannot meet large ones in contests determined by productive capacity. This advantage in production, however, necessarily creates competitive disadvantages in adapting to change. Large ones cannot keep up with small ones in adapting to change (3.2.3 Complementary Opposites).

2. *Momentum creates two types of large organizations and two types of opportunities*. An organization doesn't get large without developing a great deal of momentum. Vital organizations with great momentum create opportunities by reshaping the competitive landscape, opening up new ground for new smaller organizations. However, all momentum fades over time. Large organizations with fading momentum encourages a new crop of competitors in the areas that they once controlled. These competitors feed off the fading organization (7.5 Momentum Limitations).

3. *Large organizations create sameness which creates the need for variety.* During their vital growth stage, the productive power of large organizations drive out the smaller, more varied, but less productive organizations. In doing so, they create a more homogeneous environment. This new environment is never perfect. It comes with a new set of unmet needs. These needs are small at first, easier for small organization's to see and address (3.2 Opportunity Creation)

4. *Strength comes from unity and focus rather than size.* People mistakenly think that size is strength. The larger an organization is, the more problems it has with unity and focus. Different parts of the organization develop separate missions and what benefits one part of the organization can be very destructive to other parts. This is especially true in the internal competition for resources between new growing parts that represent the future and the older established parts the create the most resources (1.7 Internal Strength).

5. *Loss of unity and focus creates openings*. If we think in terms of strategic positions, the problems with size become apparent. Larger organizations cover more ground, but they cannot be equally strong everywhere. Their size also slows them down, making it very difficult for them to change direction and stay united (3.4.1 Unity Breakdown).

6. *Size limits opportunity*. Size also makes it more difficult to find suitable new positions. Small opportunities are more common than large opportunities. The larger an organization's size, the rarer suitable opportunities are. Most openings are too small to provide them with meaningful opportunities. As their existing positions naturally degrade overtime, large organizations find it difficult to find new positions to accommodate them. This forces them into less and less profitable and tenable competitive arena (3.4.2 Opportunity Fit).

7. *Size makes large organizations slow to react to change*. Their size also slows them down, making it more and more difficult for them to change direction. Changing direction and keeping united is even more difficult. The decision loop through the organization's hierarchy takes more time in large organizations than small ones. As changes come both from the environment and from competitive challenges, large organizations are slow to react. This slow reaction also creates opportunities for competitors (3.4.3 Reaction Lag).

Illustration:

I am tempted to give examples from military history such as Alexander the Great, leading a force of less than 40,000 destroying Darius's Persian army estimated to be about 600,000 in the Battle at Issus , but let us look at some modern business examples that are easier to appreciate.

1. *The same size that is an advantage in production is a disadvantage in competitive maneuvering*. When IBM was big, Microsoft could outmaneuver them. When Microsoft was big, Google could outmaneuver them.

2. *Momentum creates two types of large organizations and two types of opportunities*. Google and Apple create new markets in the building momentum phase. Others such as Microsoft and WalMart are still growing, but coasting on their momentum. The vast majority are companies such as Sears, GE, AIG, Citibank, NY Times, etc. whose momentum has faded and are passing away.

*3. **Large organizations create sameness which creates the need for variety.*** The standard environment created by Microsoft Windows created a huge application market for PCs. We are about to see the same thing take place again for Google's Android phones.

*4. **Strength comes from unity and focus rather than size.*** 70-80% of new jobs are created by small businesses, not large. Over any twenty years, about 80% of the Fortune 500 of America's largest companies is replaced.

*5. **Loss of unity and focus creates openings**.* Starbuck's just brought out an instant coffee, which it is selling hard. This is creating a rift within the company and between the company and its customers. ***Size creates limitations***. When Starbuck's started opening stores across the street from each other, we should have seen the writing on the wall.

*6. **Size makes large organizations slow to react to change**.* Merck's slow reaction to news of heart problems from their arthritis drug Vioxx in 2004 created legal problems that continue today.

3.4.1 Unity Breakdown

Description: Sun Tzu's eight key methods regarding the conflict between size and unity.

"Another [commander] has subcommanders who are angry and defiant; they attack the enemy and fight their own battles."

Sun Tzu's The Art of War 10:2:17

"United we stand, divided we fall."

George Pope Morris

General Principle: Growth in the size of an organization naturally decreases its unity and focus.

Situation:

The mistake is thinking that size equals strength. We think of size in competition like children on a playground. Those who are bigger can bully. We want to get big so we won't be bullied. Because we are taught linear thinking , this seems to make sense. The problem is that competition doesn't follow the same rules of scale. Strength in competition is not defined by size. We think that if we grow, competition will get easier but it often gets more difficult. Size works against the real source of strength in competition. Large competitors can be intimidating, but they cannot be strong in the way that Sun Tzu defines strength.

Opportunity:

When we understand the problems of size, we learn to leverage the size of our opponents against them. Sun Tzu teaches that strength comes from a strongly shared mission not from size. From a single, clear mission flows focus and unity, which are the true components of strength. While the key elements that make up a strategic position are the same for any size organization (13.2 Element Scalability), strength from focus and unity does not scale. Opportunities are openings, arising from need, but all openings and needs are limited in size (3.2 Opportunity Creation). Eating one ice-cream sundae is good. Eating two isn't necessarily better. Eating ten is a form of torture.

Key Methods:

The following seven key methods describe how we look for opportunities in unity breakdown.

1. The first place we look for opportunities is in where unity and focus breaks down. Unity and focus are the source of strength. Strength arises from our shared mission, but because mission is the core of all strategic positions, a breakdown of unity and focus affects all five key aspects of a position. The larger the organization, the harder it is to maintain focus and unity. This creates weakness, which is an opportunity for others (1.7 Competitive Strength).

2. As organizations grow, smaller groups within them separate themselves. Each separate need that an organization fills has a limited size. Large organizations grow by serving many needs. Growth creates multiple missions. Different missions divide large organizations. We use the word "divisions" to describe the internal separations in of large organizations. These divisions naturally separate to create weakness within the organization (1.6.1 Shared Mission).

3. The logical division of labor requires internal connections that can break down. The division of labor depends on both loose and tight internal couplings. Over time, this integration tends to break down. Individuals focus their groups immediate goals, drifting away from the shared mission for practical reasons. This is known in management science as "practical drift" in business methods (1.5.2. Group Methods).

4. Division weakens the power of a mission. The larger the organization, the more basic its mission becomes. Different divisions find the lowest common denominator of mission. This is also the weakest of missions. In a business, it ends up as "making money." This makes the large organization generic, blurring its distinction from the rest of its competitive arena. Without a clear mission, it is held together only by history and structure, losing the impact of focus (1.7.2 Goal Focus).

5. Division leads to weak, spread-out positions. As missions diverge, different missions lead part of the organizations in different directions. The organization's focus gets spread out over more and more ground. The different systems in the organization no longer support each other. As Sun Tzu said, an army that tries to defend everywhere is weak everywhere. An organization that does more and more things does them less and less well (4.6.1 Extremes of Area).

6. Different internal goals lead inevitably to internal battles for resources. Size is an advantage in production. This means that large organizations have more resources, but divided missions mean different priorities. Different priorities create battles within an organization over limited resources ([1.6.3 Shifting Priorities](#)).

*7. **Internal competition takes the place of external competition.** This takes the form of internal politics. Politics emerges with growth as different groups develop their own separate agendas. More and more people within the organization can gain more personally from winning internal battles than external ones. Since these battles are internal, conflict becomes unavoidable. Since conflict is the most costly aspect of competition, the costs of running the organization rises inexplicably as more resources and energy are lost in internal conflict ([3.1.3 Conflict Cost](#))*

*8. **Opportunity for smaller competitors exists in all these divisions.** Opportunity exists in openings. Large competitors create the need for more focused competitors, with clearer, sharper missions. Those competitors can take advantage of the openings on the ground created by weak, spread out positions. They can better use their resources by avoiding battle and focusing on external progress ([3.1.4 Openings](#))*.

Illustration:

This problem with unity and focus and growth is seen most clearly in the growth of government.

*1. **The first place we look for opportunities is in where unity and focus breaks down.** Both parties are in the process of discovering that larger government is less effective government. The Republicans lost their unity and focus during the Bush years. The Democrats are losing their unity and focus during Obama's presidency despite overwhelming majorities in both houses of Congress.*

*2. **As organizations grow, smaller groups within them separate themselves.** The Republicans are trying to decide if they are the small government party or simply large government "light". The Democrats, meanwhile, are fighting over whether or not universal health care must be provided for abortions and illegal aliens.*

3. The logical division of labor requires internal connections that can break down. Rules allowing members of both parties to work together have been established over the years to prevent the dominant party from over-stepping their mandate. These rules protected minority interests from being shut out of debate and the majority from power plays that alienate the public. For example, the requirement in the Senate for 60 votes for cloture. However, over the years both parties have lost sight of the value of those rules.

4. Growth weakens the power of mission. The growth of government has blurred America's founding principles based on protecting individual liberty at home and fighting for it abroad. The big political tent is, by definition, a hard mission to package. Generic missions such as "change" quickly devolve into specific questions such as "change into what?"

5. Division leads to weak, spread-out positions. These weakness demonstrates itself on how poorly the government executes every activity. Politicians complain when corporation make a measly few percentage points in profit creating goods and services, but the government cannot give away $8,000 for used cars without it costing taxpayers over $30,000 per vehicle.

6. Different internal goals creates internal battles for resources. Politicians of both parties seem less and less interested in passing good laws and more and more interested in buying political support at the taxpayers expense. No one needs to read the legislation anymore as long as they know it has their own personal earmarks in it. For each billion dollars a politician gives out in taxpayer money, they want to see a million come back to them in political donations or cheap loans or free vacation homes.

7. Internal competition takes the place of external competition. As government tries to "solve more problems" within the country, America grows weaker in its world position both economically and militarily. In the recent decision to hold 9/11 trials in NY , America's enemies are given the publicity that they want so that one political party can put the other political party on trial.

8. Opportunity for smaller competitors exists in all these divisions. As America is more consumed with its own political divisions, it becomes more and more a target for terrorist and economic attack.

3.4.2 Opportunity Fitness

Description: Sun Tzu's seven key methods describing the problems for large organization finding new opportunities that fit their size.

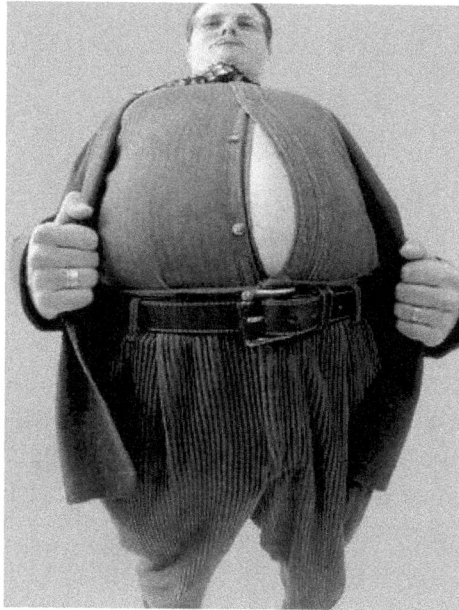

"Victory comes from correctly using both large and small forces."

Sun Tzu's The Art of War 3:5:3

"Small opportunities are often the beginning of great enterprises."

Demosthenes

General Principle: Larger organizations have more difficulty finding high-probability opportunities suitable for their size.

Situation:

Just as we confuse size with strength, we also confuse size with our capabilities to pursue opportunities. Because we are taught to think that bigger is better, we think of larger organizations as having more opportunities. The competitive reality is much more complicated. We can get into serious trouble if we fail to understand how our size relative to our competition sets practical limits on the opportunities that we can pursue.

Opportunity:

When we understand how our relative size affects our opportunities, we can identify suitable opportunities more easily. Opportunities are openings that fit our available strategic resources (3.1.1 Resource Limitations). Our resources have both size and shape. As with all competitive characteristics, the size and shape of our resources is relative. We only understand our qualities by comparing them against the position of our potential competitors (1.3.1 Competitive Comparison). Our relative size compared to our potential competitors creates both problems and opportunities in terms of finding opportunities that fit our resources.

Key Methods:

The following seven key methods describe the problems in finding opportunities that fit larger organizations.

1. ***Opportunity fit comes from matching available resources to the size and shape of openings.*** Large organizations are more likely to have a large variety of available resources but fewer opportunities to use them. Small organization are less likely to have a variety of available resources but many more opportunities to use them (3.3 Opportunity Resources).

2. ***Openings can be too large or too small to fit an opportunity.*** Successfully pursuing openings that are too big for our resources simply paves the way for larger competitors. Pioneering openings

that have too little long-term potential relative to the overall size of the organization leads to fragmentation. A number of small opportunities does not equal a big opportunity because the organization that pursues them pulls itself apart (3.4.1 Unity Breakdown).

3. Small opportunities fit our resources best when we are close to them. The vast majority of opportunities are small, local ones. These opportunities are the open spaces left between and among other existing positions. These opportunities fit our resources best when we are close to them physically or psychologically. Fit is based on proximity and affinity. Existing positions that are too distant from the need either physically or psychologically do not fit (4.4 Strategic Distance).

4. Large openings only arise on frontiers and fit those closest to them. A frontier is a new competitive arena opened by new methods. There are two common general types of frontiers. ***Frontiers for exploration*** arise when new methods open up entirely new areas of unknown potential. ***Frontiers for consolidation*** arise when new methods create the means for a large organization to displace a number of smaller, more diversified, local organizations. Both require the use of innovation. (7.3 Strategic Innovation).

5. The potential on frontiers of exploration is unknown but it always starts small. When a new competitive area is opened up by new methods, knowledge, or technology, its true potential is unknown, but it always starts out small. While some large organization's can pioneer new areas, the size of most of these opportunities will never be large and those that are large enough will take a long time to develop. Because of internal competition for resources, most mature large organization's do not have the patience to develop them (3.1.6 Time Limitations).

6. The potential on the frontiers of consolidation are better known but also usually start small. Since consolidation transforms an existing competitive arena, the general size of that arena is known. Successful consolidation almost always requires specialized knowledge only available within a competitive area. Consolidation is started by a small organization within that arena pioneering new methods that make consolidation possible. Large competitors can seldom move into an arena ripe for consolidation from the outside because they lack the specific knowledge and skills required (2.6 Knowledge Leverage).

7. People within large organizations are less capable at perceiving risks. Responsibility becomes more diffused in groups. People in groups make riskier decisions than they would ever make alone because they perceive that the others in the group are approving of that risk taking. This is known in psychology as the "risky shift." Coupled with fewer natural opportunities, this risky shift leads large organizations to pursue low probability opportunities instead of high-probability ones (4.0 Leveraging Probability).

Illustration:

Let us look at some business examples from the modern world.

1. Opportunity fit comes from matching available resources to the size and shape of openings. One example is Warren Buffett's investment firm, Berkshire Hathaway. Historically, Berkshire Hathaway grew by acquiring privately held firms. However, as Berkshire Hathaway has grown in scale, there are simply fewer and fewer companies larger enough for it to pursue. Buffett has discussed this problem a number of times, as this recent article describes: Buffett deals only with large companies because he needs to make massive investments to garner the returns required to post excellent results for the huge size to which his company, Berkshire Hathaway, has grown.

2. Openings can be too large or too small to fit an opportunity. See specific examples below.

3. Small opportunities fit our resources best when we are close to them. Here is a typical example in the pharmaceutical industry, described in an article in the The Atlantic about how the mergers in the industry is eliminating the availability of new drugs: At large companies, products that are technically promising are terminated if the marketing potential is thought to be too small. And the height of that market hurdle has risen as the profits of the large companies have grown. Today, programs that are thought to have an annual sales potential of less than $1 billion are usually stopped in their tracks. Some companies have abandoned their work in entire areas of medicine, such as antibiotics, because they believe the markets are too small to make a difference to their total sales.

4. Large openings only arise on frontiers and fit those closest to them. Frontiers for exploration are new markets such as the personal computer or internet market. Frontiers for consolidation occur in places like retailing where new innovation in communication and transportation created new methods of distribution.

5. The potential on frontiers of exploration is unknown but it always starts small. A number of large companies were directly involved in the pioneering efforts to create the first personal computers. IBM, Digital Equipment, and Xerox all did the basic research in development but lost out to relative new comers like Apple because they were all too big for the opportunity. IBM's first successful PC (after a series of failures) was more of a success for the small companies Microsoft and Intel than it was for IBM who, of course, eventually sold off its PC division. The same was true in the Internet, where large media companies such as Time/Warner invested heavily buying AOL. The result again was spectacular failure.

6. The potential on the frontiers of consolidation are better known but also usually start small. It was Wal-Mart and Costco, coming from nowhere, who revolutionized retail distribution, not the giants Sears JC Penney's, or K-Mart. Enron was very successful at consolidating the trading of energy in the form of natural gas contracts, but when they moved outside their area of expertise into other forms of trading, such as broadband contracts, the result was a spectacular financial failure and collapse.

7. People within large organizations are less capable at perceiving risks. How could Enron get into so much trouble? Inherently risky decisions were perceived as less risky because of the size of the group that seemingly approved of them.

3.4.3 Reaction Lag

Description: Sun Tzu's six key methods regarding why organizations react slower as they grow larger.

""*Take advantage of a larger enemy's inability to keep up.*
Sun Tzu's The Art of War 11:2.17

"The percentage of mistakes in quick decisions is no greater than in long-drawn-out vacillation, and the effect of decisiveness itself 'makes things go' and creates confidence."
Anne O'Hare McCormick

General Principle: The larger the organization, the slower its reaction time.

Situation:

Speed is the essence of competition. In any organization, the reactive decisions are made on the frontlines, reacting to external events. What happens to reaction time as an organization grows? Its ability to react to external events slows down. The problem in larger organizations is the coordination of response. The larger the organization, the more entangled its lines of authority. More levels of decision-makers are involved. Different parts of the organization will react to events in very different ways. While strategy arises from our reaction to external stimulus, for large organizations, that reaction becomes an internal problem.

Opportunity:

The opportunity here is for relatively small organizations to take advantage of events before their larger competitors can react. The opportunity for larger organizations is use their advantages in resources to overcome their disadvantages in initial response. Large organizations create opportunities for smaller organizations because they are, by necessity, slower to react to events. For both, the use of strategy depends heavily on speed and quickness.

Key Methods:

The basis of good strategy is fast cycle-times (1.8.3 Cycle Time). Events are happening continuously. Sun Tzu adapts to those events. Our initial response are never perfect, but the faster our reaction cycles, the more quickly we can fine-turn our response. Quick reactions cycles, even if imperfect, can make situations more difficult for our opponents (5.3 Reaction Time).

1. Internal areas of control always grow faster than external competitive interfaces. Growing an organization is like blowing up a balloon. The surface of the balloon is the competitive interface where the organization makes contact with the environment. The internal volume of the balloon is the organization's span of control.

As an organization grows, its competitive surface expands but its span of control expands much, much faster. This is mathematically true for any solid object. For a sphere, the surface grows at the rate of its size squared, but the volume grows at the rate of its size cubed (1.9 Competition and Production).

2. The demands of internal control move the organization's focus toward _executing plans._ Large organizations require more internal planning because they have a large interior volume of production resources. Production requires planning, but the focus on internal planning decreases the focus on external strategy. Those on the competitive surface of the organization must increasingly conform their decisions to existing plans. Sales plans and marketing plans have little predictive value aside from extending historical momentum into the future but they are necessary to feed production planning (1.9.2 Span of Control).

3. Existing plans slows down reaction time to unplanned external events. As planning comes to dominate organizational thinking, both recognizing external events and adjusting to them requires more time. Actions must be coordinated to plans. The minority of people who are concerned about strategy are outnumbered by the volume of people who are concerned about maintaining plans (5.2.1 Choosing Adaptability).

4. Front-line decision-makers may see what needs to be done but cannot make the case to do it quickly. Managers throughout the company have not been trained in strategy. Instead they are consciously trained to make decisions within a narrow set of boundaries. This means when unexpected events arise, front-line decision-makers are at a disadvantage as the decision is passed up through the organization hierarchy and out to different divisions within the organization. The more unusual the event, the further up the hierarchy it must go for a decision to be made (3.4.1 Unity Breakdown).

5. Information degrades as it moves through the organization decreasing decision pressure. This means that more than time is lost in clarifying what is really happening. The further decision-makers are from the front-lines, the more time it takes them to gather information about an event in order to develop a complete picture of the situation. The more people through whom information and decisions must pass, the more likely it is to hit a bottleneck or simply get lost or forgotten (2.1.1 Information Limits)

6. *Organizations are trained to execute plans not to adapt to changing conditions.* Larger armies must train their people how to change directions quickly, but other large organizations are not similarly trained. Once a decision is made, large organization's take longer to act than small ones. Coordinating large groups always takes longer than coordinating small groups. A small group of twenty people can put together a task force of five people many times more quickly than a larger group can. A useful rule of thumb to calculate the relative time of response is simply to multiply response time by the relative difference in size. If one group is twice as large as another, it will take them twice as long to respond. If it is a hundred times longer, it will take them a hundred times longer to respond to an unforeseen event (6.0 Situation Response).

Illustration:

The best example of this problem of reaction lag is in the growth of government and its delivery of services.

1. *Internal areas of control always grow faster than external competitive interfaces.* When a government is small and local, most its resources are on the surface. The elected officials deal directly with the public that they serve on a hourly basis, providing many services directly themselves. As the government grows, not only are the elected officials more and more isolated but more and more government employees work inside increasingly large bureaucracies with no public contact at all.

2. *The demands of internal control move the organization's focus toward executing plans.* As government grows larger, more and more people are devoted to writing policies, regulations, and plans. The laws themselves grow in volume and size until they are so complex that no one understands them.

3. Existing plans slows down reaction time to unplanned external events. Regulations become so confused that Treasury Secretary Geithner, who is responsible for the tax code, cannot correctly pay his income tax and Attorney General Holder cannot answer the question about whether or not those who capture bin Laden would have to read him his Miranda rights.

4. Front-line decision-makers may see what needs to be done but cannot make the case to do it quickly. Top decision-makers are largely immune from the consequences of their mistakes, but those on the front-line know that they will be held responsible for their decisions. Making decisions requires more and more diffusion on responsibility to avoid the consequences of the complex internal environment.

5. Information degrades as it moves through the organization decreasing decision pressure. Incumbents and bureaucrats are increasingly isolated from the decisions that they make, so they feel that they can concentrate on issues such as medical care and cap-and-trade, while the economy and dollar spirals downward.

6. Organizations are trained to execute plans not to adapt to changing conditions. While large companies usually punished by the market for their increasingly ineffective organizations, government simply sends tax payers a bigger and bigger bill.

3.5.0 Strength and Weakness

Description: Sun Tzu's six key methods explain how openings created by the strength of others.

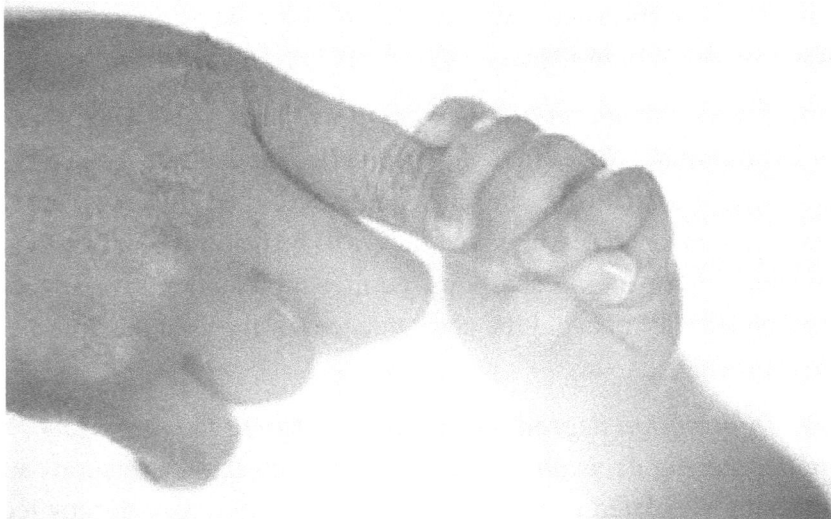

""You must adapt to opportunities and weaknesses."
Sun Tzu's The Art of War 8:2:2

"If you think a weakness can be turned into a strength, I hate to tell you this, but that's another weakness."
Jack Handy

General Principle: A competitor's strength always creates a corresponding weakness that is an opening.

Situation:

Strength draws our attention. We naturally focus on the strengths of others. One of the most common strategic mistakes is thinking that we have to duplicate the strengths of others in order to be competitive. Nothing is further from the truth. Though we are a thousand times more likely to hear about the strengths of others, especially our rivals, than we are their weaknesses, this doesn't mean that our success lies in copying them. That path only leads to duplication of effort and often to conflict as a test of similar relative strengths.

Opportunity:

Our opportunity is not in duplicating the strengths of others but in complementing them. It is the weaknesses of others that creates openings and our opportunities. Openings are difficult to see directly because people hide their weaknesses (3.2.2 Opportunity Invisibility). While people disguise their weaknesses, their strengths are easy to see and seldom disguised. Our opportunity is that we can use those strengths to identify their weaknesses. Every strength creates a corresponding weakness if we know where to look for it. It is these weaknesses that provide us with our opportunities. They are the openings that we can take leverage to our advantage. Learning how to identify weaknesses in strengths takes time and practice. Once we master these skills, every time a strength draws our attention, we can instantly find ourselves thinking about the weaknesses that this strength could engender.

Key Methods:

Weakness arises from strength in the specific ways described by the following key methods.

1. We never look for advantage by duplicating a rival's strengths. Duplicating strengths looks easier than it is. Such duplication alone cannot result in a superior position because it is a copy. At best, it creates a good copy, a second-best position. It also usually fails on economic grounds, because our rivals are always ahead of us on the learning curve (3.1.2 Strategic Profitability).

2. We can use people's strengths to predict their behavior and predictability is a weakness. People use their strengths and tend to develop their strengths over time. Once we understand where a position's strength lies, we can predict how it will be used and how it develops over time. We can also better predict what surrounding positions will be left open (2.3.2 Reaction Unpredictability).

*3. **Ground area, barriers, and stickiness each create two balancing forms of weaknesses***. These three dimensions determine the "surface" characteristics of a strategic position. Each of their six extremes creates a different specific form of weakness (4.7 Competitive Weaknesses).

*4. **For decision makers, character excesses generate weaknesses***. Sun Tzu describes five key characteristics of decision makers. We normally think of a weakness as a lack, but Sun Tzu teaches that excessive strength creates weaknesses. This is especially true when we look at a person's character. We can find opportunities in the specific weaknesses of character--over-confidence, foolhardiness, indecision, rigidity, and fussiness--arise from an excess of certain traits (4.7.1 Command Weaknesses).

*5. **Imbalances within organizations create weaknesses.*** An organization needs a balances of skills and capabilities. An overbalance in one area or another creates an organization weakness. Sun Tzu describes six specific forms of imbalances. We learn those weaknesses in order to spot the opportunities that they create (4.7.2 Group Weaknesses).

*6. **Specific forms of strength generate specific forms of weakness.*** We look for our openings by identifying the flip side of a given strength. Sun Tzu's principles list many specific forms of strength and their corresponding weakness. Fast service is good, but it means limited choices and quality. Having lot of options is good, but more options make decisions more difficult. Low prices are good, but it means less quality and service. High quality and service is good, but it means high prices. The most common example of this are the weaknesses caused by size (3.4 Dis-Economies of Scale).

*7. **More generally, we can use the calculus of emptiness and fullness to find weakness in strength***. A strength is a fullness of some resource. Every resource is generated buy a key element of a position (1.3 Elemental Analysis). Every key element is balanced by an opposing element. A surplus in one side of the equation creates a corresponding cost on the other side of the equation (3.2.4 Emptiness and Fullness).

Illustration:

Since this is such a broad topic, let us look at a variety of examples here.

1. We never look for advantage by duplicating a rival's strengths. For example, Apple is a great proprietary design company. In trying to duplicate Apple's success, a lot of competitors will focus on trying to out-design Apple. In taking this path, virtually all of them will fail. Apple's position as the design leader is firmly established both by objective facts and subjective beliefs. No one will change it until Apple starts making consistent mistakes in design (like the recessed headphones jack of the first iPhone).

2. We can use people's strengths to predict their behavior and predictability is a weakness. As self-defense martial artist once explained to me, you always know exactly where the focus of an armed attacker is. It is focused on his weapon and his weapon hand. He is vulnerable everywhere else because his attention is consumed by the weapon. His strength is his vulnerability.

3. Ground area, barriers, and stickiness create specific forms of weaknesses. The highly successful position of Coke was based on its "secret recipe," and that positioning is extremely sticky, which is usually considered a good thing because people are devoted to sticky positions. Pepsi took advantage of that stickiness by catering to changing tastes offering a sweeter product and using taste tests to promote that product. Coke could not counter that move with its own sweeter product because of the stickiness of its position, as it discovered with its failed introduction of New Coke,

4. For decision makers, character excesses generate weaknesses. Historically, highly educated and academically intelligent state leaders have been characteristically flawed throughout modern history by indecision, especially in choosing between two bad alternatives when no good alternatives are available.

*5. **Imbalances within organizations create weaknesses.*** We commonly see larger organizations grow their internal bureaucracies until they become like GM: unable to respond to market competition because their decisions are too heavily influenced by internal issues.

*6. **Specific forms of strength generate specific forms of weakness.*** For example, after years in the software business, when I hear about how "feature rich" a software product is, I instantly think about the downsides of features. More features make it difficult to learn those features. Features often get in the way of the relatively simple tasks. Features cost money to develop and support and increase the costs of software.

*7. **More generally, we can use the calculus of emptiness and fullness to find weakness in strength**. Going back to our example of Apple, the strength of great design creates weaknesses. Great design is costly. Products that provide the same functionality can be built and sold much less expensively. Those who compete with Apple on price will always find a place in the market because Apple will never see themselves as the low-cost producer.

3.6.0 Leveraging Subjectivity

Description: Sun Tzu's seven key methods regarding openings between subjective and objective positions.

""*You can be as mysterious as the fog.
You can strike like sounding thunder.*"

Sun Tzu's The Art of War 7:3:7-8

"It isn't what we don't know that gets us in trouble. It is what we think we know that ain't so."

Will Rodgers

General Principle: Many opportunities arise in the gap between objective reality and subjective perception.

Situation:

An opportunity requires two components: an opening in the environment and the resources to move into it. These resources take many different forms. A new job requires qualifications. A new business requires investment. The problem is that all resources are limited. Our resource limitations are especially a problem when we are first starting out, but, even as we advance, it always seems that each additional step forward always requires more resources than the last. The use of physical resources is like the use of force. The more force we use, the more resistance we meet.

Opportunity:

Our opportunity is in replacing the use of physical resources with intellectual leverage. We can leverage people's perceptions of our position to advance our position. There is always a gap between the objective reality and people's subjective opinions. That gap is a special type of opening that we can use as an opportunity (3.1.4 Openings). Our position is like a bottle. Since we are inside the bottle, we cannot read its label. Others can read the label, but they don't really know what is inside the bottle. All they know is what the label says. Changing the label to improve people's perceptions is easier than changing the contents of the bottle. We use this change in packaging as a leverage point to change our objective position (2.6 Knowledge Leverage).

Key Methods:

Looking for opportunities in the gap between subjective perception and objective reality is easier using the following seven key methods.

1. There is always a gap between subjective perception and objective reality. The question is not whether or not that gap exists. There is always a gap between the objective nature of reality and our human subjective ability to perceive it. The only question is whether or not we know how to leverage that gap to improve people's subjective impression of our position (1.2 Subobjective Positions)

2. We can change perceptions either through repackaging or reeducation. Repackaging simply puts known facts in a better context. Re-education is much more difficult since it means changing one set of perceptions into another.

3. Repackaging requires clarifying our position, its value, and how it has changed. This is done through the five techniques of getting agreement, pointing out trends, highlighting scarcity, authority approval, and asking for favors covered more extensively later in The Playbook (8.3.2 Distinctive Packaging).

4. Re-education requires communicating non-conforming facts that conflict with existing perceptions. Everyone thinks that their opinions are based upon facts, but perceptions usually come tfirst. After perceptions are formed, facts that don't conform to those perceptions are unconsciously filtered out. This is known scientifically as confirmation bias. It requires work to break down this bias (2.1.1 Information Limits).

5. We can only change opinions with facts not different opinions about facts. A non-conforming fact is not a different subjective interpretation of a fact. Nor can it be a piece of information that is questionable or debatable. It must be indisputably solid, but unnoticed. Pushing alternative opinions only creates reactance , people's desire to do the opposite of what they are pressured to do (2.3.1 Action and Reaction).

6. We must gather information to identify non-conforming facts that others do not see. We mistakenly think that others see the same fact that we do. Confirmation bias almost assures that others do not see what we see. Because of our different positions, we all have a different perspective. Our job is to identify what others are missing, which we do through the standard strategic technique for developing perspective (2.0 Developing Perspective).

7. We must present the non-confirming fact as surprising. If we do not draw attention to the fact as surprising, it will get filtered out through the normal process of confirmation bias. The fact may not seem surprising to us, but we must pretend that it is in order to communicate it. Surprise is always necessary when we want people to pay attention to what they would normally miss (2.1.4 Surprise).

Illustration:

As an illustration, let us examine the problem of getting someone to trust us. This is a common problem that comes up in a variety of both personal and professional issues of advancing a position.

1. There is always a gap between subjective perception and objective reality. People do not trust us because they know that they do not know us. We can never really know a person completely, but we can know them well enough to trust them.

2. We can change perceptions either through repackaging or reeducation. For our illustration, let us assume the problem is that we are known to be a little lazy. If its is true that we are a little lazy, we must repackage our laziness to its best advantage. If it is false, we must must work on reeducation.

3. Repackaging requires clarifying our position, its value, and how it has changed. The first step is clarifying the boundaries and benefits of our laziness. If we recognize that we are lazy in less important areas, we can claim to be prioritizing our efforts. We can also claim that one of the benefits is that our laziness has always spurred us to find more efficient and effective ways of working.

4. Re-education requires communicating non-conforming facts that conflict with existing perceptions. If we really are not lazy, the facts of our industriousness must exist.

5. We can only change opinions with facts not different opinions about facts. Here, we must make sure that we *are* really industrious and that we are not simply deluding ourselves.

6. We must gather information to identify non-conforming facts that others do not see. We must collect the date that proves how hard we work in measurable non-subjective terms: hours of work, number of tasks performed, etc.

7. We must present the non-confirming fact as surprising. If we just say, "You think I am lazy, but here are the facts," we will trigger reactance. However, if we start from a position of "Wow, I was surprised to find out that I did so much last month. I always thought I was pretty laid back about this stuff," we have a much better chance of being heard.

3.7.0 Redefining the Comparison

Description: Sun Tzu's eight key methods on redefining a competitive arena to create relative mismatches.

""You can divide the ground and still defend it."
Sun Tzu's The Art of War 6:3:15

"It was classic divide and conquer."

David Vise

General Principle: Competitors can be divided into different categories of comparison to uncover a hidden opening.

Situation:

Competition is based on making comparisons. The problem is that there are just some types of comparisons in which we are never going to look as good as we can. We get measured against the wrong competitors in the wrong ways. We can seem trapped by fate into comparison where we simply cannot stand out or rise up. In these situations, we cannot find openings. We are dominated by an environment in which we are a square peg in a world of round holes.

Opportunity:

Though opportunities are created by our environment, we can shape our environment by shaping how comparisons are made. How comparisons are made is based upon a subjective decision. This choice either divides one set of contestants or one set of judges from another. This choice defines the "battle ground". Sun Tzu described the battleground as infinite because it can be divided in an infinite number of ways. We can use division to reveal openings that don't exist from any standard perspective. When we cannot measure up on an existing yardstick, we may have the opportunity to invent new yardsticks for comparison. Yes, we must adapt to objective reality, conforming our strategy to real world conditions instead of trying to control them (3.2.1 Environmental Dominance). However, the subjective measures by which comparisons are made are infinitely variable.

Key Methods:

To redefine a competitive arena to produce more favorable comparisons, we must use the following key methods.

1. The way in which positions are compared is dynamic.
People are always finding better ways to make comparisons. We can climb up the rungs of a ladder that already exists or we can reinvent the ladder. We make the choice based on how easily we can sell people on the idea of a new ladder where we already own a high rung. In the social sciences, framing describes the collection of concepts that people use to use understand and respond to events. We often have the ability to create new frames that divide that competitive space in innovative, new ways. We can then identify holes that are invisible from the ordinary ways in which those spaces are evaluated (1.1.1 Position Dynamics).

2. ***The opportunity for dividing the ground must exist in the*** ***environment.*** We cannot invent that ladder out of whole cloth. A new basis competition only works if others can easily see the value in a new framework for comparison. Those who judge must be rewarded in some way for using the new basis of comparison (3.1.2 Strategic Profitability),

3. ***We must understand the current basis for how our ground*** ***is currently divided.*** This means that we must have a broad perspective on our competitive arena. We must understand how the rankings within it are currently made and why (2.4.1 Ground Perspective).

4. ***List the characteristics that are currently used for comparison.*** What are the current methods of competitive comparison? This is, of course, different for every competitive arena. These are the common characteristics that bring a group of competitors, creating a specific competitive arena (1.3.1 Competitive Comparison).

5. ***List potential areas of comparison that are currently overlooked.*** There are four common ideas we can use for inspiration here: a) finer distinctions that create smaller groups, b) distinctions that make bigger groups, b) distinctions than emphasize change or rate of change rather than static conditions, and c) distinctions that are made in similar types of competitive arenas (2.6 Knowledge Leverage).

6. ***We identify overlooked characteristics that give us a clear*** ***advantage.*** We identify comparisons in which we can excel and in which others do well. These characteristics obviously emphasize our strengths. These depend upon our current position and our relative capabilities (3.5 Strength and Weakness).

7. ***There must be an advantage*** *__for others__* ***in using our new*** ***yardstick.*** We want others to use this yardstick because it improves our position, but they will not use it unless it is in their best interests to do so. The new frame must help them understand the competitive arena better so that they can make better comparisons and choices. There are often empty niches for comparisons waiting to be filled. No one sees those niches because no one asks these questions. This potential for benefit in using a new yardstick has to exist in the situation, both for ourselves and for others. (1.6.1 Shared Mission).

8. We must be able to promote the value of seeing the ground in this new way to others. This goes back to the concept that we must make claims in order to get rewarded. A new yardstick does us no good unless we can get people to use it (8.2 Making Claims).

Illustration:

Let us illustrate these key methods by examining the positioning of a business in an existing marketplace.

1. The way in which positions are compared is dynamic. Since I personally prefer working in more dynamic competitive arenas, redefining ground is my preferred way of identifying openings and competing. Let us examine how I positioned my software company before I sold it.

2. The opportunity for dividing the ground must exist in the environment. We got into the software market because it was fast growing. Quickly growing competitive arenas create more opportunities for dividing the ground as more complexity emerges.

3. We must understand the current basis for how our ground is currently divided. Since we grew our company into our market niche for over a decade, we understood how the game was played.

4. List the characteristics that are currently used for comparison. In our area of software--order processing systems for large, multinational manufacturers, comparison was usually made on the basis of detailed feature sets. The purchasing decision was based on which software package had the best feature set.

5. List potential areas of comparison that are currently overlooked. We could have tried to go into more detailed descriptions of features, but the list was already beyond human comprehension. We could have looked at areas of computers, for example, Apple, and competed on the basis of a more exciting user interface.

6. *We identify overlooked characteristics that give us a clear advantage.* Our product was built to make it easy to tailor our product to meet specific needs. A concept that we called, modifiable-bydesign.

7. *There must be an advantage for others in using our new yardstick.* We changed the decision away from choosing software by comparing endless lists of competing features. Instead we asked if the potential customer wanted to a) adapt their business processes to fit the software and then freeze those processes or 2) adapt the software to fit their process and continue modifying the software as their business changed while retaining the ability to keep those modifications when they moved to a new version of the software.

8. *We must be able to promote the value of seeing the ground in this new way to others*. Needless to say, this was a fairly easy decision and we quickly became the number one accounting product on our platform, Unix servers. \

3.8.0 Strategic Matrix Analysis

Description: Sun Tzu's four key methods regarding two-dimensional representations of a strategic battleground.

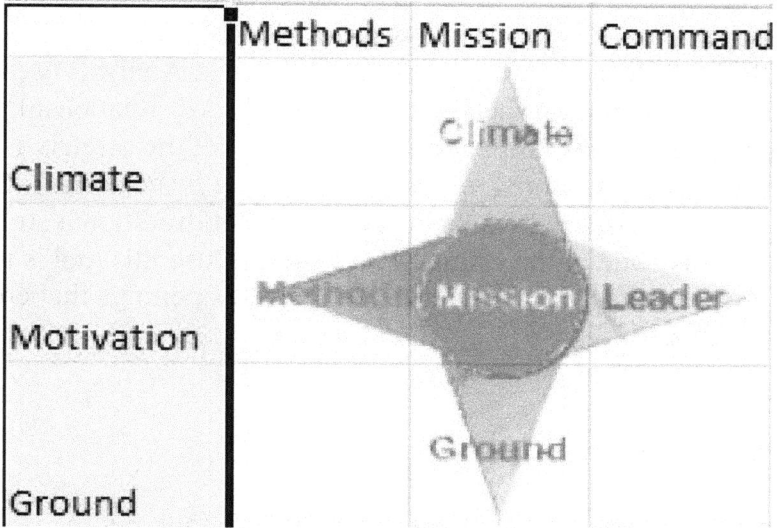

	Methods	Mission	Command
Climate		Climate	
Motivation	Methods	Mission	Leader
Ground		Ground	

"You can recognize the opportunity for victory; you don't create it."

Sun Tzu's The Art of War 4:1:10

"There exist limitless opportunities in every industry. Where there is an open mind, there will always be a frontier."

Charles Kettering

General Principle: Mapping situations using the five elements in a matrix makes openings easier to see and predict.

Situation:

As we can see from this section of The Playbook, there are many types of openings and the concept of "openings" can get very conceptual. The problem is that, as humans, we are wired primarily for visual perception. When our methods are purely conceptual, we miss many of our potential opportunities because we cannot "see" the openings involved.

Opportunity:

One of the most sophisticated ways to discover openings is using Strategic Matrix Analysis. Strategic Matrix Analysis uses the Stratrix, a visual tool for helping people see the key relationships among a given set of competitors. The purpose of the Stratrix is to provide a two-dimensional representation of the five dimensions (mission/climate/ground/leader/methods) used in traditional strategic analysis. One of the primary ways we can use this tool is to map competitive arenas in order to identify the openings that create opportunities.

Key Methods:

There are many different uses of the Stratrix tool, but the purpose of this article is simply to introduce the tool and its use in discovering opportunities.

	Low Price	Quality	Custom
Novel			
Standard			
Mass			

1. The generic Stratrix is three-by-three, nine-celled matrix.
The three columns of the Stratrix represent the major components of an competitor: a) methods, b) specific mission, and c) command. The three rows of the stratrix represent the major components of the competitive environment: 1) climate, 2) general motivations, 3) ground. Following the normal compass map of the five key elements (1.3 Elemental Analysis).

2. The rows and columns are modified to reflect the unique *character of the competitive arena*. Since each of the five dimensions represented in the matrix has many different defining characteristics, a special Stratrix can be designed to compare only those characteristics seen as the most relevant in a given competitive situation. We usually use the matrix to organize the characteristics already used to divide groups of competitors in a given arena (3.7 Defining the Ground). In this version, we compare the positioning of various companies and products. The columns represent various types of sellers--a) low price, b) quality c) custom. The rows represent types of customer markets--1) the market for novelty, 3) the market for standards, 3) the mass market.

3. Relative competitive positions are mapped on the Stratrix.
The Matrix is used to map relative positions. Each relevant competitor will have both a location and take up a certain amount of "space" on the map. The space represents the mental space owned by the competitors. Using this tool, we can chart in two dimensions the positions that competitors occupy in five dimensions. This allows us to see their relative position to each other.

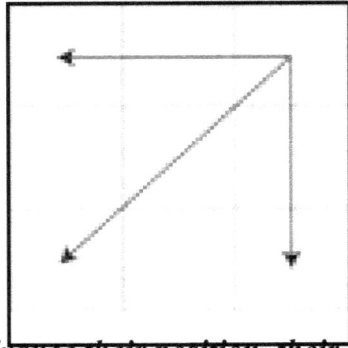

As competitors advance their position, their positions tend to move down and to the left. One important aspect of the Market Analysis Stratrix is that we can use it to predict the paths of competitors in a competitive arena. That path starts at the top, since new position are created by climate and moves down as they establish themselves on the ground. They also move from right to left, from command, making decision, to methods, as those methods become more established (1.1 Position Paths).

Illustration:

Let us say that there are three competitors in a market. Blue is a company like Apple sells cutting edge, high-quality products that have become standard in a few areas. Red appeals more to the standard and mass markets with combining quality and low price. Green focuses more on low price and standards.

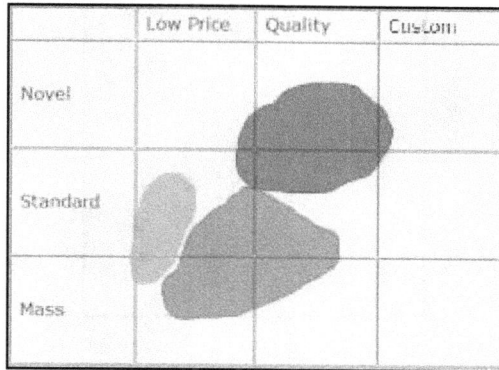

	Low Price	Quality	Custom
Novel			
Standard			
Mass			

The question is, where is the potential opening? In real life, most people just look at the tiny openings between competitors: areas of quality that are missed by Blue and Red, the areas of standards missed by Red and Green. New competitors entering this market might even miss those tiny openings, instead going after areas already occupied by one of the major existing competitors. These "me-to" products would almost certainly fail because there is no opening and therefore, no opportunity.

The real potential openings in this market are the cells that are almost entirely empty for any type of more customized product or for a low-priced novel product. If a competitor can get to one of these positions, they know that they will not face competition in these areas. They cannot know the value of these positions before exploring them (3.1.5 Unpredictable Value), but they can know that this positions represent open ground.

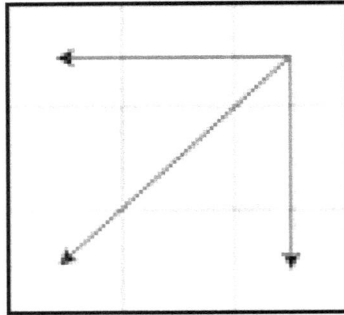

As these organizations develop and grow, they migrate from the upper right-hand corner down toward the lower left-hand cell. Blue sells very novel products today, but success makes it hard to maintain novelty. If successful, products that were once novel move into the mass market. Smart competitors enter markets in the upper right-hand box (very novel, custom products) taking the highground from existing products. Then, as they grow, their leading edge sucks the life of their competitions railing edge.

Sun Tzu's Playbook

Volume 4:
Probability

About Probability

You cannot pursue every opportunity you discover. You must be selective. Opportunities represent potential positions. Each position has its own unique character. Each has its own limitations. Each offers its own unique probabilities for success. This chapter covers how you can identify the "high-probability" opportunities for success.

To calculate these probabilities, you must understand your current position's potential as a stepping-stone to future positions. You must evaluate the potential and limitations hidden in every competitive position. You cannot invest in positions that are difficult to defend. You cannot move into positions that are dead ends.

Different Forms of Opportunity

In evaluating the potential of a given opportunity, we start with the concept of "ground form." In Sun Tzu's system, the ground is the basis of competition. Different competitive arenas are different types of ground, but these different types of ground all have a form. Sun Tzu's principles define four forms, each of which offers its own advantages and challenges in terms of choosing an opportunity.

In this volume, we describe these four forms very generally as "tilted," "fluid", "soft," and "neutral." However, in writing about Sun Tzu's principles, we have used a variety of other terms as well, including "uneven," "rapidly changing," "uncertain", and "solid." The terms used are less important than the key methods describing them, but here we provide a quick overview

"Tilted" or "uneven" forms represent an unbalanced areas. Physically, Sun Tzu described them as "mountains." In a modern social context, we have describe them as a business market have many small potential customers are dominated by a few very large customers. These forms are important because the force of gravity give some positions an advantage. We use their gravity to fight "downhill."

"Fluid" or "rapidly changing" areas are dominated by climate, that is, the forces of change. Sun Tzu describes this as water. In modern terms, we talk about areas such as technology that change rapidly. The advantage in these areas comes from the direction of change. We call this direction the "flow" or "currents" of change.

"Soft" of "uncertain" areas are dominated by confusion, rumors, and a lack of solid information. Sun Tzu described them physically as "marshes." In modern society, they are any area where most people have proven to be undependable. The advantage in these areas comes from whatever stability or solid information we can find.

"Neutral" or "solid" areas are the opposite of the other three. They are just right. They are even, stable, and certain. In these area, there is no forces at work, such a gravity, currents, or stability, that give an advantage to one position over another.

You can use the topography of an opportunity against your competitors in any of these four areas. You must not treat all spaces as if they were the same. You must adapt to the unique conditions in the place, just as you adapt to the changing character of your enterprise.

Physical and Psychological Space

Most of the principles in this volume deal with the idea of "space" or "area." In picking an opportunity, you must be able to defend your existing position long enough to move to another one. How easily you can defend your position and eventually move to a better position is determined by the aspects of its "space," discussed in this chapter. Some positions are easy to defend; others are more difficult. Some positions are difficult to advance while others make advancing easy.

There is nothing new in any of these situations. They have occurred a million times in competition, but every situation will not occur in every campaign. You cannot predict if or when they will occur.

Positions exist both in physical space and mind space. Your job has a physical location. Its location describes its physical relationships with customers, competitors, and suppliers. Your role also has a psychological location. Its psychological position maps how your customers, competitors, and suppliers position you in their mental image of the marketplace.

As we move deeper into the information age, physical market space is becoming less important while psychological or mental space is becoming more important. Affinity trumps proximity. Advances in transportation and communication make physical proximity less important.

All positions have shape. Physical spaces have shape. Psychological spaces have shape. Positions, a combination of both, have shape. Though it is easier to discuss shape in physical terms, the most important forces shaping markets today are psychological. Your success depends more upon people's perceptions than upon physical location. It doesn't matter how physically close people are if you are psychologically remote.

Because it exists primarily in people's minds, a position is subjective. Each customer and competitor defines it a little differently. Your position is both subjective and relative. It is defined only by how people mentally compare you with your competitors.

Like physical space, the psychological space of the market also has three dimensions. These dimensions are area, obstacles, and dangers. These terms have very specific meanings in the science of strategy.

"Area" measures the range of psychological territory that a position covers. For example, a position may address a small number of needs for a small group of people. Such a position covers a very small market area. A position may also address a wide variety of needs for a large group of people. Then the position covers a market area. The more area in a position's space, the more difficult that space is to defend.

"Barriers" refer to the number of problems you encounter in moving from one position space to another. Think of these problems or obstacles as "barriers to entry." The more barriers in a space, the more time, effort, or resources it takes to navigate that space. A position space that is easy to get into has few barriers to entry. A position space that is difficult to get into has many barriers to entry. The more barriers in a space, the easier it is to defend but the harder it is to advance into it.

"Dangers" refers to the type of risks you encounter as you move out of certain types of positions. Some positions are challenging because you cannot leave them without weakening your position. Other positions are dangerous because if you attempt to leave them, you destroy them and cannot return to them. Both dangers make advances difficult.

Positions in Six Extremes

There are no absolutes in strategy. Everything is relative. Comparing every unique aspect of your position to all the unique aspects of your competitors is too complicated so we simplify. You can gauge the potential of a given competitive position by comparing it to the six extreme variations of the three dimension. We call these extremes the six benchmarks.

You examine positions one dimension at a time. For area, you compare your position to the smallest position area and largest position area. For barriers, you compare your positions to positions with the most barriers and the fewest. For dangers, you compare positions to the challenges of niches and peaks. By examining each of these six benchmark regions one at a time, you get a sense of the restrictions of any given position.

In this volume, you will learn to Sun Tzu's terminology for comparing positions using these benchmarks. You will also learn their related strengths and weaknesses. This is done in the terms of complementary opposites. Confined positions are the opposite of spread-out positions. Barricaded positions are the opposite of wide-open positions. Fragile positions or niches are the opposite of optimal positions or peaks.

You can see the restrictions in your own position by comparing it to each of these six benchmark regions. A position cannot be, at the same time, both confined and spread out since these are both opposite extremes of area. However, a position or potential position can be confined and barricaded and fragile.

Once you understand the shape of your position or potential position in terms of the six benchmark regions, this analysis will tell you how easily that position will be to establish, defend, and advance. You will also know how you must utilize that particular type of space.

Internal Imbalances

To understand your choices, you have to consider the restrictions created by the nature of any organization upon which you rely. Certain restrictions expose certain weaknesses in an organization. The six flaws of organizations are amplified by the restrictions in the six benchmark position. You can diagnose these weaknesses to predict how a given organization will respond to the restrictions of a position space.

Six weaknesses can handicap any organization. They affect both your own organizations and your competitors' organizations. The presence of these flaws makes it difficult for any organization to take advantage of any position space. However, each of the benchmark handicaps is exaggerated by one particular set of restrictions.

Self-destructive organizations result from a lack of mission. Their problems are most apparent in confined positions. Overextended organizations have to pull back from their position. Their greatest weakness is spread-out positions. Distracted organizations suffer from self-satisfied leadership. They have the most problems in barricaded positions. Barricaded positions are easy to defend but they require concentration. Inefficient organizations waste their resources. They have the most difficulty in wide-open positions. Wide-open positions invite competition. Prices are pressured in markets with few barriers to entry. Undisciplined organizations require not only good leadership judgment, but leadership control over the organization. They are most vulnerable in fragile positions. Fragile market positions require discipline. Untrained organizations have poor systems. They have the most problems in optimal positions. Optimal market positions require minimal decision-making on the part of the enterprise's leadership.

The potential of a given position arises as an interaction between the form of its space and the weaknesses of the organization. An organization can be understood in terms of the relative strength of it leadership, its systems, and the focus and unity it gets from its mission. If you analyze your organizations and your competitors' organizations, you are able to predict their options for defending or advancing their positions.

Knowing a Position's Potential Before Moving

You must understand the potential of your position before moving into a new position. You must understand how to use area, barriers, and dangers in order to advance your current position. You don't want to move into positions that make future advances more difficult. Each position must be a stepping-stone. This is the only way to build success over time.

You must choose or shape the organizations upon which you rely to fit the nature of your position. You do not have to do everything well in every position. You develop the qualities that are critical in your specific position space. You focus on bringing your resources together in confined spaces, on courageous leadership in spread-out positions, on focus in barricaded positions, on efficient systems in wide-open positions, on disciplined leadership in fragile positions, and on effective systems in peak positions. This is how you are profitable in these various situations.

You must respond to the mistakes your competitors make. You challenge them directly when they misjudge their position. Forget your original plans in the given situation. You cannot plan for every opportunity. You must go after opportunities that arise from a competitor's mistakes.

If you examine your current position and potential position, you can know when pursuing a new position will be too costly. Spread-out positions look big enough for unlimited expansion, but they result in a mismatch of your resources with position size. Open positions look easy to get into, but you have to have efficient systems to survive in them. You have to have the resources to invest to surmount the barriers to entry in barricaded positions. You must avoid pursuing positions hat will cost you more than they will ever return.

Your advances must pay for themselves in terms of giving you more resources not just win recognition. Get out of any positions that cannot pay off. Success demands that you make create an advantage, adding value to your environment. This is how you build your position over time. This is how you ensure your success.

All positions have shape and form. The shape of the positions you inhabit determines how easy it will be to defend and expand your position.

There are proven benchmarks for gauging position potential. Six benchmark positions represent the purest forms of extreme, static conditions. These benchmarks define the ways in which each of these six positions must be utilized.

Every organization has weaknesses and strengths. To make the most of the potential hidden within your position, you must know what elements within your organization need to be developed.

Your ability to harvest position's potential determines your future. You may know that the organizations to which you belong really work within a given type of space. You must also know that your competitors are poorly suited for that space. Finally, you must also know exactly how to use your resources in that space. If you understand your position and its dynamics, your success is assured.

4.0 Leveraging Probability

Sun Tzu's nine principles for making better decisions regarding our choice of opportunities.

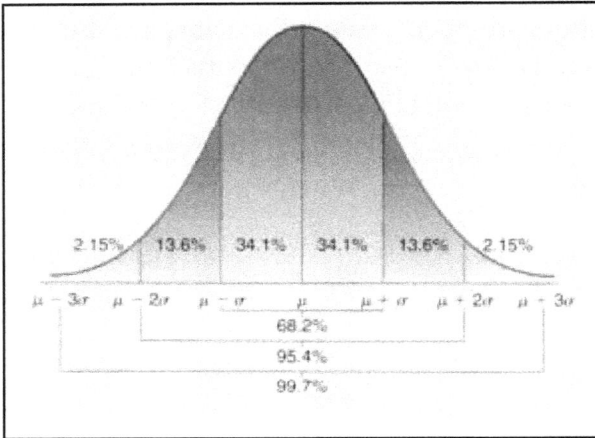

"Your numbers determine your calculations.
Your calculations determine your decisions.
Your decisions determine your victory."
Sun Tzu's The Art of War 4:4:12-14

"Probability is expectation founded upon partial knowledge."
George Boole

General Rule: We must choose the least expensive opportunities that lead to the most rewarding positions.

Situation:

An opportunity is any opening that we have the resources to pursue, but it is a mistake to pursue every possible opportunity. Most openings are unlikely to offer real rewards. Sun Tzu's science is exploration, designed to increase our probability of success over time. We cannot be successful if we chase after every opening, going in one direction then in another. Our resources are limited. We can only do one thing at a time. Openings must lead to positions. We cannot afford to pursue positions that we are not likely to win. We also must not choose positions that are not likely to take us where we want to go.

Opportunity:

The key is identifying high-probability opportunities. These are opportunities that lead to positions that pay for themselves. This is the topic of all of the articles in this section of our Playbook. We have limited time and resources (3.1.1 Resource Limitations). We want to devote those resources to pursuing opportunities. Those opportunities must lead to positions that we can win. Those positions must be those that are the most likely to pay, both in the short term and long term (3.1.2 Strategic Profitability). While nothing can tell us the true potential of an opportunity before we explore it, we can compare opportunities by characteristics that have, in the past, proven to make a big difference in identifying those opportunities that lead to great positions.

Key Methods:

These ten key methods define how we leverage probability to our advantage.

1. ***To leverage probability, we must think both of opportunities and positions as stepping stones.*** Opportunities are openings to a position. Positions move us toward our goals. We must consider where each step leads before we take it. Pursuing any opportunities has costs. Only positions can return rewards. Using high probability opportunities determines how easily and inexpensively new, valuable positions are won, defended, and advanced (1.1 Position Paths).

2. ***To leverage probability, we need only the ability to compare the general odds.*** Success doesn't require that we make perfect choices about our moves, but choosing the probabilities makes our

success more certain over time. We can never know exactly where a specific opportunity will lead so we compare opportunities based upon how we see the probabilities involved. Only from these comparisons can we get a quick idea of the future potential profitability of exploring an opportunity (1.3.1 Competitive Comparison).

3. ***Our probability of a successful move depends both on our starting point and destination.*** Successful moves improve our position. Our current position only makes certain opportunities available. Our choices in pursuing opportunities can either open or close doors for us. Both our current position and desired future position have different limitations that we must consider in making our moves. We want to move in directions that open us to more and better opportunities over time. (4.1 Limitations and Potential).

4. ***To leverage probability, we must choose non-action when high-probability opportunities are unavailable.*** Though we talk in terms of choosing among opportunities, we always have the opportunity to choose not to pursue any current opening. When we choose non-action, we are conserving resources so we have them to pursue future opportunities (4.2 Choosing Non-Action).

5. ***To leverage probability, we must work with rather than against the forces in our environment.*** We increase our chances of success if we leverage the forces in our current position and future positions. We must consider how these forces can work for or against us before we make our move (4.3 Ground Forms).

6. ***To leverage probability, we must choose close opportunities instead of distant ones.*** Proximity is one of the primary keys in determining probability. How close we are to openings, both physically and psychologically, largely determines whether or not we are likely to succeed using a given opportunity to move forward. The closer a future opportunity is to our current position, the easier it is to win. Proximity is measured both in physical space and mental knowledge. In moving forward, we must as much as possible stick to what we know and understand (4.4 Strategic Distance).

7. ***To leverage probability, we must judge opportunities based upon their appearances.*** We cannot know opportunities before we explore them but we can see certain surface conditions. Before we

explore a position, we must consider its size, its barriers to entry, and how "sticky" it is. Size must match capability. Barriers of entry can be expensive to surmount, but they can also provide protection once they are surmounted. "Stickiness" is more complicated to judge, but it determines how easy it will be to move forward from a position (4.5 Opportunity Surfaces).

8. *To leverage probability, we must consider our internal weaknesses before moving to a new position.* Internal weaknesses are weaknesses of command and methods. No judgments about future position can be made without also considering the capabilities of the person or organization seeking to fill that position. The characteristics of organizations and their leaders make them better suited for some positions than others (4.7 Competitive Weaknesses).

9. ***To leverage probability, we must consider the long-term trends in selecting opportunities.*** Some directions are supported by long-term climate changes, others are not. We choose to pursue opportunities based not only upon their immediate rewards, but upon their future potential. Ideally, we want to move in directions that open us to more and better opportunities over time. Opportunities that we are likely to have pay off, both in the short term and long term (4.8 Climate Support).

Illustration:

Let us illustrate these principles by thinking about the challenges faced by salespeople in picking which prospects to pursue.

10. ***To leverage probability, we must think both of opportunities and positions as stepping stones.*** We pursue the prospects that we are most likely to close and which lead us to move prospects and better prospects in the future.

11. ***To leverage probability, we need only the ability to compare the general odds.*** As a salesperson, we cannot expect every prospect to buy, but we want to pursue only the prospects that are the most likely to buy. We can only know the most general characteristics about prospects before pursuing them so we have to compare them generally or as general groups to decide how to act.

12.   ***Our probability of a successful move depends both on our starting point and destination.*** Our most probable future customers are determined by who our current customers are. Our choice of the prospects we pursue determines both the size and quality of the customer base we work ourselves into. For example, if a car salesperson has sold some expensive luxury cars in the past, he can increase his focus on those customers in the future.

13.   ***To leverage probability, we must choose non-action when high-probability opportunities are unavailable.*** A salesperson cannot afford to choose every customer. Every low-probability, low-profit customer he wastes time on means less time for pursuing high-probability, high-profit customers.

14. ***To leverage probability, we must work with rather than against the forces in our environment.*** If we go after customers who have high-turnover, we must work against the environment.

15.   ***To leverage probability, we must choose close opportunities instead of distant ones.*** We need to go after customers who are both physically and psychologically close to us. ***To leverage probability, we must judge opportunities based upon their appearances.*** A salesperson must consider the size of the prospect base, its ability to pay, and how likely it is to produce repeat customers.

16.   ***To leverage probability, we must consider our internal weaknesses before moving to a new position.*** A salesperson cannot pursue prospects who don't fit with either his temperament or his company's processes.

17. ***To leverage probability, we must consider the long-term trends in selecting opportunities.*** A salesperson should sell to customers and markets that are growing rather than shrinking.

4.1 Future Potential

Five key methods regarding the limitations and potential of current and future positions.

"Some commanders are not skilled in making adjustments to find an advantage.
They can know the shape of the terrain.
Still, they cannot exploit the opportunities of their ground."

Sun Tzu's The Art of War 8:1:16-18

"Continuous effort - not strength or intelligence - is the key to unlocking our potential."

Winston Churchill

General Rule: Current and future positions have different limitations that potentially determine future moves.

Situation:

Making choices means eliminating existing options in the hope of discovering better future options. Our past decisions have restricted our current options. Our current decisions will restrict our future options. Every move to a new position puts us on a new path. If we get on the wrong path, we can find fewer and fewer opportunities in the future. We cannot pretend that we can always go back and correct our mistakes.

Opportunity:

Every move to a new position can open up new opportunities while closing down others. Most moves do both. Our first consideration must be where pursuing an opportunity leads in terms of future opportunities. Even successful positions are temporary (1.1.1 Position Dynamics). We must evaluate our opportunity based both upon the potential rewards they offer and the future opportunities they offer. The path has many branches. Each time we choose among different opportunities, we are choosing a certain future. Our opportunity is in thinking before we move about the best way to choose not only among future positions but future paths (1.1 Position Paths).

Key Methods:

The following six key methods describe Sun Tzu's view of future potential.

1. We choose based on probabilities because our knowledge of potential is limited. In improving our choices, choosing the best path is a matter of working from what we know for certain to what is the most uncertain. We move in the general direction of "improving our position" as determined by the general goals of our mission rather than to a specific position because the value of positions is always unknown (2.1.1 Information Limits).

2. All progress begins with the potential of our current position. We do not know where our journey will end, but we know for certain where it must begin. Our current position consists of two components that are critical in picking the best possible opportunities (1.0 Strategic Positioning).

3. We must understand all of the potential in our current position. We can know our current position better than we know where an opportunity will lead. Our ***potential*** includes all elements of our current position, including both resources and abilities, that facilitate movement. Our ***limitations*** are the elements of our current position that hinders our movement (3.1.1 Resource Limitations).

4. We must choose openings in the direction that maximize current potential. The potential and limitations of our current position depend on our direction. A seeming limitation can become an advantage given a certain choice of direction. Our limitations make it easier for us to make decisions because they eliminate choices with a low probability of success. We are often too close to our situation in time to see how conditions naturally reverse themselves in different directions. If we are able to overcome what appears to be a limitation related to our current positions today, it can be transformed into more potential in the future (3.2.5 Dynamic Reversal).

5. We must choose opportunities that do not constrict our future potential. Long campaigns especially should open up more potential opportunities since they are a long-term commitment to a direction. We should avoid commitments to directions that offer only one possible goal, which may prove, as we get closer to it, less attractive than it seemed at a distance. The problem with choosing these types of paths is that, by investing heavily in meeting a certain set of requirements, we can get "locked into" a path. The more we invest in a certain path, the more difficult it becomes to leave that path. In the end, such a path may offer relatively few rewards given the costs (6.2 Campaigns).

6. We must choose openings that lead to more and better potential choices. The most common paths to success are not commitments to long campaigns that follow sets of required steps. This often means choosing directions whose requirements we can meet along the way rather than in advance. The best opportunities are short moves in directions where even more openings seem to lie.

Each of these moves should have the potential to be profitable in its own right. Even if they are not immediately profitable, they explore a profitable direction, offering more potential directions of movement (5.4 Minimizing Action).

Illustration:

Let us look at these key methods and how they might apply to the path of someone who has the potential to become President of the U.S. t

1. We choose based on probabilities because our knowledge of potential is limited. No one can plan a path from childhood to the presidency, but we can make choices that maximize our potential in that direction.

2. All progress begins with the potential of our current position. We cannot control our circumstances at birth, but as long as we are not born a foreign citizen, any current position qualifies for being President.

3. We must understand all of the potential in our current position. If we were born into a rich, politically connected family, we have more potential. If we went to Idaho University instead of Yale or Harvard, we have less potential. Coming from a broken home used to be an obstacle, but it no longer is.

4. We must choose openings in the direction that maximize current potential. Going to Harvard and/or Yale and getting a degree in law opens up more opportunities in general but not everyone has those options. Certain disadvantages, such as having a physical handicap, being from a broken home, or being born a minority may have once seemed like limitations to becoming president, but they are no longer. Some day, perhaps even graduating from Idaho University may cease being an obstacle.

5. We must choose opportunities that do not constrict our future potential. While we may not be able to go to Harvard, we can all avoid dropping out of school. Choosing certain types of behavior and getting caught at it publicly can eliminate future opportunities.

6. We must choose openings that lead to more and better potential choices. Most law or business degrees from an Ivy League college don't lead to the White House, but they lead to a lot of other good things as well.

4.2 Choosing Non-Action

Sun Tzu's seven key methods about choosing between action and non-action.

"There are roads that you must not take.
There are armies that you must not fight.
There are strongholds that you must not attack.
There are positions that you must not defend.
There are government commands that must not be obeyed."

Sun Tzu's The Art of War 8:1:9-14

"Insanity: doing the same thing over and over again and expecting different results. "

Albert Einstein

General Principle: To pursue opportunities, we must choose when and when not to act.

Situation:

We must walk the line between drifting along in life and fighting useless battles. Though we may not realize it, most of the decisions that we make are choices of non-action. In many situations, choosing not to react can be the best choice. However, the habits and inertia of non-action can become deadly. It is always easier to continue doing what we have done in the past than go in a different direction. We must not act only when action is forced upon us because those situations are defined by our lack of options. We must make the choice to pursue opportunities. If is too easy to fail to act in the face of opportunity because our bias is toward non-action omission bias. These choices require a change of direction, which is hard. However, chasing after every possible opportunity doesn't lead to success either because we have limited resources and time. Danger lies in both directions.

Opportunity:

We dramatically improve success by knowing how to balance action and non-action. We must decide which opportunities to pursue and which not to pursue. when we are not pursuing a new direction, we must gather information about new directions to pursue. Learning to see opportunities is half the challenge (3.0 Identifying Opportunities). Eventually, we must pursue the best opportunity that we have long before taking action is forced upon us by our situation. We must know instantly what situations to avoid. We must know quickly which opportunities to pursue. We must change our direction by choice not circumstance.

Key Methods:

Before we can understand the more detailed methods for separating high-probability opportunities from their lower-probability cousins, we first must understand the principles governing action and non-action and our choices.

1. *Non-action frees up the resources that we need for future action.* We must see non-action and actions as requiring each other. Our decisions to act are made possible by earlier decisions not to act. Actions use resources. Constant action is prevented by limitations of resources. When we choose non-action, it makes most resources available for future actions (3.1.1 Resource Limitations).

2. *Most of our decisions for non action are based on habit and reflex*. Most of our decisions are made automatically without analysis.We simply act out of habit and training without having to think about it. This isn't a bad thing. Instant gut decisions are better decisions, especially in areas that require expertise (6.1.1 Conditioned Reflexes).

3. *Too many decisions for non-action simply continue or repeat past behavior unthinkingly.* On a second-to-second or minute-to-minute level, we need to continue what we are doing to get tasks done. On this micro-decision level, finishing what we are doing at the moment is important. We would never complete any task if we are continually distracted by events. In larger blocks of time, we must get from one task to the next. On this macro-decisions level, our habits are less beneficial. We can fall into set patterns of behavior that lock us into doing what we have always done, which can only get us what we have always gotten or less because of the laws of diminishing returns (2.3.3 Likely Reactions).

4. *We must choose non-action because most events do not require a response*. Because modern communications expose us to more events, we must be more selective in our reactions. Most events are simply noise, the back and forth lapping of the waves. We must reserve our actions for the important shifts in conditions, the rising and falling of the tides. Another way of saying this is that we must do what is important not merely what is urgent. We must resist two psychological biases, the primacy effect and recency effect , which unduly influences our choices of actions. The primacy effect is our tendency to respond to the first demands on our time. The recency effect is our tendency to respond to the more recent demands on our time (5.1.1 Event Pressure).

5. *We must use non-action to create time to weigh potential opportunities.* Instead of using all our time in habit or responding to events, we must set aside time to weigh new opportunities. We need to develop a habit of thinking about opportunities. Opportunities seldom interrupt our lives as events do. By their very nature, they are hidden. We must take the time to think about them and consciously decide whether or not they are worth pursuing (3.2.2 Opportunity Invisibility).

6. *We must consciously reject low-probability opportunities, choosing non-action.* We must not make the mistake of thinking that we must pursue every opportunity that comes along. We can do only one-thing at time. We have limited resources. Most opportunities have a low-probability of success. If we commit ourselves to pursue a low-value opportunity, we will not have the resources to pursue a better opportunity when it comes along. We must know which opportunities we can eliminate from consideration (3.1.1 Resource Limitations).

7. *We must stop doing other tasks to make time to act on an opportunity that has a high probability of success.* We must make time because we cannot take time to act quickly on high probability opportunities. If we want to advance our position, we **_must_** pursue opportunities. This requires the time to do so. However, we must not act on every opportunity. We must pursue **_only_** those opportunities that meet the criteria defining high-probability opportunities. We cannot know how long an opportunity will last. All opportunities have a limited shelf life. We do not know when a better opportunity will come along. We must explore all high-probability opportunities as quickly as we can. They will not improve over time (3.1.6 Time Limitations).

Illustration:

Let me illustrate these principles in the context of what I am doing now, re-writing this Playbook article.

1. ***Non-action frees up the resources that we need for future action.*** I had to choose not to do something else in order to write this article.

2. ***Most of our decisions for non action are based on habit and reflex***. My decision to re-write these articles was already made months ago when I committed to our Today's Article on Warrior's Rules program. When I am not traveling, I know when I get up that I am going to do at least one such article and schedule it for publication.

3. ***Too many decisions for non-action simply continue or repeat past behavior unthinkingly. My day often starts on auto-pilot.*** Normally, I get up around six, review the morning's news on-line, and often start editing an article. Since these are rewrites, I spend my first minutes rearranging the existing text to our new standards without thinking much about content. Most mornings I am interrupted by a few phone calls, perhaps a radio interview. A couple of hours after being up, I start coffee and maybe do some kitchen cleanup. Until this point, I am still waking up, operating largely out of habit. Then I start to deal with the day's events and look for opportunities.

4. ***We must choose non-action because most events do not require a response***. As I review the morning news, often in the context of preparing for the coming day, I am looking for opportunities to do an "Strategy in the News" article. In the past, before I was as busy as I am today, I felt pressure to write a new news article every day as well. Now, I choose not to because I have better uses for the time.

5. ***We must use non-action to create time to weigh potential opportunities.*** If I don't see any opportunities to dramatically improve a Rules article, I simply correct a few things or add an image. This allows me to get onto other routine work, such as answering my email or testing new website features, as quickly as possible. Today, I found this article extremely incomplete, not mentioning several key points on non-action and offering no illustration of the principles.

6. *We must consciously reject low-probability opportunities, choosing non-action.* The <u>format for Playbook articles</u> makes openings for improvement rather clear. Many existing articles are missing components: descriptions of the situation and opportunity, poorly explained steps or missing illustrations of the steps. All are quick, easy openings to fill. In filling them, these articles are generating a bigger and bigger following for Sun Tzu's ideas.

7. *We must stop doing other tasks to make time to act on an opportunity that has a high probability of success.* If I find an opportunity for a "Strategy in the News" article, I always do it immediately rather than try to get back to it. Same with adding to a daily Rules article. If I see a way to improve it, I do it now, knowing that I won't get back to it for some months and by then will have lost the idea.

4.3 Leveraging Form

Sun Tzu's seven key methods on how we can leverage the form of a territory.

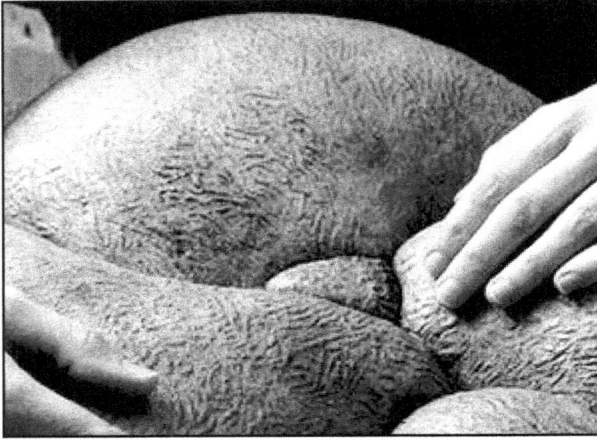

"You can find an advantage in all four of these situations."

Sun Tzu's The Art of War 9:1:25

"Let us, my friends, snatch our opportunity from the passing day."

Horace

General Principle: We should favor opportunities that leverage gravity, the currents of change, and exclusive dependability.

Situation:

The most important form of space only exists in our minds. Strategy leverages our mental mapping of the contested territory. We must evaluate opportunities based on the form of our opportunity. The forms of physical strategic space is easier to understand, but they are becoming less important in our competitive decisions. The forms of psychological strategic space are more difficult to understand, but they are becoming increasingly important. As we move deeper into the information age, understanding the shape of our opportunities in psychological space is difficult without useful analogies that connect to our sense of physical space.

Opportunity:

In applying Sun Tzu's ideas, we use physical analogies to represent many aspects of psychological spaces. These analogs use both the objective and subjective dimensions to compare the characteristics of potential positions (1.2 Subobjective Positions). We can see and more easily comprehend relationships in physical space. We use this understanding to apprehend the key difficulties with our opportunities that exist primarily in the psychological space of competition. In using these analogies to pick the best opportunities, it is often easier to use the process of elimination. We look for defects in opportunities that eliminate them from consideration. No opportunity is perfect, but some opportunities are too difficult to pursue.

Key Methods:

This following eight key methods describe what we must know to leverage the form of an opportunity.

1. Our opportunity for leverage depends on the form of the contested territory. An opportunity is an opening. Though its space is empty, its forms exists in the context of a given type of territory. How we can leverage the territory to take advantage of an opportunity depends on that form. Form is important both in choosing opportunities and in choosing our actions to react to situations (6.7.1 Forms Adjustments).

2. The opportunity to leverage form exists as inequality in a territory. This inequality can be seen as a type of openings, from which all opportunities spring. Sun Tzu describes four forms of territory: mountains, rivers, marshes, and plateaus. In physical space, these forms of territory determine how easily we can move into a new position, defend it, and move on from it. We adapt these same concepts from physical space into the psychological space of competition. The first three of these four forms are dominated by features which can be leveraged. In each of these three spaces, one direction or specific location has a specific advantage over other locations in their immediate vicinity. We abstract these physical forms into mental models that we can apply to analogous situations in psychological space (2.2.2 Mental Models).

3. Tilted forms define territories in which we can leverage gravity. These spaces are dominated by uneven features that Sun Tzu describes as mountains. In physical terms, the force of gravity gives an advantage in these areas to some positions over others. In psychological terms, gravity exists were opinions tilt strongly in one direction. These are often areas where the opinions of a few key people or organizations are much more important than those of most people or organizations (4.3.1 Tilted Forms).

4. Fluid forms define territories in which we can leverage the direction of flow. These spaces are dominated by the flow of change that Sun Tzu describes as rivers. In physical terms, the direction of the flow gives an advantage to one position over another. In psychological terms, currents exists wherever the direction of change favors some positions over others (4.3.2 Fluid Forms).

5. Soft forms define territories in which we can leverage the rare areas of support. Soft forms are dominated by non-supporting features. In physical terms, dependable ground is rare in these areas and therefore valuable. In psychological terms, dependability is important because most features in the environment is uncertain and easily changed (4.3.3 Soft Forms).

6. Neutral forms define territories that offer few opportunities for leverage. On neutral ground, the three characteristics that can be leveraged to create an advantage--gravity, current, and dependability--are unimportant. They can exist in small degrees, but the advantage or disadvantage that they offer is not necessarily decisive. One neutral ground, success is determined by characteristics other than form. We cannot leverage form against others, and they cannot leverage form against us (4.3.4 Neutral Form).

7. High probability opportunities are those where we can leverage form against our opponents. In non-neutral forms, the best opportunities are those favored by gravity, current direction, or exclusive dependability. The worst opportunities are those in which these forces can be leveraged against us. We compare opportunities and potential positions based upon these characteristics (1.3.1 Competitive Comparison).

Illustration:

Let us illustrate these ideas by using them to describe different types of markets.

1. Our opportunity for one type of leverage depends on the form of the contested territory. All marketplaces have a shape in which we can look for opportunities.

2. The opportunity to leverage form exists as inequality in a territory. To see the form of a marketplace, we must think about why one position in that market is better than another.

3. Tilted forms define territories in which we can leverage gravity. The U.S. market for textbooks is an tilted form of ground. While each state makes its own public school purchasing decisions, a few large states, specifically California, Texas, and Florida, set the standards for all the rest because of the size of their markets.

4. Fluid forms define territories in which we can leverage the direction of flow. The high-tech market is a fluid form of ground. They typical high-tech company must reinvent their product line every three years, making decisions about the direction of the fast-changing current of tastes and technology.

5. Soft forms define territories in which we can leverage the rare areas of support. The political arena is an soft form of ground. Political promises are not more solid than the predictions about the effect of various laws and programs. Voters are best sticking to the few areas of certainty, if they can find them.

6. Neutral forms define territories that offer few opportunities for leverage. A grocery store is a neutral form of ground. It is dominated by the average decision-maker, relatively slow changing products, and a high-level of consistency.

*7. **High probability opportunities are those where we can leverage form against our opponents**.* Textbook makers need the favor of the big states to generate an economic volume of sales. Tech companies need the support of the trends. Voters want something to depend on. Decision is easy. Don't print the unfavored books. Don't promote the old technology. Don't vote to the fuzziest promise.

4.3.1 Tilted Forms

Sun Tzu's six key methods regarding space that is dominated by uneven features.

"To win your battles, never attack uphill."
Sun Tzu's Art of War 9:1:4

"The object in life is not to be on the side of the majority, but to escape finding oneself in the ranks of the insane."
Marcus Aurelius

General Principle: Seize the high ground.

Situation:

If we can see where the ground is tilted heavily in favor of some positions, we can more easily spot high probability opportunities. In physical space, this tilt of ground is as easy to see because it creates slopes, hills, and mountains. It is harder to determine in the psychological dimension of competition where the ground is tilted based on opinion. In some areas, we have as many different opinions as people. In others, opinions tend to pile up into different camps. Sometimes the resulting tilt of the ground is based simply on the number of people with a set opinion. The problem is that our herd instinct is based on the idea that each person's opinion is equal to that of others. On many types of tilted ground, this average opinion matters less than the opinions that dominate among the key decision-makers, those that decide the competition.

Opportunity:

When the ground is tilted, we must get the force of gravity on our side. Even those with only the most basic understanding of strategy see the value of working from the high ground. When we control the physical high-ground, the force of gravity works in our favor. The same is true of psychological space, only the tilt is determined by opinion, specifically the opinions of the decision-makers who "judge" the context.

Sometimes this "tilt" is the opinion of the crowd. Quite often, however, it is the tilt of the opinions of a few key decision makers or influencers. High-probability opportunities can be defined by our ability to seize the high ground in any situation, recognizing the use of gravity in social situations and psychological situations as well as physical ones.

Key Methods:

In the psychological space of modern competition, we have to think about the mental landscape of a territory instead of the physical space.

1. On tilted forms of ground, some positions are "higher" than others. Height exists when one part of an area rises above others. In physical situations, the difference is in physical height. In social situation, "height" is determined by the relative weight of people's opinions. On relatively flat ground, opinions are varied, without any opinions clearly dominating the others. On tilted ground, a few opinions of groups or certain individuals can rise above those of others (1.3.1 Competitive Comparison).

2. When the tilt depends on broadly shared views, gravity takes the form of popular opinion. This is the realm of our herd instinct.Different groups can have different opinions just as there are different mountains within a mountain range. To know the lay of the land, we must know the tilt of the group in which we find ourselves. We must understand its strong prejudices and how they distinguish that group from surrounding groups (1.6.1 Shared Mission).

3. When the tilt comes from key positions, gravity arises from a relatively few individuals. In these situations, a few people's opinions are counted much more heavily than the opinion of the crowd. In these situations, "height" comes from another bias, called *authority bias.* Under the influence of authority bias, the average decision is heavily influenced by few rather than by the many. We call those with gravity "authorities," "the powerful," "experts," "influencers," or "opinion leaders" (1.5.1 Command Leadership).

4. On tilted forms of ground, gravity gives an advantage to the high ground. This works for both senses of "gravity," the physical force and the psychological force where more of seriousness is given to a few opinions, either broadly shared or arising from a few people. This disparity between the perceived value of some opinions over others creates high ground that can be leveraged. This gravity can arise either from the physical power of these positions, say from control or wealth of resources, or from the subjective power of these positions to tilt the influence of others (1.2 Subobjective Positions).

5. On tilted ground, we must position ourselves on the high ground. Seizing the high ground, means taking positions that are supported by the force of gravity. We want to get either the physical force or the social force on our side. To see the In terms of choosing the best tilted opportunities, we must clearly see where the forces of gravity are. If there are obvious centers of gravity, an advantageous opportunity is defined by an opening that is supported by the opinions of one of those centers of gravity. A defective opportunity is defined as one that goes against the gravity of one of those centers of gravity (4.0 Leveraging Probability).

6. *On tilted ground, we can find common denominators among competing centers of gravity*. In situations where there are competing tilts among major centers of gravity, taking one side or another can be as dangerous as it is advantageous. In general, we want to find the common inclinations that these major players share. In physical terms, we want to stick to the valleys, which represent the common ground among the big players (3.1.3 Conflict Cost).

Illustration:

Many famous battles are fought on hills because the high ground always gives an strong advantage to the force that occupies it first. Gettysburg was one of the most famous that was decided largely on the basis of the fact that the Union was able to occupy the high ground.

But we see this same effect in every competitive arena where height is at work.

1. *On tilted forms of ground, some positions are "higher" than others*. In business, certain marketplaces have tilted forms when they are dominated by a few dominant tastes. For example, there are a many good ways to make pizza and no single way dominates the market in America as a whole. However, as you travel across the country, you will find strong regional preferences such as Chicago style or New York style.

2. *When the tilt depends on broadly shared views, gravity takes the form of popular opinion*. Most Americans prefer tomato sauce on their spaghetti. If we want to open an Italian restaurant, we must offer tomato sauce as an option if we want to satisfy customers. No matter how good our Alfredo sauce or clam sauce, most are going to order tomato sauce.

3. *When the tilt comes from key positions, gravity arises from a relatively few individuals*. In the textbook market in the U.S., certain large states--Texas, California, Florida, and New York--set the standard for the textbook industry. When a publisher wins a book contract in one of those states, they have seized the high ground.

4. On tilted forms of ground, gravity gives an advantage to the high ground. If we work as employees, the management hierarchy of our organization represents a slope of gravity. The opinions of those higher in the hierarchy have more gravity than those lower on the hierarchy.

5. On tilted ground, we must position ourselves on the high ground. Within a large organization, high-probability opportunities are those that favor the goals, opinions, and prejudices of those high-up within the hierarchy. Seizing the high ground, means taking positions that support or side with the organization's force of gravity.

6. On tilted ground, we can find common denominators among competing centers of gravity. One division leader may favor one type of product while a competing division leader will favor another. They will both support a marketing program that promotes their differing priorities equally well.

4.3.2 Fluid Forms

Sun Tzu's six key methods on selecting opportunities in fast-changing environments.

"Never face against the current."
                    Sun Tzu's The Art of War, 9:1:13

"The art of progress is to preserve order amid change."
                    Alfred North Whitehead

General Principle: We must leverage the direction of change instead of fighting against it.

Situation:

Accelerating change affects more and more of the world. When we are trying to select the best opportunities, change creates a problem. Decision-making depends on good information. Good information is easier to get in stable environments because information is so quickly outdated in fast-changing situations. However, opportunity also depends on change. Faster-changing situations create more opportunities than stable ones. As change increases past a certain point, good information about the future becomes impossible to get. Environments that create the most opportunities are, by definition, the same ones on which we have the worst information.

Opportunity:

Even though our information about fast-changing situations is relatively poor, in these situations, we actually need less information. Only one factor is important, especially when considering high-probability opportunities. This factor is the direction of change, the direction of the currents of change. In situations dominated by change, a high-probability opportunity is supported by the direction of change. Our judgments can safely focus on that single issue.

Key Methods:

The following six key methods define the ways in which we use opportunities on fluid ground.

1. Fluid ground combines the elements of climate and ground. We normally think of change as an aspect of climate. All competitive arenas are influenced by climate, but fluid forms of ground are much more strongly influenced by climate shifts than any other form of ground. Fluid opportunities are in areas whose dominant feature is the dynamics of change. Any competitive arena where the conditions change quickly, dragging everything with them into the future, defines this form of ground (1.4.1 Climate Shift).

2. On fluid ground, positions are carried forward by the trends of change themselves. In most competitive arenas, we advance our position only by putting energy into making our moves. On fluid ground, the ground itself is moving. We can create superior positions with very little work by using the direction of change to our advantage (1.1.1 Position Dynamics).

3. The more fluid the ground, the more temporary our current position. Change erodes existing positions. On fluid forms of ground, the force of change can erode our position as fast as we build it up. We end up running the Red Queen's race, running faster and faster just to stay in the same place. In a best case scenario, the force of change carries us forward, building up our position for us while we just maintain our position (1.1.1 Position Dynamics).

4. *On fluid ground, we must get the currents on our side*. On fluid ground, we have to be concerned about the direction of change. We call this direction the flow of the **current**. The direction of the currents favors some directions of change over others (8.7.1 Evaluating Existing Positions).

5. *On fluid ground, the question is never where the opportunity is today, but where it will be in the future*. On fluid ground, opportunities are created and outdated extremely quickly. We must look further ahead in making our moves, positioning ourselves to take advantage of an opportunity quickly, before it passes us by (1.8.1 Creation and Destruction).

6. *During peak periods of change, we must not attempt a move on fluid ground*. The currents of change on fluid ground will wax and wane, but when change reaches it height, we should never attempt to pursue a fluid opportunity. In the book, Golden Key to Strategy , these situations are described as *change storms*. Pursuing an opportunity during a change storm is extremely risky with a low-probability of success. Change storms are growing more common as the pace of change is increasing everywhere. (4.2 Choosing Non-Action).

Illustration:

Let us take our illustrations from my background in the world of high-tech software. I got out of the software business in the late nineties because of my understanding that I was working on fluid ground.

1. *Fluid ground combines the elements of climate and ground*. During the late nineties, the software business was the perfect example of a fluid opportunity. The average lifespan of technology was about three years.

2. On fluid ground, positions are carried forward by the trends of change themselves. To stay current with the fast-changing technology, we had to completely redevelop our software products every three years. We "surfed" the various waves of change in the industry.

3. The more fluid the ground, the more temporary our current position. When we sold our company in 1997, the company that purchased it didn't understand the nature of fast-changing terrain. The result is that they ended up closing down the division that our company represented after three years because they didn't know how to keep the current of change on their side.

4. On fluid ground, we must get the currents on our side. In software right now, the direction of change favors applications that utilize the server cloud of the web rather than those that stand isolated on the desktop. It also favors applications that can be used both on phones as well as desktops. Today's software, and perhaps even today's businesses, are about making connections rather than simply performing tasks.

5. On fluid ground, the question is never where the opportunity is today, but where it will be in the future. On phone, the first dominant platform was the iPhone, but the android rapidly became more popular because it is a broad standard sold by many different vendors. Those developing applications that focus solely on the iPhone could easily miss the shift. The question as of this writing is where Windows 8 will be the future.

6. During peak periods of change, we must not attempt a move on fluid ground. Change storms can take many forms. Personal change storms can arise from death, divorce, a move to a new town, marriage, the birth of a child, and so on. In organizations, change storms arise with new management, mergers, and downsizing. In software, in can mean the introduction of many new competing platforms, where the eventual winner is far from certain.

4.3.3 Soft Forms

Sun Tzu's six key methods regarding space that is dominated by non-supporting features.

> "*You may have to move across marshes.*
> *Move through them quickly without stopping.*"
> Sun Tzu's The Art of War 9:1:15-16

> "*We sail within a vast sphere, ever drifting in*
> *uncertainty, driven from end to end.*"
> Blaise Pascal

General Principle: Soft opportunities can be used only as transitional positions.

Situation:

Soft ground offers us little solid support. Sun Tzu's analogy for soft ground is marsh land. Soft terrain can seem appealing as an opportunity because no one holds a position on it, so it seems empty. However, it is open for a reason: it cannot support anyone over time. These areas tend to swallow those that try to use them. They are characterized by uncertainty, a lack of solidity, and limited visibility. On this ground, we tend to get bogged down because the ground does not support a position. Their uncertainty is different from the normal limitations on our knowledge, known as "the fog of war." Here, what we are uncertain about is how well the ground will support us. We cannot get a good fix on our position.

Opportunity:

If we choose our opportunities correctly, each position works as a stepping stone to the next. Even though we cannot hold a long-standing position of soft ground, we can use these positions as transitional position. We learn how to recognize and use their uncertainty as a shortcut from one longer term position to another. We can get a relative advantage on this ground, using our relatively better knowledge against our opposition. In moving through these uncertain situations, we must avoid straying from our path and losing the traction we need to maintain our progress. When we master the skills of dealing with opportunities on soft ground, our probability of success improves dramatically.

Key Methods:

The key methods for recognizing and utilizing soft forms of ground are below.

1. On soft ground, the gravity of uncertain opinions tends to bog us down. On tilted ground, gravity is the tilt of opinion. On fluid ground, currents are determined by the direction of change. On soft ground, it is the opinions that are soft, changing direction under pressure. The opinions on soft ground cave under pressure. This ground offers the poorest information giving us the poorest ability to predict the future (2.1.1 Information Limits).

2. On soft ground, most existing positions are uncertain. In the psychological space of modern competition, soft opportunities are characterized by a lack of the key areas of support that we need to develop a permanent position. Perhaps the most common soft forms of ground shaped by our own indecision or the indecision of others (2.1.2 Leveraging Uncertainty).

3. *This lack of support can take five forms*. Soft forms of ground are defined by the following problems:

- A lack of physical resources (2.4.1 Ground Perspective)
- A lack of temporal resources (2.4.2 Climate Perspective)
- A lack of decisive character (2.4.3 Command Perspective)
- A lack of skills and systems (2.4.4 Methods Perspective)
- A lack of shared motivations (2.4.5 Mission Perspective t)

4. *Soft opportunities are only __transitional__ positions.* We can only use them as an intermediate step as part of a longer campaign. We use them to move from our current position to another desired position. Of course, all positions are temporary since all positions degrade over time, but soft positions can never truly support us and can only be used for transition (1.1.1 Position Dynamics).

5. *We must only pursue soft opportunities when there are no alternative paths*. Given their dangers, we pursue these transitional opportunities only when they are necessary to get from where we are to where we desire to be. If an alternative path that avoids soft ground is available, we should always use it (6.2 Campaigns).

6. *We cannot stop moving on soft ground*. This is the opposite of how we respond during a change storm on fluid forms of ground. On fluid ground, we stop and wait for the environment to stabilize (4.3.2 Fluid Forms), but on soft ground, we cannot stop. We get trapped in *indecision bogs* if we stop moving. Indecision bogs are more dangerous than change storms because they are more difficult to identify. Storms are noisy, disruptive, uncontrollable, and hard to miss. Bogs are quiet and serene on the surface. They wait so patiently to suck us in. Getting trapped on soft ground is often excused as "keeping our options open." We cannot leave critical decisions unresolved for long periods of time (3.1.6 Time Limitations).

7. When challenged, we must find the most solid ground available within these soft areas. These area lack some forms of key support, but they don't lack all support. We must identify which of the five key resources of ground, climate, character, methods, or mission are the most abundant. Only then can we get the most out of them, converting them into the resources that we lack (8.1.1 Transforming Resources).

Illustration:

It is a lot easier to understand soft forms of ground through a couple of illustrations from personal relationships and our professional career.

1. On soft ground, the gravity of uncertain opinions tends to bog us down. Two common examples are a) personal relationship in which a couple cannot decide to commit to marriage or not, and 2) spending time in college which is a preamble to starting our real career.

2. This lack of support can take five forms. Soft personal relations are a problem when we cannot decide to break up or go forward (lack of command support). If we get bogged down in these soft relationships, they can waste literally years of our their lives without developing our personal life. The same is true of time in college when we lack a mission or spend time getting an education without developing any real skills.

3. Soft opportunities are only _transitional_ positions. Soft romantic relations are transitional to finding permanent commitment. Going to college is another classical example of a transitional soft opportunity. Going to college does not support us financially (lack of ground support), instead it costs us. We go through college to get a degree to help us in our careers, but many people get bogged down in college, ending up wasting years of their life there and, too often, end up graduating with a degree that has little or no value in their career.

4. We must only pursue soft opportunities when there are no alternative paths. All romantic relationships start out as soft situations. We cannot know beforehand if the person is right for us. People get into these relationships with the goal of finding a permanent relationship. Many types of careers demand a college degree.

5. *We cannot stop moving on soft ground*. Couples who live together but do not marry are making this mistake. Young people who attend college but never graduate are another.

6. *When challenged, we must find the most solid ground available within these soft areas.* In college, this means taking courses that have solid value in the marketplace. People are more likely to get through college studying something like science and business than they are something soft such as liberal arts. In relationships, this means setting deadlines for making decisions.

4.3.4 Neutral Forms

Sun Tzu's seven key methods for evaluating opportunities with no dominant ground form.

"On a level plateau, take a position that you can change."

Sun Tzu's The Art of War 9:1:22

"But some fell into good ground, and brought forth fruit, some an hundredfold, some sixtyfold, some thirtyfold."

Mat 13:8

General Principle: Neutral competitive ground forms offer the broadest range of potential positions.

Situation:

When the ground has a distinctive form, we can know where its advantages and disadvantages are. Form is a valuable key for evaluating the potential of opportunities. When a given ground lacks a distinctive form, it is more difficult to know where its advantages and disadvantages lie. We have clear principles for how to evaluate and pursue opportunities on unequal, fast-changing, and uncertain ground. When the ground lacks any of these forms, we need a different set of key methods. There is a danger in using the same rules for evaluating form on less distinguished ground.

Opportunity:

Neutral ground is the most flexible form of ground for competition. Since Sun Tzu's system is based on our ability to adapt to situations, this form of ground gives us the most options. Unequal, fast-changing, and uncertain ground are dominated by forces that may give some positions an inherent advantage over others. We leverage the nature of the ground to our advantage. We can filter out opportunities that put us in a disadvantageous position of these forms of ground. On neutral ground, there a more types of advantageous positions. In many ways, it is the ideal ground for competition, but we still need to understand the principles for best utilizing it.

Key Methods:

We need to understand the following key methods to best utilize neutral ground.

1. Neutral ground is relatively flat, stable, and solid. The advantages and disadvantages of tilted, fluid, and soft ground are relatively unimportant on neutral ground. The force of form--the gravity of inequality, the currents of change, and the uncertainty of support--are always present, but on neutral ground they are not strong enough to become a dominate factor in our decision about the quality of an opportunity (1.3.1 Competitive Comparison).

2. Neutral ground is __not__ simply a combination of other forms of ground. Ground forms in combination are more complicated than neutral ground. A combination of factors makes it more difficult to identify high-probability opportunities. The competing forces involved are difficult to gauge accurately and the best decision is to avoid complex ground. Neutral ground is the opposite of complex ground. On neutral ground, these forces are mostly irrelevant (4.2 Choosing Non-Action). *Gravity still exists on neutral ground but it is not decisive*. Few competitive arenas are completely flat. Gravity, both physical and social, is always subtlety in play. The gravity of opinions may carry a little more weight in one direction than another but other factors are more important. We want to satisfy a broad range of opinions rather than a specific one. Though broad opinions are much less passionate than specific ones, we still want to hold the high ground, when we can find it (4.3.1 Tilted Forms).

3. Neutral ground does not have powerful, dominant currents. It may have seasonal cycles of change, and change may drift in one direction or another, but those eddying currents have a tendency to even out over time (4.3.2 Fluid Forms).

4. We can see and trust our footing on neutral ground. Neutral ground can support us. While our information is always limited in competitive situations, we can be relatively certain of our standing. We always want to choose positions where our information is the most solid, but this advantage is limited (4.3.3 Soft Forms).

5. On neutral ground, distance and dimension are more important than form. This makes neutral ground opportunities more appealing than those on the three other forms of ground. Neutral ground is a level playing field. Worrying only about distance and dimension makes these opportunities simpler and easier to evaluate (4.4 Strategic Distance , 4.5 Opportunity Surfaces).

6. The best positions on neutral ground are those that we can easily change. The best opportunities are those that lead to such positions. We always want positions that we can adapt to changing conditions, but this is more important on neutral ground because this form of ground offers more freedom of movement. The shape of other forms of ground constrain our movements (1.8.2 The Adaptive Loop).

Illustration:

Let us use the grocery store to demonstrate the characteristics of a ideal form of market.

1. Neutral ground is relatively flat, stable, and solid. Most of the products that we see in the grocery store are on neutral ground.

They are aimed at the average consumer. The brands involved do not change dramatically from year to year. The consumer product market provides solid financial support for these brands.

2. Neutral ground is _not_ simply a combination of other forms of ground. A good example of combination ground would be the music market. This market is not neutral, but very tilted because a few large companies and big artists have traditionally determined music popularity, distribution, and radio play. It is also fluid, because it is in transition from physical distribution, where people buy CDs, to electronic distribution. It is soft, because the market doesn't support most musicians. This combination makes it nearly impossible to identify a high-probability opportunity in the music market. Even winning on American Idol is not a guarantee of success.

3. Gravity still exists on neutral ground but it is not decisive. At the grocery store, it doesn't hurt to have the Good Housekeeping Seal of Approval, but it doesn't determine any products success or failure.

4. Neutral ground does not have powerful, dominant currents. In the grocery store, at various times, tastes may drift over time say, between smooth or chunky styles of peanut butter, but overall, the market is stable.

5. We can see and trust our footing on neutral ground. Milk, eggs, and all the rest of the products in the grocery store can depend on solid financial and cultural support as long as they maintain their position.

6. On neutral ground, distance and dimension are more important than form. How the competing grocery store brands do in the market have more to do with how convenient they are to buy and how well they are entrenched in the three opportunity dimensions of area, barriers, and stickiness.

7. The best positions on neutral ground are those that we can easily change. What is the most common message on packages in the grocery store? New and Improved. Most brands take positions that they can easily change. Some, such as Coca Cola, with its New Coke, found they weren't in such a position.

4.4 Strategic Distance

Sun Tzu's nine key methods regarding relative proximity in strategic space.

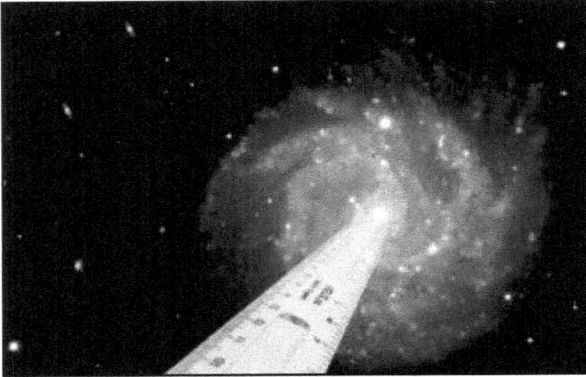

"The ground determines the distance.
The distance determines your numbers."
Sun Tzu's The Art of War 4:4:10-11

"If a man take no thought about what is distant, he will find sorrow near at hand."
Confucius

General Principle: The greater its distance, the less the value of an opportunity.

Situation:

There is a danger hidden in improved communication. While improved communication is incredibly valuable, it means that we can hear about opportunities from anywhere in the world. This fact can lure us into the dangerous strategic error of thinking that distance no longer matters in choosing our opportunities. There are two mistakes in this thinking. First, it assumes that distance is simply a physical measure of space. Second, it assumes the communication alone eliminates the problems of distance.

Opportunity:

In picking high-probability opportunities, one of the most important characteristics is distance (4.0 Leveraging Probability). The further a new position is from our current position, the lower the probability of successfully moving to it directly. In a single lifetime, people can advance their position unbelievable distances, but those advances are made one step at a time. We pick close-by opportunities for the same reason we climb up stairs instead of leaping to the top of buildings in a single bound. Smaller moves are easier and much more likely to be successful.

Key Methods:

While everyone instinctively recognizes the importance of distance, the Warrior's Rules regarding distance are sophisticated, covering many aspects of distance that are easily overlooked.

1. Distance is both physical and intellectual. Distance always measures space, but there is objective space and subjective space. Physical space and intellectual space both contain distance. ***Distance*** describes the differences in space and knowledge *separating* two positions. We must move over distance to get from one position to another. We can be physically close and intellectually close in different ways. This stems from the objective and subjective nature of positions (1.2 Subobjective Positions).

2. Closer openings are always better than more distant ones. In choosing the best opportunities, we must make a simple comparison of distance. Openings that contain or create more distance are never as good as the alternatives that contain or create more closeness (5.5.2 Distance Limitations).

3. Both physical and intellectual distance are measured in differences. These two types of distance are different, just as the subjective and objective positions are different. We can be physically close to someone without being intellectually close to them. We can be intellectually close without being physically close. Distance measures a degree of difference. In space, we can measure it in feet and miles, meters and kilometers. Intellectual distance measures the differences in knowledge and perspective (1.3.1 Competitive Comparison).

4. Both distance from our current position and distance from people decrease success probability. Successful moves are more likely in the short-term if they keep close to our current position. They are also more likely to succeed in the long term if they bring us closer to more people. Opportunities close to where we are are more probably successful than those further away. Opportunities that bring us closer to more people are more probably successful (4.0 Leveraging Probability.

5. Proximity is physical closeness, the opposite of physical distance. Originally, the concept of "being at the right place at the right time" was focused on physical location. The more people we are close to, the easier it is to make connections and the more successful we are. (4.4.1 Physical Distance).

6. Physical proximity increases our probability of success. In searching for proximity to other people, people move from the country to cities and from small cities to large ones. Large organizations are housed in large office buildings, complexes, and campuses because physical proximity is valuable. People in cities and office buildings all enjoyed the strategic advantage of being close to each other. People who were close to others are generally more successful to people than people whose positions enjoyed fewer advantages of proximity (2.6 Knowledge Leverage).

7. Affinity is intellectual closeness, the opposite of intellectual distance. In the mental landscape, we are further away from those with different goals, different views of the future, different skills, and different personalities. A personal affinity for a position makes it intellectually attractive. This is based on a feeling of identification with that position. Affinity leads to connection among people of similar interests. It can mean a similarity in positions, but it less often means identical positions than it does compatible or, more to the point, complementary positions (4.4.2 Intellectual Distance).

8. *Affinity is growing more important in determining success*. Proximity is still very important, but because of technological change, affinity is becoming more important. Advances in transportation and especially communication have decreased the impact of physical proximity. The growing access of people everywhere to a wider variety of alternatives is making *affinity* increasingly more important. Because of all the new forms of communication and transportation, people are connecting with others more and more on the basis of their affinities, the intellectual and emotional closeness that they share. The challenge in evaluating opportunities is the changing nature of distance in the world today as physical distance becomes less important and intellectual and emotional distance becomes more important ((1.4.1 Climate Shift).

9. *Physical and intellectual distance can create each other over time*. This is just like subjective and objective positions creating each other as complementary opposites.When we are physically close to people, we tend to get intellectually closer. If we are intellectually close to people, we want to get physically closer. The reverse is also true. If we are physically distant over time, we will become more intellectual distant (3.2.3 Complementary Opposites).

Illustration:

Let us look at how we can use these key methods to evaluate different job opportunities.

1. *Distance is both physical and intellectual*. A job opportunity that requires us to master more new skills is less likely than one that requires us to master fewer new skills.

2. *Closer openings are always better than more distant ones*. A job opportunity that requires us to move a great distance is never as good as one that doesn't.

3. *Both physical and intellectual distance are measured in differences*. A job opportunity that associates us with people with whom we have little in common is worse than one that associates us with people with whom we have more in common.

4. Both distance from our current position and distance from people decrease success probability. A job that isolates us from contact with people is less likely to bring success than one that puts us in contact with many people.

5. Proximity is physical closeness, the opposite of physical distance. Jobs that improve our proximity to those whose decisions affect our future are better than those that distance us from those people.

6. Physical proximity increases our probability of success. A job opportunity that requires a long daily commute is not as good as one that doesn't.

7. Affinity is intellectual closeness, the opposite of intellectual distance. Jobs that put us in contact with those with whom we share many things are better than those that put us in contact with those with whom we share little.

8. Affinity is growing more important in determining success. More and more businesses are being shaped by their ability to attract people with a similar mindset as well as needed skills.

9. Physical and psychological distance can create each other over time. Over the long term, we will tend to share the thinking of those with whom we work and tend to physically get together with those with whom we share our thinking.

4.4.1 Physical Distance

Sun Tzu's six key methods regarding the issues of proximity in physical space.

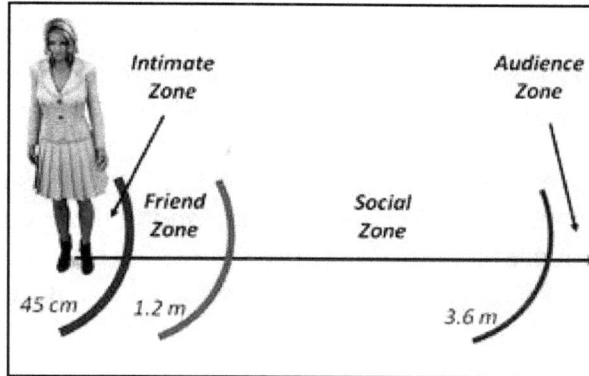

"You must analyze the obstacles, dangers, and distances. This is the best way to command."

Sun Tzu's The Art of War 10:3:4-5

"Distance lends enchantment to the view."

Mark Twain

General Principle: : The greater its distance, the less the value of an opportunity.

Situation:

Space: the final frontier. We can explore more space, but does broadening our activities uncover better opportunities? Going greater distances certainly increases our costs. The mistake is think-ing that it automatically increase our rewards. The grass may look greener on the other side of the fence, but is that an illusion? The rewards of any opportunity are impossible to know before exploring it. Distant opportunities often seem bigger just because of a trick of perspective. Such opportunities are exotic and different, but that fact makes them more risky as opposed to more certain.

Opportunity:

We can use physical distance to prioritize opportunities. Physical distance is easy to compare (1.3.1 Competitive Comparison). We know for certain that a move from New York to New Jersey is shorter than a move from New York to California. In picking the best opportunities, we look for small movement in physical space that can dramatically improve our position. Remember, to advance our position, we must make only profitable moves. This means we must think about the cost of each move. Among these costs is cycle time because increasing distance also creates increases in the time it takes us to get feedback on the effectiveness of our activities (1.8.3 Cycle Time).

Key Methods:

Sun Tzu offers the following six key methods related to physical distance.

1. Production is duplicated over physical distance more easily than competitive strategy. The problems with physical distance are a matter of external differences. Competition depends much more on external conditions than production systems, which rely more on internal organizations. The central problem with physical distance is getting good local information about dynamic, external condition, which vary widely from region to region (1.9 Competition and Production).

2. Leadership is always local because it cannot be projected over physical distance. Someone must take the responsibility to make decisions on the spot. Leaders must see and be seen to understand the situation. This is often done by gut decisions that unconsciously process more information than we can put into words. Communication doesn't replace physical presence. Physical presence always provides better information than communication systems. Strategy depends on oneon-one relationships and those relationships are impossible to develop and maintain given physical separation. Our contact networks in remote places are never going to be as complete or reliable as local ones (2.3 Personal Interactions).

3. *Physical distance is always costly to navigate.* The higher our costs, the lower our likelihood of success. High-probability opportunities include a minimum of costly distance. Physical Distance necessitates two forms of costs. ***Transportation costs*** are the costs created by moving between places. Communication costs are the costs of communication. Strategy depends upon making moves that pay and the higher the costs, the less probably it is that given more will pay (3.1.2 Strategic Profitability).

4. *The costs of physical distance can be mitigated but not eliminated.* While modern technology has dramatically reduced the physical cost of transportation and communication, it cannot eliminate those costs. Even in an era of instant communication, we do not eliminate the differences in time zone or language that are part of physical distance. Those difference create many different costs, including the frequency of errors and the cycle time needed to correct such errors. The further we have to travel to take advantage of an opportunity, the more costly it will be to pursue that opportunity (4.4 Strategic Distance).

5. *Separation over physical distance can lead to separation of goals.* Shared goals hold organizations together. The larger organizations are, the more difficult it is to maintain common goals. Size is not always a matter of number of people. It is always a function of the physical distance separating those people (3.4 Dis-Economies of Scale).

6. ***The best moves forward are always local ones, covering only a minimum of physical distance.*** We must learn to prefer opportunities that are physically close to where we are now. When we pick actions with which we explore an opportunity, we want to pick the closest moves, but this philosophy must start with picking the right opportunities (5.5.2 Distance Limitations).

Illustration:

Consider the challenge of opening new sales offices in distant locations.

7. ***Production is duplicated over physical distance more easily than competitive strategy.*** Opening remote hamburger stands, which are production locations, is much easier than opening remote sales offices.

8. ***Leadership is always local because it cannot be projected over physical distance.*** At each local sales office, an individual must take responsibility for making it work. That individual must learn from someone with more experience about how to make those decisions. That means that he must be transferred there, trained by someone on site a period of time, or move someone else for training for a period of time.

9. ***Physical distance is always costly to navigate.*** When we have opened new distant sales offices, we are going to have to spend more money to operating them than ones that are closer to us. The transfer and training described above is just the start. So these offices are always going to be less profitable over time.

10. ***The costs of physical distance can be mitigated but not eliminated.*** New technology, such as video conferencing, help, but do not eliminate the problem with leadership, management, and creating relationships.

11. ***Separation over physical distance can lead to separation of goals.*** People in different sales offices are going to develop different goals depending on their local conditions.

12. ***The best moves forward are always local ones, covering only a minimum of physical distance.*** Local salespeople are always going to have a higher probability of success than distant ones.

4.4.2 Intellectual Distance

Sun Tzu's six key methods regarding the challenges of moving through intellectual space.

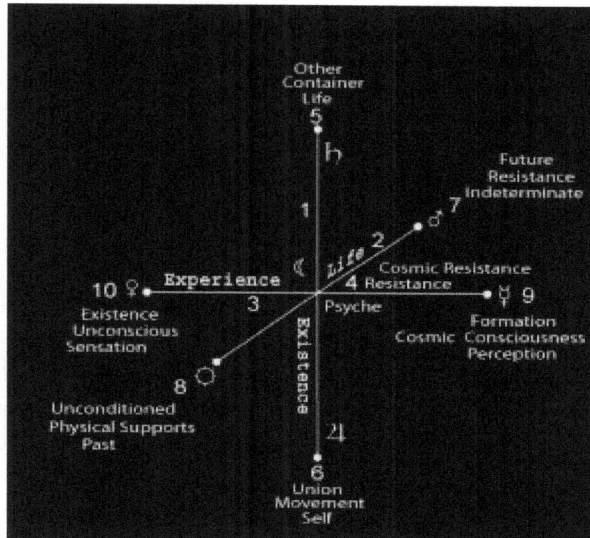

> *"You can be close to an ally and still part ways."*
> Sun Tzu's The Art of War 1:4:14

> *"The most painful thing about mathematics is how far away you are from being able to use it after you have learned it."*
> James Newman

General Principle: The best opportunities are those that pay off with the least new learning.

Situation:

The less we know about an opportunity, the better it looks. This is a central challenge when picking high-probability opportunities. The challenge is worse in this new era of communication, where intellectual distance seems to be minimized by our communication systems. Unlike physical proximity, intellectual affiliations and differences are difficult to identify, quantify, and compare. Intellectual closeness and distance are much more varied and complex than physical closeness. People that are intellectually close in some areas of affinity can be very distant than others. Unity based on affinity and opposed to proximity is relatively fragile and tentative.

Opportunity:

The intellectual terrain has always been more important than the physical terrain in strategic competition. It also offers many more opportunities. Those who understand the principles of intellectual distance have a tremendous advantage in our more competitive world.Gauging intellectual distance is more difficult than physical difference, but it can be simplified by a single concept: learning. Just as travel covers physical distance, learning covers intellectual distance. Distance is a measure of differences (4.4 Strategic Distance). Our differences in goals, attitude, knowledge, character, and skills make up intellectual distance (1.3 Elemental Analysis). The more learning pursuing a given opportunity requires, the more distant it is from our current location.

Key Methods:

The key methods regarding intellectual distance are perhaps even more fundamental than those regarding physical distance.

1. All strategic moves to a new position require learning to cross intellectual distances. While a given strategic move to a new position may or may not require a physical move to a new location, they always require mastering new knowledge. We may not travel physical distance, but we must work to travel intellectual distance. It is measured in how much work we must do to get from one intellectual place to another. This learning is a measure of effort and time, in the same way that traveling physical distance is measured in effort and time. (2.6 Knowledge Leverage).

2. We can travel intellectual distance in the five elemental dimensions. The dimensions of mission, climate, ground, command, and methods represent five different types of learning. We can "move" by learning 1) new motivations, 2) new trends of change, 3) new competitive arenas--their players and rules, 4) new people, and 5) new skills and systems (1.3 Elemental Analysis).

3. Learning to navigate intellectual distance requires investment. The higher these costs, the lower our likely success. High-probability opportunities include a minimum of costly distance. Intellectual distance necessitates two forms of costs. **Communication** costs are the investments needed to acquire new knowledge. Learning costs are the investments required to integrate that knowledge into our decision-making. Strategy depends upon making moves that pay and the higher the costs, the less probable it is that given move will pay (3.1.2 Strategic Profitability).

4. These costs of covering intellectual distance can be mitigated but not eliminated. While modern technology has dramatically reduced the cost of communication, it cannot eliminate the cost of learning. No matter how available the information, it requires time and effort to integrate it into our decision-making. This costs including the frequency of our errors and the cycle time needed to correct such errors. The more we have to learn to take advantage of an opportunity, the more costly it will be to pursue that opportunity (4.4 Strategic Distance).

5. Organizations must learn together to stay united when crossing intellectual distances. Shared goals hold organizations together. The larger organizations are, the more difficult it is to maintain common goals. Size is not always a matter of number of people. It is always a function of the differences in their knowledge levels. Different knowledge creates different perspectives and goals, which divide organizations (3.4 Dis-Economies of Scale).

6. The best moves forward reuse existing knowledge to minimize the crossing intellectual distances. In other words, we try to minimize learning. We must prefer opportunities that are intellectually close to where we are now. When we pick actions with which we explore an opportunity, we want to pick those which are mostly familiar to us (5.5.2 Distance Limitations).

Illustration:

As an illustration of these principles, let us think about our careers and how we pursue them both within and without organizations.

1. All strategic moves to a new position require learning to cross intellectual distances. An individual once had to rely upon a position within an organization--a position in the mental landscape not the physical one--for his or her situation. Moves up in the organization require learning a little broader area of responsibility. However,

2. We can travel intellectual distance in the five elemental dimensions. For example, any move from one job to another entails a change in climate, a change in command, and changes in systems. Moving from a job as an assembly line worker to a sales job is a bigger change than moving from selling to one group of customers to selling to different customers because it requires more learning.

3. Learning to navigate intellectual distance requires investment. Because of limitations in learning, people's options are limited in terms of pursuing opportunities. Many, perhaps most, once aspired to stay with the same organization their entire career, moving up the corporate ladder rather than striking out on their own because of the loss of affinity, the shared knowledge within the organization. This strengthened the competitive position of organizations, but it weakened the competitive position of individuals. The factory town was the hallmark of individuals being trapped by an organization using proximity, which is physical closeness, and affinity, which is intellectual closeness.

4. These costs of covering intellectual distance can be mitigated but not eliminated. Individuals are increasingly freed from their dependence on organizations for their career positions by improved communication. Using telecommuting, people can work anywhere in the world, associating with others in the value chain based upon their personal as opposed to organizational knowledge. Using on-line shopping, people can buy products anywhere in the world. However, the knowledge of any one person is still limited, even with access to the internet. A formal organization still has a more diverse set of intellectual skills than a single individual.

5. Organizations must learn together to stay united when crossing intellectual distances. The concept of the corporation was built on minimizing intellectual distance: a group of people working together toward a shared goal develop an affinity for each other. Today, we are seeing all types of groups form around all types of affinities, shared forms of caring, in cyberspace. This means that individuals must learn and master more strategic skills to navigate the challenges of the new world order. Organizations at every level, business and state, provide less and less protection from competitive pressure. Longer term, this shifts the strategic balance to individuals who develop strategic skills and, based on those skills, position themselves at the future crossroads of opportunity.

6. The best moves forward reuse existing knowledge to minimize the crossing intellectual distances. Home isn't just a physical location, but an intellectual place. As the saying goes, "Home is where the heart is." One of the fundamental changes underlying our current financial crisis it that organizations no longer enjoy the competitive benefits of exclusive affinity among people that they once did. The advantage is shifting from organizations at every level to individuals. We see this in every competitive arena from sports to politics, the competitive issues are less about the organizational affinity and more about the individual affinity.

4.5 Opportunity Surfaces

Sun Tzu's six key methods on judging potential opportunities from a distance.

"You must analyze the obstacles, dangers, and distances. This is the best way to command."
                                        Sun Tzu's The Art of War 1:4:14

"It is easier to perceive error than to find truth, for the former lies on the surface and is easily seen, while the latter lies in the depth, where few are willing to search for it."
                                        Johann Wolfgang von Goethe

General Principle: The surface characteristics of an opportunity are their area, barriers, and holding power.

Situation:

To pick high-probability opportunities, we must make judgments from a distance before investing in the opportunity. We eliminate the most distant opportunities because we cannot see them clearly.

We are warned not to judge a book by its cover, but we must judge opportunities by their surface characteristics. We want to conserve our resources by pursuing our best opportunities. We need tools to help us determine which opportunities are likely to be best.

Opportunity:

Sun Tzu's strategy is the science of what happens on the front-lines, on the boundaries, where one person or organization makes contact with the outside world. Using a living cell as an analogy, strategy is not the programmed instructions of the cell's DNA. It is the interactive process on the surface of the cell, the cell's membrane that adapts to external conditions from moment to moment. When it comes to judging opportunities, the surface is particularly important. From a distance, we can only see the surface of an opportunity. While the value of an opportunity may, like gold, be buried deeply in an opportunity, the most common problems are right on the surface if we know how to look. Our ability to choose the best possible opportunities depends on our ability to eliminate opportunity surfaces that can prevent our progress now and in the future (1.1 Position Paths).

Key Methods:

The following key methods describe the key surface characteristics of an opportunity and how we use it.

1. We can make decisions about surface characteristics from a distance. Distance describes the differences *separating* two positions. We cannot know the true value of opportunity without making a move to explore the depth of the opportunity. We can only see it from a distance. What we see from a distance is just its surface, so we must make our judgments based on that surface (3.1.5 Unpredictable Value).

2. We can observe three surface characteristics called area, barriers, and holding power. Strategic area describes the amount of surface. Barriers describes the roughness of a surface. Stickiness describes the holding power of a surface. We have to examine three of the surface characteristics to eliminate the worst opportunities. These characteristics tell us a great deal about the future potential of an opportunity (4.1 Future Potential).

3. *Area describes the amount of surface that must be covered.* Area measures the breadth and range that a future position encompasses. Area describes the differences in space and knowledge *within* a given position. A position can attempt to control a small or broad territory. The more area in a strategic surface, the broader the space and/or knowledge that must be mastered to take advantage of that opportunity. This can be either an advantage or disadvantage depending on the specifics of our situation (4.5.1 Opportunity Area).

4. *Barriers describes the roughness of a surface.* Barriers refer to the number of obstacles encountered in moving from one position to another. Think of these obstacles as "barriers to entry." In physical space, these obstacles can have a number of different forms: differences in elevation, depth of water, and uncertain footing. In intellectual space, these translated into the knowledge barriers: hierarchies, change, and uncertainty. The more barriers around a certain opportunity, the more specialized and rare the skills and resources required to navigate that surface. While more area requires more resources, more barriers require not only more resources but specific types of skills and resources. Barriers create strategic spaces that are easy to defend but difficult to advance (4.5.2 Opportunity Barriers).

5. *Holding power describes the stickiness or slipperiness of a surface.* This is the most complicated characteristic of a strategic opportunity. Sun Tzu described it as "dangers" because this characteristic in holding an occupant prevents movement and progress. The lack of holding power, slipperiness, is also a problem since it makes holding a position difficult. In the mental landscape, holding power is often determined by how strongly a position is understood and remembered versus how easily it is confused and forgotten. Both sticky and slippery spaces are easy to defend and difficult to advance but for very different reasons (4.5.3 Opportunity Holding Power).

6. Surface characteristics allow us to eliminate the problematic opportunities. As we study these characteristics, we discover that, unlike distance, these characteristics are neither simply good or bad, but they do determine both the limitations and potential of different opportunities. More or less surface area, barriers, and holding power have very different affects on our ability to make progress using a given opportunity. They affect all three aspects of progress, our ability to 1) advance into a position, 2) defending that position while we hold it, and 3) advance from that position in the future. (4.4 Strategic Distance).

7. Surface characteristics can mislead us about the potential of opportunities. Many of the principles describing the advantages and disadvantages of these three characteristics are non-intuitive. Advantages that make it easy to get into a position can turn to disadvantages when it comes time to move on from that position. Without knowing these principles, we can see "obvious" advantages and easily miss the more subtle disadvantages (4.1 Future Potential).

Illustration:

For an illustration, let us imagine that we have a chain of retail stores and are evaluating various rental location for opening a new store.

1. We can make decisions about surface characteristics from a distance. We can know that location is the key, but we cannot know the true potential of a location before we open the store.

2. We can observe three surface characteristics called area, barriers, and holding power. In evaluating potential locations, we can only observe these three characteristics if we ask and consider them.

3. Area describes the amount of surface that must be covered. We can evaluate the size of potential in a variety of ways. How big a community does a location serve? How distant are the nearest direct competitors? How busy is the location in terms of existing traffic? Does the size of the retail space meet our needs?

4. *Barriers describes the roughness of a surface.* How much remodeling does the space require? How easy is it to obtain local licenses and permits? How easy will it be to negotiate a reasonable rental rate in the area?

5. *Holding power describes the stickiness or slipperiness of a surface.* How long a lease are we obligated to? If the store fails, can we get out? How easily can we expand at the location? If the store succeeds, can we grow? What happens to the rental rates over time?

6. *Surface characteristics allow us to quickly eliminate the problematic opportunities.* Where do the excess or lack of these qualities create problems or costs in moving into the location, adapting it over time, and moving out of it in the future.

7. *Surface characteristics can mislead us about the potential of opportunities.* Some characteristics will make it easy to move in but hard to move out. Others will make the position easier or more difficult to keep the store profitable over time.

4.5.1 Surface Area

Sun Tzu's seven key methods for choosing opportunities on the basis of their size.

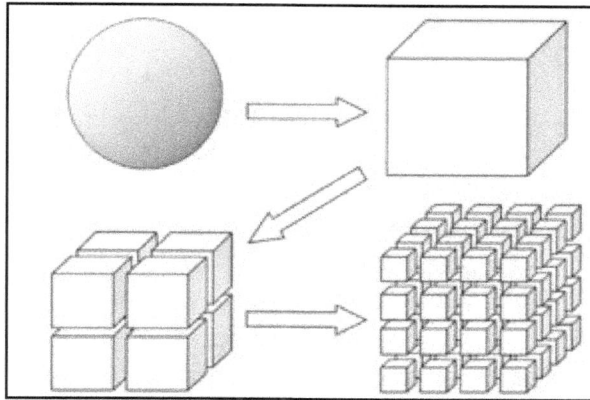

"Victory comes from correctly using both large and small forces."

Sun Tzu's The Art of War 3:5:3

"So never lose an opportunity of urging a practical beginning, however small, for it is wonderful how often in such matters the mustard-seed germinates and roots itself."

Florence Nightingale

General Principle: Large and small opportunities offer very different types of advantages.

Situation:

Surface area measures the apparent size of an opportunity. We mistakenly think that the bigger the opportunity, the more likely it is to lead to success. However, the advantages coming from the size of an opportunity can be very misleading. We think that we need a "big break" to be successful. We think that big breaks depend solely upon luck. However, the advantages of big opportunities often disguise extremely costly dangers. We can easily mistake the size of the territory in which the opportunity arises for the space within the opportunity itself.

Opportunity:

As we learn more about gauging the size of an opportunity, picking high-opportunity opportunities become much easier. Once we understand what the "size" on an opportunity really means, we can gauge how well a given opportunity fits our unique abilities to utilize it (3.4.2 Opportunity Fit). With the right perspective on opportunity size, we avoid costly mistakes regarding picking opportunities that seem closer than they are because of their size (4.4 Strategic Distance). One of the most important ways we benchmark opportunities is identifying those that are too spread out and those that are too confined (4.6.1 Extremes of Area).

Key Methods:

Below are the key methods that describe the use of opportunity area in comparing the potential of opportunities.

1. Opportunity area is different from opportunity distance. Opportunity area evaluates the breadth and range of territory that a future position encompasses. The space covered by position is different from that separating positions. Area is the extent, range, or and capacity ***within*** an opportunity, the expanse of the region it covers. Distance is the space ***separating*** different positions, the investment that must be made to explore an opportunity from an existing position. Opportunity area contains and covers distance to the extent that opportunities exist as opening between existing positions. Area and distance are similar, existing both in physical and intellectual space and measured in differences. (4.4 Strategic Distance).

2. Opportunity area measures the range of physical and intellectual capacities. Positions exist both on physical and mental landscapes. We can measure physical area in the feet and miles, meters and kilometers an opportunity covers. We measure intellectual area in the range of knowledge and skills an opportunity requires to address. An opportunity is an opening and physical space and intellectual space both measure the extent or capacity of that opening. These two aspects of area stem from the dual objective and subjective nature of positions (1.2 Objective and Subjective Positions).

3. The area of the competitive landscape is measured by the number of optional positions available. Since a position is a combination of the characteristics of mission, climate, ground, command, and methods, potential positions on a competitive landscape is a combination of those characteristics. As the possible characteristics get multiplied together defining optional positions, this number of options grows very large. The area of an given opportunity or opening describes a small subset of the competitive landscape with a more limited number of combination of characteristics (1.3 Elemental Analysis).

4. The larger the opportunity area, the more resources required to fill it. We can often see the size of an opportunity more easily if we think about the resources required to pursue it. We explore opportunities with the excess resources that we do not need for maintaining our current position. Physical space must be traveled. Intellectual space must be covered. The larger the area, the more needs, time, materials, decisions, and skills that opportunity requires required to cover it. "Big" opportunity areas require more range and depth of resources than small opportunity areas (3.4.2 Opportunity Fit).

5. Small areas of opportunities are much more common than large ones. Opportunities are openings, often in the form of unsatisfied needs. The vast majority of opportunities exist as empty spaces between existing positions. The spaces between large competitors tend to be filled by smaller competitors and the spaces between those smaller competitors are what remain. This is why small openings are much more common than large ones. Large areas of opening only exist on the periphery of most existing positions, created as new areas of opportunity are opened up or created by new methods (3.2 Opportunity Creation).

6. Small opportunities can eventually lead to larger ones. Since opportunities are unmet needs, one unmet need can lead to another opportunity in a chain. Like following a vein of gold in a mine, small threads of opportunity can lead to gradually large, unrecognized areas of need. Working on the periphery of existing positions can lead to the periphery of all existing positions (3.7 Defining the Ground).

7. The larger the opportunity area, the more probably a partial fit becomes. Opportunities are openings that we can fill and needs that we can satisfy. Opportunities have a shape and size and our resources have a shape and size. The larger the area of an opportunity, the more likely it is that our available resources will fit part of that opportunity. Our resources are always limited (3.1.1 Resource Limitations).

8. Large and unfilled opportunities attract more competition. While all opportunities are difficult to see, larger opportunities are easier to see than small ones. Because of their size, they can be seen at a greater distance. Once we begin to fill an opening, it instantly becomes easier for others to see. Since larger opportunities are more difficult for us to fill, when we pursue large opportunities, we expose them to other potential competitors (3.2.2 Opportunity Invisibility).

Illustration:

Let us illustrate these principles discussing the choosing of a geographically large sales territory versus a smaller one. This is an interesting problem because salespeople often prefer large territories because they think that they hold more potential prospects.

1. Opportunity area is different from opportunity distance. The area a new sales territory covers is different from the distance it takes to get to that territory. Taking over a distant territory may require a commute or even moving to even get to it. Traveling within the territory is different than getting to it.

2. *Opportunity area measures the range of physical and intellectual capacities*. A geographically large territory may or may not contain more prospects but always contains more distance, the space between the prospect. A better measure for a sales territory is the population within it. Another way to measure the intellectual extent of a territory is the range of products that a salesperson must learn to represent or the number of different types of businesses he must address. Sales territory can also be measured in terms of the size of the customers it addresses. A geographically large territory can contain only a few large customers while a geographically small territory can contain a large number of small customers.

3. *The area of the competitive landscape is measured by the number of optional positions available*. The size of a sale territory can be measured by the physical territory it covers, by the number of prospects within it, by the number of different products sold within it, by the number of orders it generates, by its total sales volume, by the sales commission it generates, and on. While some of these characteristics may correlate with one another, others do not. For example, a territory that generates the most sales volume could have a few very large customers rather than the most customers.

4. *The larger the opportunity area, the more resources required to fill it*. It takes more time to cover a geographically or demographically large territory. The larger the territory, the less frequent the visits to potential prospects and existing customers. The more products and types of business a territory covers, the greater the range of sales knowledge that is required on the part of the salesperson.

5. *Small areas of opportunities are much more common than large ones*. As a market and company matures, sales territories tend to get whittled down, smaller and smaller. Large sales territories are more common in new, unproven companies and industries.

6. *Small opportunities can eventually lead to larger ones.* Success in a small territory can lead to a large one. Success in selling small customers can lead to selling large ones.

7. *The larger the opportunity area, the more probably a partial fit becomes.* Salespeople offering new technologies open up large areas of application. They tend to find more diverse areas of applications, most of which offer a partial solution and none of which offer a complete solution.

8. *Large and unfilled opportunities attract more competition.* If a given salesperson is successful selling to certain new markets, more salespeople will pursue that market. Many poorly fitting applications of new technology tend to attract those offering better fitting applications.

4.5.2 Surface Barriers

Seven key methods regarding how to select opportunities by evaluating obstacles.

"Everyone confronts these obstacles on a campaign."
Sun Tzu's The Art of War 11:1:30

"The greater the obstacle, the more glory in overcoming it."

Molier

General Principle: We must compare opportunities by the difficulty, number, and familiarity of their barriers.

Situation:

Barriers describes the difficulties in filling the opening presented by given opportunity. Barriers are obstacles that block our access to the opportunities. While opportunities are always difficult to see, opportunity barriers can be either readily apparent or nearly invisible. When apparent, these barriers can completely discourage us from pursuing high-probability opportunities. When barriers are difficult to see, they can lure us into pursuing opportunities that have a very poor chance of success.

Opportunity:

Without barriers, the openings that define opportunities would be quickly filled without our efforts. In other words, without barriers, the needs that create opportunities would not exist. The nature of a given opportunity's barriers separates our opportunities from opportunities best suited to others (3.4.2 Opportunity Fit). Like distance, barriers create a cost to pursuing an opportunity, but unlike distance, that cost is not determined by proximity but capability (4.4 Strategic Distance). Barriers can be good or bad depending how well they fit our capabilities. While they increase the costs in some aspects of using a given opportunity, they can also decrease those costs over time (4.6.2 Extremes of Barriers).

Key Methods:

The following key methods describe how to understand the nature of barriers in comparing our opportunities.

1. Opportunity barriers describe the physical and intellectual obstacles blocking an opening. In physical space, these obstacles can be differences in elevation, moving water, and soft ground. In intellectual space, we meet social barriers, knowledge barriers, personality barriers, changing trends and so on. Obstacles describe any surface condition making transition slower or more difficult (4.5 Surface Characteristics).

2. Barriers are measured in difficulty, number, and familiarity. We usually discuss the size of barriers in terms of how difficult or easy they are to surmount. A small barrier requires less effort or investment than a large one. A few large barriers can be much more of an obstacle than many small barriers. The wild-card is familiarity. The more familiar we are with a given type of barrier, the more we know whether it is easy or difficult to surmount (3.2.1 Environmental Dominance).

3. Probability of success is determined by internal resources as well as external conditions. The advantage or disadvantage comes from the specific nature of the barriers, our internal resources, and how our resources compare with those of potential competitors. The barriers and competitors are external conditions, but our resources are internal (4.6.2 Extremes of Barriers).

4. The more barriers, the more costly it is to pursue an opportunity. Costs are increased in both the time and money it takes to advance to the new position. The higher the costs, the less the reward so the larger the number of barriers, the less likely it is that the reward pays off (3.1 Strategic Economics).

5. Barriers make it less costly to defend a position. This is the defensive side of the equation. Positions blocked by barriers may be more expensive to win, but they are less expensive to defend (4.6.3 Barricaded Conditions).

6. Advantages in overcoming barriers are a matter of resource fitness. Surmounting barriers isn't just a matter of investment. Investing more doesn't guarantee success. Success is often a matter of having the right capabilities to surmount a particular type of barrier. If the barrier is a mountain, mountain climbing and equipment gives us the resources we need. If the barrier is a lake, having a boat is valuable. If the problem requires sales skills, sales resources are important. If it demands product development, development skills are important (3.1.1 Resource Limitations).

7. Picking the best opportunity is a simple comparison of opportunity barriers and available resources. While opportunity barriers can get very complicated if our goal was to thoroughly analyze them, fortunately, in actual practice, this is seldom necessary. Once we consider the barriers involved and the resources required, we should be able to see in a flash which opportunities fit our particular resources. If others have a better set of resources to meet the challenges of a particular opportunity, we should not pursue it (1.3.1 Competitive Comparison).

Illustration:

Let us consider the barriers in pursuing different careers.

1. Opportunity barriers describe the physical and intellectual obstacles blocking an opening. Learning means covering a lot of ground but that ground has few barriers, just about anyone can do it. As opposed to managing a fast-food franchise, becoming a nuclear scientist or a professional level athlete offers a host of barriers.

2. Barriers are measured in difficulty, number, and familiarity. There may be a lot of different tasks to learn in order to run a fast-food franchise, but none of those tasks are particularly difficult and most are familiar. The barriers to becoming a professional athlete are extremely difficult but familiar. In contrast, the barriers to becoming a nuclear scientist are both difficult and unfamiliar.

3. The more barriers, the more costly it is to pursue an opportunity. Working in a fast-food franchise is much less costly than starting one. The costs of pursuing a professional career are amplified by the low probability of success.

4. Barriers make it less costly to defend a position. A career in nuclear science or as a professional athlete is much easier to maintain than to establish. A fast-food franchise, however, is always facing new competition.

5. Probability of success is determined by internal resources as well as external conditions. Different people have different capabilities. For some people, doing what is necessary to run a fast food chain may be much more difficult than learning nuclear science or becoming an athlete

6. Advantages in overcoming barriers is a matter of resource fitness. The skills involved in becoming a nuclear scientist or a professional level athlete are extremely difficult to master and well beyond most people's capabilities. In the case of more professional athletes, those capabilities have a time limit as well.

7. Picking the best opportunity is a simple comparison of opportunity barriers and available resources. Even if we have the opportunity to become a professional athlete and some of the resources required, that opportunity has a lower probability of success because of the height of the barriers involved.

4.5.3 Surface Holding Power

Sun Tzu's seven key methods regarding sticky and slippery situations.

"You cannot leave some positions without losing an advantage."

Sun Tzu's The Art of War 10:1:24

"It keeps users engaged, so it keeps our site sticky. We've already turned browsers into buyers, and that's all that matters."

Meredith Medland

General Principle: Holding power makes positions easy to defend and hard to change.

Situation:

Some positions are sticky, making it difficult to move on from them. Others are slippery and very difficult to hold onto. When we are examining our opportunities, the relative holding power of a new position the most easily overlooked of all its characteristics. While misunderstandings about opportunity size and barriers are common, these characteristics are usually considered. This is not true for holding power, which is seldom considered at all. This is unfortunate because holding has tremendous influence on our probability of success both in using a position and moving on from it.

Opportunity:

Since holding power is so easily overlooked, understanding it gives us the ability to see more deeply into the nature of a position than others. More importantly, it enables us to avoid the problems associated with too much or too little holding power in a position (4.2 Choosing Non-Action). Understanding holding power also allows us to make better decisions about how to utilize a given opportunity as a stepping stone in making progress (1.1 Position Paths). As with all surface characteristics, mastering Sun Tzu's idea of holding power gives us a concrete concept that we can observe and evaluate before pursuing an opportunity.

Key Methods:

The following six key methods describe how to understand the value of holding powers in gauging different opportunities.

1. Holding power describes adhesion and repulsion of a potential position. Holding power is the strength of the connection between a position and its holder. In physical space, this holding power describes how sticky or slippery an area is. Sticky positions have a great deal of holding power so moving from them is costly in terms of resources. Slippery positions have very little holding power so keeping to them is costly. In intellectual space, these ideas translate into how concretely position is understood and sticks in the memory (4.5 Surface Characteristics).

*2. **In more stable environments, holding power appears as friction**.* When we describe holding power in terms of stickiness and slipperiness, we infer some fluidity to the ground. The antonym of both sticky and slippery is dry. Environments range from stable to fluid. In more fluid environments, change acts like lubrication. When opportunities lack fluidity, that is, when the ground is very stable, holding power appears as the presence of friction making the ground easier to hold but more costly to move out upon (4.3.2 Fluid Forms).

*3. **An abundance of holding power makes it less costly to maintain a position**.* The friction of holding power keeps values aligned, slows down events, makes resources more dependable, creates relationships among people, and stabilizes processes. Holding power makes positions much less costly to defend (1.1.2 Defending Positions).

*4. **A lack of holding power makes it more costly to maintain a position**.* In slippery situations, it is difficult to hold to values, events move more quickly, resources are unreliable, connections break down, and processes vary wildly. Such positions are expensive to defend (1.1.2 Defending Positions).

*5. **An abundance of holding power makes it more costly to change a position**.* This is easier to understand if we think of holding power as friction, the costs of movement. Friction is a form of conflict. It affects all five elements of a position. It creates conflict among changing goals, eats up time, wears out materials, prevents people from working together, and overheats processes (3.1.3 Conflict Cost).

*6. **A lack of holding power makes it less costly to change a position**.* Without friction, positions are more slippery, making movement easier. This is like lubricating a machine. We can adapt our goals, save time, not get worn out, come together easily, and move processes along smoothly (3.1.3 Conflict Cost).

7. Picking the best opportunity is a simple comparison of holding power with our need for movement. While understanding opportunity holding power can seem complicated, comparisons of opportunities are usually simple. In these situations, the value of holding power depends on how long we want to hold to a given position. The more transitory a position, the less important holding power becomes. The more long-term we want to hold a position, the more important holding power becomes (1.3.1 Competitive Comparison).

Illustration:

Let us use these concepts to look at website design.

1. Holding power describes adhesion and repulsion of a potential position. In the case of website design, the nature of the opportunity depends on what we are looking for: many visitors that pass through and move on or fewer visitors that stay for a long time. Sticky websites will encourage visitors to stay. They will have longer articles, more content, and many links to that internal content. Huffington Post and YouTube are designed as sticky websites. Slippery websites will encourage visitors to move on. They will have shorter articles, less internal content, and many links to that outside content. Instapundit and Drudge are slippery websites.

2. In more stable environments, holding power appears as friction. Most websites have constantly changing content, but some websites, for example, educational organizations, will demand a certain amount of adhesion as a cost of access.

3. An abundance of holding power makes it less costly to maintain a position. Websites with good holding power will tend to maintain their audiences with less effort. Websites with less holding power must constantly change their content in order to keep attractive visitors.

4. A lack of holding power makes it more costly to maintain a position. The most common key used when cruising the web is the Back key. People visit a site and quickly return from where they came.

5. *An abundance of holding power makes it more costly to change a position*. Websites with good holding power cannot change their direction very easily. They hold their audiences but they are also held captive by the expectations of those audiences, forced to serve those expectations. Huffington Post must service a certain type of political audience, with a certain kind of story, slanted in a specific way.

6. *A lack of holding power makes it less costly to change a position*. Instapundit can post about anything that Glenn finds interesting.

7. *Picking the best opportunity is a simple comparison of holding power with need for movement*. There is a market for a range of websites, from very sticky to very slippery and through all points in between. The differences have more to do with the goals and capabilities of those who run them.

4.6 Six Benchmarks

Five key methods regarding simplifying the comparisons of opportunities.

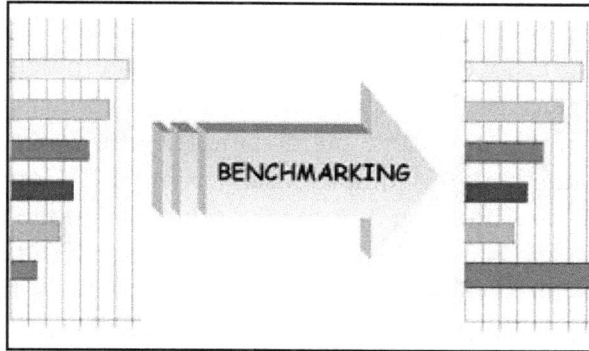

"You must be able to lead your men deeply into different surrounding territory.
And yet, you can discover the opportunity to win."
Sun Tzu's The Art of War 11: 5:14-16

"We are all faced with a series of great opportunities brilliantly disguised as impossible situations."
Charles R. Swindoll

General Principle: We use the six extremes in strategic space as benchmarks to evaluate future positions.

Situation:

Evaluating opportunities is one of the most sophisticated aspects of Sun Tzu's system. This is especially true given the limited amount of information we have before exploring opportunities. Twenty different key methods describe the surface characteristics of opportunities that separate good opportunities from poor ones.

In the real world, we simply do not have time to compare all these characteristics rigorously. All alternative opportunities are impossible to identify. Facts and opinions vary. Most characteristics resist quantitative analysis.

Opportunity:

Fortunately, Sun Tzu offers a simple methodology. To pick the best opportunities, we use a simple mental model to help us recognize the pattern of future probabilities. These models make our decisions as simply a possible but no simpler. The yardstick that we use throughout strategy is simple comparison (1.3.1 Competitive Comparison). In evaluating our opportunities, we judge the surface characteristics we can see by benchmarking against the extremes of such characteristics (4.5 Surface Characteristics). With a general understanding of those characteristics, we can map opportunities, graphically separating high probability opportunities from low probability ones.

Key Methods:

There are no absolutes in strategy. Absolute measurements of the future are particularly impossible. By definition, decisions depending on such measures have a lot of probability of success.

1. Area, barriers, and holding power are the dimensions that measure an opportunity. Sun Tzu's strategy depends on the relative advantages in different positions. We use these three dimensions to evaluate potential positions. Thinking of these three categories as physical dimensions allows us to compare the positions of opportunities quickly and easily (4.1 Future Potential).

2. To compare area, barriers, and holding power, we only need to understand their extremes. To compare positions, we don't need exact measures. We need only to identify the *boundaries* of measurement, the extremes at both ends of the scale. From these boundaries of the minimum and maximum states, we create the simplest possible scale for comparing relative positions of opportunities (1.3.1 Competitive Comparison).

3. The extremes of area, barriers, and holding power define six benchmarks. We call these extremes the six **benchmark positions**. The method we use is to compare the potential of future competitive position against the six extreme variations of opportunities (4.5 Opportunity Surfaces).

- Spread-out positions cover a maximum of area.
- Constricted positions cover a minimum of area.
- Barricaded positions have a maximum of barriers.
- Wide-open positions have a minimum of barriers.
- Fixed positions have a maximum of holding power.
- Sensitive positions have a minimum of holding power.

4. These extremes define the potential of future positions in terms of advance and defense. The issue in pursuing an opportunity is not simply advancing a position, but defending it as well. Because all positions are paths, we have to look at how easy a given opportunity is to advance into and how easy it is to advance from (1.1 Position Paths). Spread-out positions are hard to defend and advance.

- Confined positions are easy to defend and advance.
- Barricaded positions are hard to get into and easy to defend.
- Wide-open positions are hard to defend but easy to advance.
- Fixed positions are hard to leave but easy to defend.
- Sensitive positions are easy to leave but risky to advance.

5. We compare these benchmarks not only to other opportunities but also our current position. We can see the potential and restrictions in any position by gauging it against other positions with these six benchmark positions, but even if we are not looking at other alternatives, we can compare an opportunity to our current position. The goal is just to quickly get a relative comparison. This process immediately gives us a better feeling for the possibilities of new opportunities and of our current position. We cannot see true potential and restrictions in our current position until we compare it against other alternatives against the six benchmark positions (4.2 Choosing Non-Action).

- In thinking about the amount of area an opportunity targets, is it more confined or more spread out?
- In thinking about the barriers of the target position, is it more wide-open or more barricaded?
- In thinking about the stickiness of the target positions, is it more fixed or more sensitive?

Illustration:

Let us use an illustration from sales competition, specifically, a salesperson selecting which new type of prospect to pursue. The more specific the problem, the easier these key methods are to apply, so we will make some assumptions regarding our salesperson's available options.

1. Area, barriers, and holding power are the dimensions that measure an opportunity. Since his current position is secure, he has a lot of time to invest in developing his territory, but since he plans to stay in his current market for a couple of more decades, he wants to make moves that continue to yield results for a long period of time. His biggest current problem is his inability to keep his current customers, who are easily lured away to competing products.

2. To compare area, barriers, and holding power, we only need to understand their extremes. The salesperson recognizes that there is no perfect group of customers but that the most desirable group likes at the certain extremes rather than in any mid-range. The choices are a specialized small medical market, a generic but large wide-open business market, or a market of individuals who are attracted to novelty.

3. The extremes of area, barriers, and holding power define six benchmarks. The medical market is small, requires specialized knowledge, is slow to change, and hard to contact. The generic business market is wide open, has few barriers and is relatively easy to contact. The market of individuals is in between in size, but has little holding power.

4. *These extremes define the potential of future positions in terms of advance and defense.* This medical group is easy to defend, but will require more work to win over because penetrating the market requires learning specialized knowledge so it is is protected by certain barriers. These customers tend to group together and makes changes only when required since they are hard to sell. While this market will be hard to win, it tends to stay with existing providers.

5. *We compare these benchmarks not only to other opportunities but also our current position.* The salesperson picks the medical market, not only because it is more stable than his other alternatives but because it is more dependable over the long term than his current market.

4.6.1 Spread-Out Conditions

Sun Tzu's five key methods for recognizing opportunities that are too large.

"Some field positions are too spread out."
Sun Tzu's The Art of War 10:1:45

"Perception is strong and sight weak. In strategy it is important to see distant things as if they were close and to take a distanced view of close things."
Miyamoto Musashi, *Book of Five Rings*

General Principle: Spread-out positions pull us in too many directions at once, creating strategic weakness.

Situation:

The bigger the opportunity, the more attractive it always appears, especially at a distance. Since opportunities are openings, a big opening seems to offer plenty of room with lots of potential.

Unfortunately, openings that are too large offer many more disadvantages than advantages. This raises another challenge. How do we identify opportunities that are "too large?" In comparing opportunities, we can see when one offers more area than another, but what defines "too" large?

Opportunity:

When we evaluate potential opportunities, we can easily get seduced by opportunities that are too large if we don't have a benchmark for identifying them (4.6 Six Benchmarks). We learn the distinctive characteristics of the benchmark for a maximum of area as a key point of comparison. We can then use that benchmark to identify positions that are so large that they can potentially cause problems for us.

Key Methods:

When we evaluate opportunities by their size, we recognize spread-out positions, those that are "too large" in area, by the following key methods.

1. Spread-out opportunities look like they have great potential. Most people are attracted to spreadout positions because they seem to lead to bigger and better things. They are so large that they are attractive even at a distance. Unfortunately, this mindset forgets that we are working in a competitive environment and the further that we must go, the less likely our success (4.4 Strategic Distance).

2. Spread-out positions are those that stretch our resources. Good strategy tells us to avoid spreading ourselves too thinly. Strength arises from concentrating resources. Our time is always limited. We can juggle only so many balls at a time. Add one ball too many and they all come crashing down. Spread-out regions are "too large" opportunities relative to the size of our resources to explore and develop them. They spread our limited resources too thinly across too large of a strategic area (3.1.1 Resource Limitations).

3. Spread-out positions require multiple, simultaneous points of focus. If our position pulls us in many different directions at once, we cannot defend it. Spread-out positions require us to divide our attention among many different points. Focus on a single, clear goal creates unity and strength (1.7.2 Goal Focus).

4. *Spread-out positions undermine a group's unity.* Problems arise occupying a position or pursuing an opportunity pulls people apart. All opportunities require some expansion, but problems arise when people are so distant from one another, physically or intellectually that they lose their unity as a team (1.7.1 Team Unity).

5. *Spread-out positions are difficult to defend.* Since they must be defended in multiple places at once, spread-out positions are the source of openings for others. Spread-out positions are an invitation to our opponents. Spread-out positions are weak because they invite attack. Big territories are hard to defend. They leave too many openings for our opponents to attack us (1.7 Competitive Strength).

Illustration:

Let us consider pursuing a career in music as a rock guitarist, a common mistake that wastes the talents and energy of so many young people.

1. *Spread-out opportunities look like they have great potential.* We see the big successes in the music business, we do not see the millions of struggling musicians.

2. *Spread-out positions are those that stretch our resources.* Since music does not provide enough income to support most musicians, they must pursue other careers as well, in exciting industries like fast-food service.

3. *Spread out positions require multiple, simultaneous points of focus.* Spreading their time between music practice, looking for gigs, trying to form a group, and working at a regular job, most musicians don't make progress on any front.

4. *Spread-out positions undermine a group's unity.* Music groups come together and quickly fall apart as their inability to support themselves pull members in different directions.

5. _Spread-out positions are difficult to defend._ Even when some progress is made in forming a group, developing a reputation, and getting gigs, there are always lots and lots of competitors waiting in the wings who are willing to work for less to get notoriety.

4.6.2 Constricted Conditions

Sun Tzu's five key methods for identifying and using constricted positions.

"Some field positions are constricted.
Get to these positions first."

Sun Tzu's The Art of War 10:1:33-34

"A single day is enough to make us a little larger or,
another time, a little smaller."

Paul Klee

General Principle: Pick constricted opportunities over spread-out ones.

Situation:

Small opportunities are easy to miss, even when they are right in front of us. Since opportunities are openings and all openings are difficult to see, the smaller the opening the more difficult it is to see. The problem is that small opportunities always seem constricting. We need to practice seeing and embracing small opportunities because they offer many more advantages than large openings.

Opportunity:

When we evaluate potential opportunities, we need a benchmark to help us identify opportunities that are so small that they are easy to miss (4.6 Six Benchmarks). We learn the distinctive characteristics that define the minimum of area for improving our position. We can then use this benchmark to identify positions that are small but can potentially enhance our position at a minimum of cost.

Key Methods:

When we evaluate opportunities by their size, we recognize spread-out positions, those that are "too large" in area, by the following key methods.

1. Constricted opportunities look like they have little potential. Remember, opportunities are openings or needs that no one is filling. Constricted positions are so small that they can only be seen if we are close to the need they represent. Because of this, only a few people are in a position to recognize these opportunities. Unfortunately, most people miss the fact that these constricted positions actually do lead to bigger and better things. (4.4 Strategic Distance).

2. Constricted positions are those that we have more than enough resources to fill completely. We all have limited resources, but we almost always have plenty of resources to fill constricted resources. All that is required to take advantage of constricted opportunities is our commitment to them. We are only vulnerable when pursuing these opportunities if we do not commit ourselves to filling the position completely. We only have to juggle things if we have more balls than we have hands. Juggling seems exciting because failure is just a misstep away. Constricted opportunities may not seem very exciting, but we have a high-probability of successfully pursuing them. (3.1.1 Resource Limitations).

3. Constricted positions of a very narrow point of focus.
Strength arises from concentrating resources. If our position narrows our focus, we can easily win it and defend it. Constricted positions require us to focus our resources on a single small area. Focus on a single, clear goal creates unity and strength. Both are the primary sources of strategic strength (1.7.2 Goal Focus).

4. Constricted positions enhance a group's unity. We think that working closely together creates friction, but more often a group that works together closely becomes more tightly bonded. When people are physically, philosophically, and intellectually close to one another, they develop closer bonds in their unity as a team (1.7.1 Team Unity).

5. Constricted positions are easy to defend. These positions allow whoever holds them to control them naturally and easily. Niches are easy to defend because we can fill them completely, leaving no openings for others. While this is impossible if we pursue opportunities that are much larger than our resources, it is easy if we pursue opportunities that are smaller than our resources. (1.7 Competitive Strength).

Illustration:

To illustrate constricted positions, let us consider a good marriage, the most constricted and most powerful position of them all.

1. Constricted opportunities look like they have little potential.
We are told how restricting a marriage is. How old-fashioned. Men and women are both encouraged to open themselves to the wonderful world of multiple, simultaneous and sequential relationships, disposing of their current relationship whenever they feel the urge.

2. Constricted positions are those that we have more than enough resources to fill completely. No matter how limited our resources, we are endowed by our sex with unique resources that fulfill the needs of the opposite sex.

3. Constricted positions of a very narrow point of focus. In a marriage, we are focused on making our partner happy above everything else because we recognize that our happiness depends on theirs.

4. Constricted positions enhance a group's unity. Like any team, a man and a woman who are devoted to their marriage combine the very different but totally complementary strengths of each sex into the cause of mutual success.

5. Constricted positions are easy to defend. A spouse in a marriage can maintain their marriage much more easily than finding a new relationship as long as they put in the effort to maintain it.

4.6.3 Barricaded Conditions

Sun Tzu's seven key methods regarding the issues related to the extremes of obstacles.

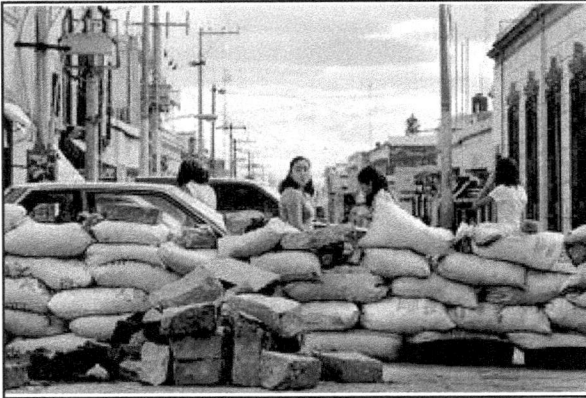

"Some field positions give you a barricade."
Sun Tzu's The Art of War 10:1:39

"If you can find a path with no obstacles, it probably doesn't lead anywhere."
Frank A. Clark

General Principle: Barricaded positions are hard to win but easy to defend.

Situation:

It is a mistake to think of barriers as a problem instead of an opportunity. When we evaluate potential opportunities, we must consider the number and types of obstacles that we will encounter in pursuing them. Obstacles are any natural characteristic that makes taking advantage of a specific opportunity difficult. Barriers to entry can be physical, but more often they are psychological and intellectual. The most common barrier to entry to any opportunity is a lack of specific knowledge.

Opportunity:

Opportunity exists as openings (3.1.4 Openings). Openings only exist when there are barriers of entry preventing them from being filled easily (4.5.2 Surface Barriers). To help us analyze the potential opportunities, we use the benchmark called barricaded positions. These are positions defined by the most extreme barriertts. We use them as a benchmark to help us understand the issues related to positions that have a maximum of barriers (4.6 Six Benchmarks).

Key Methods:

The following seven key methods define the nature of barricaded positions and how they are won.

1. Barricaded positions are the benchmark for the most barriers to entry. Competitors are blocked from getting into these positions by either physical or intellectual obstacles. Barricaded positions have a great number of obstacles, very large obstacles, or very unfamiliar obstacles. A few large barriers can be much more of an obstacle than many small barriers (4.5.2 Opportunity Barriers),

2. The more barricaded the position, the more costly it is to pursue. Barriers can only be overcome by an investment. Depending on the type of barrier, that investment can take the form of effort, time, or other strategic resources. These costs represent the initial commitment required to explore an opportunity. The less available the resources required, the less the probability that a given position will be initially profitable (3.1.2 Strategic Profitability).

3. Winning a barricaded position often requires a campaign. Campaigns are a series of moves toward a longer-term goal. The main purpose of campaigns is surmounting barriers. Familiar barriers, where the obstacles are well understood, are surmounted by repeating the steps in previous similar campaigns. Since they often require campaigns, these positions are costly and time-consuming to acquire (6.2 Campaigns).

4. ***The degree of cost depends on the position from which we approach the barriers***. The best opportunities are those in which we find a key or angle that gives us easy entry into a barricaded position. Different types of barricades require different types of skills and resources to surmount. If we have those specific skills and resources to surmount the barricade more easily than others, we must always take advantage of the barricade (3.3 Opportunity Resources).

5. ***Barriers make it less costly to defend a position***. While barriers decrease the initial profitability of a position, they lower the costs of maintaining a position over time. Once we are behind the barrier, the barrier protects us from would be competitors, decreasing our costs of competition. If a position is difficult to achieve when it is empty, it is invulnerable once we have filled it (3.1.3 Conflict Cost).

6. ***We get an advantage when we get behind the barriers first.*** If a barrier can be surmounted, it will be surmounted. We realize the potential of these opportunities by establishing ourselves in barricaded positions before our competitors do. Once we are in these positions, those same barriers to entry protect us (5.3.1 Speed and Quickness).

7. ***After winning a barricaded position, we must make it visible.*** Barricaded positions are often obscured by their barricades. We must be recognized for winning the value of a barricaded position. If we are seen as having a dominant position in these areas, we will win the support of others. We can only lose these positions to competitors if we abandon them.

Illustration:

A good illustration of a barricaded position is one that is protected by copyright law. For our example, let us use the example of pharmaceutical companies.

1. Barricaded positions are the benchmark for the most barriers to entry. Before any company can sell a new drug in the American market, it must navigate a series of campaigns. The drug companies know that only a small percentage of the drugs they attempt to develop will surmount the barriers involved.

2. The more barricaded the position, the more costly it is to pursue. New drugs must be researched. they must be able to protect that drug by patents so that it cannot be copied by those not paying for development. Then they must be tested to the satisfaction of the FDA in the US. The drug must go through the FDA approval process. They must be covered by insurance. They must then be marketed both to doctors and consumers.

3. Winning a barricaded position often requires a campaign. Each step in this process requires a separate strategic move. Big pharmaceutical companies, having gone through these campaigns before, have the resources necessary to complete these campaigns.

4. The degree of cost depends on the position from which we approach the barriers. Since the drug companies approach these barriers with experience in surmounting them, they are much better positioned than any doctor or scientist who discovers a new drug on their own. Over time, we developed skills in surmounting specific kinds of barrier.

5. Barriers make it less costly to defend a position. Once the drug is proven, the company developing it has it protected by patents for a certain span of time before it can be copied by generic drug makers. The length of time of protection, depends on how quickly they can negotiate the barriers involved, since patent protection starts long before the drug is proven and approved.

6. We get an advantage when we get behind the barriers first. The first drug company to develop a new drug has a certain advantage. One that develops a new category of drugs has a huge advantage.

7. After winning a barricaded position, we must make it visible. Part of the process is promoting the drug to doctors and patients. Because the barriers are temporary, they need to grow the recognition of the drug as quickly as possible.

4.6.4 Wide-Open Conditions

Six key methods regarding the issues related to an absence of barriers.

"You can attack from some positions easily.
Other forces can meet you easily as well.
We call these unobstructed positions.
These positions are open."
                              Sun Tzu's The Art of War 10:1:7-11

"Where there is an open mind there will always be a frontier."
                              Charles F. Kettering

General Principle: Establish wide-open positions quickly and make them visible.

Situation:

It is a mistake to think that the best opportunities are those that have the fewest possible barriers to entry. While obstacles make taking advantage of a specific opportunity difficult, the absence of barriers creates an opposite problem where taking advantage of an opportunity is too easy, not only for us but for everyone. Areas without barriers are highly competitive environments where it is difficult to find any competitive advantage unless we understand our situation.

Opportunity:

Opportunity exists as openings (3.1.4 Openings). This logic suggests that the most open situations would provide the most opportunities. However, wide-open positions are one of the many non-intuitive situations in strategy that require the reverse of our normal perspective (3.2.5 Dynamic Reversal). To help us analyze the potential opportunities, we use the benchmark called wide-open positions to help us understand the issues related to positions that have no barriers to entry (4.6 Six Benchmarks).

Key Methods:

The following key methods define the nature of wide-open positions and how we must handle these opportunities.

*1. **Wide-open positions are the benchmark for the positions with** no **barriers to entry.*** There are no real obstacles, physical or intellectual, preventing us or anyone else from getting into these positions. These opportunities are like fragile bubbles, protected only because people do not see them (3.2.2 Opportunity Invisibility).

*2. **The more open the position, the less costly it is to pursue.*** Barriers require an investment. Depending on the type of barrier, that investment can take the form of effort, time, or other strategic resources. These costs represent the initial commitment required to explore an opportunity. The less available the resources required, the less the probability that a given position being initially profitable (3.1.2 Strategic Profitability).

*3. **Winning a wide-open position requires quick, direct action**.* Since these opportunities have no barriers, they do not require long campaigns. The main purpose of campaigns is surmounting barriers. These positions must be established quickly, without going through a series of steps (5.3.1 Speed and Quickness).

4. We must avoid conflict in pursuing wide-open positions. As we know, conflict is always expensive. The threat of new competition tends to depress the value of this position both initially and over the longer term. Low-barrier opportunities are high-probability opportunities but they are usually low-profitability opportunities. (3.1.3 Conflict Cost).

5. We must maintain the supporters and resources we win to produce profits from these positions. As non-intuitive as it sounds, the secret to using opportunities in wide-open areas is not better competitive skills but better production skills. Maintaining existing supporters of our position is less costly than winning new supporters so we must offer as much value as we can for as little cost. More efficient forms of internal operation can make these inherently marginal positions profitable enough to justify holding them, at least for a time (1.9 Competition and Production).

6. While hard to defend, wide-open positions make good stepping stones. While the lack of barriers increases the likelihood of winning a position, they raise the costs of defending a position over time. Since there are no barriers to entry, any success we find simply attracts more competitors, decreasing the relative value of our effort by increasing our competition. Often, the main value of wide-open positions is in using them as a stepping stone to a new, less open position (3.1.2 Strategic Profitability).

7. After winning a wide-open position, we can create barriers with visibility. Wide-open positions have great visibility and lend themselves to self-promotion. We establish a position in these areas, we can create recognition for our position. Since mind space is limited even when an opportunity is wide-open, our recognition can create a more dominating position (8.3 Securing Rewards).

Illustration:

Any business that requires little training and no real capital investment defines a wide open position. So do relationships that lack any kind of commitment or investment. For our illustration, let us think about a window-washing business.

1. Wide-open positions are the benchmark for the positions with no barriers to entry. Anyone can start a business washing windows of businesses and homes.

2. The more open the position, the less costly it is to pursue. Window washing requires no investment in learning, skill development, or equipment.

3. Winning a wide-open position requires quick, direct action. Since lots of people would like their windows washed at a reasonable price, all we need to do is get out there and talk to them.

4. We must avoid conflict in pursuing wide-open positions. We cannot try to win away the customers of other window washers.

5. We must maintain the supporters and resources we win to produce profits from these positions. We must keep all existing customers, contacting them regularly to see if they need their windows cleaned again. We must get more efficient over time at both finding new customers and cleaning windows.

6. While hard to defend, wide-open positions make good stepping stones. We must look for opportunities to expand our business, into carpet cleaning or other forms of maintenance for existing customers

7. After winning a wide-open position, we can create barriers with visibility. If we get well known for providing good service, we can maintain our business.

4.6.5 Fixed Conditions

Sun Tzu's nine key methods regarding positions with extreme holding power.

"You cannot leave some positions without losing an advantage."

Sun Tzu's The Art of War 10:1:24

"For every mountain there is a miracle."

Robert H. Schuller

General Principle: Fixed positions cannot be left without losing an advantage.

Situation:

When we evaluate potential opportunities, we must consider what it means to have a great deal of holding power either in our current position or in a future position. Extreme holding power in our current position creates an unseen danger in moving on from where we are. Moving into a position with holding power offers both benefit and challenges. The biggest danger is not understanding what we are getting into. Whenever people talk about a "lack of an exit strategy," they are talking about the problems encountered in positions with extreme holding power. Sun Tzu described these conditions as "propped up," which we translated as "supporting" in the original text.

Opportunity:

We do not need an exit strategy if our current position satisfies all our needs. Our usual goal is to continually improve our position, but when life gives us the best it can offer, our opportunity is in recognizing it. Since most of us seldom reach such peaks, the value of understanding fixed positions is as benchmarks for analyzing our opportunities. We need to understand how positions with a great deal of holding power can create challenges in moving forward. We can build up these positions over time, but we cannot relinquish them without taking a step backwards. We can safely move into fixed position if we understand the permanent commitment that this position entails.

Key Methods:

The following seven key methods describe the identification of use of fixed positions.

1. Fixed positions are the benchmark for the most amount of position holding power. This holding power gives the position a great deal of permanence. In real life, some positions are much more fixed than others, but few positions are absolutely fixed for all time. We used the concept of fixed positions as a relative point of comparison, as a way of comparing positions and opportunities (4.6 Benchmarking Opportunities).

2. Fixed positions have so much holding power that we cannot move out of them. This holding power has many different affects on a position. In our Sun Tzu English translation, we translated fixed positions as "supporting" positions, for their advantages they offer. In many of our adaptations of Sun Tzu to modern competition, we use other terms, for example, *peak* positions in Golden Key to Strategy and **optimal** positions in 9 Formulas for Business Success.In The Playbook, we often reference the "stickiness" and "friction" of these holding powers (4.5.3 Opportunity Holding Power).

3. People closely identify us with our fixed position. In the intellectual aspect of positions, fixed positions are powerful because they stick in the mind. Because they stick in the mind, people gravitate toward them. Since getting mind-space is so difficult to win, this stickiness is a great advantage. One we never want to lose though it does come with cost of being "stuck" with a firmly attached label (1.2 Subobjective Positions).

4. Fixed positions are easy to defend. Since they offer many resources and are superior to all surrounding position, these positions are natural defense points. While opponents can get through barriers given enough time and resources, they cannot wear down a fixed position because it is supported by the environment, which is stronger than any competitor (3.2.1 Environmental Dominance).

5. We must carefully choose a fixed position before we are locked into it. There are many advantages in being in a fixed position, but we must be careful about making such commitments. We are going to be locked in these sticky positions for a long time, perhaps forever. We can only move out of them at a cost. The only time to consider if we want a fixed position is before we get into them. Leaving a fixed position is always costly (1.1 Position Paths)

6. Fixed positions are advanced by growth. When we are in fixed positions, we advance our position by growing it rather than by using it as a stepping stone to a new position. We extend our existing position over time, using the fixed position as an anchor point (1.8 Progress Cycle).

7. Opponents will attempt to entice us out of a fixed position. Competitors will desire our position, but they cannot win it from us. They will try to get us to abandon it. If we try to move out of fixed positions, we immediately run into problems. Even if rivals cannot take over our old position, if we let ourselves get enticed away from a fixed position, we are weakening in comparison with competitors (1.3.1 Competitive Comparison).

8. *We cannot move away from fixed positions without going downhill.* Fixed positions are advantageous compared to all surrounding positions. We are stuck in these because holding power offers an advantage that we cannot afford to lose. Using one physical analogy, fixed positions are like mountain peaks. They are the peak because there are no higher positions around them. However, unlike mountain peaks, we can stay on them because their "height" is the control of resources that they offer us (3.3 Opportunity Resources).

9. *Fixed positions and sensitive positions can reverse over time.* Positions can loose their holding powers with changes in the environment. These types of positions are the opposite extremes of holding, but, given a change in environmental conditions, these positions can follow the dynamics of reversal because of changes in the environment. Over time, a fixed position can loosen into a sensitive position and a sensitive position can get set in stone and become a fixed position (3.2.5 Dynamic Reversal).

Illustration:

The classic example of an attempt to move away from a fixed position was the attempt to change the "secret formula" of Coca-Cola with an introduction of the New Coke in 1985.

1. *Fixed positions are the benchmark for the most amount of position holding power.* CocaCola's secret formula had the greatest holding power in the soft drink industry.

2. *Fixed positions have so much holding power that we cannot move out of them.* Because of the secret recipe, Coca-Cola had built a dominating position since the drink was introduced in 1886. The recipe was changed in 1903 with the removal of the coca leaf (the source of cocaine) that was part of its original formula, but it remained unchanged since then.

3. *People closely identify us with our fixed position.* For many years, Coke's identity was built around their secret recipe.

4. Fixed positions are easy to defend. Coke was the "real thing." All other colas were positioned as imitators trying to duplicate the secret formula.

5. We must carefully choose a fixed position before we are locked into it. In the case of Coke, they discovered the holding power of the recipe rather than choosing it.

6. Fixed positions are advanced by growth. Coke brought out other drinks, including diet versions, but the center of their product line was always the original recipe Coke. **Opponents will attempt to entice us out of a fixed position.** Pepsi enticed Coke with their "taste challenge," which appeared to demonstrate that, without the brand awareness, people preferred Pepsi on the basis of taste alone. A classic example of using the gap between subjective and objective positions to an advantage (3.6 Leveraging Subjectivity)

7. We cannot move away from fixed positions without going downhill. Coke never tried this until 1985, when it discovered the penalties of trying to move first hand. New Coke, with a new formula, was introduced replacing original Coke in response to Pepsi's taste tests. The result was a disaster and they quickly returned to the old formula, but not without wasting a lot of resources.

8. Fixed positions and sensitive positions can reverse over time. When Coke was first introduced, its formula was not a fixed position. It's cocaine-based formula was a sensitive position that, once abandoned, could not be returned to. However, over time, the new formula became a fixed position.

4.6.6 Sensitive Conditions

Six key methods regarding the affects of positions with no hold-ing power on pursuing opportunities.

*"These are entangling positions.
field positions are one-sided."*
                              Sun Tzu's The Art of War 10:1:16-17

*"All politics takes place on a slippery slope. The most
important four words in politics are 'up to a point."*
                                                George Will

General Principle: We can only advance from sensitive posi-tions when our success is certain.

Situation:

When we are advancing our position, a lack of holding power either in our current position or in a future position can have disastrous effects. When evaluating future position, we must take these effects into account. A lack of holding power in our current positions makes moving on from where we are a one-way proposition. When moving into a position with little or no holding power, we must consider what that means to our next move. The danger in positions without holding power is not from our opponents but from losing our supporters. Whenever people talk about "getting on a slippery slope," they are talking about the dangers encountered in getting into position lacking holding power. Sun Tzu described these conditions as "hanging," which we translate as "entangling" in our translation.

Opportunity:

Since our strategic goal is to make continuous progress, we need to understand how positions can create challenges in moving forward. Sensitive positions can be valuable stepping stones if we know how to safely move into and out of them.

Key Methods:

The following key methods describe the benchmark to recognizing and dealing with positions with too little holding power.

1. Sensitive positions have no holding power. This lack of holding power has many different consequences. It means they are so slippery that we cannot return to them. Sensitive positions are loose in the sense of the opposite of fixed positions. Sun Tzu described them as entangling positions. In Golden Key to Strategy , we describe them as "one-way" positions because we cannot return to them. In 9 Formulas for Business Success , we described them as fragile positions because they are easily destroyed. The thinking behind both terms will become clear (4.5.3 Opportunity Holding Power).

*2. **Sensitive positions are difficult to hold onto while new positions are being established.*** To use a physical analogy, we usually
try to advance our position like climbing a ladder. We stand on our
current position, gradually transferring our weight to a better position. This works fine as long as we aren't supporting ourselves on a
sensitive position. When we advance from a sensitive position, the
position falls away as we take our weight off of it. We cannot return
to it. Hence, it is a fragile and oneway position (1.1.2 Defending
Positions),

*3. **Sensitive positions depend on a commitment**.* Even though
they are slippery, we can hold onto them but only if we are completely committed to them. Sensitive positions aren't bad positions
as long as we stay in them. Their weaknesses only appear in transition from them as we must eventually do (1.1 Position Paths).

*4. **We destroy sensitive positions when we try to move out
of them.*** The very act of moving out of them destroys them. We
cannot get back into them. If we try to advance from a sensitive
position and fail to establish a new position, we cannot return to our
old position (1.8 Progress Cycle).

*5. **Moves from sensitive positions must succeed the first time.***
Sensitive positions are challenging because our advance from them
to a new position must succeed the first time. This means they must
have the highest probability of success. If our move to a new position fails, we put ourselves exactly without a position entirely. Since
our first priority is always defending our existing position until we
establish a new one, we can only advance out of these positions
when we are certain of our new position (5.6.1 Defense Priority).

*6. **Fixed positions and sensitive positions can reverse over
time.*** These two types of positions are the opposite extremes of
holding power, but, given a change in environmental conditions,
these positions can follow the dynamics of reversal. Over time, a
fixed position can become more sensitive and a sensitive position
can get set in stone (3.2.5 Dynamic Reversal).

Illustration:

These sensitive, one-way, fragile positions are common, more common than most people think. When we quit a job or get a promotion, we usually cannot go back to our old position if our new position doesn't work out. Any position that depends largely on an exclusive relationship based on trust is a sensitive position. We have already described marriage as a constricted position because sane people limit themselves to a single spouse, but marriage is also a sensitive position.

1. Sensitive positions have no holding power. A marriage does not stick no matter what we do. If we violate our commitment, we endanger it.

2. Sensitive positions are difficult to hold onto while new positions are being established. We cannot establish a new romantic relationship and hold onto a marriage.

3. Sensitive positions depend on a commitment. Violate the commitment and the marriage falls apart.

4. We destroy sensitive positions when we try to move out of them. In almost every case, we cannot return to our spouse after a divorce.

5. Moves from sensitive positions must succeed the first time. People move to new relationships, but if those relationships do not work, they cannot go back.

6. Fixed positions and sensitive positions can reverse over time. Marriage was once a fixed position. People could not move from it without suffering desperate consequences. Because of changes in social mores, it has become a sensitive position.

4.7 Competitive Weakness

Sun Tzu's six key methods on how certain opportunities can bring out our weaknesses.

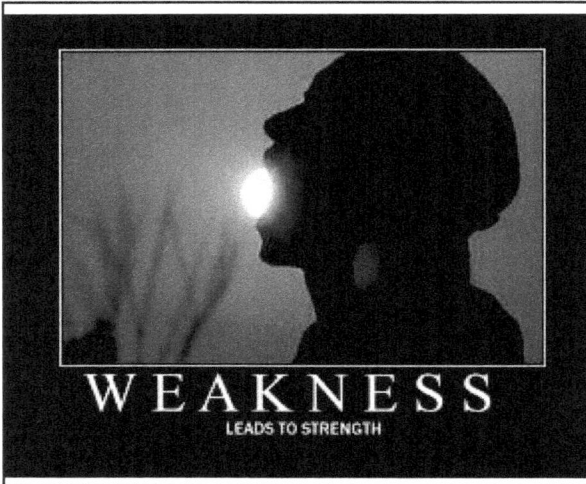

"You must know all about these six weaknesses.
You must understand the paths that lead to defeat."
            Sun Tzu's The Art of War 10:2:31-32

"It's about human failings, human failings amplified by
technology. Men are not angels. Our Constitution was
written by people who understood that human nature has
many flaws."

                                Lee Tien

General Principle: The six benchmark positions expose organizational weaknesses arising from character flaws.

Situation:

To pick the best possible opportunities, we must avoid putting ourselves in a bad position. Pursuing the wrong opportunities brings out our weaknesses. These situations fail to take advantage of our strengths. Most of us do not realize that picking the wrong opportunities can create or emphasize previously hidden weaknesses.

Opportunity:

We can see problem situations from a distance on the surface of opportunities (4.5 Surface Characteristics). We use the six benchmarks of surface characteristics to identify our potential weaknesses (4.6 Six Benchmarks). To successfully avoid the danger of moving into the wrong situations, we start with considering our fitness for a given opportunity in terms of our strengths and resources (3.4.2 Opportunity Fit). We must then consider our flaws and weakness as well. Those weaknesses arise in two areas: our character of decision-making and our organizational connection to others.

Key Methods:

We use the six benchmarks of an opportunity surface to identify potential misfits using the following key methods:

1. Weakness in a future position arises at the intersection between its nature and our fit. We think of an organization as our methods, decision-making and resources. This organization must fit the opening of an opportunity. If is does, moving into that opening creates value. If our organization is unsuited to the nature of a space, moving into that space creates a disaster (3.4.2 Opportunity Fit).

2. The character flaws of decision-makers create organizational weakness. Weaknesses in our execution arise from flaws in our decision-making. Using elemental strategic terminology, command leadership determines group methods (1.5 Internal Elements , 1.5.2. Group Methods).

3. *The five command weaknesses create six organizational weaknesses.* The five command characteristics are intelligence, caring, courage, discipline, and trustworthiness. The five character flaws are the lack of these command characteristics. In interacting with others, these five flaws create organizational weakness. While these weaknesses appear in the way an organization fails at certain opportunities, the source of these problems are in the way we make decisions (4.7.1 Command Weaknesses).

4. *The six opportunity benchmarks can also be used to uncover six common flaws in organizations.* Few organizations lack flaws. Opportunities also have flaws as identified by the six benchmarks. Combining the wrong opportunity with the wrong organization is a disaster either in advancing into a given position or defending it. These flaws hurt every type of organization subtly in every situation.They are exaggerated in wrong form of opportunities (4.7.2 Organizational Weaknesses).

5. *These flaws in a rival organization can create our opportunities.* These six organizational weaknesses can affect any organization: our own or any rival. While we usually find opportunities by seeing the strength of our opponents, our examination of the surface of an opportunity can also help us identify potential traps for opponents (3.5 Strength and Weakness).

Illustration:

Taking a cue from the initial quote above, let us use the illustration of why, despite its good intentions, statism and socialism in all its forms, always fails.

1. *Weakness in a future position arises at the intersection between its nature and our fit.* Failed states and societies always blame their opponents and the conditions with which they must deal. They never realize that "the fault is not in our stars but in ourselves."

2. *The character flaws of decision-makers create organizational weakness*. This is most clearly seen in various totalitarian states because they always start as a cult of personality. The fundamental mistake is confusing the strength of unity with the strengths of a single decision-maker.

*3. The five command weaknesses create six organizational weaknesses.*These strong leaders imprint their excess confidence on the states that they create. The leaders condone their bad decisions by the needs of the state, but, more importantly, all their followers condone doing evil in the name of the leaders intention of creating a greater good.

4. The six opportunity benchmarks can also be used to uncover six common flaws in organizations. Totalitarian states will handle many aspects of internal control initially very well, their weaknesses always appear over time as the state must adapt to changing circumstances. This ability to adapt to the nature of emerging opportunities expose the fragility of their rigid systems regulating their citizens.

5. These flaws in a rival organization can create our opportunities. The continuous rise of totalitarian states on the Utopian promises of strong leaders lead eventually to their fall and the creation of many openings for individuals.

4.7.1 Command Weaknesses

Sun Tzu's ten key methods on the character flaws of leaders and how to exploit them.

"Know all six of these weaknesses.
They create weak timing and disastrous positions.
They all arise from the army's commander."
　　　　　　　　Sun Tzu's The Art of War 10:2:7-9

"The wise know too well their weakness to assume
infallibility; and he who knows most, knows best how
little he knows."
　　　　　　　　Thomas Jefferson

General Principle: Five character flaws are open to five forms of attack and create six organizational flaws.

Situation:

We can be poorly suited to an opportunity based on our character. An area of weak character leads to mistakes in making choices about positions. Though these mistakes appear as organizational weaknesses, they arise from character flaws. Organizations reflect those who guide them. Weakness in command leads predictably to certain types of weakness in organizations.

Opportunity:

Sun Tzu teaches that making the right strategic decisions requires intelligence, caring, courage, discipline, and trustworthiness. Each of the five areas of character relates to a specific elemental aspect of our position (1.3 Elemental Analysis). Understanding the connection between character, positions, and organizations allows us to see the opportunities that we can take advantage of better than others. We can avoid pursuing the wrong opportunities if we know ourselves and know our rivals.

Key Methods:

The following key methods describe how the five character flaws create six organizational forms of weakness.

1. A lack of intelligence leads to ignorance of the ground. The key methods work with both meanings of intelligence: our IQ and the quality of our information. Ignorance means not recognizing conditions that persist over time. In Sun Tzu's strategy, we call them "ground features." We are all ignorant about many aspects of what is changing in the future, that is climate conditions. It is a leader's absolute duty to know the nature of the ground that he and his people are moving into (1.4.2 Ground Features).

2. Ignorance of the ground leads to organizations that are outmaneuvered. When leaders fail to recognize conditions that persist over time, they cannot use the ground to their advantage and opponents can use the conditions of the ground against them. The easiest way to leverage their ignorance against them is through surprise.For example, when they do not realize where the high ground lies, opponents can secretly seize the high ground and use it to their advantage (2.1.4 Surprise).

3. The lack of caring leads to the inability to create a higher, shared mission. When we say "caring," we mean our dedication to the mission. This is almost always the result of selfishness. Selfish leaders do not remain leaders for long (1.6.1 Shared Mission).

4. Lack of a shared mission leads to self-destructive organizations that fall apart. The easiest way to leverage this weakness against leaders is through division, separating them from their supporters. The best leaders are servants of their shared mission and, through their shared mission, servants of their followers (9.2.5 Vulnerability of Organization).

5. The lack of courage means the inability to deal with climate. This means the inability to face the challenges of the future. Fear of making mistakes is normal, but leaders have to rise above it. If navigating the future were easy, people wouldn't need leaders to guide them (1.4.1 Climate Shift).

6. A inability to deal with climate leads to over-extended organizations. Over-extension arises from the fear of letting go, making decisions about what is valuable and what is not. The easiest way is use a use a lack of courage is through deception, using misinformation and disinformation to control leaders who want to play it safe (2.4.2 Climate Perspective).

7. The lack of discipline means failing in methods. This is the inability to execute on decisions. A leader who lacks discipline will make good decisions but lack of the persistence necessary to see them through difficult times (1.5.2. Group Methods).

8. Failing in methods leads to untrained and undisciplined organizations. Untrained organizations do not know what to do. Undisciplined organizations just don't do it. Strategic reflexes must be trained to keep organizations together. The easiest way to leverage a lack of discipline is by challenging it by opposing attempted moves. This is what strategy calls "battle," meeting an opponent so that they have to respond. Undisciplined leaders are unable to over-come the obstacles that confront them (6.0 Situation Response).

9. The lack of trustworthiness means losing the respect of others. Leaders must make the hard choices and they must make them correctly. As leaders, we must make our decisions quickly and clearly. If we do not make the tough decisions, followers lose trust in our leadership (1.5.1 Command Leadership).

10. The lack of clear decisions leads to disorganization. Organizations arise out of the leader taking responsibility and follow-ers accepting the leader's decision. Where decisions are sloppy, lazy, and unclear, there is no organization. The best way to oppose untrustworthy leaders is simply challenging them for their position. This is called siege. If people are untrustworthy, they leave them-selves open to being replaced in their responsibilities (2.4.3 Com-mand Perspective).

Illustration:

We will need a variety of examples from a variety of competitive domains to illustrate all these failures.

1. A lack of intelligence leads to ignorance of the ground. When Time/Warner bought AOL, they didn't understand the nature of the internet and the world wide web.

2. Ignorance of the ground leads to organizations that are out-maneuvered. The AOL environment that Time/Warner had hoped to use to deliver paid content was soon outdated by the free content on the broader Internet.

3. The lack of caring leads to the inability to create a higher, shared mission. In organizations such as the UN, the bureaucrats that rise to the top are more focused on their personal careers than any solid philosophy.

4. Lack of a shared mission leads to self-destructive organiza-tions that fall apart. Because its various members put their self-interest above everything, the organization is useless in terms of action against countries such as Iran.

5. *The lack of courage means the inability to deal with climate*. As overseas cars became more popular, US car makers needed the courage to identify a position that they could defend instead of drifting into a more difficult future.

6. *A inability to deal with climate leads to over-extended organizations*. Instead, companies such as GM and Ford all bought overseas car companies, such as Saab and Jaguar. Eventually, they had to sell them off.

7. *The lack of discipline means failing in methods*. Dell rose to become the largest computer manufacturer due to their innovative sales of computes over the web. However, their organization's quick success never allowed them to develop solid operating methods.

8. *Failing in methods leads to untrained and undisciplined organizations*. Operational problems in support (Dell Hell) and questions about financial irregularities started to erode people's trust in the organization.

9. *The lack of trustworthiness means losing the respect of others*. We are seeing this problem demonstrated right now with President Obama's administration. People on the right and left are quickly losing trust in the administration's direction and commitment.

10. *The lack of clear decisions leads to disorganization.* The inability of the Democrats to pass legislation despite huge majorities in each house of Congress is due entirely to the lack of organization.

4.7.2 Group Weaknesses

Sun Tzu's six key methods regarding organizational weakness and where they fail.

"You must know all about these six weaknesses. You must understand the philosophies that lead to defeat."

Sun Tzu's The Art of War 10:2:31-32

"There are two kinds of weakness, that which breaks and that which bends."

James Russell

General Rule: The six benchmark positions expose six common forms of organizational weaknesses.

Situation:

Flaws in leaders lead to flaws in organizations. All organizations are flawed in some way, but the flaws in organizations become fatal when we put them in inappropriate situations. A weak organization is one that pursues the wrong opportunities. We must avoid putting our organizations in a bad position. We cannot put our group in the wrong place at the wrong time by pursuing those opportunities that highlight the groups weaknesses.

Opportunity:

Five weaknesses in character leads to six forms of organizational weakness (4.7.1 Command Weaknesses). These six forms of organizational weakness can be matched against the six benchmarks that are used to analyze opportunities (4.6 Six Benchmarks). From this process, we can know which opportunities are most likely to create serious problems for a given organization. An objective appraisal of our opportunities relative to our particular group is a huge advantage. We can avoid these weaknesses before pursuing the wrong opportunities.

Key Methods:

These are six key methods describing the six weaknesses of groups and the ground that exposes them:

1. Spread-out positions expose overextended organizations. Overextended organizations are already trying to do more than they can do well, failing to expect competition. Their leaders want more ground than they realistically can control. The spread-out position is often chosen by overextended organizations. More focused competitors are usually stronger in specific areas. By spreading too few resources over too much ground, overextended organizations cannot defend their position at any point of attack and are forced to retreat (4.6.1 Spread-Out Positions).

2. Confined positions expose self-destructive organizations. Self-destructive organizations suffer from a lack of mission. Their leaders let each group develop its own separate goals and priorities. In Sun Tzu's strategy, unity is strength. The advantage of confined regions is that they are easy to defend, physical closeness is not unity. If the organization is not united, it falls apart. Without a clear, uniting mission, people follow their own personal goals. These enterprises will self-destruct over time, especially on confined ground where everyone must work together closely (4.6.2 Constricted Positions).

3. Barricaded positions expose disorganized organizations. Disorganized organizations take their eye off of the ball. The safety of a barricaded position allows their leadership to grow overconfident and fall out of touch with the changes of climate. Relying on the natural barriers to competition, these organizations lack direction and gradually decay over time. Such negligence is quickly punished in most positions, waking people up to what is changing, but in barricaded positions, negligence grows and grows leading to chaos (4.6.3 Barricaded Positions).

4. Wide-open positions expose clumsy organizations. Clumsy organizations cannot adapt to the moves that their rivals make because they don't understand the ground. They have the most difficulty in wide-open positions that have few barriers to entry. Like spread-out positions, wide-open positions invite competition. Competitors must act and react quickly to use this position. In a wide-open position, clumsy organizations are too slow are easily outmaneuvered by competitors (4.6.4 WideOpen Positions).

5. Fixed positions expose untrained organizations. Untrained organizations consist of people who have failed to learn proven methods. This weakness occurs in stable, fixed positions, where leaders take their positions for granted, failing to emphasize training and hiring trained people. In these organizations, good decisions are wasted because they cannot be executed. Since fixed positions are usually optimal positions in a competitive arena, the usually result is that these organizations fall down from their peaks (4.6.5 Fixed Positions).

6. Sensitive positions expose undisciplined organizations. Undisciplined organizations suffer from leadership that is too lax. These organization are most vulnerable in sensitive positions where execution must be precisely controlled. Sensitive positions do not forgive bad decisions.

7. Organizations get entangled in sensitive positions, naturally slipping out of them into weaker positions and unable to return to them. Sensitive positions rely on great decisions about when to defend these positions and when to move from them (4.6.6 Sensitive Positions).

Illustration:

We will continue with a variety of illustrations that parallel those given in 4.7.1 Command Weaknesses :

1. Spread-out positions expose overextended organizations. American car companies, specifically GM, is a great example.

2. Confined positions expose self-destructive organizations. The example is the UN, which fails whenever it has to focus with a specific situation in the world.

3. Barricaded positions expose disorganized organizations. President Obama's administration is a good example.

4. Wide-open positions expose clumsy organizations. Time/Warners' movement into the Internet with the acquisition of AOL is a classic example.

5. Fixed positions expose untrained organizations. Coke's introduction of New Coke is the classic example.

6. Sensitive positions expose undisciplined organizations. Dell's losing its leading position in computer sales is a good example.

4.8 Climate Support

Sun Tzu's eight key methods to help us choose new positions based on future changes.

"Don't attack into the wind."

Sun Tzu's The Art of War 12:2:14

"When in doubt, predict that the present trend will continue."

Merkin's Maxim, Murphy's Laws

General Rule: Choose opportunities that are built up by trends in climate.

Situation:

To make the best decisions about pursuing opportunities, we not only have to consider current conditions but the direction in which those positions are likely to change. So far we have looked at future positions from their more static (ground) conditions of distance, form, surface, and fit. Now we need to think about future positions from the perspective of how those positions are going to be naturally built up or eroded by the current trends.

Opportunity:

Success requires adapting to the environment not trying to control it (3.2.1 Environmental Dominance). Our positions are advanced in two ways: by what we choose to do and by what the environment does naturally on its own (1.1.1 Position Dynamics). In the first case, we use time and effort ro move to better and better positions like stepping stones (1.1 Position Paths). In the second case, we stay in a position because the trends in that environment are naturally moving that position up. By choosing the right positions, we can use them like escalators, improving our position effortlessly.

Key Methods:

The following key methods describe the use of trends in picking the best opportunities.

1. We must not only identify trends but identify how long those trends are going to last. Of course, it takes strategic skills to identify positions that are going up and effort to move into them. Most strategic mistakes are mistakes of timing: abandoning trends just as they are about to catch on or, much more common, jumping on a trend just as it is about to change. People are naturally skeptical of trends. Most people don't necessarily buy into them until everyone else does. However, by definition, once *everyone* buys into a trend, the trend is over because there is no one else left to buy into it (7.4 Timing).

2. When a trend goes too far, we must prepare for it to naturally reverse itself. In Sun Tzu's strategy, we have a clear explanation for this phenomena. We think about trends of change as being driven by the competing forces that we call complementary opposites (3.2.3 Complementary Opposites). These forces create a balance. To understand opportunity, we think about this balance in terms of emptiness and fullness. Emptiness is the opening that defines opportunities. Fullness is the crowded state that leads to costly conflict (3.2.5 Dynamic Reversal).

3. *A trend measures the movement of people from emptiness to fullness.* As people start to move to a new open position, a trend begins. This movement supports the people that got to that position first, improving their position as the crowd comes in behind them (3.2.4 Emptiness and Fullness).

4. *At some point, the new opening gets over-crowded.* The good ground is taken. The opportunities are fewer. People stop coming in and those who are there start to leave. Depending on the nature of the ground, they either go back to where they were before, or go onto some other new territory that has just been opened up (3.1.4 Openings).

5. *Success depends totally on how we use the trend.* If we were one of the first to a new opening, we are going to do very well. However, if we come in later, after the needs have been filled, our efforts in competition with those who were there first and have deeper knowledge cannot be profitable (2.6 Knowledge Leverage).

6. *When we are in the middle of a trend, it always looks like it is going to last forever.* It never does. The more popular a trend becomes, the closer it is to reversing itself (3.1.6 Time Limitations).

7. *We can guess on the lifespan of an opportunity by its surface characteristics.* The strategic tools for determining how long a trend will last, whether it is at the beginning or end of the trend, are the same three dimensions that we have been using for picking the best opportunities (4.5 Surface Characteristics):

- ***The larger the ground for the trend, the longer the trend will last.*** The more people that are potentially involved, the more people that can potentially jump on board, The smaller the area, the fewer people it affects, the shorter it will last.
- ***The more barriers there are, the slower the trend will develop and the longer it will last.*** Trends that go suddenly straight up in one direction are suspect. The rate of increase cannot be sustained.

- ***The more holding power a trend has, the longer it will last.*** The combination of memorability and deep appeal that make up holding power is the most difficult dimension to quantify but we can see their affects over time. The longer trends have lasted the more likely they are to continue to last.

  8. *Move when a trend shows signs of exhausting itself.* Good strategy starts with accepting that neither we nor anyone else can know trends for certain. In our journey, we are going to make mistakes. We are going to choose positions that are going up and going down. We have to be willing to adapt through our movements to what is actually happening. Both long trend and short trend can be used to support a position. We can always move to a new position as a trend exhausts itself, but to do so we must have some feel for the length of trends to use the best timing (1.8.2 The Adaptive Loop).

Illustration:

Let us look at the trend in the markets driving up the price of gold.

1. We must not only identify trends but identify how long those trends are going to last. If we are going to invest in gold, we have to know if that investment is long or short-term.

2. When a trend goes too far, we must prepare for it to naturally reverses itself. While gold has been going up since the dollar was disconnected from it, at some point in the future, the price of gold will start to decline in price, at least temporarily, because it is over-bought. When there are no more buyers, the price must decline.

3. A trend measures the movement of people from emptiness to fullness. Think of the "boom towns." When gold was discovered, people flooded into an area. In the case of the price of gold today, people are not so much moving into gold as moving away from paper money, fiat money. As long as there are more people who begin to think that printed money is less solid than gold, gold will continue to go up.

4. At some point, the new opening gets over-crowded. At some point, everyone who is going to invest in gold will have invested. They will start to move to other types of value.

5. Success depends totally on how we use the trend. Money can be made when the price of gold goes up or down depending on whether we go long or short.

6. When we are in the middle of a trend, it always looks like it is going to last forever. Since this is a very long-term trend, starting in the 1930s, it looks like it will continue forever.

7. We can guess on the lifespan of an opportunity by its surface characteristics.

- **The larger the ground of the trend, the longer the trend will last.** There are a lot of people in the world, such as the Chinese, that are just getting the opportunity to buy gold. Many others, because of recent financial crises, are growing less trusting in paper money.
- **The more barriers there are, the slower the trend will develop and the longer it will last.** In the past, there were many restrictions and physical difficulties in buying gold. Most of those have gone away, which is why gold has been going up more quickly. The only barriers left are psychological: other investments are seen as more rational.
- **The more holding power a trend has, the longer it will last.** Gold has had value for most of human history.

8. Move when a trend shows signs of exhausting itself. At the time this was written, the price of gold had risen quickly. These price increases must sustain themselves. These will be corrections. In a given week, the price of gold can decline by 5%. The big question at any point remains: what do people trust more: currency, stocks and bonds, or gold? The fact that gold is appearing on that list for the first time tells us something about the times.

4.9 Opportunity Mapping

Five key methods regarding a two-dimensional tool for comparing opportunities probabilities.

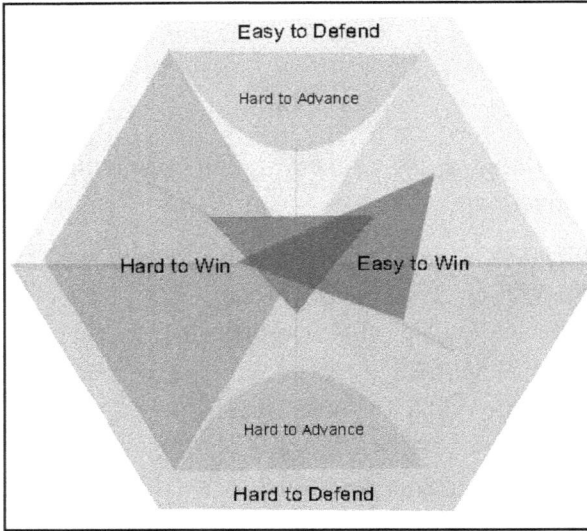

"You can recognize the opportunity for victory; you don't create it."

Sun Tzu's The Art of War 4:1:10

"A good map is both a useful tool and a magic carpet to far away places."

Anon

General Rule: Graphically mapping opportunities using the six extremes of surface characteristics makes their potential easier to see.

Situation:

Sun Tzu's three dimensions—distance, barriers, and dangers—that describe opportunities and their six extremes provide a lot of information to consider in evaluating opportunities. As humans, we tend to consider one or two things that jump out at us rather than the complete picture. When our methods are purely conceptual, we miss many of our best opportunities because we cannot "see" the key characteristics of the opportunity involved.

Opportunity:

We are wired primarily for visual perception. A simple way to identify the best opportunities is by mapping them according to the six benchmarks (4.6 Six Benchmarks). We can use a mapping tool that we call the Opportunity Map. The Opportunity Map is a visual tool to see the relative advantages and disadvantages of various opportunities. The Opportunity Map provides a two-dimensional representation of the three dimensions (area/barriers/holding power) used to identify the highest probability opportunities.

Key Methods:

The Opportunity Map is a training tool, used to practice comparing opportunities. The key methods for using the hexagon of the Opportunity Map as a tool for visualizing the relative merits of different opportunities are as follows.

1. The Opportunity Map *is a hexagon showing the six bench marks as extremes on three axes.* The line between each of the benchmarks represents a range. The area range is between the extremes of confined and spread-out areas. The barrier range is between barricaded and wide-open areas. The holding power range is between fixed and sensitive or sticky and slippery areas, if that works better. (4.6 Six Benchmarks).

2. We can evaluate our current position or a future opportunity by where we think it falls on each scale. We do this simply by marking where we think that opportunity falls on each of these three ranges. Is it more barricaded or open, confined or spread-out, fixed or sensitive. *See example below.*

3. We then connect the three marks to create a triangle. This triangle represents where the position sits on the Opportunity Map.

4. We then replace the six benchmarks map with the characteristic map. This map breaks the hexagon into five regions. The regions show how difficult the position will be to win, defend, and advance. The triangle will overlap several areas, but it will fall more into some than others. The higher it is, the easier it is to defend. The more to the right is, the easier it is to win. The more centered it is, the easier it is to advance. High probabilities are easy to win, defend, and advance.

5. By mapping several opportunities, we can easily compare where they fall. Obviously, we are looking for opportunities that are more in the upper, right section where positions are easier to win and defend.

Illustration:

We will illustrate the key methods above through actual illustrations.

1. The Opportunity Map **is a hexagon showing the six bench marks as extremes on three axes.** The value of these benchmarks is that they are not exact measures, but simply comparisons of positions between two extremes. *See example below.*

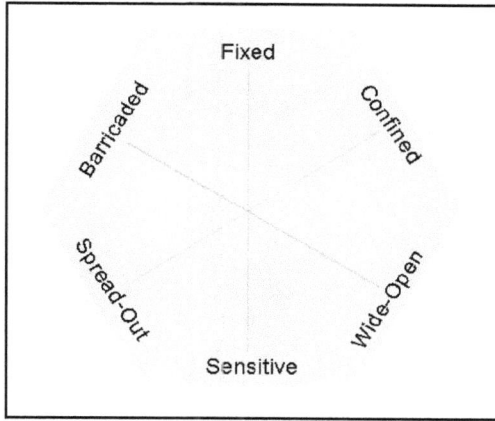

2. *We can evaluate our current position or a future opportunity by where we think it falls on each scale.* In this case, we see this opportunity as more barricaded than open, more confined than spread-out, and perhaps a little more sensitive. *See example below.*

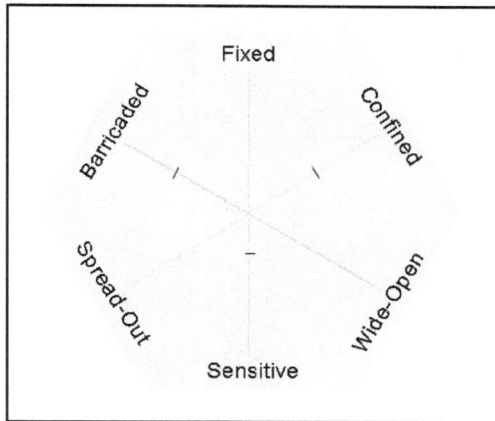

3. *We then connect the three marks to create a triangle.* How large the triangle is doesn't matter, just where it falls in the hexagon. *We then replace the six benchmarks map with the characteristic map.* The first opportunity we charted above falls mostly in the

easy to defend region, but it is split evenly between easy and hard to win. *See example below.*

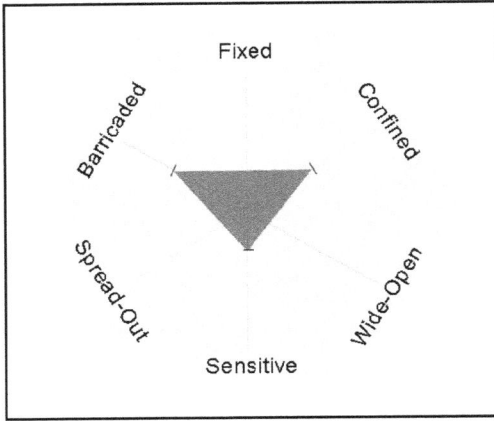

4. By mapping several opportunities, we can easily compare where they fall. In comparing the first opportunity with a second, we can see that both are easier to defend but the second opportunity is much easier to win. This makes the second opportunity a better choice. *See example below.*

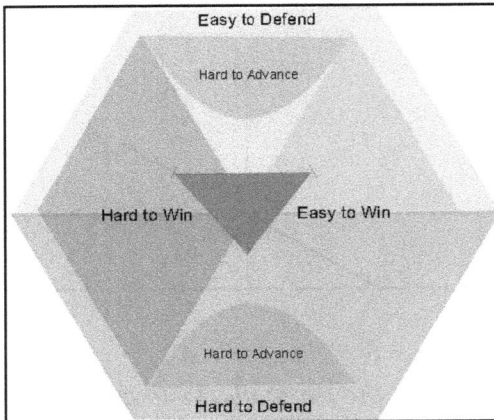

5.

6. By mapping several opportunities, we can easily compare where they fall. The area covered by the triangles show their relative advantages. *See example below.*

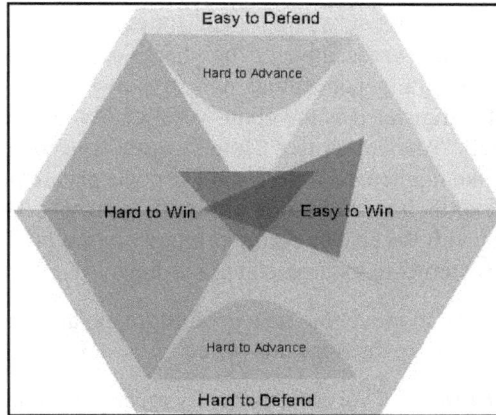

Glossary of Key Concepts from Sun Tzu's *The Art of War*

This glossary is keyed to the most common English words used in the translation of *The Art of War*. Those terms only capture the strategic concepts generally. Though translated as English nouns, verbs, adverbs, or adjectives, the Chinese characters on which they are based are totally conceptual, not parts of speech. For example, the character for conflict is translated as the noun "conflict," as the verb "fight," and as the adjective "disputed." Ancient written Chinese was a conceptual language, not a spoken one. More like mathematical terms, these concepts are primarily defined by the strict structure of their relationships with other concepts. The Chinese names shown in parentheses with the characters are primarily based on Pinyin, but we occasionally use Cantonese terms to make each term unique.

Advance (*Jeun* 進): to move into new **ground**; to expand your **position**; to move forward in a campaign; the opposite of **flee**.

Advantage, *benefit* (*Li* 利)**:** an opportunity arising from having a better **position** relative to an **enemy**; an opening left by an **enemy**; a **strength** that matches against an **enemy's weakness**; where fullness meets emptiness; a desirable characteristic of a strategic **position**.

Aim, *vision, foresee* (*Jian* 見)**: focus** on a specific **advantage**, opening, or opportunity; predicting movements of an **enemy**; a skill of a **leader** in observing **climate**.

Analysis, *plan* (*Gai* 計)**:** a comparison of relative **position**; the examination of the five factors that define a strategic **position**; a combination of **knowledge** and **vision**; the ability to see through **deception**.

Army: see **war**.

Attack, *invade* (*Gong* 攻)**:** a movement to new **ground**; advancing a strategic **position**; action against an **enemy** in the sense of moving into his **ground**; opposite of **defend**; does not necessarily mean **conflict**.

Bad, *ruined* (*Pi* 圮)**:** a condition of the **ground** that makes **advance** difficult; destroyed; terrain that is broken and difficult to traverse; one of the nine situations or types of terrain.

Barricaded: see **obstacles**.

Battle (*Zhan* 戰)**:** to challenge; to engage an **enemy;** generically, to meet a challenge; to choose a confrontation with an **enemy** at a specific time and place; to focus all your resources on a task; to establish superiority in a **position**; to challenge an **enemy** to increase **chaos**; that which is **controlled** by **surprise**; one of the four forms of **attack;** the response to a **desperate situation;** character meaning was originally "big meeting," though later took on the meaning "big weapon"; not necessarily **conflict**.

Bravery, *courage* (_Yong_ 勇): the ability to face difficult choices; the character quality that deals with the changes of **CLIMATE**; courage of conviction; willingness to act on vision; one of the six characteristics of a leader.

Break, *broken, divided* (_Po_ 破): to **divide** what is **complete**; the absence of a **uniting philosophy**; the opposite of unity.

Calculate, *count* (_Shu_ 數): mathematical comparison of quantities and qualities; a measurement of **distance** or troop size.

Change, *transform* (_Bian_ 變): transition from one **condition** to another; the ability to adapt to different situations; a natural characteristic of **climate**.

Chaos, *disorder* (_Juan_ 亂): conditions that cannot be **foreseen**; the natural state of confusion arising from **battle**; one of six weaknesses of an organization; the opposite of **control**.

Claim, *position, form* (_Xing_ 形): to use the **ground**; a shape or specific condition of **ground**; the **ground** that you **control**; to use the benefits of the **ground**; the formations of troops; one of the four key skills in making progress.

Climate, *heaven* (_Tian_ 天): the passage of time; the realm of uncontrollable **change**; divine providence; the weather; trends that **change** over time; generally, the future; what one must **aim** at in the future; one of five key factors in **analysis;** the opposite of **ground**.

Command (_Ling_ 令): to order or the act of ordering subordinates; the decisions of a **leader**; the creation of **methods**.

Competition: see _war._

Complete: see _unity._

Condition: see **ground.**

Confined, *surround* (_Wei_ 圍): to encircle; a **situation** or **stage** in which your options are limited; the proper tactic for dealing with an **enemy** that is ten times smaller; to seal off a smaller **enemy**; the characteristic of a **stage** in which a larger **force** can be attacked by a smaller one; one of nine **situations** or **stages**.

Conflict, *fight* (_Zheng_ 争): to contend; to dispute; direct confrontation of arms with an **enemy**; highly desirable **ground** that creates disputes; one of nine types of **ground**, terrain, or stages.

Constricted, *narrow* (_Ai_ 狹): a confined space or niche; one of six field positions; the limited extreme of the dimension distance; the opposite of **spread-out.**

Control, *govern* (_Chi_ 治): to manage situations; to overcome disorder; the opposite of **chaos.**

Dangerous: see **serious.**

Dangers, *adverse* (Ak 阨): a condition that makes it difficult to **advance;** one of three dimensions used to evaluate advantages; the dimension with the extreme field **positions** of **entangling** and **supporting**.

Death, *desperate* (_Si_ 死): to end or the end of life or efforts; an extreme situation in which the only option is **battle**; one of nine **stages** or types of **terrain**; one of five types of **spies**; opposite of **survive**.

Deception, *bluffing, illusion* (_Gui_ 詭): to control perceptions; to control information; to mislead an **enemy**; an attack on an opponent's **aim**; the characteristic of war that confuses perceptions.

Defend (_Shou_ 守): to guard or to hold a **ground**; to remain in a **position**; the opposite of **attack**.

Detour (_Yu_ 迂): the indirect or unsuspected path to a **position**; the more difficult path to **advantage**; the route that is not **direct**.

Direct, *straight* (_Jik_ 直.): a straight or obvious path to a goal; opposite of **detour**.

Distance, *distant* (_Yuan_ 遠): the space separating **ground**; to be remote from the current location; to occupy **positions** that are not close to one another; one of six field positions; one of the three dimensions for evaluating opportunities; the emptiness of space.

Divide, *separate* (_Fen_ 分): to break apart a larger force; to separate from a larger group; the opposite of **join** and **focus**.

Double agent, *reverse* (_Fan_ 反): to turn around in direction; to change a situation; to switch a person's allegiance; one of five types of spies.

Easy, *light* (_Qing_ 輕): to require little effort; a **situation** that requires little effort; one of nine **stages** or types of terrain; opposite of **serious**.

Emotion, *feeling* (_Xin_ 心): an unthinking reaction to **aim**, a necessary element to inspire **moves**; a component of esprit de corps; never a sufficient cause for **attack**.

Enemy, *competitor* (_Dik_ 敵): one who makes the same **claim**; one with a similar **goal;** one with whom comparisons of capabilities are made.

Entangling, *hanging* (_Gua_ 絓): a **position** that cannot be returned to; any **condition** that leaves no easy place to go; one of six field positions.

Evade, *avoid* (_Bi_ 避): the tactic used by small competitors when facing large opponents.

Fall apart, *collapse* (_Beng_ 崩): to fail to execute good decisions; to fail to use a **constricted position**; one of six weaknesses of an organization.

Fall down, *sink* (_Haam_ 陷): to fail to make good decisions; to **move** from a **supporting position**; one of six weaknesses of organizations.

Feelings, *affection, love* (_Ching_ 情): the bonds of relationship; the result of a shared **philosophy**; requires management.

Fight, *struggle* (Dou 鬥**):** to engage in **conflict**; to face difficulties.

Fire (*Huo* 火**):** an environmental weapon; a universal analogy for all weapons.

Flee, *retreat, northward* (*Bei* 北**)** :to abandon a **position**; to surrender **ground**; one of six weaknesses of an **army**; opposite of **advance**.

Focus, *concentrate* (*Zhuan* 專**):** to bring resources together at a given time; to **unite** forces for a purpose; an attribute of having a shared **philosophy**; the opposite of *divide*.

Force (*Lei* 力**):** power in the simplest sense; a **group** of people bound by **unity** and **focus**; the relative balance of **strength** in opposition to **weakness**.

Foresee: see **aim**.

Fullness: see **strength**.

General: see **leader**.

Goal: see **philosophy**.

Ground, *situation, stage* (*Di* 地**):** the earth; a specific place; a specific condition; the place one competes; the prize of competition; one of five key factors in competitive analysis; the opposite of **climate**.

Groups, *troops* (*Dui* 隊**):** a number of people united under a shared **philosophy**; human resources of an organization; one of the five targets of fire attacks.

Inside, *internal* (*Nei* 內**):** within a **territory** or organization; an insider; one of five types of spies; opposite of *Wai*, outside.

Intersecting, *highway* (*Qu* 衢**):** a **situation** or **ground** that allows you to **join**; one of nine types of terrain.

Join (*Hap* 合**):** to unite; to make allies; to create a larger **force**; opposite of **divide**.

Knowledge, *listening* (*Zhi*: 知**):** to have information; the result of listening; the first step in advancing a **position**; the basis of strategy.

Lax, *loosen* (*Shii* 弛**):** too easygoing; lacking discipline; one of six weaknesses of an army.

Leader, *general, commander* (*Jiang* 將**):**
the decision-maker in a competitive unit; one who **listens** and **aims**; one who manages **troops**; superior of officers and men; one of the five key factors in analysis; the conceptual opposite of fa, the established methods, which do not require decisions.

Learn, *compare* (*Xiao* 效**):** to evaluate the relative qualities of **enemies**.

Listen, *obey* (*Ting* 聽**):** to gather **knowledge**; part of **analysis**.

Listening: see **knowledge**.

Local, *countryside* (_Xiang_ 鄉): the nearby **ground**; to have **knowledge** of a specific **ground**; one of five types of **spies**.

Marsh (_Ze_ 澤): **ground** where footing is unstable; one of the four types of **ground**; analogy for uncertain situations.

Method: see **system**.

Mission: see **philosophy**.

Momentum, *influence* (_Shi_ 勢): the **force** created by **surprise** set up by **standards;** used with **timing**.

Mountains, *hill, peak* (_Shan_ 山):uneven **ground**; one of four types of **ground**; an analogy for all unequal **situations**.

Move, *march, act* (_Hang_ 行): action toward a position or goal; used as a near synonym for <u>dong</u>, act.

Nation (_Guo_ 國): the state; the productive part of an organization; the seat of political power; the entity that controls an **army** or competitive part of the organization.

Obstacles, *barricaded* (_Xian_ 險): to have barriers; one of the three characteristics of the **ground**; one of six field positions; as a field position, opposite of **unobstructed**.

Open, *meeting, crossing* (_Jiao_ 來): to share the same **ground** without conflict; to come together; a **situation** that encourages a race; one of nine **terrains** or **stages**.

Opportunity: see <u>advantage.</u>

Outmaneuver (_Sou_ 走): to go astray; to be **forced** into a **weak position**; one of six weaknesses of an army.

Outside, *external* (_Wai_ 外): not within a **territory** or **army**; one who has a different perspective; one who offers an objective view; opposite of **internal**.

Philosophy, *mission, goals* (_Tao_ 道): the shared **goals** that **unite** an **army**; a system of thought; a shared viewpoint; literally "the way"; a way to work together; one of the five key factors in **analysis**.

Plateau (_Liu_ 陸): a type of **ground** without defects; an analogy for any equal, solid, and certain **situation**; the best place for competition; one of the four types of **ground**.

Resources, *provisions* (_Liang_ 糧): necessary supplies, most commonly food; one of the five targets of fire attacks.

Restraint: see **timing.**

Reward, *treasure, money* (_Bao_ 賞): profit; wealth; the necessary compensation for competition; a necessary ingredient for **victory**; **victory** must pay.

Scatter, *dissipating* (_San_ 攽): to disperse; to lose **unity**; the pursuit of separate **goals** as opposed to a central **mission**; a situation that causes a **force** to scatter; one of nine conditions or types of terrain.

Serious, *heavy* (_Chong_ 重): any task requiring effort and skill; a **situation** where resources are running low when you are deeply committed to a campaign or heavily invested in a project; a situation where opposition within an organization mounts; one of nine **stages** or types of **terrain.**

Siege (_Gong Cheng_ 攻 城): to move against entrenched positions; any movement against an **enemy's strength**; literally "strike city"; one of the four forms of attack; the least desirable form of attack.

Situation: see **ground.**

Speed, *hurry* (Sai 馳): to **move** over **ground** quickly; the ability to **advance positions** in a minimum of time; needed to take advantage of a window of opportunity.

Spread-out, *wide* (_Guang_ 廣): a surplus of **distance**; one of the six **ground positions**; opposite of **constricted.**

Spy, *conduit, go-between* (_Gaan_ 間): a source of information; a channel of communication; literally, an "opening between."

Stage: see **ground.**

Standard, *proper, correct* (_Jang_ 正): the expected behavior; the standard approach; proven methods; the opposite of surprise; together with **surprise** creates **momentum.**

Storehouse, *house* (_Ku_ 庫): a place where resources are stockpiled; one of the five targets for fire attacks.

Stores, *accumulate, savings* (_Ji_ 糧): resources that have been stored; any type of inventory; one of the five targets of fire attacks.

Strength, *fullness, satisfaction* (_Sat_ 壹): wealth or abundance or resources; the state of being crowded; the opposite of Xu, empty.

Supply wagons, *transport* (_Zi_ 輜): the movement of **resources** through **distance**; one of the five targets of fire attacks.

Support, *supporting* (_Zhii_ 支): to prop up; to enhance; a **ground position** that you cannot leave without losing **strength**; one of six field positions; the opposite extreme of gua, entangling.

Surprise, *unusual, strange* (_Qi_ 奇) : the unexpected; the innovative; the opposite of **standard**; together with **standards** creates **momentum**.

Surround: see **confined.**

Survive, *live, birth* (_Shaang_ 生): the state of being created, started, or beginning; the state of living or surviving; a temporary condition of fullness; one of five types of spies; the opposite of **death.**

System, *method* (_Fa_ 法): a set of procedures; a group of techniques; steps to accomplish a **goal**; one of the five key factors in analysis; the realm of groups who must follow procedures; the opposite of the **leader.**

Territory, *terrain*: see **ground.**

Timing, *restraint* (_Jie_ 節): to withhold action until the proper time; to release tension; a companion concept to **momentum.**

Troops: see **group.**

Unity, *whole, oneness* (_Yi_ 一): the characteristic of a **group** that shares a **philosophy**; the lowest number; a **group** that acts as a unit; the opposite of **divided.**

Unobstructed, *expert* (_Tong_ 通): without obstacles or barriers; **ground** that allows easy movement; open to new ideas; one of six field positions; opposite of **obstructed.**

Victory, *win, winning* (_Sing_ 勝): success in an endeavor; getting a reward; serving your mission; an event that produces more than it consumes; to make a profit.

War, *competition, army* (**Bing** 兵): a dynamic situation in which **positions** can be won or lost; a contest in which a **reward** can be won; the conditions under which the principles of strategy work.

Water, *river* (_Shui_ 水): a fast-changing **ground**; fluid **conditions**; one of four types of **ground**; an analogy for change.

Weakness, *emptiness, need* (_Xu_ 虛): the absence of people or resources; devoid of **force**; the point of **attack** for an **advantage;** a characteristic of **ground** that enables **speed**; poor; the opposite of strength.

Win, *winning*: see **victory.**

Wind, *fashion, custom* (_Feng_ 風): the pressure of environmental forces.

The *Art of War Playbook* Series

There are over two-hundred and thirty articles on Sun Tzu's competitive principles in the nine volumes of the *Art of War Playbook*. Each volume covers a specific area of Sun Tzu strategy.

About the Translator and Author

Gary Gagliardi is recognized as America's leading expert on Sun Tzu's *The Art of War*. An award-winning author and business strategist, his many books on Sun Tzu's strategy have been translated around the world. He has appeared on hundreds of talk shows nationwide, providing strategic insight on the breaking news. He has trained decision makers from some of the world's most successful organizations in competitive thinking. His workshops convert Sun Tzu's many principles into a series of practical tools for handling common competitive challenges.

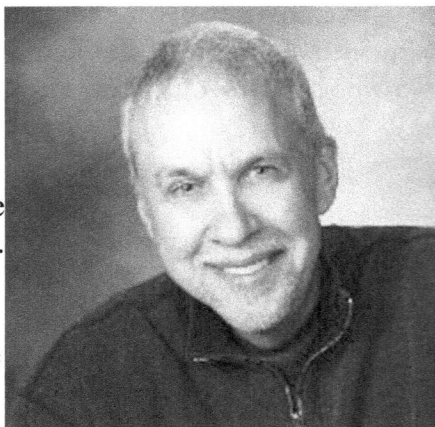

Gary began using Sun Tzu's competitive principles in a successful corporate career and when he started his own software company. In 1990, he wrote his first *Art of War* adaptation for his company's salespeople. By 1992, his company was on *Inc. Magazine's* list of the 500 fastest-growing privately held companies in America. He personally won the U.S. Chamber of Commerce Blue Chip Quality Award and was an Ernst and Young Entrepreneur of the Year finalist. His customers—AT&T, GE, and Motorola, among others—began inviting him to speak at their conferences. After becoming a multimillionaire when he sold his software company in 1997, he continued teaching *The Art of War* around the world.

Gary has authored several breakthrough works on *The Art of War*. Ten of his books on strategy have won book award recognition in nine different non-fiction categories.

If you enjoyed this work, contact the author at Garyg@SunTzuS.com and let him know. He enjoys communicating with interested readers.

Art of War Books by Gary Gagliardi

9 FORMULAS FOR BUSINESS SUCCESS:
THE SCIENCE OF STRATEGY

THE GOLDEN KEY TO STRATEGY:
EVERYDAY STRATEGY FOR EVERYONE

SUN TZU'S THE ART OF WAR PLUS THE ART OF SALES:
THE ART OF WAR FOR THE SALES WARRIOR

SUN TZU'S THE ART OF WAR PLUS THE ART OF SALES:
THE ART OF WAR FOR THE SALES WARRIOR

THE ART OF WAR PLUS THE CHINESE REVEALED

THE ART OF WAR PLUS THE ART OF MANAGEMENT:
THE ART OF WAR FOR MANAGEMENT WARRIORS

THE ART OF WAR PLUS THE ART OF MANAGEMENT:
THE ART OF WAR FOR MANAGEMENT WARRIORS

MAKING MONEY BY SPEAKING:
THE SPOKESPERSON STRATEGY

THE WARRIOR CLASS:
306 LESSONS IN STRATEGY

THE ART OF WAR FOR THE BUSINESS WARRIOR:
STRATEGY FOR ENTREPRENEURS

THE ART OF WAR PLUS THE WARRIOR'S APPRENTICE

THE ART OF WAR PLUS STRATEGY FOR SALES MANAGERS

ART OF WAR FOR WARRIOR MARKETING:
STRATEGY FOR CONQUERING MARKETS

THE ANCIENT BING-FA:
MARTIAL ARTS STRATEGY

STRATEGY AGAINST TERROR:
ANCIENT WISDOM FOR TODAY'S WAR

THE ART OF WAR PLUS THE ART OF CAREER BUILDING

THE ART OF PARENTING:
SUN TZU'S ART OF WAR FOR PARENTING TEENS

Gary Gagliardi's Books are Available at:

SunTzus.com
Amazon.com
BarnesAndNoble.com
Itunes.apple.com

www.ingramcontent.com/pod-product-compliance
Lightning Source LLC
Chambersburg PA
CBHW060846220326
41599CB00017B/2402